STREAMLINED ID

Streamlined ID: A Practical Guide to Instructional Design presents a focused and generalizable approach to instructional design and development—one that addresses the needs of ID novices as well as practitioners in a variety of career environments. Emphasizing the essentials and "big ideas" of ID, *Streamlined ID* presents a new perspective that aims to produce instruction that is sustainable, optimized, appropriately redundant, and targeted at continuous improvement.

The book features an enhanced version of the classic ADDIE model (Analysis, Design, Development, Implementation, and Evaluation) that emphasizes the iterative nature of design and the role of evaluation throughout the design/development process. It clearly lays out a systematic approach that emphasizes the use of research-based theories, while acknowledging the need to customize the process to address a variety of pedagogical approaches: Instructivist, Constructivist, and Connectivist.

The book opens with an overview of the basics of ID and each subsequent chapter describes major activities in the ID process with step-by-step instructions and tips for streamlining the process. Numerous job aids serve to maximize the efficiency and effectiveness of your design efforts. Each chapter highlights key concepts and provides additional exercises and assignments based on the work of Benjamin Bloom. *Streamlined ID* is an ideal reference guide for optimizing professional practice.

Miriam B. Larson is an Adjunct Assistant Professor who teaches courses in instructional design and technology for the University of Tennessee, Knoxville, and for Virginia Tech. She has over 30 years of experience designing instruction for organizations in a variety of career environments.

Barbara B. Lockee is Professor of Instructional Design and Technology and Associate Director of Educational Research and Outreach in the School of Education at Virginia Tech.

STREAMLINED ID

A Practical Guide to Instructional Design

MIRIAM B. LARSON
UNIVERSITY OF TENNESSEE, KNOXVILLE
& VIRGINIA TECH

AND

BARBARA B. LOCKEE
VIRGINIA TECH

WITH ILLUSTRATIONS
BY
MIKAELA L. FUCHS

Routledge
Taylor & Francis Group

NEW YORK AND LONDON

First published 2014
by Routledge
711 Third Avenue, New York, NY 10017

Simultaneously published in the UK
by Routledge
2 Park Square, Milton Park, Abingdon, Oxon OX14 4RN

Routledge is an imprint of the Taylor & Francis Group, an informa business

© 2014 Taylor & Francis

The right of Miriam B. Larson and Barbara B. Lockee to be identified as
authors of this work has been asserted by them in accordance with sections
77 and 78 of the Copyright, Designs and Patents Act 1988.

Library of Congress Cataloging in Publication Data
Larson, Miriam B.
    Streamlined ID : a practical guide to instructional design / by Miriam B. Larson and Barbara B. Lockee.
    pages cm
    Includes bibliographical references and index.
    1. Instructional systems—Design. I. Title.
    LB1028.38.L37 2013
    371.3—dc23
    2012042463

ISBN: 978–0–415–50517–8 (hbk)
ISBN: 978–0–415–50518–5 (pbk)
ISBN: 978–0–203–11875–7 (ebk)

Typeset in Minion
by Swales & Willis Ltd, Exeter, Devon

Printed and bound in the United States of America
by Edwards Brothers, Inc.

Dedication

This book is dedicated to my husband, my children, and my parents, who supported and encouraged me throughout the long process.—Miriam

To Chase, who graciously accepted my "homework" alongside of his. Thank you for your understanding and your never-ending patience.—Barbara

Contents

This Book: At a Glance   viii
Acknowledgments   xii

1.   Mastering the Basics   1

2.   Analyzing Needs to Define the Project   20

3.   Analyzing to Identify the Learners   41

4.   Analyzing the Contexts of Instruction   60

5.   Analyzing the Content and Project Scope   91

6.   Identifying the Outcomes and Aligning Instruction   115

7.   Assessing Learning   131

8.   Selecting Strategies: The Heart of Instructional Design   149

9.   Selecting Technologies That Support Instruction   181

10.   Designing and Delivering an Effective Message   203

11.   Producing and Implementing Instruction   220

Glossary   251
References   263
Index   275

This Book: At a Glance

Why Streamlined ID?

This book presents a simplified, yet detailed approach to designing instruction for a wide range of purposes and career environments. It includes step-by-step instructions to aid novices in designing learning experiences, as well as detailed job aids that will serve as a reference for more experienced designers as they practice their craft. We've made an effort to incorporate what we believe to be the most commonly used methods and theories from the field, as well as those on the horizon that appear promising.

We do, however, agree with others in the field of Instructional Design and Technology (IDT) who've called for a more responsive and rapid process for designing learning experiences and environments. We've noted that many books on instructional design are geared for a specific career environment (higher education, K-12, business and industry, health care, and/or government/military) and often do not provide globally applicable guidelines for the practice of ID. Therefore, this book presents a global and *streamlined* approach to instructional design and development—one that we believe meets the needs of ID novices *and* practitioners in a *variety* of work settings by emphasizing designs that are:

> **Sustainable**—Sustainable instruction is designed and developed with the future in mind. The resources and time devoted to the design/development effort is planned and adjusted to reflect the expected lifespan of the instruction, its importance and complexity, its need for future updating and maintenance, and the possible future need to scale the instruction up or down in size and scope to meet demand.
>
> **Optimized**—Optimized instruction is efficient and useful. It does what it is supposed to do in the most efficient manner possible, and it maximizes functionality, usability, and productivity. Ideally, optimized instruction is designed so that it can be reused for different purposes and audiences.
>
> **Appropriately Redundant**—While too much redundancy can frustrate or annoy a learner, appropriate redundancy refers to providing the content in multiple formats so that it is accessible to all learners. Redundancy also refers to provisions that allow the learner to review the instruction again whenever necessary, and at a pace that meets his or her needs.
>
> **Right-Sized**—Instructional project "creep" is the well-known problem that evolves when you try to design instruction that is everything to every learner, or when multiple stakeholders make requests that end up "supersizing" the learning experience. When you practice right-sized ID, you stick to the essential content, and use techniques that give

learners options for accessing additional, nice-to-know, or remedial content if and when it is needed.

Continuously Improving—The IDT field has always emphasized review and revision to improve the quality of instruction and learning. An iterative approach that features frequent formative and usability testing throughout design and development serves to help designers "get it right" earlier in the process. It also helps to focus all stakeholders on the need to continuously improve.

How Is This Book Organized?

We've chosen to stick with a classic model of instructional design that is familiar to those in the field—with a twist. The classic ADDIE model—an acronym for "Analysis, Design, Development, Implementation, and Evaluation" (Allen, 2003)—has a simplicity that underscores the streamlined approach we've taken. That said, we emphasize throughout the book that the ADDIE ID process is *iterative*, not linear, and that it should be used in a way that reflects responsiveness to the surrounding contexts of instruction. We also emphasize that *evaluation* is not merely one piece of the model, but that you should consider how you evaluate your instruction throughout the design/development process, since this approach promotes continuous improvement. To that end, we briefly describe evaluation in the first chapter and then highlight how it should be factored into the process in subsequent chapters.

Each chapter contains items that exemplify key design principles:

- **Inquiring Minds Want to Know …** provides questions about the chapter contents to focus your attention on items you should be sure to remember and understand.
- **Jargon Alerts!** highlight potentially confusing and duplicate terms used in the field of Instructional Design and Technology (IDT).
- **Notable Non-Examples** feature stories of what *not* to do in your design practice, and immediately precede a section on …
- **… What's Involved?** providing step-by-step instructions based on best practices. We've placed as much of the content for each chapter in handy job-aid-type tables that we hope you will be able to use frequently in your professional practice.
- **Streamlining** suggestions follow the content for each activity in design and development.
- **Evaluation** factors applicable to each activity are addressed, as well as examples of how ID activities vary between **Different Career Environments**.
- **Bloom Stretch** exercises are included to help you monitor and extend your own learning. We use Bloom's Revised Taxonomy of Educational Objectives (Anderson & Krathwohl, 2001; Krathwohl, 2002) as a framework with exercises that address four levels of Bloom's thinking skills taxonomy: *Apply, Analyze, Evaluate,* and *Create.* (We address the first two levels, *Remember* and *Understand*, at the beginning of each book chapter.)

Test Your Understanding With a Bloom Stretch

- At the close of each chapter, a **Diving Deeper** section refers to the resources available on the book website.
- As you read, you may find it helpful to refer to the **Glossary** of IDT terms and the **References** cited at the back of the book.

To keep this book as streamlined as possible, we've placed some of the resources online at www.routledge.com/cw/larson, where they can be more easily updated:

- **Practical Exercises and Examples**, including additional Bloom Stretch suggestions, worked examples, case studies, and problems to check your understanding of the chapter concepts;
- **Job Aids**, including worksheets for major activities in the ID process and process charts; and
- **Recommended Resources**, including current trends and issues, books, articles, and Internet links for further information on the topics addressed in the chapter.

Who Might Use This Book and How?

I'm ...	I have to ...	I will use this book ...
An Instructor in Higher Education or K-12	• Move some of my courses to an online format. • Adjust my courses to better address the needs of those who will employ my students. • Quickly develop several new courses. • Teach students to design instruction or training.	• As a guide to adjust my instruction for an online environment. • To determine what future employers need from my students. • To help me streamline the course development process, and/or work more effectively with faculty course development experts. • To provide my students with a solid resource for learning instructional design and an easy-to-use reference for their future ID practice.
A Course Developer or Technology Coordinator in Higher Education or K-12	• Support others in the design of face-to-face, blended, and/or fully online courses. • Help others use technology effectively to support learning. • Provide materials to help others design and develop instruction.	• To provide a basis and guide for collaborating with others in the design of instruction. • As a source of best practices to share with others as they design and implement technology-supported instruction. • As a source of job aids for designing instruction.
A Trainer in Business and Industry, Health Care, Government, or Military	• Produce and/or deliver instruction that will improve the performance of employees. • Rapidly produce instruction on new products, services, procedures, or processes. • Produce instruction to respond to applicable standards, regulations, or certification requirements. • Justify training development and implementation efforts.	• As a quick reference guide for producing instruction that improves performance in measurable ways. • To help me streamline the ID process so I can keep my organization competitive and employees current with just-in-time instruction or job aids. • To help me produce instruction that prepares others to meet standards, regulations, or certification requirements. • As a guide for using theory, evaluation results, and/or cost-benefit analyses to justify training.
An Independent IDT Consultant	• Produce instruction quickly and in a cost-effective manner to maintain an acceptable profit margin. • Either do all steps in the design/development process myself, or work with SMEs or an ID team or subcontractors.	• To streamline my design/development process. • As a reference for best practices and ideas. • As a guide for effective collaboration and contribution to IDT team efforts, or to work successfully with stakeholders and subcontractors in the IDT process.

Who Are Erma and Ernest?

There are several "big ideas" in IDT that should be internalized by everyone practicing in the field. There are also many common misconceptions that can hamper the effectiveness of designers, and that, if known, can prevent mistakes and avoid delays in the design/development process. Erma and Ernest will serve as guides throughout this book to highlight these big ideas and misconceptions (or, in ID talk, to provide an "advance organizer").

Acknowledgments

We would like to thank the graduate students from the University of Tennessee's IT570 and IT578 instructional design and development classes for their helpful feedback on the book, as well as those who read through draft versions of the book, including Rhonda Phillips, Susan Sutton, and Jeanne Anderson. Many thanks to Ireta Ekstrom, who provided insights on instructional design practice in health-care environments. We also thank Kibong Song for his assistance with compiling and reviewing our References and the development of our Glossary; both tasks were of significant help to us.

Many thanks go to Alex Masulis and Madeleine Hamlin at Taylor & Francis/Routledge for their support and assistance through the writing process—we greatly appreciate the opportunity to share our work with the many practitioners of instructional design, thanks to you!

Finally, a big thank you to Miriam's daughter, Mikaela Fuchs, whose incredible artwork makes this volume complete and hopefully conveys the sense of pragmatism and levity that reflect the authors' perspectives.

1
Mastering the Basics

A COMMON OCCUPATIONAL HAZARD:
ID EXPLANATION FRUSTRATION

You are wired to learn, and that's good, because learning helps you adapt and survive in a world that is changing at an ever-increasing rate. In this era of information overload, the new currency is *the ability to learn*. As a result, learning is a key concern for:

- Businesses with changing products, services, competitors, and business conditions;
- Governments struggling to ensure an adequate quality of life for its citizenry, while adjusting to changing economic, political, and societal factors;

- Military organizations faced with global political changes, and new technologies and methods for securing populations;
- Institutions of higher learning tasked with anticipating and communicating an evolving knowledge base and meeting the changing needs of society and students;
- Health-care organizations challenged by changing health needs, demands for research, the application of new knowledge, and the implementation of new methods; and
- K-12 educators who must not only learn new knowledge and methods, but must also prepare future generations to learn and adapt in a constantly changing world.

Change characterizes every aspect of life in the 21st century. As a result, lifelong learning is crucial to the survival of individuals and societies, and therefore there is an ongoing, critical need for *effective learning experiences and environments.* Well-designed instruction captures the attention of learners and prompts them to interact with the content. It also helps learners focus on what's important, aids them in organizing new information and making connections to previously learned material, and provides memorable experiences that help them apply new knowledge. The field of Instructional Design and Technology (IDT) has evolved to address this critical need for well-designed learning environments and instruction. Yet, instructional designers do more than just design. They also:

- analyze problems to determine if instruction is a valid solution;
- identify and limit the scope of instruction to ensure its relevance and ability to meet critical needs;
- select appropriate media and delivery modes; and
- develop, implement, and evaluate the success of instruction.

With such a broad range of responsibilities, it's easy for instructional designers to become mired in complexity and discouraged from taking a creative approach. That's why it's important to know how to design effective instruction, *and* when and how to *streamline* the process.

Inquiring Minds Want to Know …

- Where did the field of Instructional Design and Technology originate?
- What does it mean to be a competent instructional designer?
- What is the *Kirkpatrick four-level model of evaluation* and how is it used to improve an instructional design?
- What factors and processes are involved in designing instruction, and how can the process be streamlined?
- What do I need to remember and understand from this chapter?

  ⇒ The distinction between systematic design and systemic design;
  ⇒ The difference between "hard skills" and "soft skills";
  ⇒ The range of meaning for the terms: learning, instruction, technology, design, grounded design, competency, *asynchronous* and *synchronous learning*, media comparison studies, stakeholders, formative and summative evaluation;
  ⇒ The difference between a well-structured and an ill-structured problem;
  ⇒ Different career environments where IDT is practiced;
  ⇒ The range of competencies expected of proficient instructional designers;
  ⇒ The principles of streamlined instructional design;

⇒ Different ways to classify learning environments; and
⇒ The importance of learning theory and research in IDT.

Jargon Alert!

What's in a name? There are many different job titles used for those who design instruction and many diverse degree programs that produce practitioners. Knowing the range of titles and terms can be of value when you are searching for helpful research or career positions. Some applicable fields include: *instructional design and technology, instructional or educational technology, instructional systems design, learning sciences, technical communications, adult learning, performance technology, instructional psychology, online teaching and learning, e-learning, training and development,* and *open and distance education.* Job titles vary both by industry and sector, and you'll even find inconsistencies within a particular field. The range of job titles includes: *instructional technologist, distance learning coordinator, librarian, media specialist, instructional systems specialist, learning architect, learning experience designer,* and even *learning product design engineer!* If you've been perusing the job ads, you can probably add a few to the list.

The Nature of Learning and Instruction

You learn in many ways: through your senses and experiences, by reflecting on those experiences, and by interacting with and watching others. You learn from everyday life. You learn intentionally and serendipitously; from both formal and informal instruction and experiences. Educators define learning in many ways but most would agree that it "occurs when experience causes a relatively permanent change in an individual's knowledge or behavior" (Woolfolk, 2005, p. 190), and some would also emphasize the change in a learner's connections to knowledge sources (their knowledge networks).

At a very basic level, instruction is "that which facilitates and supports learning" (Spector, 2001, p. 309). Since educators differ on the definition of *learning*, it's easy to see why they might also differ on the definition of *instruction* (Reigeluth & Carr-Chellman, 2006). The distinguished educator John Dewey (1938) defined instruction as a social activity with a key aim to prepare students to become more capable learners in the future. IDT pioneers Robert Gagné and Leslie Briggs (1974) defined instruction as "a human undertaking whose purpose is to help people learn" (p. 3), explaining that it is accomplished through a set of events external to the learner, as well as through internal self-instruction. They therefore concluded that teacher-led instruction is just one form, since instruction could be also accomplished through events generated by physical objects and experiences. Bruner (1966) broadly defined it as "an attempt to shape intellectual growth" (p. 1), and Glaser (1976) described it as "the conditions that can be implemented to foster the acquisition of competence" (p. 1). Reflecting a different theoretical perspective, Biggs (1999) characterized instruction as "a construction site on which students build on what they already know" (p. 72). More recently, Stephen Downes (2012) stated that Connectivist learning experiences "create an environment where people who are more advanced reasoners, thinkers, motivators, arguers, and educators can practice their skills in a public way by interacting with each other ..., [and other] people can learn by watching and joining in" (p. 508). You can experiment with design methods to produce instruction that matches any and all of these definitions, and this book will provide plenty of ideas for pursuing that goal.

So What's Involved? The Field of Instructional Design and Technology

Imagine that you are attending your high school reunion. Having sent previous, *numerous* emails to correct the reunion coordinator's records (explaining that you work as an *instructional* designer, not an industrial or interior designer), you arrive at the event to face yet another challenge. You meet an old friend and she asks you, "Now, can you tell me just what an instructional designer is? What do you actually *do?*" Would she understand and be able to accurately convey what you do to others? What if you called yourself an *instructional technologist?* Would your friend be able to distinguish your career from that of an information technologist at her company?

If you were ultimately unsuccessful in conveying the essence of your work, you could take comfort in knowing that you are not alone. Those working in the field of Instructional Design and Technology (IDT) frequently remark that answering questions about what they do is difficult—even with their relatives! This is true for many reasons: the field of IDT is constantly changing and expanding; the field is broad and IDT professionals do many different things and work in many different public and private career environments; and the field has many names (as noted previously).

The discipline of instructional design emerged primarily during the 20th century and experienced an enormous boost as a result of the military training needs of World War II (Reiser, 2001a, 2001b). Influences that have shaped the field, however, can be traced all the way back to the early Greek philosophers Aristotle and Plato, who pondered the nature of knowledge and truth and whether they are external or internal to a person (Saettler, 2004). While the nature of IDT is continually evolving and foundational tenets are frequently challenged, two practices continue to be central to the field: the use of systematic instructional design procedures and the use of media for instructional purposes (Reiser, 2002).

The field of IDT has evolved over several decades and has a broad knowledge base. It has been characterized as both an art and a science, because it is one of the creative design fields and is rooted in research-based methods and learning theories (Moore, Bates, & Grundling, 2002; Skinner, 1954). An early pioneer in the field, Florida State University educator Robert Morgan (Branson & Reiser, 2009), reiterated Dewey and Piaget's call for a *science of education* (Dewey, 1929; Piaget, 1969). Morgan, along with colleagues Robert Gagné, Leslie Briggs, and Robert Branson, developed elements of a systematic approach that eventually became known as Instructional Systems Design (ISD) (Tomei & Balmert, 2001). ISD represents a very structured approach to the design of educational experiences and it makes use of contributions from a variety of fields (see Figure 1.1). Management science contributes systems theory, planning, cost analysis, and scheduling; the learning sciences contribute learning research, theories, developmental psychology, and systematic design; and communications technology contributes communications theory, and the media and methods necessary to deliver instructional messages (Larson, 2004).

For many years, the IDT field was known merely as Instructional Technology (IT). The term "IT" was originally equated with instructional media. However, the definition of the word "technology" has evolved, and the field has broadened to emphasize both "hard" skills (technical competencies) and "soft" skills (design skills, effective communication, analysis skills, change management, etc.). It also now encompasses areas as diverse as learning sciences and Human Performance Technology (HPT). As a result, "IT" no longer communicates an accurate picture of the scope of the field … Not to mention the fact that the field of Information Technology (IT) has stolen our abbreviation!

In their popular text on current issues in the field, Reiser and Dempsey (2007, p. 3) also refer to the field as *Instructional Design and Technology (IDT)*. The title is a good one because it communicates the importance of both soft skills (design skills) and hard skills (technology skills) in professional practice. However, since technology is always changing, it is the soft skills that distinguish

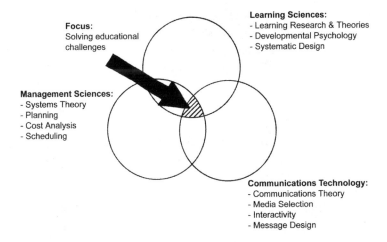

Focus:
Solving educational
challenges

Learning Sciences:
- Learning Research & Theories
- Developmental Psychology
- Systematic Design

Management Sciences:
- Systems Theory
- Planning
- Cost Analysis
- Scheduling

Communications Technology:
- Communications Theory
- Media Selection
- Interactivity
- Message Design

Figure 1.1 Contributions to the Field of Instructional Systems Design

IDT practitioners from other "IT" professionals, because these skills persist over time and apply across contexts. In a reflection of this emphasis on soft skills, a leading professional organization for the field, the Association for Educational Communications and Technology (AECT) defines IDT as "the theory and practice of design, development, utilization, management, and evaluation of processes and resources for learning" (Seels & Richey, 1994, p. 1). In this book we focus on the soft skills necessary for professional practice, we explain how hard and soft skills interact to produce well-designed and effective instruction, and we describe how you can streamline the process to meet the demands of any design challenge.

The Nature of Design

As mentioned earlier, design is a part of many different disciplines. What is design and how does it differ across disciplines? Architects design living spaces; engineers design everyday objects, software interfaces, and industrial systems; and graphic designers and artists design visual messages. How does the type of design they do compare to the design carried out by teachers, trainers, and instructional designers?

In his classic book *The Design of Everyday Things* (2002), Donald Norman elaborates on how product designers often fail to attend to the needs of those for whom they are designing. Norman cautions against becoming a "self-centered designer" (p. x) who chooses a solution because he or she finds it personally pleasing rather than choosing it for how it will serve the end user. Can we draw any parallels between product design and instructional design? Can we make any generalizations about the practice of design? Yes, across disciplines and job tasks, *design*:

- Is a complex endeavor involving knowledge of many disciplines;
- Is a learning process;
- Is a reflective conversation with the materials of the situation;
- Is dependent on the context of the situation;
- Is iterative;
- Can be improved through collaboration and multiple perspectives;
- Is a goal-directed process;
- Produces something with practical utility;

- Involves generating solutions for ill-defined problems;
- Involves transforming design requirements into design specifications;
- Involves a combination of technical skills and creativity, rational and intuitive thought processes. (Norman, 2002; Rowland, 1993; Schön, 1987)

Norman (2002) emphasizes that, ultimately, good design is "an act of communication between the designer and the user" (p. xi). The success of the designer's message is dependent on how well the designed product explains itself. In the case of instructional design, the learner must be able to relate to and understand the instruction, particularly if it is stand-alone without the benefit of a "live" instructor to explain it. Norman goes on to describe certain design principles that apply to product design. We can apply these principles to instructional design, as well:

- Provide learners with a conceptual model to aid their understanding;
- Provide *feedback* so learners understand the effect of their actions; and
- Build in constraints that make it impossible for the learner to do something the wrong way, and affordances that make it easy to perceive how to do something the right way.

Take away a valuable tip from Norman to apply to your ID practice: *become an astute observer of people, of instruction, and of the way they interact.* As you refine this ability, you will be able to identify problems *and* offer effective instructional solutions.

The Nature of Design Problems

We've mentioned design for instruction and the design of products, but design is a creative process that is carried out in almost every field, with some of the most commonly recognized fields being architecture, engineering, and software development. In all of these fields, design involves *problem solving* and is regarded by many as an *ill-structured* process because it frequently deals with ill-structured problems (Jonassen, 1997; Rowland, 1993). Solving *well-structured* problems is a straightforward process because it's generally easy to analyze the existing situation, identify the problem and all the parameters involved, define the ideal situation, and follow structured, straightforward methods to solve the problem. For example, there are well-established and appropriate methods to use for changing the tire on a car or truck. Well-structured problems *do* exist in the IDT field; however, the more challenging design problems are those that are ill-structured.

In contrast, an ill-structured problem is not well-defined, many of its elements are unknown or are not consistent, the goals are often unclear, and there are multiple possible solutions. There are no obvious right answers or solutions because ill-structured problems are usually complicated by varying factors and conditions. The designer must simultaneously understand multiple facets: the needs and characteristics of multiple learners, the many constraints and resources involved in the situation, the different conditions occurring in multiple contexts, and the multiple perspectives of the populations involved. Consider this contrast between a well-structured and ill-structured design challenge, taken from the field of architectural design:

> *Well-structured challenge*—An architect is given a specific budget and timeline and is tasked with adjusting a standard townhouse design for the size of a level building site, and producing a cookie-cutter plan for a complex that has already been duplicated numerous times in the city.
> *Ill-structured challenge*—An architect is given an unlimited budget, a problematic building site, very few goals and constraints, and a vague client request that cutting-edge green

technology be used. This version of the problem is much more ill-structured and challenging. If the architect is an expert with a highly developed knowledge base in his field, his vast experience may make the task less complex for him and he may be able to quickly accomplish the job. However, the problem would remain ill-structured for him if he knows next to nothing about green technologies.

Now consider an ill-structured challenge from the IDT field. How easy do you think it would be to train graduate geology students to predict the impact of a potential tsunami caused by a 9.0-point earthquake, 50 miles offshore in multiple areas where there have been no previous earthquakes? And what if you also wanted them to be able to provide recommendations for precautionary measures in those areas? Imagine the complexity of making recommendations for both high-population First World countries, and high- and low-population Third World countries! In such a situation, there are many unknowns, and the recommendations would require these graduate students to have knowledge in areas other than geology, including sociology and culture, demographics, geography, and more.

The challenge of ill-structured design problems is clear: you must understand and consider all the content, learners, contexts, systems, and conditions involved; generate multiple alternative solutions; select and justify a solution; and then implement that solution and adjust it based on feedback. This challenge illustrates the value of using an iterative, systematic, and systemic design process (addressed later in this chapter.)

The Nature of Technology

When you mention the word "technology," educators typically envision physical *products* such as computers, videos, DVDs, mobile tablets, and electronic white-boards … even pencils are a form of technology! However, many do not realize that the word "technology" has both a "*product*" meaning, and a "*process*" meaning. The etymology of the word *technology* hints at this process meaning. The word comes from the Greek *tekhnologia*, which means "a systematic treatment of an art or craft" (Garrison & Anderson, 2003, p. 33). Therefore, instructional technology as a *process* refers to the systematic treatment of the craft of designing instruction, through the application of learning theories and the use of technology *products* to support solutions to educational problems.

In its infancy, the field of IDT emphasized instructional media and the use of audiovisual materials. Over time, the field has evolved to emphasize two main areas that reflect the product and process meanings of instructional technology:

1. The use of different types of *physical media* to communicate instructional messages and support teaching and learning; and
2. The use of *systematic approaches* to analyze learning needs, and to design, develop, implement, and evaluate instructional materials to meet those needs.

The effective use of media and systematic processes, supported by research-based theories, prepares you to practice instructional design in a variety of other fields, yielding a career that is satisfying and continually interesting. In the same way that veterinarians apply biological theories to the care of animals and accountants apply mathematical theories to solve financial challenges, instructional designers apply theories from many fields (including learning science, educational psychology, media, communications, systems, and more) to solve educational problems and meet educational needs.

Systematic and Systemic Design

To produce instructional products, IDT professionals use a *systematic* design process. Smith and Ragan (2005) define Instructional Design (ID) as: "the systematic and reflective process of translating principles of learning and instruction into plans for instructional materials, activities, information resources, and evaluation" (p. 4). In the following section, you will read about the many steps involved in a typical, systematic instructional design and development project.

Effective instructional design is also *systemic*. A *system* is an interdependent set of items that form a unified whole, and therefore systemic design is holistic, and considers all the systems that impact, and are impacted by, the learner. Since human beings are social, we tend to be part of several systems that impact how we learn. For example, a learner enrolled in a university course is part of that offering of the course, which is in turn part of the course offerings at a specific institution of higher education. That institution may be part of a state system of elementary, secondary, and post-secondary schools, which, in turn, is part of the system of education offered in the United States, which is part of the U.S. government and society. Potentially, what occurs in one of those systems can influence components in all related systems.

Considering systemic influences may enable you to design better instruction, or may merely ensure that you acknowledge project constraints over which you have no control. For example, if you were designing a unit of instruction for fifth-graders on writing short stories, how do you think it would impact the success of your materials if you discovered that the parents of 50% of the children in the class had read books to their children regularly since kindergarten, while the parents of the other 50% had never read to their children at all? Or, how might the availability of funding for web-based courses influence your decision on whether to use a face-to-face or a web-based format for your college biological field methods course? Systems issues are *contextual* issues, and instructional designers must address them because they ultimately impact how, and how well, the target audience learns (context issues are addressed in Chapter 4). Your observation and thoughtful reflection about the systems and interactions involved in a particular project will enable you to produce more effective instruction.

ADDIE: An Iterative Design Process

This book highlights just one of the numerous models that exist to guide the design of instruction. Figure 1.2 illustrates the classic, systematic ADDIE model of instructional design, with a slight adjustment. The acronym "ADDIE" is typically described as standing for the process phases of Analysis, Design, Development, Implementation, and Evaluation (Allen, 2006). In this book, we'd like to emphasize that the model elements represent *activities* rather than phases or stages, and that these activities are carried out repeatedly, or *iteratively*, throughout the life of an instructional product. Our version of the model uses the verb form of these activities to indicate action, and its shape emphasizes the iterative nature of the process involved.

Note that the center of the model includes the symbol for infinity labeled with the phrase *continually improve*, because this process really *can* seem to go on forever. And it should! If you're not improving the instruction, you should be continually improving your design and development skills. A list of the components addressed by each ADDIE activity follow, and the words "Review/ Approve/Revise" are repeated between each major activity to emphasize that the designer evaluates and seeks input from *subject matter experts (SMEs)* and stakeholders, revising and improving the instruction at multiple points during the process.

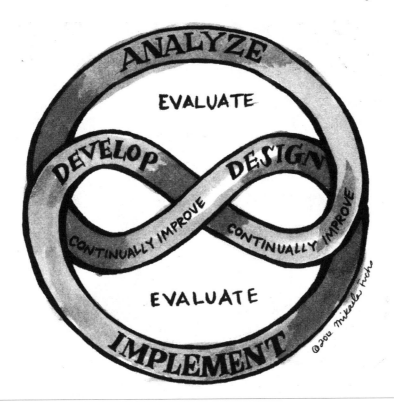

Figure 1.2 The Iterative ADDIE Model

Analyze ...

- Problem, Expectations, and Needs
- Goals, Resources, and Constraints
- Learners
- Contexts
- Content, Prerequisites, and Priorities

REVIEW/APPROVE/REVISE

Design ...

- Learning Outcomes and Sequencing
- Aligned Outcomes, Assessments, and Strategies
- Message, Media, and Delivery Systems
- Evaluation Plan

REVIEW/APPROVE/REVISE

Develop/Produce ...

- Project Management Tools
- Adaptations of Existing Materials
- Prototypes
- Final Instruction
- Implementation Guidelines

REVIEW/APPROVE/REVISE

Implement ...

- Instruction and Learning Experiences
- Feedback Collection
- Evaluation and Revision Tracking

REVIEW/APPROVE/REVISE

Evaluate and Continually Improve throughout *the Process Using ...*

- Reviews and Feedback Analysis
- Formative Testing and Observations
- Summative Evaluation
- Revisions
- Examination of Teamwork and ID Process

Evaluation

Planning for a successful design means *beginning with the end in mind.* You should have a concrete picture of what success will look like for your learners, and should evaluate your instruction against that benchmark throughout your project. The evaluation process is both *formative* (ongoing during design, development, and implementation activities) and *summative* (appraised after completion and implementation of the instruction). For example, when an artist steps back to analyze a picture, she is in the process of painting, she is conducting a formative evaluation. When her clients view the painting in a gallery, it is being summatively evaluated.

You will note that in the illustration of the ADDIE model, the word *evaluate* is placed in the background to emphasize its ongoing nature throughout the process. *Continuous evaluation* produces feedback that facilitates *continuous improvement* of the instruction. In the late 1950s, Donald L. Kirkpatrick developed what has become one of the most popular models for evaluating instructional programs (see Table 1.1). Kirkpatrick's four-level system of evaluation is primarily summative, since it is used to evaluate instruction after development and implementation. However, the first two levels of his model can also be used formatively to gauge learner satisfaction and monitor learning. Beyond that Kirkpatrick stresses that, to produce accurate results at any of the levels, you must plan for and conduct appropriate measurements at the *beginning* of a project and *throughout* the design/development process (Kirkpatrick & Kirkpatrick, 2006). To illustrate how this might be accomplished, each chapter of this book includes notes on evaluation considerations during different portions of the design/development effort.

At the start of any instructional design/development project, you should consider the main evaluative questions that you would like to be able to answer at the end of the project. With your stakeholders, develop a list of broad guiding questions—or *key questions*—that your evaluation will address. Russ-Eft and Preskill (2001) state that most program evaluations have from three to twelve key questions designed to focus and guide the entire evaluation process. They indicate that the questions should be broad and general, grouped by theme or category (or by Kirkpatrick level), and prioritized by those that *must* be answered versus those that would be *nice* to answer. The number of questions you identify will vary based on the number of Kirkpatrick's levels you intend to address. Chapter 11 provides more information on evaluation.

Table 1.1 Kirkpatrick's Four-Level Evaluation Model

Level	What the Level Measures	Questions and Measurement Example (How would you *like* to be able to answer these questions after implementation? Ponder them *early* to guide your design!)
I Learner Reaction	Evaluations conducted at this level measure the reaction and satisfaction of learners with the learning experience. A positive reaction can enhance learning, and may indicate that the instruction successfully addressed learner interests, attention, and motivation.	How did the learners to react to the learning experience? Were they satisfied with the instruction and did they find it relevant to their needs? Were they engaged in the instruction and did they complete it? Example: Use "smiley face" attitude questionnaires or course evaluations to gauge learner reaction.
II Learning	This level of evaluation measures the extent to which participants acquire the intended knowledge, skills, and attitudes as a result of the instruction. This is also known as *assessment.*	Did the learners acquire the intended knowledge, skills and desirable attitudes? What did they learn from the experience? Example: Administer a posttest on the content to gauge learning gains.
III Behavior	This level evaluates to what degree the learner applies what was learned in the final work context (e.g., in a job, in the next course, in life). Application of new learning is not only dependent on what has been learned, but also by the final performance/work context. Provide support and accountability in that context by implementing and tracking processes and systems (i.e., drivers) that reinforce, monitor, encourage, and reward performance of critical behaviors on the job. This level also known as "Performance" or "Transfer."	How did the instruction affect long-term learner behavior or performance? Was the learning transferred to the work or performance environment? Is the learner actually *using* what they learned? If not, why not? Is it because they didn't learn it or are there administrative or motivational challenges preventing the application of the learning? Example: Some time after the instruction, observe the learner in the job setting or use a performance test to determine if the new knowledge and skills are being applied in authentic settings.
IV Results	Measuring and reporting results enables you to justify the cost of the learning experience by demonstrating its value to the sponsoring organization. Your results should clearly illustrate the "impact" of the instruction on the organizational goals it was designed to achieve. Monitor leading indicators of success. Identify desired outcomes and take benchmark measurements at the beginning of the project, and then remeasure following the instruction to demonstrate results/impact.	Did improvements in learner performance (resulting from the instruction) affect organizational goals? Did the learning event impact productivity, job placement, graduate school acceptances, retention, etc? What is the return on investment (ROI) or return on expectations (ROE) of the instructional effort? Example: Analyze job placement and retention figures to judge the value or worth of the instructional program and its objectives.

Adapted from: Kirkpatrick and Kirkpatrick (2006).

Principles of Streamlining

There are numerous methods and metrics available to use for each activity listed in the ADDIE process, but you may not have the time or resources to complete all of the ADDIE activities for every project you design. This book is based on the idea that, in most cases, the entire design/ development process can be *streamlined* (made more efficient and effective) by taking short-cuts or using faster and simpler methods. The use of faster and simpler methods frees up more time for "testing" the instruction so you can produce more efficient and effective instruction. (A notable exception to the use of this approach would be the development of critical, life-and-death instruction for which the stakes are often too high to rush the process.) With this approach in mind, note the following five Principles of Streamlining that can help you design and develop instruction more efficiently and effectively:

1. *Practice Sustainable ID*—Whenever possible, design with the future in mind. In many design fields, research has identified sustainability as a key priority (Manfra, 2005). Sustainability is a key concern in IDT, as well. Ask yourself: What is the life expectancy of the instruction? How long will it be used? How often will it need updating? Has maintenance and updating been planned for in the budget? Is the design scalable so that it can easily be expanded to meet the needs of a wider audience?

2. *Practice Optimized ID*—Whenever possible, design so that all or portions of the instruction can serve multiple purposes. Ask yourself: Can the components of the instruction be used by multiple courses or training applications? Are there other needs in the organization that the instructional elements could also address, such as providing informational material for *knowledge management* systems, or marketing materials? Should the instruction be developed as a series of *learning objects*, or a set of case studies that could serve multiple functions? Might the instruction be recycled in the future and, if so, how can it be designed to make its reuse and revision an easy task? Are there existing materials that can be used or slightly adjusted to meet all or a portion of the need? If there are existing materials that need revision, what is the least change that can be made for the greatest effect?

3. *Practice Redundant ID*—Now, this principle must be applied carefully, because if you force a learner to view redundant materials they can become frustrated and annoyed. However, it is always wise to provide access to redundant instructional elements as a backup plan, in case the main *delivery system* fails or cannot be accessed by all learners. Ask yourself: If a learner does not have the correct equipment or has a disability that prevents them from accessing all elements of the instruction, how can I provide an alternate format or means of delivery?

4. *Practice Right-Sized ID*—Stakeholders often communicate conflicting needs or propose a multitude of purposes for an instructional project. As a result, you can end up with "supersized" instruction that goes way beyond the immediate need or that, in attempting to meet all needs, really doesn't adequately meet anyone's needs. Take a right-sized approach, and for any given design project ask yourself: What is the essential material that must be covered versus the nice-to-know material? How can I produce high value per volume of instruction? What topics are likely to hold long-term constant value or apply to the widest audience? What topics hold special value and cannot be easily obtained from other sources? If the instruction will be used in multiple locations or for multiple purposes, can I produce a generic version that can be locally and easily customized? Can I start on a small scale and develop a design that works and then add components that repeat the basic design plan with applicable variations, as time and money allow?

5. *Practice Continuous Improvement*—This is a cornerstone principle of all instructional design, and it underscores the iterative nature of the process. Surprisingly, it also aligns well with a philosophy of streamlining, because when an instructional designer tests their ideas and *prototypes* early and often with key stakeholders and representatives from the target audience, it results in instruction that continually gets more accurate and more effective at meeting the identified needs.

Each chapter in this book addresses how ADDIE activities can be streamlined according to these principles, and provides examples to help you design more efficient and effective instruction.

Learning Environments

Across the span of your career, you will likely design instruction for a variety of different learning environments. You might develop instruction for individuals, as well as for collaborative groups.

You will probably also develop instruction for both asynchronous and synchronous learning activities. *Asynchronous* instruction occurs when individuals are involved in learning activities outside the constraints of place and time. Note these examples of asynchronous instruction:

- A written correspondence course that can be completed at the learner's home or work location;
- Online self-study materials that can be completed by learners from a personally convenient location, at any hour of the day or night; and
- An online course that requires learners to post comments and reply to course peer comments on a virtual discussion board that is accessible at any time and from any location with Internet connectivity.

Synchronous learning involves groups of individuals learning at the same time and in the same physical *or* virtual place. Note these examples of synchronous learning activities:

- Traditional face-to-face courses and workshops;
- Online classes that meet in real time by means of audio or video-conferencing equipment;
- Online webinars and presentations that allow for audience-presenter interaction.

Asynchronous and synchronous learning activities can be carried out in almost any learning environment, although some spaces are better suited for fostering the type of interaction that collaborative strategies seek to facilitate.

You might be tasked with designing instruction that is highly structured, directed, and formal. Or you might be asked to design unstructured, informal learning experiences that allow the learner to self-direct and control what they access and the time, place, path, and/or pace of instruction.

As technology advances, new possibilities for learning activities and environments are continually being conceived and developed. The variety of possibilities can be confusing, and since instructional design is rarely carried out in isolation you should become familiar with some of the more common classification systems for learning environments so that you can communicate with others during design discussions. These learning environment classification systems are typically illustrated as matrices that chart two conditions on a continuum.

Time and Place Where and when is the instructional interaction taking place? Dan Coldeway's quadrants are often used to categorize distance learning environments as well as other learning environments (Simonson, 2003). The four quadrants of his matrix plot time and place to illustrate four categories of learning environments: same time/same place instruction (such as traditional face-to-face classrooms), same time/different place instruction (synchronous distance education, often delivered via interactive telecommunications technologies), different time/same place instruction (such as individualized online tutorials available for student use in a library media center), and different time/different place instruction (asynchronous distance learning).

Content and Geographic Location Where and when is the instructional interaction taking place? This matrix is used primarily in K-12 settings, and plots the amount of content delivery from offline to online, and geographic location on a continuum from supervised brick-and-mortar schools to remote locations. Possibilities include offline content in a supervised school setting (e.g., a traditional classroom), offline content in a remote setting (e.g., home study without online content), online content delivery in a supervised school setting (e.g., Internet activities carried out at a school and supervised either locally or by virtual teachers), or online content delivery in a remote location (e.g., a state or district virtual high school or via mobile applications), among others (Staker & Horn, 2012).

Collaboration and Self-Direction How much group collaboration and individual initiative is required? This matrix illustrates how varying degrees of collaboration and self-direction can distinguish certain learning environments. The four quadrants include low collaboration/low self-direction (e.g., a teacher-delivered lecture followed by a traditional assessment), low collaboration/high self-direction (e.g., an individual student research project), high collaboration/low self-direction (e.g., teacher-identified problems and student-led brainstorming for solutions), and high collaboration/high self-direction (e.g., a team-selected and team-executed project).

There are many other categorizations that are helpful to use in design discussions, one of which addresses the categorization of instructional strategies by the nature of the learning environment. Weston and Cranton's (1986) model groups teaching methods into four categories: instructor-centered, individualized, interactive, and experiential. They emphasize that the selection of appropriate strategies is dependent on many factors, including the prior knowledge of the learners, the instructional objectives, the available resources, the context, and the subject matter.

Fortunately, today's technologies enable people to learn anytime, anyplace, with anyone, anywhere, online or offline, collaboratively or individually. Such environments may be technology-enhanced physical spaces or virtual spaces enabled by technology. Learning occurs in formal spaces such as classrooms, and informal places such as coffee shops, aboard mass transportation, and in hallways. Even in formal spaces, the previously traditional lecture format is increasingly giving way to learning activities that include group work, student-led presentations, and a variety of interactions between students and with the instructor. Many face-to-face instructors are "flipping" their content, requiring students to consume content outside of class time so they can use the face-to-face time to clear up *misconceptions*, discuss content, and facilitate activities that allow students to apply their new knowledge and skills (Berrett, 2012).

Learning environments can often feature either, or both, *synchronous* activities (occurring in real time) and *asynchronous* activities (occurring at a time and place convenient for the learner). Here is a sampling of environments for which you might eventually design instruction:

- *Traditional Face-to-Face*—Face-to-face (F2F) environments include traditional K-12 classes and university courses, business training classes and workshops, traditional apprenticeships, teaching labs, and enrichment classes offered by community and religious or civic organizations. In such environments, the majority of activity occurs in real time, although these courses are increasingly supplemented with online materials. The Sloan Consortium Reports use the term "web-facilitated course" (Allen & Seaman, 2007; Picciano & Seaman, 2007) to describe face-to-face courses that deliver up to 29% of the content online.
- *Online*—In these learning environments the instruction is primarily delivered online via the World Wide Web, via an internal company intranet system, or via a mobile environment such as a smartphone or tablet (at least 80% of the content is delivered online for these courses, according to Sloan).
- *Blended or Hybrid*—These environments typically consist of a combination of face-to-face and online activities (the Sloan Consortium sets the percentage of online activity for blended courses at 30–79%). However, note that some organizations define "blended" differently.
- *Personal Learning Environments (PLEs)*—PLEs include the tools, communities, and services that make up an individual's learning environment, enabling them to access, select, and organize a broad range of resources to pursue their own learning goals and direct their

own learning (Educause, 2009). PLEs may also include *job aids* that provide just-in-time information to help employees perform at or beyond expected levels.

- *Performance Support Systems*—Network-based knowledge systems are designed to support performance by delivering information to individuals and groups at the moment they need it (Piskurich, 2000). Most are *electronic performance support systems (EPSS)* that provide employees or learners with what is referred to as *just-in-time* or *point-of-need* access to reference documentation, tutorials, job aids, and other materials through a user interface.

The Importance of Learning Theory and Research

There are many factors that influence learning, and these elements and circumstances are the focus of many research studies in the field of instructional design. Much of the research is based on certain assumptions about knowledge and how people learn that educators and researchers from a variety of fields have proposed as *formal learning theories.*

Studying these learning theories and the assumptions upon which they are based will equip you to thoughtfully question their applicability to specific learning problems and to make informed decisions about content treatment and appropriate instructional strategies. However, even if you understand the theories and assumptions and have a firm idea of their proper application, you may not always be free to select the theory base for your instructional design. Besides considering whether certain learning assumptions apply to a particular design problem, you should also consider the perspectives of your target learners and those of your client or major stakeholders. Chapter 4 provides more details on assumptions about learning and learning theories, which represent just one of the many *contexts* that influence the design of instruction.

Regardless of career environment, knowledge of learning theories is almost always cited as desirable in IDT job ads. Competent instructional designers have knowledge about a variety of learning theories and learning assumptions and know how to use them as a basis for their designs. In addition, they justify their designs by using valid *research* on measures that best support those assumptions. If you know the research and you can use it effectively for justification, your design will be grounded in theory and research, and will be more likely to foster learning success.

Caution!

As you study the research, note that there are many *media comparison studies* that attempt to illustrate the value of mediated instruction over traditional instruction (i.e., instruction that utilizes more advanced technologies than traditional technologies like face-to-face lectures and handouts, per Heinich, 1968). These studies also try to compare the learning that results from instruction delivered by two different technologies. Such studies are typically flawed, because in social sciences research there are just too many human variables that you cannot control for in an experimental study. Comparison studies typically result in findings that claim "no significant difference" between the learning results for the compared treatments. A major critic of such studies, the noted researcher and theorist Richard Clark wrote a classic article (1983) that argued that instructional media made excellent *vehicles* for storing and delivering instructional messages, but were not responsible for learning. Instead, learning is promoted by factors such as the instructional content, the strategies used to promote learning, and the engagement of the learner in the learning activities. It is essential to remember that instructional designers should select technologies to *support specific instructional strategies* (addressed further in Chapter 9).

Instructional Design Career Environments and Competencies

Since learning generally occurs in every human interaction and relationship, people who design instruction work in many fields and in both formal and informal learning environments. For example, instructional designers are employed in higher education, K-12 education, business and industry, government, military, health-care, and non-profit organizations. In each of these environments, the different values, priorities, and purposes for education impact the way in which ID is carried out. For example, note how the competencies listed in Table 1.2 differ by career environment. The requirements for the extent of an instructional design and its justification also tend to differ by career environment. For some business environments, you must have a detailed design document complete with a *return on investment (ROI)* study to justify your efforts, while in K-12 environments you provide objectives and a lesson plan. This book highlights some of those differences through explanations and examples.

Because the field is so broad, the role of an instructional designer also ranges widely. The title of instructional designer is applied to instructors who develop and teach their own materials; to those who work with subject matter experts (SMEs) to develop classroom or online courses; and to design team members producing portions of stand-alone content for corporations and universities. In any of these roles, your knowledge of how the different technologies foster and support learning will enable you to make effective choices as you design instruction. Of course, as Norman (2002) says, "technology changes rapidly; people change slowly" (p. xiv), so the ability to observe people and how they interact with technology is also essential.

Over the years, different professional groups have come up with lists of competencies for instructional designers. The International Board of Standards for Training, Performance and Instruction (ibstpi) defines a *competency* as "an integrated set of skills, knowledge, and **attitudes** that enables one to effectively perform the activities of a given occupation or function to the standards expected" (see http://www.ibstpi.org). Often, instructional design competencies vary by career environment. For example, skill in the methods used for human performance improvement (HPI) is a competency cited by organizations geared more to business and industry environments. Table 1.2 provides a list of competencies unique to specific career environments.

Based on your career goals, you can consult one or more of the lists of competencies and standards developed for IDT. Organizations with competency lists and/or standards include the American Society for Training and Development (ASTD), the International Society for Performance Improvement (ISPI), the Association for Educational Communications and Technology (AECT), the Society for Information Technology and Teacher Education (SITE), the International Society for Technology in Education (ISTE), the Society for Applied Learning Technology (SALT), and the National Council for the Accreditation of Teacher Education (NCATE). Links to some of these lists are provided on the book website. Ultimately, all effective instructional designers carry out a process of design that is systematic, systemic, and iterative (Cennamo & Kalk, 2005). Consider your career goals, and then do a little research to figure out the specific competencies required for competent instructional designers in the career environment of your choice.

Taking a "Deep" Approach to IDT

If you are a novice instructional designer, or even an experienced designer, we hope that you will take a *deep approach* to learning about instructional design and technology throughout your career. Research shows that when learners are committed to forming a personal understanding of the topic under study, they will take a deep approach that includes active engagement and interest in the topic. While this book describes a streamlined approach to the ID process, we'd like to emphasize that the more you understand about the practice of ID and about different

Table 1.2 Unique or Emphasized Areas of Competency for Specific Career Environments

Career Environment	Area of Competency and Specific Skills
Business and Industry	• The basics (ability to think, write, and communicate orally and to make wise and wide use of instructional design and technologies) • Communication competence (writing and technical writing, public speaking and presentation skills, ability to justify and communicate a sound business case for training solutions) • Interpersonal relationship competence (motivation, coaching, persuasion, leadership, negotiation, team skills, cross-cultural awareness) • Analytic competence (critical thinking, problem definition and problem solving, performance gap analysis and strategy/intervention application, business research skills) • Project management competence (project/resource management, contracting and outsourcing skills, customer-oriented outlook) • Business competence (systems thinking, organizational and industry knowledge, change management and coping, global solutions, cost-benefit analysis and return on investment studies, knowledge of business trends like performance improvement and emotional intelligence) • New technology literacy and competence (knowledge of recent technologies, evaluation of new technologies, online teaching/designing and distance education abilities)
Higher Education	• Teaching experience • Interpersonal skills • Knowledge and/or experience in multimedia technologies and computer-based instruction • Expertise and track record in research • Knowledge of, and experience in, applying learning theories to instructional designs • Production of grant proposals • Knowledge and/or experience in telecommunications and distance learning
K-12 Education	• Knowledge and skills to meet federal and state standards • Library media specialists require information specialist skills, resource selection skills, cooperative planning skills
Military	• High level of training and familiarity with technologically advanced systems • Knowledge of technological simulation systems • Training methods for digitized tasks • Knowledge of Distributed Mission Training (DMT), combining live, virtual, and constructive simulation • Knowledge or experience in program evaluation and needs assessment • Knowledge of adult learning
Government	• Training for learners with less formal education preparation • Knowledge of federal and state codes and regulations • Ability to apply for and obtain federal- and state-funded grants • Project management, oversight and evaluation of training consultants and services • Contracting IDT services • Knowledge of adult learning
Health Care	• The basics (ability to think, and communicate—both written and oral—and to make wise and wide use of instructional design and technologies) • Communication competence (especially technical writing) • Interpersonal relationship competence (team skills, cross-cultural awareness) • Analytic competence (critical thinking, problem definition and problem solving, performance gap analysis and strategy/intervention application) • Project management competence (project/resource management, customer-oriented outlook) • Business competence (systems thinking, organizational and industry knowledge) • New technology literacy and competence (knowledge of recent technologies, evaluation of new technologies) • Knowledge and skills to meet federal and various licensing standards • Work with and compile information from a broad range of sources (medicine, nursing, other health-care specialties to create the knowledge base as well as incorporating information from the library, articles, research, best practice, and specialists) • Learning assessment background or experience—especially authentic assessment • Knowledge of adult learning principles • The ability to develop training for learners with less formal education preparation than you or more formal education preparation.

Source: Bartell (2001); Cabral-Cardoso (2001); I. Ekstrom (personal communication, October 6, 2012); Grimwald (2001); Larson (2004); Tasker & Packham (1993); Trimby (1982)

**Test Your Understanding
With a Bloom Stretch**

Apply	Apply your understanding of systems theory to identify the different systems involved in your choice of a specific educational system. Briefly describe how each subsystem impacts the other systems involved. For example, you could describe the systems in your state's public education organization, those involved in a multinational company, the systems that interact in a Third World health organization, military or governmental training systems, or the interaction of various subsystems that impact an institute of higher education.
Analyze	Do an Internet search to find three examples each of good and bad instruction. Provide a bulleted list for each example that briefly describes the good and bad design elements.
Evaluate	Locate a list of criteria for online instruction and then use that list to evaluate one of the good and one of the bad examples of instruction you found for the "Analyze" activity, above.
Create	Pick and choose from the various competency lists available to create a table of competencies that you could use for personal professional development. For each competency, the table should state the desired competency or standard, the sponsor organization, a rating of your own proficiency for that competency or standard, and your ultimate proficiency goal.

technologies, the more competent you will be as an instructional designer. Commit now to be a lifelong learner in the field and take a deep approach to learning that includes:

- An intention to understand;
- Active interest and personal engagement;
- Relating new ideas to previous learning;
- Gaining an overview of the topic;
- Creating outlines and structures;
- Questioning and using evidence critically;
- Seeking the central point;
- Drawing conclusions;
- Seeing the purpose of a task or seeing it in its wider context (McCune & Entwistle, 2000).

Ultimately, effective IDT is a combination of all the *concepts* discussed in this chapter. It is broad and varied; involves product and process; is systematic, systemic, and iterative; is supported by learning theory and research; and much, much more. Begin now to take a deep approach, and, as you read about concepts that we touch on in this book, mark those that you'd like to know more about so you can revisit the topics in the future. We encourage you to consult the resources recommended at the end of each chapter under "Diving Deeper" and on the website for each chapter, and to seek out activities that allow you to explore the depth and breadth of practice in the field of IDT.

Diving Deeper

Want to know more? Much of what you've read in this chapter represents just the "tip of the iceberg," and when your schedule allows it we encourage you to go deeper to learn more about the topics addressed. The website for this book provides exercises and resources for further study on the following topics:

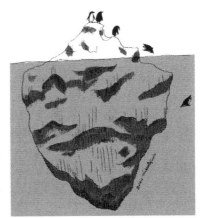

- **Practical Exercises and Examples**—A completed IDT competency goals worksheet.
- **Job Aids**—A worksheet for identifying personal IDT competency goals.
- **Resources**—Recommended resources on the history of the IDT field, instructional design competencies, learning environments, and other instructional design models.

2
Analyzing Needs to Define the Project

ERMA STRUGGLES TO DEFINE THE PROJECT.

At the beginning of a project, designers gather and analyze a wealth of information to define the main problem and the basic needs involved. Often, those needs can be met with instruction, *but not all problems have an instructional solution,* so some needs must be addressed through other means. Analyzing the problem and needs helps you define the *scope* of a project, which is also impacted by the type and amount of resources available, and any limiting constraints. For instruction, the project scope is also influenced by learner needs and characteristics, contextual factors, and the content itself. Ideally, you analyze all these things simultaneously, but since design is typically collaborative and fraught with conflicting stakeholder expectations, defining the scope may take longer than expected (especially if you have to act as a mediator between parties to gain consensus). Consequently, defining the project scope is a bit like trying to nail gelatin to the wall—the process tends to fall apart frequently and requires that you return repeatedly to your analysis data to reconsider it throughout the life of the project. In this chapter, you'll examine streamlined analysis methods that you can use to define the scope of a project.

Inquiring Minds Want to Know ...

- How do you determine whether a problem, challenge, or opportunity has an instructional solution?
- Who are the stakeholders involved in the instructional design process?
- How do you identify the essential or critical needs that must be met?
- How do instructional needs translate into instructional goals?
- What resources should be identified for a project and what type of constraints might impact and shape the project scope?
- What do I need to remember and understand from this chapter?

    ⇒ Some common roles and responsibilities in the instructional design process;
    ⇒ What is meant by "the gap between what is and what should be";
    ⇒ The meaning of the terms "needs analysis," "project scope," "curriculum alignment," "instructional alignment," and "instructional goals;" and
    ⇒ The analysis activities involved in determining the project scope.

Defining Terms: Needs, Problems, and Opportunities

When the communication theorist David Berlo stressed that *meanings are in people, not in words* (1960), he was referring to the fact that our understanding of language is based on our experiences. Naturally, if our experiences are different from those of others, we may be using the same words but have a completely different understanding of their meaning. When you move a word from one context to another, it is likely to change meaning. For example, to an individual learning the English language, a letter containing the sentence "Since we last saw you, Sally has grown another foot" could either mean Sally is quite a bit taller or that she now needs three shoes. To maximize the commonage between this book and your experience, and to minimize the chance of miscommunication, there are a few terms that require definition.

As noted above, instructional design projects are typically initiated to solve a *need.* Needs come in several forms, such as a *problem* (e.g., high self-inflicted injury rates among workers operating hand tools); a *challenge* (e.g., maintaining college enrollments in the face of competition from online degree programs); or an *opportunity* (e.g., training rural teachers to make use of a gift of cutting-edge technology). To streamline this book, we'll use the generic term "problem," trusting that you'll remember that instruction can just as easily be initiated to meet a challenge or take advantage of an opportunity.

Part of your job is to gather, sort through, and analyze information to determine if instruction is actually the best solution. This activity is known as *needs analysis,* or *needs assessment.* Some writers use these terms interchangeably (as we will in this book), while others distinguish between the two, stating that "needs assessment identifies and prioritizes needs, while needs analysis breaks needs down and suggests causes of and solutions to needs" (Benjamin, 1989, p. 12). To our way of thinking, this is all part of the same process, since you really need to understand the causes and potential solutions before you can effectively prioritize needs.

Jargon Alert!

The terms *needs analysis* and *needs assessment* aren't the only ones used to describe information-gathering and analysis activities. There are many others used in various career environments, including these types of analyses: *gap, front-end, goal, performance, learning, audience, delivery, critical incident, discrepancy, root cause, organizational, operational, opportunity, cost-benefit, job* or *task*, and *criticality*, just to name the most common analyses used! Take your pick—there are subtle similarities and differences among the terms and you can choose one based on the methods you want to use and the content and situation you must analyze. Often, an employer or client will *tell* you which method to use. If not, do a little Internet research on the terms and make the decision based on your understanding and needs. A needs analysis is just one type of analysis used in identifying the scope of a design project. Since it often overlaps with other analyses, make sure you and your key stakeholders are in agreement on the definition of the terms being used.

Notable Non-Examples

The purpose of instruction is typically to *meet an educational need, solve an educational problem, or address an instructional challenge.* You'll note the use of the modifiers "educational" and "instructional" in the previous sentence. So what happens when the solution to a problem is *not* instruction, but the stakeholders and designers are either ignorant of that fact or willfully overlook it? Take a look at these non-examples to learn what *not* to do when identifying the scope of an instructional design project.

> *Faulty Assumptions at 30,000 Feet*—According to ID folklore (might be true or false, but either way it makes our point), there once was an airline executive who was served wine in a water cup when flying first class on her own company's plane. Disturbed that the flight attendants did not know to serve wine in the proper wine glass, she initiated an elaborate training program to teach the attendants the proper wine service practices. Shortly after the implementation of this training effort, she again rode in first class on one of her company's planes. She ordered wine, confident that it would be served in the correct glass. Imagine her dismay when, once again, she was served wine in a plastic water cup! She immediately questioned the attendant to find out if he had attended the training course. Upon discovering that he had completed the training, the frustrated executive asked:
> "Then why did you serve my wine in a plastic water cup??!"
> As she listened to the attendant's reply, the executive gained a new understanding of the problem and realized the futility of her solution:
> "Why, we haven't had those wine glasses in stock for about six months. Procurement says they've been on back order forever!"
>
> *Addressing First Things, First*—An urban elementary school in Florida was struggling to bring up the test scores of their disadvantaged students. Their efforts to create engaging, effective instruction were failing until they partnered with a local YMCA's after-school program. It turns out many of the children came from homes where they did not, for whatever reason, receive an adequate evening meal. As a result, they did not sleep well on an empty stomach and frequently fell asleep in class the following day or were distracted to the point where they could not concentrate on their lessons. By partnering with local food service businesses that were willing to donate their surplus, wholesome food, the YMCA's

Kid's Cafe program was able to offer an after-school meal to these children. After this basic need was met, the teachers reported that the children were much more attentive in class, and were making increased academic progress.

Caution!

Both of these stories illustrate plainly that the success of any instructional effort begins with a thorough understanding of the problem and needs that should be addressed. Not all needs can be met with instruction, and even when instruction is the solution there are often other factors that must also be addressed to ensure success. The information in this chapter will help you avoid having your design become the topic of a Notable Non-Example due to a faulty analysis of the problem and needs.

So What's Involved? Analyzing to Define the Project

On paper, the analysis of needs looks like a simple process, but in truth it can get quite complicated, since it is carried out in conjunction with analyzing the target learners, the contexts of the instruction, and the content. All the analysis activities that apply to an instructional design project follow. Steps 1–4, 8, and 9 are covered in this chapter and address analyzing needs and other factors to define *goals* and the scope of an instructional project. Steps 5–7 are addressed in Chapters 3–5, as noted.

1. *Identify Stakeholders and Expectations*—Identify all key stakeholders and their expectations, including the primary target audience impacted by the problem and potentially influenced by any solutions (e.g., learners, users, employees).
2. *Identify Project Roles and Responsibilities*—Determine the roles and responsibilities of all those involved in the project. Seek to gain consensus and approval on project expectations.
3. *Define the Problem(s) and Analyze the Needs*—Identify the problem, challenge, or opportunity to be addressed, the causes or indicators, the resulting needs, and solution alternatives. If one or more of the needs can be effectively addressed with instruction, identify broad goals for the instruction.
4. *Gather Data on Needs, Resources, and Constraints*—Determine what you need to know about potential needs, resources, and constraints, and the data that will support the need for instruction. Select appropriate tools and initiate the data-gathering and analysis activities. Analyze the resources available to meet the needs and any additional resources that are required. Identify any constraints that will limit the project design, budget, and/or schedule.
5. *Analyze Learner Needs and Characteristics*—(covered in Chapter 3) Identify the primary target learners, and any secondary learner groups. The target learners are often identified for you by a client or by the situation itself; however, there may be secondary learner groups that have not been identified, but whose characteristics could exert a substantial influence over the content or format of the instruction.
6. *Analyze Contexts*—(covered in Chapter 4) Identify aspects of the learning and *performance contexts* that will impact the instructional design, the cultural context of the instruction, and the theoretical basis for the design.
7. *Analyze Content*—(covered in Chapter 5) Determine the boundaries of the content to be covered, any prerequisites, and the type of learning outcomes to be addressed.

8. *Refine and Translate Needs into Goals*—Consider the information from all the different analyses and translate the resulting needs into *goal statements* that can be reviewed and approved by key stakeholders.

9. *Seek Approval of the Project Scope and Plan*—Provide key stakeholders with a summary of your analysis and your recommendations for the project scope, and seek their approval of your plans.

Identifying Stakeholders and Their Expectations

Every project has a set of key groups and individuals who are interested and involved in, and are potentially impacted by, the instruction you design (Figure 2.1). *Stakeholder* refers to people who have a "stake" or claim concerning the nature of the instruction being designed, and who have certain expectations for the nature of that instruction. The type of stakeholders involved in a project often varies by career environment, but could include one or more of the following:

- Clients, owner/operators, managers, shareholders, employees, tax accountants, the client's customers, your customers, suppliers, partners, trainers or training coordinators;
- The general public, tax payers, government officials, government agencies;
- School administrators, school districts, parents and parent organizations, teachers, grant recipients, grant providers;
- Community and social service organizations, people served by aid agencies, funding agencies, accreditation and credentialing organizations;
- Department heads, faculty and staff, alumni, undergraduate students, graduate students, postdoctoral and research staff;
- Patients, doctors, nurses, or other medical professionals;
- Learners of all types and ages;
- And, of course, your own boss.

Figure 2.1 Stakeholders

Each stakeholder could have different expectations for the purpose, goals, and intended results of the instruction. There are many reasons that instruction is developed and many purposes it might be expected to fulfill. Instruction is developed to:

- *Inform* or instruct learners;
- *Encourage collaboration* to solve problems or creatively construct innovations;
- *Improve performance*;
- *Foster transfer* of learning to new situations;
- *Provide just-in-time information* for those who need it on the job.

In addition to opinions on the purpose for the instruction, stakeholders may expect a certain format or content, or may expect the instruction to be accessible and to accommodate special needs. Certain groups may expect a full-blown instructional workshop designed to improve performance, while others may only want job aids that provide concise information at the time of need. You may even encounter a wide range of opinions on the needs of the learners, or even about who the learners are for the project! Conflicting opinions on the purposes, needs, and final deliverables are common, so you should collect stakeholder expectations as early as possible to gain consensus, manage the expectations and obtain approval for your understanding of the project scope and results. Keep in mind that many instructional programs, designed to meet valid needs, fail because the sponsor's expectations or motives were not accurately interpreted and could therefore not be effectively managed or considered in the design. Finally, the most important concept to convey to your stakeholders is that the original, agreed-upon design can and probably will change!

Identifying Project Roles and Responsibilities

In addition to having expectations for your project, stakeholders are those who have key roles and responsibilities in the venture. Who is the client or initiator of the project? Who has funding and approval authority? Who will provide resources or information? Who will be impacted by the instruction or other interventions implemented to address identified problems? Who will do the actual design and development work? Depending on the career environment, the purpose of the instruction, and budget and time constraints, these roles and responsibilities may be carried out by an entire team or by a single individual. Examples of typical responsibilities for IDT projects include instructional design, graphic design, programming, scheduling, tracking, commissioning work, managing the budget and schedule, course maintenance, course meetings and minutes, instructional product testing, status reporting, collecting and setting expectations, and, often, "educating" the client about the value-added contributions of the design effort.

In almost all cases, there will be a client or initiator for the project. The client generally has funding authority and provides final approval of the scope and all other major deliverables. *You* may actually be the client if you will also teach the materials you develop, or if you are developing instruction that you intend to use to impress a potential employer. When you are the client, you must make sure to acknowledge your biases, assumptions, and preconceived notions, and to thoroughly research the needs of your target learners rather than fabricate or imagine their needs based on the instruction that you want or feel you need to design.

Typically, you will either be the content specialist or you will work with one or more "SMEs"— *subject matter experts*—who provide content information and review the instructional materials at various points in the process. If you are working on the project alone, you should have your materials reviewed by an impartial SME who is, preferably, external to the situation and yet aware of the needs and characteristics of the target learners. Some SMEs know the content well and have also taught it, while other SMEs may not understand what you are trying to do and therefore provide limited help or are downright uncooperative. Ideally, an SME knows the content, is willing to help, and is also knowledgeable about your target audience.

If you are part of a project team, it may include a project leader, graphic designer, multimedia specialist, programmer, web developer, instructional designer, and/or a marketing specialist. One person may fill several roles. A team approach is ideal, since projects typically benefit from the time and talents of all members of a design/development team, and businesses and organizations are increasingly adopting team-based approaches to produce goods and services. If you use a team approach, be sure to establish group norms and standards for working together and attempt to ascertain whether team members differ with regards to quality standards and work habits. It is also advisable to establish consistent quality standards, use templates and established formats, formalize your communication, and track progress and provide team members and supervisors with regular progress reports and lists of action items.

Defining the Problems and Analyzing the Needs

To adequately define the problem situation, you must identify all probable causes and analyze the resulting needs. Mapping this out involves identifying the existing situation or problem ("what is"), the desired situation ("what should be"), and the resulting gap between the two, or the *needs* (Figure 2.2).

Figure 2.2 Needs Analysis

Consider this simplified example: Sam is a 21-year-old computer analyst whose parents call to say they are coming to visit for the first time since Sam started working and moved into an apartment. They are arriving in time for lunch. Being new to the kitchen (he usually eats fast food), Sam decides to prepare his favorite dish, Chicken Pot Pie, and looks in the cookbook his mother gave him three years ago. After removing the shrink wrap from the cookbook, he reads the recipe and looks in his pantry to assess what he has and what he needs from the corner grocery store. He realizes that, not only is he missing some of the ingredients, he doesn't have enough utensils and he doesn't know how to work the gas stove in his apartment. If his only problem was a lack of ingredients and utensils, the solution to Sam's problem would be non-instructional—he could just go to the store for the items. However, there's more to the gap than missing items. The gap between *what is* (Sam's knowledge of how to work an electric stove) and *what should be* (knowing how to work a gas stove) reveals Sam's need for instruction on gas-stove cooking. After an unsuccessful search for the operator's manual for the ancient gas stove, Sam decides to take his parents out to lunch.

Scale and Purpose

The scale of your analysis is determined by what you are going to do with the information when the investigation is complete. Will you write up a report, formally present the data to key stakeholders, or merely file away the results? Realistically speaking, will anyone care about the information you uncover? Is the client determined to develop a training program regardless of the real needs? Is the School Board truly interested in hearing about the real issues and do they want desperately to avoid spending money needlessly or on the wrong project? You can use information from a needs analysis for many purposes:

- As justification and support for the problem solution you recommend;
- As a basis for estimating the time and schedule required to implement the proposed solution;
- To develop performance outcomes for instruction;
- To evaluate the success of the implemented solution;
- As a basis for rating the criticality of instructional content (e.g., rating "need to know" versus "nice to know" content);
- To prioritize needs and the resulting projects designed to address those needs;
- As a basis for estimating the costs or budget for proposed solutions; or
- As the basis of a report or presentation to communicate the needs analysis results.

Ultimately, a needs analysis is conducted to collect data that will be used to make appropriate decisions and to help you prioritize the identified needs (King, 1998, p. 21). However, even if there is a compelling reason to conduct a thorough needs analysis, designers often abbreviate or skip it due to a lack of time. For your own benefit as a designer (and to guard yourself from future attack by disgruntled stakeholders), you should try in some way to verify the need for instruction. It can be very frustrating to discover at the end of a project that the assumed needs were flawed or non-existent.

If a client or employer has provided you with information on the needs and characteristics of the target learner, then you should verify that information. As noted above, the client may not have an accurate picture of their learners' needs, or they may have other reasons for the project that have nothing to do with learner needs. For example, suppose your employer asks you to produce a series of videos of one of their sales trainers who has been very successful at training customers to use the products purchased from the company. The videos will be shown to other company sales staff newly tasked with training customers. You may suspect that the success of the trainer to be recorded is primarily due to his personality and the well-written technical manuals that he gives to the customers. Because of this, you may also be concerned that the videos will merely be "talking head" training products that do little to help the sales staff master their new job tasks.

In this situation, gathering evidence to support or refute your suspicions would provide you with a clear picture of the needs of the target learners and the demands of the task. If your employer rejects your evidence, you would at least be aware of the challenges ahead. You could then attempt to add features to the videos to address the true needs and result in effective instruction, despite the constraints placed upon you by your employer.

You can also identify needs by analyzing the organization's short- and long-term goals and its culture and climate, and comparing that information to key stakeholder expectations about what the proposed instruction will do for the organization. Are their expectations unrealistic considering the culture and climate of the organization? Are their expectations in line with the organization's stated goals? Additional needs will result from an analysis of the learners themselves (covered in Chapter 3), and an analysis of the content, task, or job involved (and the knowledge, skills, and attitudes required by those tasks or jobs) (covered in Chapter 5).

Instructional and Non-Instructional Solutions

Some needs may mistakenly be interpreted as requiring an instructional solution, when instead they may require another type of solution. Or, there may be a variety of needs that require both instructional and non-instructional solutions. Therefore, the basic needs assessment process should be designed to determine both what the needs are and whether they can be met through instruction. If you identify a problem that results from a lack of skills, knowledge, or information, it can generally be met through instruction or provision of a job aid. Problems resulting from a lack of motivation are also sometimes addressed with instruction. However, as illustrated in the first Notable Non-Example, your problem and needs analysis may uncover situations that are better addressed through non-instructional solutions, including changes in policies or procedures, administration, logistics or work-flow; or the provision of feedback, motivational rewards, or job aids and other performance supports. It is also common to address problems with a combination of instruction and other measures. Table 2.1 lists some sample problems with alternative solutions.

Table 2.1 Sample Problems and Alternative Solutions

Problem (What Is)	Desired Goals (What Should Be)	Gap (Resulting Needs) and Possible Solution Alternatives
Company profits are too low to cover expenses with an adequate profit margin.	Management wants to increase profits by 25%.	Increase profits through increased productivity, new products, better marketing, and/or training to reduce inefficiency.
District high school students are scoring low on tests measuring global awareness.	Students should score 100/126 on the Global Awareness Profile test.	Increase student global awareness through a new course in Comparative World Culture and Government; student exchange programs; language instruction requirements; inclusion of daily foreign news clips in all social science classes.
Increasing frequency of suicide amongst active military and veterans.	Suicide rates among active military personnel and veterans should be at or below suicide rates in the general society.	Improve diagnosis, treatment, and follow-up care for those with post-traumatic stress and traumatic brain injuries. Improve deployment preparation and build resilience of soldiers prior to deployment. Provide post-service counseling and placement services to reduce the number of homeless, unemployed veterans, paying particular attention to the plight of female veterans. Along with compensation and disability services, emphasize the abilities and future possibilities for wounded warriors. Improve the ability of military leaders to listen, provide focus, encourage, and aggressively advocate for their men and women. Educate military spouses and families about the issue and provide counseling and resources.

Basic Needs

There are certain basic individual needs that, if not met, can interfere with an individual's ability to learn, as illustrated in the second Notable Non-Example for this chapter. Abraham Maslow (1954, p. 236) promoted the view that all humans possess a biologically based core of needs, goals, values, satisfactions, and frustrations that affect their personality and behavior. Maslow's famous *hierarchy of needs*, illustrated in Figure 2.3, is used today in many fields. Maslow referred to it as a hierarchy, suggesting that the needs listed at the bottom must be met before those at the top; however, there may be situations where this may not be the case. Some people neglect or forgo lower needs (such as food or safety) to pursue higher ones (such as social and fulfillment needs), and some simultaneously pursue the fulfillment of multiple need levels. For example, some anorexic teens forgo food because they believe that by being thin they will belong and be loved, and some thrill seekers engage in activities that threaten their safety in order to fulfill a need for attention, esteem or fulfillment. Can you think of situations where some of these needs should be considered

Figure 2.3 Maslow's Hierarchy of Needs

prior to attempting to instruct a learner or group of learners? (Chapter 3 provides a more detailed coverage of the impact of learner needs and characteristics on the design of instruction.)

Gathering Data on Needs, Resources, and Constraints

Valid needs are supportable by data. Once you have a general idea of the needs involved, determine what data should be collected to support the need for instruction. Determine which questions to ask and the items to research to verify or further *elaborate* on the needs. What type of information will tell you if the needs are valid? Should you analyze existing *performance* or analyze future organizational goals to determine how performance goals should be adjusted? Be sure to plan your investigation carefully to minimize the time required to complete it.

The right tools can make the data gathering and analysis process more efficient and effective. Basically, you must decide on the methods and tools required to identify the difference between what *is* and what *should be*. For instructional solutions, the gap between these two consists of the knowledge, skills, and attitudes required by the learner. The methods and tools you select to investigate needs should support your efforts to: *ask, observe,* and *study*.

Most needs analysis efforts involve some type of interviews (individual and focus group), questionnaires or surveys, and observations. With these methods, designers may use *think-aloud* protocols, consultation with a panel of experts, analysis of online discussion boards, forums, chats, and messaging, and web statistics and *learning analytics*. Get feedback on any surveys or interview questions you intend to use from others who have expertise in developing such instruments, especially if your conclusions must be based on statistically valid and reliable data. Such experts can help you determine the size and makeup of a sample group of your target population, your method(s) of data collection, and how you should analyze and compute the results.

Observations can be made with live visits (random, or approved and scheduled), or can analyze approved video or audio recordings and photographs. Helpful tools include observation guides, recording sheets or checklists, rating scales, demographic forms, frequency count forms, and field notes. During observations, you may note things like:

- Actual activities as compared to stated activities;
- Undocumented procedures, methods, or management operations;
- Reactions of individuals attempting to complete required job tasks in less-than-optimal conditions;
- Quality and nature of products, assignments, or discourse and
- Physical atmosphere, learning environment, climate, or seating arrangements.

Some designers use more rigorous methods to yield results that will be carefully considered in "go/no-go" funding and authorization decisions. Others use methods designed to quickly verify needs that have already been identified. Select the methods and tools that align best with the scope of your investigation. Table 2.2 lists a variety of methods and tools for analyzing needs.

Table 2.2 Methods and Tools for Needs Analysis

People to Ask	Things to Observe	Things to Study/Analyze
• Key stakeholders • Members of the target audience or population • Upper, middle, and line managers • The target population's supervisors and subordinates • Co-workers or peers of the target population • Human resource personnel, school counselors, etc. • The organization's clients, customers, vendors, and competitors • Industry experts and commentators • Business experts in training, management, and strategy • Students and instructors • Administrators, School Board members, and PTA members	• Employee on-the-job behavior and skills; student classroom behavior • Employee or student desire for self-development and improvement • Supervisor behavior: assignment of work, planning and scheduling, instruction of subordinates, handling of grievances, job pride or interest, coordination skills, recognition and motivational skills • Instructor behavior: questioning ability, explanations, instructional delivery, grading behavior, encouragement and recognition of learners • Communication: written and oral instructions, information flow down, up, and across the organization, verbal oral and written expressive ability, semantic difficulties • Technical, administrative, and supervisory job knowledge and ability, and problem-solving ability • Factors related to morale: personal friction, blame-shifting, complaints, attention to work, leadership or support, style of leadership, clarity of purpose, feelings of belonging to the organization, communication of employee worth, recognition of accomplishments, job security • Demonstrations, instruction, presentations, performances, etc. • Cultural and class interactions, levels of support and cooperation, decision making, power relationships, flexibility, and adaptability • Levels of participation, attitudes, motivation, satisfaction, and engagement • Facial expressions, gestures, and postures	• Relevant literature, journal articles, books, and legal records about the problem or topic under study • Previous evaluations, needs analyses, inspection reports, audit reports, and organization or management studies; previous studies of the target population and/or their jobs • Organizational mission/vision statements, goals, criteria, and metrics, projections, short- and long-term plans, brochures, and newsletters, procedures, manuals, handbooks, job aids, and tools • Relevant individual and group employee records: employment records, test results, absences and tardiness, sick leave usage, merit ratings, composition of supervisory force, turnover rates, accident severity and frequency ratios, grievances and complaints, accident and incident reports • Relevant student records: absenteeism, tardiness, sick days, SAT and ACT scores, end-of-course scores, adequate yearly progress, graduation rates, dropout rates, college admissions rates, behavior incidents, participation in extracurricular activities, dual enrollments, AP and honors courses • Job descriptions, hiring qualifications, firing records, exit interviews, and recruiting records • Experience and training of supervisors or faculty, written reactions to past training • Work samples and performance appraisals • Work and work-flow: productivity reports, production bottlenecks, fluctuations in production, reports on public or customer satisfaction with products or services, nature and location of backlogs, records of high cost, waste, or excessive errors • Programs in other organizations similar to those being proposed

You should also ask key stakeholders to provide their opinions on the nature of the problem(s), the causes or indicators, the resulting needs, and the solution alternatives they would recommend. Encourage them to brainstorm several problems, causes, and solutions and to identify what they think the learner needs to know, do, and believe. Keep in mind that stakeholders often see the problem from different viewpoints and therefore have a different idea of the appropriate solutions (see Table 2.3). For example, it is not unusual to discover a discrepancy between what the client or project initiator thinks the learner needs to know, do, and believe, and what the target learners think they need to know, do, and believe. If you discover major differences in expectations, you should discuss the discrepancies with key stakeholders as soon as possible. If the stakeholders agree that the target learner opinions are valid, you should change the intended content for the instruction. However, if the stakeholders discount the opinions of the target learners, make sure that the instruction communicates its own relevance so that the learners are motivated to engage in the content.

Table 2.3 Differing Views of Problems and Solutions

Problem or Existing Situation (What Is)	Desired Situation (What Should Be)	Individual or Group Questioned	Possible Causes or Indicators	Solution Alternatives
Widgets are being assembled in the wrong order and, as a result, assembly takes longer and productivity is reduced.	Increased productivity resulting from using the fastest widget assembly method possible, while maintaining required quality standards.	Employees	Employees indicate that they didn't know they were assembling the widgets in the wrong order.	Provide feedback to employees.
		Employees	Employees know they are assembling widget components in a different order than instructed, but their method is easier and there is no incentive for them to increase productivity.	Provide rewards for proper assembly, including merit pay, privileges, recognition, or management development.
		Employees	Employees report that the assembly order is complicated and hard to remember.	Provide a job aid or other performance support to provide assembly instructions when employees need a reminder.
		Employees	Employees don't know how to properly assemble the widgets.	Provide training.
		Line Managers	Employees are unmotivated.	Provide rewards for proper assembly, including merit pay, privileges, recognition, or management development.
		Line Managers	Employees are actually using a faster assembly method, but they are only picked up once a day and there is insufficient room in Shipping to hold the manufactured widgets until they can be boxed, so they are placed in another building until they can be packaged.	Change the work-flow by picking up the widgets more frequently and hiring more packers, or move shipping to a larger location with plenty of storage room.
		Upper Management	Line managers are not instructing employees on the correct method of assembling widgets.	Review procedures with managers. Authorize and initiate training.
		Upper Management	The lead line manager has personality issues and employees are slowing the process to make him look bad.	Initiate conflict resolution, provide Human Resources counseling for the lead line manager, and/or assign a new lead line manager.

Once you've gathered the information on problems, causes, and solution alternatives, you may find it helpful to graphically illustrate the information to show the relationships involved, using mind maps, flow charts, Venn diagrams, or other graphic tools. An Internet search will yield a variety of analysis tools designed to trace a problem back to its root causes and contributory factors, including timelines, narrative chronologies, time/person grid, fishbone diagrams, and barrier analyses. The website for this chapter includes examples of methods and instruments you can use to collect the perceptions and expectations of stakeholders, productivity and performance figures, and other data for analysis.

Constraints and Resources

From the first day you learn of a project, you should take note of any *constraints* that might limit its scope. Often, the scope of content in an instructional design project is heavily influenced by standards, guidelines, certification requirements, and regulations that apply to the career environment of the organization. There may be other constraints that dictate the content, format, or timeline for your instruction, as well. For example, key stakeholders may ask you to adhere to a particular style of writing or graphic design, the project may be constrained by the demands of historical accuracy or salary limits, internal consistency may be a priority, and there may be limitations on length, size, or scope. Of course, the instructional designer can rarely escape time and budget constraints, but there may also be geographic constraints, cultural constraints, technological constraints (e.g., bandwidth), or quality control standards, government regulatory issues, and industry standards that serve to constrain the project.

Some consider the market analysis that companies frequently require for design projects to be a constraint. However, a thorough market analysis can also have a positive effect on the availability of resources and can convince stakeholders to champion your project. Whenever possible, let the project constraints inspire you to design creative solutions.

Ultimately, the goal of every instructor or instructional designer is to help learners be successful. Yet, it is important to acknowledge that there are some factors that impact learning over which you have no control. Such factors represent constraints or contextual issues that can nullify or enhance the urgency of a particular goal, and may represent situations that require a solution other than instruction. In the realm of K-12 education, Marzano, Pickering, and Pollock (2001) conducted a meta-analysis of thirty-five years of educational research to reveal key factors that impact student academic achievement. The resulting factors, categorized as *school-level factors*, *teacher-level factors*, and *student-level factors*, illustrate that the classroom teacher has limited control over a majority of the factors involved (see Table 2.4). Can you think of measures and interventions to implement at the school and student levels to enhance and support teacher-level efforts, and vice versa?

Table 2.4 Marzano's Factors Impacting Student Academic Achievement

Level	Factor Affecting Student Achievement
School	1. Guaranteed and viable curriculum
	2. Challenging goals and effective feedback
	3. Parent and community involvement
	4. Safe and orderly environment
	5. Collegiality and professionalism
Teacher	6. Instructional strategies
	7. Classroom management
	8. Classroom curriculum design
Student	9. Home atmosphere
	10. Learned intelligence (knowledge of facts, generalizations, and principles) and background knowledge
	11. Motivation

In addition to classroom management, the influential teacher-level factors are *curriculum design* and *instructional strategies*, illustrating the importance of the instructional design process. However, the research shows that *student factors* (home atmosphere, learned intelligence and background knowledge, and motivation) exert the most influence on student achievement. While such factors are typically out of the designer's control, you should still consider how you might address them in your design. For example, an instructional unit designed to increase students' out-of-class reading practices should definitely take the students' home environment into account. In this situation, you might provide parents with a list of ways to encourage their child's reading practices. In addition, if you analyze your learners to determine the range of background knowledge and typical motivators, you will be able to incorporate design elements to provide remediation or better motivate the learners.

These types of situational factors can constrain what designers are able to do in other career environments, as well. For example, in a business environment, *employee*-level factors (corresponding to student-level factors) might include an individual's commuting stress or complications and potential problems with a spouse or roommate (home atmosphere factors). *Company*-level factors (corresponding to school-level factors) might include pay incentives and environmental safety. Such factors can impact the learner's ability to concentrate or their motivation to learn or work. What institutional and individual factors can you identify for your instructional project, and what might you do to minimize their impact? Are there factors influencing the learning effort over which you have no control? (Chapter 4 addresses a variety of *contextual* factors that can impact the instructional design.)

Resources must also be identified at the start of the project. You should seek to determine if there is existing instruction that can be leveraged for the project, and whether you can tap into any available human resources, expertise, or funding. Be sure to determine the time required for development of the instruction, since that will impact your project schedule. Other applicable resources include available job aids, simulations, web resources, equipment, communications systems, materials, SMEs, instructors, and support personnel. As the project shapes up, take note of resources required to address the expectations of stakeholders and your own design ideas. Be sure to include an early request for these resources as you seek approval for the project scope.

Refining and Translating Needs Into Goals

As you compile and analyze the data you collect, you will be able to refine your needs statements. You should distinguish between real needs and perceived needs that have no basis in the data. Identify those needs that can realistically be addressed, as well as those that likely cannot be addressed by you or the organization. You must also distinguish between the needs that can be met with instruction and those that will require other solutions. Then, prioritize the needs to enable you and the key decision makers to identify those that should have precedence. Questions like these can help you as you prioritize: How many people will benefit? Is the need a prerequisite to meeting other needs? How do other similar organizations meet these needs? What is the cost/benefit or return on investment (ROI) of meeting this instructional need? Are there any constraints that nullify a need or increase its urgency?

Often, it is difficult to prioritize needs that all seem to be of a critical nature. In such cases, the use of a priority mapping technique can help you identify those needs that are more interrelated with other needs and factors and which therefore may need to take precedence. A priority map illustrates the needs graphically, presenting the needs in circles and connecting them with lines that indicate dependencies and relationships. The higher the number of *other* needs dependent on a need, the higher the priority of that need.

You can use available online data analytics to study what you've collected or you can use analysis software to make your own calculations and comparisons. Analyze how your data compares to information from a literature review, to results for groups similar to your target population, or do a meta-analysis of yours and several other studies. Look for trends, similarities, and differences in the data, and compare averages with outlier data. You should also compare the data you've collected on needs to the other analysis data you've gathered.

At the same time that you are working to identify the purpose, needs, and goals of the instruction, you are also carefully analyzing the needs of the target learners and the instructional contexts and content (these analyses are covered in future chapters). As the designer, you consider the information from all these analyses and translate the resulting needs into *goal statements* that can be reviewed and approved by key stakeholders.

As noted, instruction may not represent an appropriate solution for some of the needs you identify. Goals for *non*-instructional solutions might include:

- Providing a robust incentive program to encourage employees' use of the company's knowledge management system to continuously improve their skills.
- Providing low- to no-cost breakfasts for qualifying low-income elementary students, to improve their ability to concentrate in school.
- Reducing aircraft accidents due to preventable mechanical failures by increasing the manpower assigned to routine maintenance tasks.

When you present the results of your analyses, you will present both instructional and non-instructional goals; however, since this book is about instructional design, we will focus on instructional goals. Willis (1993) defines *instructional goals* as "broad statements of instructional intent," (p. 54) and these goals establish a direction for learning.

In this book, *instructional goals* are defined as broad statements of instructional intent, written in terms of what the instruction or learner will do, that can later be broken down into more specific learning outcomes. (Chapter 5 provides more on analyzing goals and Chapter 6 addresses how to refine goals into more detailed and specific learning outcomes or objectives.)

The key here is to remember to keep your instructional goals broad and continually revisit and adjust them as the project becomes better defined.

What Factors Shape These Goals?

Instructional goals should reflect the nature of the knowledge, skills, and attitudes—the learning—that the instruction is designed to facilitate, and they are frequently shaped by:

- The needs and characteristics of the target learner(s);
- The needs of the organization;
- Applicable learning standards for a federal, state, district, or local school system;
- Certification, competency, or accreditation requirements;
- The best practices identified for a particular field;
- Requirements established by funding sources;
- The needs of current and future employers;

- The requirements of post-secondary and graduate institutions; and
- The needs of a society.

The wide range of factors in this list underscores why it's important to consider the results of *all* the different analyses as you develop the instructional goals. To illustrate, suppose you are designing a program of study for a Master's degree for teaching secondary biology in the state of Maryland. The goals you establish for the program of study should address the Maryland Teacher Technology Standards and the National Standards for Secondary Biology Teachers, as well as any special university departmental requirements, and the requirements of the school districts where you hope to place your graduates. The goals should also reflect the needs of teacher candidates who have disabilities, who speak English as their second language, or who are located remotely from the university. Finally, the goals might also be influenced by societal needs, such as a critical demand for science teachers in the state.

In an ideal scenario, instructional goals are also shaped by educational or training *research* or, in other words, what has *worked* in the past. Scientifically based research results are valuable because they provide educators with methods and materials that are likely to be effective in positively impacting learner achievement. However, as mentioned in the previous chapter, such results should be evaluated critically to ensure that the strategies recommended are right for your instructional situation and the needs of your learners. For example, you should ask:

- Does the research clearly indicate that the instructional materials or strategies advocated will work for learners, content, and contexts similar to those for which I am designing instruction?
- What is the nature of the evidence reported? Was it published in a peer-reviewed, respected journal or a popular magazine or newspaper? Does it provide guidance for practical applications?
- Was the study rigorously and systematically researched with careful observations and conclusive evidence? Or were there many uncontrolled factors that could have interfered and call into question the author's claims of causes and effects?

Often, *best practices* can be used as a basis for one or more instructional goals. Many industries have established best practices that are designed to result in high-quality goods and services. Best practices are used in the education sector, as well. Several years ago, Chickering and Gamson (1987, 1999) identified seven principles of good practice for undergraduate education. Their original article on the principles was based on the current educational research, and since that time many more articles have reported the results of studies that tested the practicality and effectiveness of those principles (1999). According to Chickering and Gamson (1987), good practice in undergraduate education:

1. Encourages contacts between students and faculty.
2. Develops reciprocity and cooperation among students.
3. Uses active learning techniques.
4. Gives prompt feedback.
5. Emphasizes time on task.
6. Communicates high expectations.
7. Respects diverse talents and ways of learning.

In today's K-12 educational environment, teachers must consider state and nationally dictated *standards* when identifying goals for instruction, and their instruction is often subject to politically influenced curriculum decisions. Do educators actually have any say in the design of the curriculum and instruction they use? Frankly, *yes*, because even pre-packaged and standardized content has to be put into context for students if they are going to learn the material in a meaningful and useful way. If the 2008 ISTE Educational Technology Standards for students and teachers are taught in isolation from other content and life tasks, the goal of preparing students and teachers to use technology as a tool for lifelong learning will not be realized (refer to the ISTE NETS Standards for teachers at http://www.iste.org/).

To effectively design instruction that provides a context for students, the designer must know both about the curriculum to be taught and the standards students are to meet. In such cases, the instructional goals should convey two types of alignment: curriculum alignment and instructional alignment. *Curriculum alignment* refers to instruction that reflects the district, state, and national standards or goals for learning. Examples might include goals for adequate yearly progress, or the curriculum standards for a specific grade or subject area. *Instructional alignment* means that the instructional design reflects a match between learner objectives, instructional activities, and classroom assessments. This type of alignment will be covered in more detail in future chapters, but here's a common phrase used in instructional design to describe this alignment between objectives, activities and testing:

Tell them what you're going to teach them, teach them, and then test them on it.

Both types of alignment also apply to other learning environments (business, government, military, health industries, etc.). In these environments, instructional goals must be aligned to organizational profit goals, certification requirements, procedural requirements, quality standards, and industry standards. What *standards, requirements, or other factors* will impact your instructional goals?

How Specific Are Instructional Goals?

Identifying instructional goals often involves decisions about the level of specificity to use. Some individuals and organizations establish very specific goals:

- *"Sales employees will increase sales by 5% by becoming more knowledgeable about customer needs."*

... while others establish more general or broad goals:

- *"The English curriculum will teach students to write effective essays."*

Some write goals in terms of what the learners will do:

- *"Learners will use effective oral presentation skills to report on their research."*

... while others write them in terms of what the instructor or instruction will do:

- *"The wireline operator training program will provide instruction on the latest technology for downhole surveying."*

Breaking the goals down into a main (or terminal) instructional goal and several related or supporting goals can help you make decisions on content sequencing and the level of detail to be included. Many organizations like to see an overall terminal goal stated in very broad terms, with several supporting goals that address different strategies that will be used to achieve the terminal goal. Chapter 5 provides more information on goals and determining the *knowledge, attitudes, skills, and interpersonal skills (KASI)* that support the attainment of those goals.

Seeking Approval of the Project Scope and Plan

Once you have analyzed the needs and translated them into instructional goals, you should summarize your analysis results and seek approval of your definition of the project scope and your proposed plans. Different situations and projects will dictate how you report your analysis data and the type of justification that might be required for your recommendations. In some cases, a client or employer may require that you demonstrate the value of the solutions and link them to the organization's goals, mission, or vision statement. They may also want you to demonstrate the benefits of implementing your proposed measures, providing a financial forecast and market analysis. You may have to present detailed specifications or merely provide an overview of the plan. To justify the expense of producing training or implementing another intervention, you may have to calculate the ROI or describe how the proposed solution will add value to the organization. The results of your analysis can be written up in a proposal, a report, a design document, or can be presented in some other format. Things that are helpful to address in a needs analysis include:

- Project background, link to organizational mission, proposed learners;
- Needs categories and needs;
- How the needs were determined and confirmed;
- Political, ethical, and legal considerations;
- Priorities for meeting the needs and justification;
- Methods used to determine needs, and groups and individuals consulted;
- Conclusion and final summary goal or purpose statement.

A clear picture of the needs, constraints, and resources for the project can provide support for efforts to justify your instructional design project. When you accurately pinpoint and provide data to document valid business needs, job performance needs, training needs, individual learner or student needs, and institutional needs, you provide convincing evidence that the instructional project is essential to meeting those needs.

A key part of this process is aligning project goals (developed from your needs, as covered previously) with the strategic goals of the organization for which you are designing instruction. Will the proposed instruction support a departmental program, address curriculum standards, or meet accreditation requirements? Will the instruction support your company's mission statement, organizational goals, or the CEO's vision? Will it bridge the gap between what is and what should be? If so, what criteria must be met to illustrate success? Finally, some organizations may also require that you figure the return on investment (ROI) to justify your instructional design project. However, be cautious in your use of the data, making sure that the numbers are presented to inform the stakeholders as well as support your claims. You don't want to be described in this way by those consuming your analysis:

> He uses statistics as a drunken man uses lamp-posts ... for support rather than for illumination!
>
> (author unestablished, possibly Andrew Lang, 1844–1912)

te for this chapter includes examples of how different designers have presented their ysis results and instructional goals for stakeholder approval.

Thinking About Evaluation …

As noted in Chapter 1, you must *begin with the end in mind* if you want to effectively evaluate your instruction. Throughout your design/development process, *but especially as you are defining the project scope*, you must consider which levels of Kirkpatrick's (1998) model to address in later evaluation efforts.

- *Level I Reaction*—Evaluation measures implemented for Kirkpatrick's (1998) first level are designed to gauge the reaction of learners to the instruction. This is why it is important to compare and attempt to align the expectations of key stakeholders with the expectations of the target learners. You may produce instruction that meets key stakeholders' expectations, but if the learners are not happy with the instruction, their dissatisfaction may eventually ruin the satisfaction of the key stakeholders. In addition, if you do not identify and adequately record and communicate what you see as project constraints, those constraints could hamper the proper development and implementation of the instruction and negatively influence learner satisfaction.
- *Level II Learning*—To adequately measure learning progress, you must have solid instructional goals that accurately address the identified needs. Think about the type of assessments you might use to measure progress toward those goals. Are the goals and assessments practical and logistically possible? Do the goals represent valid needs? Is it even possible to measure the type of learning described in your goals?
- *Level III Behavior*—Evaluating a change in learner behavior or *transfer* of learning involves determining whether your learners are using the new knowledge or skills learned, and it is typically measured several months or more after the instruction. Find out whether your key stakeholders want you to measure behavior change and transfer and whether you will have the kind of access necessary to do so. Depending on your career environment, gauging a change in behavior and skill and knowledge transfer could mean that you need to obtain access to the workplace, to the next course in a program sequence, or to the battlefield.
- *Level IV Results*—Evaluating results or the ultimate impact of instruction involves measuring how it contributes to organizational goals. As a result, you must determine the kind of results desired by key project stakeholders. Do stakeholders expect the instruction to: improve productivity, increase sales, reduce turnover, enhance the reputation of the institution, increase job placement of graduates, increase volunteerism, reduce death and injury, improve surgery survival rates, or improve test scores? Once you have an idea of the expected results, you can identify the type of benchmark measurements to take at the beginning of the project and the type of resources you will need to conduct a result or impact evaluation at the end of the project.

Streamlining Project Definition and Needs Analysis

So in what way can the process of defining the project and analyzing needs be streamlined? Here's a list of things you can do to make this process more efficient and effective:

- **Optimize**—Use existing documents, records, and statistics to verify the needs instead of conducting extensive interviews and gathering data through observations and surveys. You can often justify needs on the basis of test results, dropout or failure rates, behavior incident reports, accident or injury reports, complaints, lawsuits, union or employee grievances, accreditation results, and/or evaluation reports. What type of records exist in your field or career environment that could be used as a short-cut for defining and justifying needs?

- If working with a team, **optimize** by assigning one person to continue the analysis activities while others move on to develop interim content documents and prototypes for early feedback. Pull all team members together periodically to compare the data from ongoing analysis with the early design plans.

- A clear option for **optimizing** is to skip the needs assessment altogether! If your client or boss is convinced of the need and has made it clear what he or she wants, respect those wishes (*especially* if he or she is likely to resist or impede your attempts to verify the need).

- **Sustainable**—If it's clear from the very beginning of the project that instruction is not the best option, recommend that a job aid, performance support system, or other administrative or logistical solution be employed (of course, indicating your willingness to help with the implementation, to ensure your job security!).

- **Continuous Improvement**—Collect the opinions and expectations of a small sample of stakeholders and, with their permission, post those results to a central discussion board (physical or virtual), asking for additions or comments. This will serve to publicize multiple viewpoints and generate discussion among stakeholders that will speed up the process, gain consensus, and help narrow and refine the resulting list of needs.

Different Career Environments, Different Perspectives

- Different types of analyses and different tools are emphasized in the various career environments. For example, in K-12 environments, administrators and teachers may perform observations to identify needs, or they may compare learner data to identify discrepancies in ability or instructional practice that represent needs to be addressed.

- In business environments, the pervasive emphasis on profitability has popularized needs analysis methods and benchmarking practices that allow the designer to do a post-training analysis of the return on the training investment (ROI). Organizations that follow a Human Performance Improvement (HPI) model often conduct *performance effectiveness assessments* to determine skill and knowledge deficiencies and operational indicators (King, 1998, p. 21), or they use a *front-end analysis* to define and describe a problem, hypothesize about the causes, test the hypotheses, determine solution alternatives, and weigh the relative costs of each alternative (ibid.).

- Designers working in the health-care career environment produce large volumes of instruction on health-related and critical life-and-death topics for several different audiences, including practicing physicians, residents, medical students and interns; hospital and health organization administrators and staff; nurses; patients; and those in the pharmaceutical and health-care equipment industries. Designers who may or may not have a medical education develop initial education programs, continuing education programs, and regulatory instruction. The quality of content is critical because the stakes for inaccurate instruction are high, placing the health and wellbeing of both patients and health-care workers at risk. As a result, standards for medical schools and hospitals are rigorous, such as those established by the Liaison Committee on Medical Education (LCME) and the Joint Commission on Accreditation of Healthcare Organizations (JCAHO), and therefore designers work closely with SMEs and conduct regular evaluations of instructional materials. Medical practice, like design, is ill-defined (it is both an art and a science) and requires a combination of objective content, and heuristic and problem-solving skills. To establish what is needed for instruction, designers use critical incident analysis, gap analysis and observations, expert advisory groups and Delphi forums, and they gather much of their justification for identified needs from surveys, interviews, and focus group sessions with health-care workers, patients, and community members.

Test Your Understanding With a Bloom Stretch

Apply	Apply your understanding of problem identification and needs analysis to identify both instructional and non-instructional needs for your family, community, or work environment. Identify several solution alternatives and briefly describe how each solution would impact other factors involved in the situation.
Analyze	Do an Internet search to find three examples of needs analyses carried out for your choice of a career environment and topic. Can you also find examples of instructional and non-instructional goals for your career environment?
Evaluate	Develop or find a list of criteria for needs analyses and use it to evaluate one of the sample needs analyses on the book website or another needs analysis of your choice.
Create	Create a list of resources to share with others on your choice of a topic discussed in this chapter. Some topics to consider: problem identification and definition, needs analysis methods and tools, and instructional goals.

Diving Deeper

Want to know more? When time allows, we encourage you to go deeper to learn more about the topics addressed in this chapter. The website for this chapter provides exercises and resources for further study on the following topics:

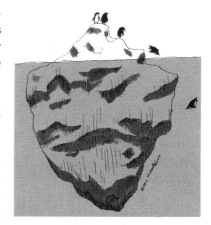

- **Practical Exercises and Examples**—Worked examples and case studies for needs analysis, constraints analysis, and resource analysis.
- **Job Aids**—Sample needs survey and needs analysis reports, and questions to ask to determine needs.
- **Resources**—Typical IDT project roles and responsibilities, and recommended books, articles, and URLs on project needs and scope definition.

3
Analyzing to Identify the Learners

RITA DECIDES IT'S TIME TO SHOW ERNEST
THE RESEARCH ON INDIVIDUAL DIFFERENCES

The learner is your customer. Those identified to use your instruction represent the "consumers," and a systematic approach will place them at the very *center* of your design efforts. A learner-centered design is said to be the most powerful contribution to effective instruction resulting from a systematic approach (Brigg, Gustafson, & Tillman, 1991). When you prioritize the learner, their needs and abilities impact the design of the instruction in many ways. For example, consider how the instructions for identifying minerals would differ for these three audiences: ninth grade earth science students, graduate geology students, and jewelry store technicians. The content might be similar, but the treatment will most likely differ based on the needs, motivations, and abilities of each audience group. Even *within* one of those groups, individual differences can impact the design.

Inquiring Minds Want to Know …

- How can I identify the characteristics and needs of the intended audience for instruction?
- In what ways do learners differ, and how do those differences impact my instructional design?
- How do I collect information on the intended audience for a particular instructional design?
- How, and how much, should I accommodate learner differences in my instructional design?
- What do I need to remember and understand from this chapter?

  ⇒ The various terms used to describe the "audience" for an instructional design;
  ⇒ The meaning and implications of terms like "individual differences," "individualized instruction," "digital immigrant," "digital native," "cognitive styles," and "multiple intelligences";
  ⇒ Questions to ask and topics to investigate concerning your audience;
  ⇒ Methods for collecting information about your intended audience; and
  ⇒ The many ways that target learners can differ and how these differences can be accommodated through an instructional design.

Analyzing the Learners

In previous chapters we emphasized that not all needs have an instructional solution, and that there are often multiple stakeholders whose needs must all be considered and prioritized when designing instruction. However, even if the need for instruction is obvious, and you've pinpointed stakeholder expectations, the final instruction can still fail to be effective if you developed it without considering the *characteristics of the target learners.* This chapter focuses on how learners and groups of learners differ, and how some of those differences can, and should, impact the design of instruction.

Jargon Alert!

There are many different terms used to describe those for whom the instruction is designed, including *target audience, learner, user, student,* and *trainee.*

Notable Non-Examples

So what happens when an instructional designer ignores the needs and characteristics of the target learner? Take a look at these non-examples to see *what not* to do when designing instruction:

Childbirth Assistance Foiled in India—Brey (1971) described a failed effort to train indigenous midwives in India during the mid-1900s, citing the following reasons for the program's failure:

1. No single group of women could be identified as indigenous midwives in the villages or urban areas.
2. There were insufficient numbers of adequately prepared auxiliary nurse midwives to serve as trainers.
3. There were insufficient vehicles to transport trainers to training locations.
4. The midwives felt that the proposed pay was insufficient.

Considering reasons 1, 3, and 4, it is evident that the program designers did not consider the target audience. They hadn't identified the availability of a group to be trained, much less their characteristics. They also failed to account for the location of the learners, since they hadn't considered the logistics of transporting trainers to them. Finally, they hadn't considered whether the proposed pay would be sufficient to motivate the learners. The training designers may have had the most well-designed and engaging training program possible, but it failed, in part because they didn't consider all the learner-related constraints and contextual factors (Allen, 2003).

USDA Training Cost Overruns—In an evaluation of the U.S. Department of Agriculture's leadership development training for staff officers in the Animal and Plant Health Inspection Service (APHIS) agency, Simao (2008) reported that design efforts were complicated by the fact that there was no standard job definition for "Staff Officers." This fact caused confusion in identifying a target audience, and the leadership training was therefore designed to try to appeal to a widely diverse job audience, including staff officers in veterinary medicine, plant pathology, agriculture, manual writing, secretarial work, and more. Evaluators concluded, "This course targets too many competencies for too broad an audience in its current design … Initially, the program was designed and budgeted for 25 participants. Between the design and delivery phase participant numbers dropped for a variety of reasons … Vendors were paid based on the initial participant numbers, which was not cost effective … The drop in attendance impacted the end of program administrative costs, because there was a funding shortfall" (Simao, 2008, B-51).

Caution!

A common mistake for both novice and experienced designers is to assume that what motivates, interests, and facilitates learning for the target audience will be similar to what motivates, interests, and facilitates learning for you. Nothing could be further from the truth, and that's why it's so important to collect and analyze information about your target audience!

So What's Involved? The Learner Analysis Process

We've listed a six-step process for analyzing the learner audience and considering the implications of that data for an instructional design. The steps are listed here and in the remainder of the chapter we'll discuss more about the "why" and "how" of analyzing your learners.

1. *Confirm the identity of your target learner(s)*—Check with all key stakeholders to make sure you know exactly who will be using the proposed instruction and, if there are several groups of learners, which group is the primary audience. (It's not a bad idea to get someone to sign off on a document stating this fact.)

2. *Determine what you need to know about your learner(s)*—You may initially be given a description or demographic data that you can analyze for accuracy and use to develop follow-up questions. Table 3.1 and resources on the book website (a *learner analysis* worksheet and survey question examples) can help you determine what other information is needed. Plan to investigate both group characteristics and the characteristics of individuals that may differ significantly from the group.

3. *Locate the desired data or identify/design tools to collect it*—Refer to Table 3.2 for examples of documents that you can analyze.

4. *Collect and analyze the data to produce a learner profile*—Once you've collected learner information, carefully analyze it to develop a profile of your target learner group and secondary learner groups. This profile should include any characteristics that are unique to individual learners or small groups of learners, even if you suspect that you will eventually decide against addressing those characteristics or needs in your design.

5. *Verify the learner profile and determine how it will impact the design*—Once you have a clear profile of the learner, have it checked for accuracy by your employer or the learners themselves. Consider what your results might mean for the instructional design (see Figure 3.1). Then, prioritize the results to determine which characteristics you must address and which ones you would like to address, given the necessary time and budget to do so. Check your priorities with your client/employer. If you have the final word on priorities and are developing instruction for the marketplace, you may need to test the market to verify that you have correctly identified your target audience.

6. *Revisit and revise your learner analysis throughout the design/development process*—Once again, we stress that instructional design is a dynamic and *iterative* process.

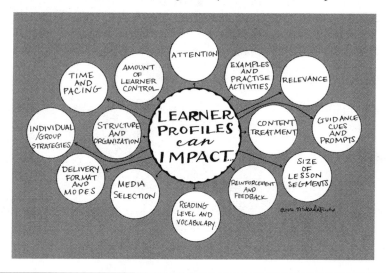

Figure 3.1 How Learner Profiles Impact Design

Why Consider Learner Characteristics?

Many needs and characteristics are common to the majority of learners within a certain age or interest group. Because of this, it is a fairly straightforward task to collect data for a profile for your target group of learners. However, within that group, there will likely be variations on how individual learners think, act, and feel. There will also be differences in the background knowledge and experience of the learners with the subject matter. If not considered, these differences may compromise the success of your instruction. For example, your web-based instruction may be perfect for 99% of your learners, but the frustrations and complaints of just one employee with a disability for which you made no accommodations, or a few users who must use a dial-up connection to access your graphics-intensive instruction, can convince your employer that there are major problems with the final product.

The bottom line is that *learner characteristics impact the effectiveness of instruction.* If your learner profiles indicate major differences in your learner population, this can impact such things as the timing and pacing of the instruction, the size of lesson segments, and the nature, difficulty, and number of examples and practice activities required. It can also influence:

- How you communicate the relevance of the instruction to learners;
- How you gain and focus learner attention;
- The type and amount of learning guidance, cues and prompts used;
- The content treatment (concrete or abstract, inductive or deductive, etc.);
- The type and amount of reinforcement and feedback;
- The reading level and vocabulary of the materials;
- The type and amount of learner control;
- The amount of structure and organization;
- Use of individual or group strategies;
- Instructional delivery formats and modes (online, face-to-face, blended, mobile, and asynchronous or synchronous); and
- The media used (Ruff & Lawson, 1990; Smith & Ragan, 2005, pp. 70–71).

These factors are summarized in Figure 3.1, and Table 3.1 lists learner characteristics and their design implications. The website for this chapter provides additional characteristics and case studies with helpful examples of how to address learner differences.

Gathering Data

There are many methods available to gather evidence to determine learner needs and characteristics (Kinzie, Cohn, Julian, & Knaus, 2002). If you have access to your learners and are not working through a "middle man," you can use surveys, focus group interviews, observation, and other means to profile your learners. Some of the information you will need to know may be available already from the client that hired you or from a school district or your employer. Note, however, that if the information you are given is from a questionable source (for example, if you doubt the information that an employer gives you about his employees), you may need to verify its accuracy.

Possible sources of data on learners are listed in Table 3.2, although note that some of the tests listed have been criticized for poorly reflecting true ability due to the impact of cultural, educational, and socioeconomic differences. Remember that the learner analysis for an instructional design project continually evolves, and you may need to go back and revise it as new information is revealed during the course of the project.

The Scope of the Challenge

There are a large number of learner characteristics to consider when designing instruction, and most situations feature unique characteristics to factor into the design. The characteristics of groups and individuals listed in Table 3.1 provide a representative list to consider. Of course,

Table 3.1 Learner Characteristics and Implications for Instructional Design

Characteristics	Implications for Design
Demographic and Group Data • Size of target audience, and sub-groups within the population • Nature of group as a whole (diversity, ability spread, job assignments, etc.) • Age range, and educational/grade level, academic major, or year in an academic program • Gender percentages • Cultural backgrounds, nationalities, ethnicities, etc. • Primary/native language • Religion • Employment/occupation • Socioeconomic status • Percentage of "traditional" vs. "non-traditional" learners • Geographic location(s) and time zones of learners	• Demographic group data indicates other questions to ask about the learner. • The diversity and range of characteristics in a learner group impacts treatment of content, mode of delivery, and amount of learner choice in the instruction. • Age range/grade (as well as primary language) determines the reading level and vocabulary to use in the instruction. It also provides clues as to interests, prior knowledge, and developmental levels. • Academic major and program year indicates familiarity with content. • Gender, culture, language, and religion give clues as to the background knowledge, frame of reference, worldview, and interests of the learners. • Employment data, such as type of job, length of employment, and other work assignments, can indicate the homogeneity of the audience's prior knowledge/experience with the topic, and their possible goals/motivators. • Socioeconomic status can serve to rule out or dictate the use of certain technologies or strategies. • Traditional/non-traditional learner ratio gives clues concerning learner lifestyles, motivations, and their preferences concerning delivery mode of instruction, amount of group work, and time available for assignments. • Location and time zone of learners may impact delivery modes for instruction.
Physiological • Sensory capabilities/impairments • Physical disabilities • Mobility and need for mobility • General health • Environmental sensitivities	• Learner physical disabilities and mobility impact the design to ensure compliance with Section 508 (technology accessibility for disabled persons). • Need for mobility may impact length of instructional segments and type of learning activities. • Health and environmental sensitivities (to light, colors, sounds, temperature, paint fumes, etc.) may constrain choices for learning environments and instructional media.
Cognitive Abilities • Intelligence • Reading level, mathematical and verbal abilities • Grade point averages (GPA) • General and specific aptitudes • Attention and focus • Learning disabilities • Mental disabilities • Metacognitive knowledge	• Learner mental abilities and their variability within the target group can impact the number of examples required, whether analogies will be effective, the time required for learning, and the amount of practice required by learners. • The attention and focusing ability of individuals with learning disabilities impacts content treatment and format, and the length of each instructional segment. • Learning and mental disabilities impact the format and treatment of content, amount and type of learner "help" provided, and amount and type of practice, feedback, and remediation. • The level of learners' metacognition (awareness of their thinking and learning processes and strategies) may indicate the amount of instruction they will need on how to approach a new learning task.
Prior Knowledge • Years of experience with topic of instruction • Specific knowledge of topic • Related coursework or experience • Range of entry level knowledge and skills (% of learners who have necessary prerequisite knowledge/experience) • Familiarity with technology	• The nature of the learners' prior knowledge and the range within a group of learners impacts content treatment, need for optional tutorials, and design of pretests to enable learners to skip familiar content. • Good design "activates" and builds on prior knowledge. • Level of technological savvy impacts choice of media. • Level of entry-level content knowledge can impact choice of visuals used. • When learners lack identified prerequisite skills, the goals of the instruction must be reconsidered.

Motivation and Other *Affective*

• Motivations, interests, personal goals, and motivation to learn • Academic self-concept and anxiety level • Beliefs • Confidence and attribution of personal success • Attitudes toward organization sponsoring instruction • Attitudes toward topic and proposed delivery system • Perceptions of and experience with specific forms of knowledge • Emotional intelligence and emotional disabilities	• Learner motivations, goals and interests can inform descriptions about the relevance of the instruction, and impact the nature of the examples used. • Learner academic self-concept, anxiety, confidence levels, and their attributions of success (to luck, others' help, ability, effort) impacts amount of reinforcement, type of feedback, and confidence-building/leveling content. • Learner attitudes about the sponsoring organization, the topic, and the proposed means of delivering the instruction inform decisions on content format, treatment, and motivational elements. • Learner perceptions about and experience with specific types of knowledge can inform content treatment and learner reinforcement. • Learner emotional stability and savvy can impact content treatment and the nature of learner group activities.

Table 3.2 Sources of Data About Learner Populations

K-12 and Higher Education Environments	Workplace Environments
• National assessments of student achievement (SATs, ACTs, etc.) • State, local, or district standards-based assessments • School-wide reading tests • Benchmark assessments supplied by textbook publishers or curriculum departments • End-of-course exam grades and percentages • Pass/fail percentages for each grade, course, or program • Absentee figures • Discipline statistics (in-school and out-of-school suspensions, expulsions, etc.) • Dropout and attrition rates • Percentage of students receiving free or reduced cost lunches, or need-based tuition aid • Measures of student socioeconomic status • Average time to graduation • Placement/employment rates for college, graduate school, and jobs • School priority comparisons (number of graduates entering college, percentage of students completing a certain amount of math, science, social studies, etc.) • AYP (adequate yearly progress) data from the previous five years • Percentage of students in AP and honors courses • Student awards and honors • Number of national merit finalists, semi-finalists, and commended students • Student involvement in extracurricular activities or school and community contributions • Individual grade or department action plan indicators (e.g., to have all English students express themselves fluently in writing, or have all fifth graders proficient in keyboarding) • Interviews or surveys of target population members, or of those who work with them • Observations of the target population or representatives of the population • Learner results from pretests on the content • Learner results from assessments on preferred instructional delivery modes, learning styles, etc.	• Hiring records and job application test results • Job descriptions • Personality, ability, or interest assessments (e.g., Myers-Briggs Personality Inventory) • Certification records and test results • Competency reports • Performance tests • Certificates earned from internal or external training programs • College transcripts • Personal development plans • Work samples • Interviews or surveys of members of the target population, or of those who work with the target population • Observations of the target population or representatives of the population • Learner results from pretests on the content • Learner results from assessments on preferred instructional delivery modes, learning styles, etc. • Results from equivalency tests (College Level Examination Program—CLEP, Defense Activity for Non-Traditional Students—DANTES, General Education Degree—GED, Graduate Records Exams—GRE) • National, state, and local demographic information • Books and articles on the interests, motivations, social development, and physical characteristics of particular age groups, developmental levels, or other demographic groups

some group characteristics vary significantly within a population, and some *continually* evolve and change over time. For example, the popular YouTube video *Shift Happens: Education 3.0* (updated yearly) reports U.S. Department of Labor facts that raise some challenging questions:

- Today's learners will have ten to fourteen jobs by their thirty-eighth birthday—how can a single college major address the needs suggested by this information?
- Many of today's college majors didn't exist seven years ago—how do we prepare students for fields that do not yet exist?
- According to the video, the amount of technical information was doubling every two years in 2009 and was expected to double every seventy-two hours by the year 2010—at that rate, how can an employee keep up with information that is needed to maintain a company's competitive edge?
- The task is to prepare learners for jobs and technologies that don't yet exist, and to solve problems we don't even know about yet. Can it be done?

The issues facing instructional designers in both public and private sectors are challenging: needs are complex and learners are different. The abilities, attitudes, expectations, and learning preferences of the current generation of learners reflect the environment in which they were raised—and that is often very different from the environment in which their teachers and workforce trainers were raised (Gibson & Slate, 2010; Oblinger & Oblinger, 2005). As just one example, consider the Table 3.1 factor, "Familiarity with technology." Educational writer Marc Prensky (2001a, 2001b, 2005) popularized two terms to describe the technology-related range of differences in today's learner population: *digital natives* and *digital immigrants.* Digital natives are those learners who have grown up with technology, are comfortable with it, and who typically use it productively in all aspects of their lives. Digital immigrants, on the other hand, are those learners who grew up *without* the technology, have adopted it in later life (or have had it forced upon them), and who are frequently uncomfortable with it.

Suppose you are designing technology-related instruction for a community college audience. It is likely that your target audience would include both digital natives and digital immigrants. How would you design the instruction to engage your digital natives, and still support your digital immigrants with the technology instructions they need? You would certainly want to both avoid overwhelming the digital immigrants and boring the digital natives. One effective strategy would be to build in "choices" in the instruction to allow digital natives to skip or "test out" of familiar content. Another option would be to provide choices in the format of the content, interspersed with self-checks and a means of review. We'll address those strategies and others in future chapters.

Narrowing the Challenge

You've seen that learner characteristics can impact the design of instruction, but it's important to know that not all characteristics have equal weight in design decisions. Frankly, not all of the factors are backed by solid research, and since your design and development time is typically limited, you may have to make some choices on what to address. The second "non-example" above illustrates that instructional efforts can fail or "blow the budget" if you design something that tries to meet the needs of every possible learner. Granted, producing effective instruction for today's complex learning environments and diverse populations often requires different approaches, different media, and different strategies. However, in the real world the majority of design projects operate under many resource constraints, and when you neglect to pursue a cost-effective design process, it tends to perpetuate the old pessimistic adage, "Fast, Cheap, and Good: Pick Two." You rarely have unlimited time and budget to meet everyone's needs, so you must often address only the most global and critical learner characteristics in your design.

So how do you decide which characteristics should be addressed? We recommend that, unless your employer or client insists that you consider a specific characteristic, you *stick with those that are supported by the research.* But here's a caveat: collect as much information about the learner as you can during your analysis (without annoying them or violating privacy rights), because, as you iteratively revisit the analysis during the design process, the additional information may inform your decisions on supporting strategies or technology, or provide an explanation for a failed *pilot test* of the instruction.

It is not unusual to be "strongly encouraged" to address characteristics that you do not feel it is cost-effective to address. For example, there are many theories on individual learning styles that have broad popular appeal and application in the business and educational fields, despite the fact that they have little empirical evidence to support them (and we'll address some of those later). Depending on the situation and the repercussions of ignoring the demands of others, you will have to make some choices:

- Acquiesce gracefully and seek to cut corners somewhere else in your schedule (and potentially compromise your design);
- Acquiesce not-so-gracefully and adopt the not-so-professional attitude, "You want it bad, you'll get it bad!" or
- Make a case for addressing the learner characteristics that you feel warrant the time and money involved by presenting the research.

If you find yourself in this situation and you decide to defend your position with the research, you'll find the overview and additional resources we present in the next section helpful as you build your case.

Research on Individual Differences

Lists of learner characteristics have grown out of ID practice, as well as research in many fields such as psychology, education, business marketing, and communications. Basically, much of this research is concerned with group behavior and how people are alike. However, researchers studying *individual differences* seek to understand how people *vary*. Differential psychologists have carried out a significant portion of the research on individual differences. Since it is possible to consider individual differences in relation to a wide variety of other topics that psychologists study (e.g., perception, cognition, problem solving, social interaction), the research base is *very* broad (Stokes-Hendriks, 2002).

Revelle (2008) explains that differential psychologists study the ABCDs of Personality: affect (feelings), behavior (actions), cognition (thinking), and desire (motivations). This research has a long and controversial history that can be traced as far back as 400 BCE, when the Greek philosopher Plato studied individual differences and described an ideal state where individuals would be assigned to the tasks for which they were best suited (Anastasi, 1958). However, the *systematic* study of how individuals differ really began in the last quarter of the 1800s, when Sir Francis Galton began developing processes to predict ability by measuring and quantifying physical and perceptual traits (Buss & Poley, 1979). Soon afterward, the Frenchmen Alfred Binet and Theodore Simon co-created an instrument that measured intelligence through such things as "memory, imagery, imagination, attention, comprehension, strength of will, and motor skills" (Stokes-Hendriks, 2002, p. 4). You may recognize Binet's name, since the Stanford-Binet Intelligence Test is still commonly used today.

As reported by Revelle, Wilt, and Condon (2011), other notable contributions were made to the knowledge base for individual differences in the areas of intelligence assessment (e.g., Spearman's general factor of ability); assessments for military selection and training; theories of personality (e.g., the "Big 5" dimensions of personality); personality inventories (e.g., the Myers-Briggs Type Indicator); instruments to measure ability, interests, and temperament (AIT) for selecting graduate students, astronauts, and Peace Corps volunteers; theories of motivation and achievement; use of technologies to study how brain activity relates to individual differences; and genetic studies that reveal the influence of heredity on ability, personality and interests (p. 14). In addition, Cronbach and Snow (1981) did extensive research on how individual differences interact with the demands of the content and learning task, the instructional treatments (or strategies and methods) used, and the structure and design of the learning environment, to produce varied and often unpredictable results. Their research has been used as the basis for several taxonomies of individual differences, and is referenced in the literature as *aptitude-treatment interaction (ATI)* research.

Since individual differences interact with so many other factors, the decision on which differences to address should be made as you consider: (1) the nature of the learner characteristics,

(2) the constraints involved in the situation, and (3) the demands of the content. For example, if you were developing an instructional series on conflict resolution, for which audience would you need to consider cultural background: an audience of adults working for an international company, or an audience of elementary students dealing with bullies on the playground? You probably responded with "It depends." The cultural background of individual employees in a multinational company would likely impact how they approach conflict on the job. If they are unfamiliar with the laws and accepted norms in the country where they are assigned to work, their cultural background should definitely be considered when designing instructional content. However, if you were designing instruction for a multicultural elementary school in a large urban city, the cultural background of individual students would also impact your design.

The reasons for educators' interest in individual differences is complex, but may be best understood with respect to the appeal of an ideal that has been around a long time in our field: *individualized instruction*. Chastain (1975) explained that "individualizing instruction means gearing the learning to the needs of the individual, not learning in an isolated context" (p. 344). However, if a designer were to try to consider every individual in this way, the development project would quickly reach the point of diminishing returns. As noted previously, you must make some decisions on which differences to address.

Here are several things to consider as you contemplate which individual characteristics to address:

1. Some characteristics play a key role in the design of instruction. In particular, variations in prior knowledge, motivational goal orientation, and intelligence have been shown to have a significant impact on the design and future success of instruction (Clark & Feldon, 2005).
2. An awareness of individual differences makes educators and instructional designers more sensitive to their role in learning (Jonassen & Grabowski, 1993).
3. Some theories on individual differences lack empirical support but have wide popular appeal, to the extent that their consideration in instructional design is mandated by school districts, company policies and practices, or certification requirements (e.g., learning styles and multiple intelligences in K-12 settings, and some personality tests in corporate settings).

Individual Differences: Things You Should Know

In this section, we will briefly describe some of the individual differences that consistently impact the design of instruction. The research on individual differences has focused on a vast range of topics like intelligence, motivation, prior knowledge, cognitive styles and controls, and learning styles or preferences. Of these, Clark and Feldon (2005) cite research to illustrate that there are *three main differences* that really deserve your attention:

> cognitive and learning styles have not proven to be robust foundations on which to customize instruction to accommodate individual differences, [but] *intelligence, motivational goal orientations, and prior knowledge* have demonstrated significant effects.
>
> (p. 105, emphasis added)

Note that there is disagreement on the nature and categorization of many of these individual differences, so we will refer you to the additional references on the book website if you wish to investigate any of the topics further.

Physical Capabilities

As a rule, the physical capabilities of your audience should always be considered in your instructional design, since that factor often affects whether your audience can even access the instruction. Section 508, an amendment to the Workforce Rehabilitation Act of 1973, requires that all electronic and information technology that is developed by or purchased by U.S. Federal agencies must be accessible by people with disabilities. Section 504 of that act, and Title II of the Americans with Disabilities Act (ADA), require school districts to provide a free and appropriate public education (FAPE) to students with disabilities that is comparable to the education being received by their non-disabled peers. The modifications and accommodations in an instructional design that are taken to meet the demands of this legislation are often referred to as "universal design" measures. (This topic will be addressed again in a future chapter.)

Intelligence and Mental Capabilities

In addition to physical capabilities, it is essential to be aware of the mental capabilities of your audience and to design the instruction accordingly. Designing instruction that is cognitively too easy for your audience may bore them and ultimately fail just as quickly as designing instruction that is cognitively way beyond your learners' mental capabilities.

In a survey of seventy years of research on cognitive abilities, Carroll (1993) described the range of those abilities as including such factors as general intellectual ability, reasoning, memory, visual and auditory perception, creativity and the production of ideas, and the speed and accuracy of mental processing. Mental capabilities vary with age, socioeconomic status, and by individual, and can impact the way in which you treat and present content, the examples you use, and the amount of structure you build into an instructional lesson. For example, Cronbach and Snow (1981) report research indicating that students of lower ability tend to be most successful when provided with a highly structured instructional environment, while high ability students tend to be most successful with low structure environments.

Cognitive or mental abilities unquestionably include intelligence, but the very concept of intelligence is a debated construct. While some theorize a general factor of intelligence (Spearman, 1904), others postulate multiple intelligences (Gardner, 1983, 2006), and the research for each theory remains inconclusive (Castejon, Perez, & Gilar, 2010). Because of this, the theory of Multiple Intelligences, while prevalent in popular instructional practice, remains controversial due to the lack of empirical evidence supporting its claims (Visser, Ashton, & Vernon, 2006a, 2006b; Gardner & Moran, 2006). (Since this is a theory you may be required to consider in your instructional designs, you can find information about multiple intelligences on the book website.)

While often classified as a cognitive control, the *attention* and focusing abilities of your learners will likely have an impact on your instructional design. The ability to attend to learning tasks varies with age, with the complexity of the content, and with the individual's interest in the topic. Clark, Nguyen, and Sweller (2006) state that "support for attention will be most important when the learners are novices, when the learning content is complex, and when the training materials are presented dynamically, requiring immediate processing" (p. 78). Of course, supports for attention are more critical when the audience includes learners with attention deficits.

Unless you are designing instruction for those with learning or mental disabilities, you will likely be able to make some assumptions about the cognitive abilities of your learners. However, you will need to be aware of the implications of cognitive load (covered in Chapters 4 and 10) and design your instruction so that you aid your learners in their attempts to understand the materials. Other common areas to consider are reading level and vocabulary, as well as mathematical ability levels (when there are computational aspects to the subject matter). The recommended reading level to target for adults varies based on the literacy of the intended audience, but is often somewhere between a sixth and ninth grade level. (Most word processing programs provide the option of displaying readability statistics that will enable you to check the reading level of the vocabulary you used in your writing.) Subject-specific terminology, jargon, and acronyms should always be defined. Ultimately, the goal is to provide cognitive accessibility to your instruction for all learners. This means you must pay particular attention to the message and information design to ensure that everyone in the learning environment can accomplish the learning goals.

Prior Knowledge and Experiences

According to learning theorist David Ausubel, "If I had to reduce all of educational psychology to just one principle, I would say this: *The most important single factor influencing learning is what the learner already knows. Ascertain this and teach him/her accordingly*" (1968, p. vi). The research overwhelmingly backs up this principle (Clark & Feldon, 2005; Jonassen & Grabowski, 1993). A learner's prior knowledge and experiences play a major role in their learning success, and significant variation in the prior knowledge of your learners can complicate your instructional design. According to Clark and Feldon (2005), "learners with low levels of prior knowledge require more extensive instructional support to minimize the level of unnecessary cognitive load imposed by the material presented ... the novice requires scaffolding to properly organize the information presented without overwhelming limited working memory" (p. 105). They emphasize that, when designers assess prior knowledge and customize the learning materials accordingly, the overall achievement of all learners can be significantly improved. The second case study example on the book website illustrates how to use prior knowledge assessments in the design of instruction, and we'll discuss strategies for customizing instruction in a future chapter.

Motivation, Goals, and Interests

Learners must have a *will* as well as the *skill* to learn, and in any given educational context, learners may differ with respect to what motivates them to learn. They may be motivated *extrinsically* (by rewards, grades, advancement, or praise), or *intrinsically* (by the relevance of the material to their own goals). With respect to instruction, just what is it that the learner must be motivated to do? Ultimately, the learner must be motivated to *make the effort to learn*. If an individual believes that effort in learning pays off, then the research shows that their belief in effort is likely to increase their academic achievement (Marzano et al., 2001). The challenge, then, is to design instructional experiences that *motivate* the learner to engage with the content and make the effort to learn.

The types of extrinsic motivators that appeal to learners vary with age and with the instructional situation. During the data collection process, you can ask older learners to rate what motivates them, while extrinsic motivators for younger learners are typically predictable by age group. However, the fastest way to motivate through instruction is to connect with the learner's personal goals and interests, or *intrinsic* motivators. Intrinsic motivation is generally believed to be a more powerful force than extrinsic motivation. (Factors and strategies that impact motivation are covered in Chapter 8.)

Motivation is just one factor in an area of learner characteristics referred to as the affective dimension. A learner's personal and learning goals exercise a substantial influence on their motivation, as do their interests. Refer again to Table 3.1 for other affective factors that impact learning and instruction.

Gender, Ethnicity, Race, and Cultural Background

Smith and Ragan (2005) provide a practical reason for considering differences in gender, ethnicity, race, and cultural backgrounds in your design:

> We consider these differences not because members of one gender or racial group process information differently, but because members of a gender, ethnic, or racial group tend to have common experiences due to their group membership that may be quite different from those had by members of other groups.
>
> (p. 50)

However, we caution you to approach these factors reflectively. Since part of your job as a designer is to be aware of how your own background might impact your design, you must take special care to avoid stereotyping. Typically, you will consider these factors to ensure that your examples and the context of your instruction are relevant and comprehensible to the learners. However, there are times when one or more of these factors can have great influence on other aspects of the instructional design. For example, several years ago, one of us was involved in planning face-to-face instruction for a group of Middle Eastern faculty who came to the United States for professional development. Due to the norms in their country, these faculty members wished to have separate male and female classes. Because the two assigned designer/instructors were both female, there was concern that the male learners would insist on a male instructor. However, we discovered through our learner analysis that the participants were most concerned that they not mix with *their own* colleagues of the opposite sex, and the male participants were therefore quite satisfied with a female American instructor.

Age and Generational Differences

Do adults and children learn differently? American educator Malcolm Knowles (1970) believed they do and he developed a theory of *andragogy* to describe how adult instruction should differ from instruction intended for children (i.e., *pedagogy*). His theory of andragogy is one of the foundational theories for today's field of adult education, despite the fact that there is still scant empirical evidence of its validity (Smith, 2002). Researchers have only recently begun to develop possible instruments to test the theory's assumptions (Blondy, 2007; Holton, Wilson, & Bates, 2009; Taylor & Kroth, 2009). Knowles's assumptions for differentiating between instruction for adults and children are often used as support for certain design features:

- *Self-concept* (adults are more self-directed in their learning, while children are more dependent on adults to indicate what is important to learn),
- *Experience* (adults have a richer source of previous experience than children),
- *Readiness to learn* (adults are more developmentally ready because their learning needs relate to fulfilling their social roles), and
- *Orientation to learning* (adults typically wish to use the information immediately, while children are oriented toward learning for future needs) (Knowles, 1970, p. 39).

Due to the typically similar age range, you will find that groups of children often exhibit more similar characteristics than groups of adults. A wide age range within a group of adult learners often results in differences in social attitudes and in knowledge of historically related topics (Gibson & Slate, 2010). However, instructional designers can make the mistake of assuming age-related differences that *do not* exist, just as often as they neglect to consider age-related differences that *do* exist. Take the previous example of the challenge to engage both digital natives and digital immigrants through instruction. You might assume that learners under the age of 30 would be more familiar with technology than would learners over the age of 30. In reality, there may be teenagers in your target audience who avoid technology and mature learners who are technologically savvy. Therefore, remember that a wide age range is one of those group demographic characteristics that should prompt you to ask additional questions about your target audience.

Oblinger and Oblinger (2005) analyzed research to come up with several generalizations about the characteristics of different generations. You may find them useful, so we have included them as a resource on the book website, but remember that such generalizations should always be confirmed through your learner analysis. Of course, if a group of adult learners includes a mix of generations, there will likely also be differences in prior knowledge and experiences. In such cases, you may be able to ascertain this information through prior knowledge questionnaires. The book website also provides a helpful table of differences between the child and adult learner along with the implications of those differences for instructional design.

Cognitive Styles, Learning Styles, and Learning Preferences

People learn in a variety of ways, and in Chapter 4 you will consider many of the theories developed to explain how people learn. However, one very common difference is in the way people perceive and process information, referred to variously as *cognitive style*, *learning style*, and *learning preference*. Cognitive and learning styles refer to the *manner in which a person perceives, processes, stores, and recalls what they are attempting to learn*. Researchers agree that people have different styles of thinking and learning, but they disagree "over the claims that these styles can be measured reliably using currently available instruments, and that tailoring instruction to match these styles (by whatever learning styles measure) improves classroom learning performance" (Terry, 2001, p. 70). The topic is highly controversial, but that hasn't stopped some from applying questionable research and promoting the use of unreliable measurement instruments to educational practice in all sectors. Instructional practices designed to appeal to various learning styles are often included in discussions about *differentiation* in K-12 settings, and in corporate settings trainers seek to accommodate types of learners identified through the use of the Myers-Briggs Type Indicator. While designing instruction to appeal to a variety of learning styles may or may not improve learning, the research *does* indicate that allowing learners to choose from a variety of learning opportunities can increase motivation, which, in turn, can improve learning success (Keller, 1987; Malone & Lepper, 1987; Marzano et al., 2001).

Clark and Feldon (2005) state that "cognitive styles and learning preferences have been advocated by some researchers for a number of years as traits that contribute to differential success in learning tasks on the basis of learners' innate approaches to learning or solving problems" (p. 103). The foundational belief behind cognitive styles is that a person's "perceptual system can be a window into the person's cognition" (Saklofske & Zeidner, 1995, p. 11). However, Clark and Feldon (2005) cite numerous research studies as support for their assessment that "these constructs have proven notoriously difficult to validate for both the stable assessment of learner characteristics and the customization of instruction to improve student outcomes" (p. 104). They conclude that cognitive and learning styles are not "robust foundations on which to customize instruction to accommodate individual differences" (p. 105).

That said, the consideration of individuals' learning styles is currently a common practice in instruction and training, and a wide variety of learning styles inventories and tests are commercially available to help educators determine those styles. It's usually a lot of fun to take those tests and to consider your own style, and doing so can make you more aware of your own styles and how they compare to the learning styles of others. However, when time and resources are short, there are several reasons *not* to collect data on and consider cognitive and learning styles:

1. *Questionable Reliability, Validity, and Faulty Measurements*—While a cognitive ability is usually measured by an aptitude or intelligence test, cognitive styles are typically measured by either objective measurement tests or self-reporting inventories. The studies using objective measures are often criticized for reliability issues over time and across domains. Coffield, Moseley, Hall, and Ecclestone (2004b) stress that the problem with self-report measures is that they "are derived from the subjective judgments which students make about themselves ... These are not objective measurements to be compared with ... [for example] the height or weight of students, and yet the statistics treat both sets of measures as if they were identical" (p. 126). In other words, an individual often consciously or unconsciously adjusts his responses to attain a desired outcome.

2. *Constraints*—In a review of learning styles models for post-16 (post-college) educational purposes, Coffield et al. (2004a) concluded that "all teacher-student interactions in post-16 learning are embedded in structures of power, regulation and control. These mean, for instance, that neither teachers nor students have the total freedom to choose the teaching or learning strategies which they may wish to adopt. There are also so many constraints on teachers and so many variables affecting learning outcomes that the differences produced through approaches based on learning styles are likely to be rather small" (pp. 14–15).

3. *Comparatively Low Returns on Individualized Instruction*—Hattie (1992) analyzed 630 students to determine that the average effect size for individualized instruction in schools was only 0.14. (*Effect size* refers to a statistical means of looking at the significance of differences in student achievement scores between a control and an experimental group.) Consequently, it is not the best use of instructor time to set up, monitor, and support individualized programs when there are large groups involved. (This may, of course, change in the future with technological advances.)

4. *Better Results with Other Interventions*—Hattie (1999) conducted a meta-analysis of educational interventions that yielded much better effect sizes than that resulting from individualized instruction. There is much wisdom in concentrating limited resources and effort on methods that provide the highest effect sizes. Here are a few for comparison: reinforcement (effect size = 1.13), direct instruction (1.04), class atmosphere/environment (0.56), peer tutoring (0.50), parental involvement (0.46), and teacher style (0.24).

In light of this information, David Merrill (2000) appears to have a practical philosophy concerning the use of information gleaned about cognitive styles and learning styles. He emphasizes that instructional strategies should be determined on the basis of the type of content or the goals of the instruction, and then, secondarily, learning styles and preferences can be used to adjust or fine-tune the strategies chosen. When you are ready to consider cognitive or learning styles, you can use the information included in Table 3.1 and the resources provided on the book website to guide your research on the styles to measure and the measurement instruments to use.

Thinking About Evaluation ...

As you analyze the learner audiences for your instruction, it is a good time to think about how you will evaluate the final instruction. How should you address the Kirkpatrick (1998) evaluation levels (Chapter 1) at this point in the process?

- *Level I Reaction*—What can you find out now about the target learner groups that will you gauge their reaction to the proposed instruction? Collecting data on learner interests and goals will help you design engaging instruction that addresses learner needs and is more likely to yield positive reactions.
- *Level II Learning*—Determining the cognitive capabilities of the learners will enable you to design instruction that is both challenging *and* achievable. In addition, collecting solid information on learner prior knowledge will set a benchmark for later evaluation of learning progress following the instruction.
- *Level III Behavior*—What information about the learners will help you determine if they are actually using their new skills and knowledge following the instruction? Is it likely that employees will be resistant to having their behavior observed during their workday? How many students go on to take another course where they would be expected to use the knowledge that they will learn in the course being designed? Considering how you might determine behavior change and transfer of learning can help you identify the information to collect regarding the learner population.
- *Level IV Results*—To adequately gauge results and the impact of your instruction on the sponsoring organization, you must identify the benchmark information to collect at the beginning of the project. How do the key stakeholders think the instruction will contribute to the accomplishment of their organizational goals? Do they expect to see increased productivity? Then you must collect information on current productivity. Do they want to reach a more diverse learner population and extend their enrollments geographically? Then you should collect data on the current learner population and geographic spread of student enrollments. Consider the alignment of the organizational goals with the goals of the instruction and determine what to collect and record about current learner characteristics to facilitate later comparisons following the instruction.

Streamlining Learner Analysis

So in what way can the process of analyzing learner characteristics and needs be streamlined? Here's a list of things you can do to make this process more efficient and effective:

- *Sustainable*—Instead of conducting extensive interviews and gathering volumes of data through surveys, use existing records about learners or observe them. (After all, surveys often just tell you what people think you want to hear!) For example, you may be able to find records that address the existing knowledge and skills that learners possess, and whether they possess the identified prerequisite knowledge and skills. What types of records exist in your field or career environment that could be used to identify learner characteristics and needs?
- *Optimized*—If it's likely that there are individuals within the learner population that have disabilities (and this is usually the case), don't waste time collecting information on those disabilities and just build in accommodations from the start of the project, following the accepted guidelines for your career environment.
- As with needs analysis, you can *optimize* team efforts by assigning one person to continue the learner analysis activities while others move on to develop interim content documents and prototypes for early feedback. Pull all team members together periodically to compare the data from ongoing analysis with the early design plans.
- Finally, you can *optimize* by using available expertise. Talk to those who know the learners well: teachers, managers, commanding officers, supervisors, and peers. They can usually

make generalizations and tell you about exceptions more quickly than if you tried to survey the learner population. As with needs analysis, if the client is convinced they have given you the essential learner needs and characteristics, avoid an argument and accept their appraisal.

- *Continuous Improvement*—Survey or conduct a focus group session with a small sample of learners to gain information on needs and characteristics. If you feel verification is necessary, post your results to a central discussion board (physical or virtual) for the entire organization, asking those who feel the results are not indicative of their own situation to contact you. This will glean information on exceptions early in the process and allow you to consider design solutions that might address those exceptions.

Different Career Environments, Different Perspectives

- Learner requirements, needs, and characteristics differ by career environment, as do the methods of learner analysis used in those environments. For example, in K-12 environments, there is currently a great emphasis on learning styles and multiple intelligences. Business and industry environments frequently use personality tests (common ones include the Myers-Briggs test and Cattell's Sixteen-Factor Personality test) and other commercial tools when employees are first hired, and the aggregated results can give you a feel for the general learner audience and any exceptions. Government and military environments have a wealth of information on disability rates, ethnic and cultural diversity, and even specific information on cognitive and physical abilities of learner groups.
- In addition, the type of information collected about learners varies due to limits on information access and/or time restrictions. In K-12 environments, institutional records provide a wealth of information on individual learners and groups of learners, but a designer may not have access to some of that information. In business and industry environments, designers may only have time to identify the training that an individual requires to improve performance and the physical and mental characteristics that will impact the effectiveness of the training, and determine whether the organization needs to provide different training to different groups of employees. Table 3.2 provides a summary of some of these career environment differences.
- Designers in health-care career environments may design instruction for *medical* learners (practicing physicians, residents, medical school students and interns), for *staff and management* learners (those working in administration for hospitals, clinics, and private practice), for *emergency medical technicians*, for *nurses* (licensed practical nurses, licensed vocational nurses, registered nurses, nurse practitioners, physician assistants, and nurse anesthetists), for *patients*, and/or for the *pharmaceutical* and *health-care equipment* industries (providing instruction for pharmacists, pharmacy technicians, and pharmaceutical and health-care equipment sales professionals). In each area the range of learners and content can be quite broad. For example, nurses (like doctors) typically can pursue a specialization in such areas as neonatal, pediatric, critical care, cardiovascular, oncology, ambulatory care, midwifery, geriatrics, forensics, those working for private agencies in home health care, and many other areas of expertise. Medical and nursing instruction is often designed by someone with a medical degree who relies on their own experience to identify learner characteristics, or by someone who works closely with an SME and relies on their experience for an accurate learner profile. Producing continuing education materials for nurses can be quite challenging because of the broad range of experience and educational backgrounds (i.e., nursing education programs range from two years to

over four years for specializations). For patient training, the prior knowledge and learner needs vary widely and designers typically seek to produce and confirm robust learner profiles that consider things like the cultural and language needs of international patients, the visual and physical needs of older adults, the needs of patients with poor reading skills, and the emotional needs of young children.

Test Your Understanding With a Bloom Stretch

Apply	Complete a learner analysis for one of the book website case studies, using the learner analysis worksheet provided.
Analyze	Select a real-world design project and classify the different groups of learners, differentiating between their needs. Decide on the target learner group and justify your decision.
Evaluate	Compare and evaluate two of the learner analyses posted on the book website, identify which one you think is more accurate or complete, and compare your evaluation results with others.
Create	Use the learner analysis worksheet from the book website to complete a learner analysis for a real-world instructional design project of your choosing.

Diving Deeper

Want to know more? The website for this chapter provides exercises and resources for further study on the following topics:

- **Practical Exercises and Examples**—Learner analysis worked examples, case studies, and exercises.
- **Job Aids**—Learner analysis worksheets and survey questions.
- **Resources**—Resources on multiple intelligences, age-related learner differences, cognitive and learning styles, and wellness needs of online learners.

4
Analyzing the Contexts of Instruction

STRETCHING A LEARNER BEYOND HER ZPD.

LEV VYGOTSKY

BF SKINNER

ZONE OF PROXIMAL DEVELOPMENT

Designers can increase their efficiency by reusing a design that has proven effective in the past. However, a previously successful design may be totally inappropriate when used for a different instructional purpose or in a different culture or locality. Design is *situated*—shaped by facets of the environment in which it occurs. So as you analyze needs, learner characteristics, and content, you must also analyze the *contexts* of instruction. What are the contexts of instruction? There are many, but here are four that have wide-ranging effects:

- *Performance context*—the environment where new knowledge and skills are to be used.
- *Learning context*—the environment where the learning experience takes place.
- *Cultural context*—the values, goals, attitudes, and practices of a society or organization that provide a frame of reference for learners, impacting how they interpret learning experiences.

- *Theoretical context*—the assumptions about how people learn that forms the basis of an instructional design.

For each project, think through the contexts to identify factors that might influence your design decisions. For example, how easy will it be to simulate the performance context in the learning context? Is the target learning population international or socially diverse? Do the stakeholders have conflicting ideas of how people learn? As design options increase, the task of analyzing an instructional context becomes increasingly complex because of the potential interactions. For example, if the learners are accustomed to formal instruction, will they be willing and able to learn in an informal environment? If the instruction must be delivered virtually, can it adequately simulate the performance context? What is the best pedagogical approach to take for content that is dynamic? Since elements from each of these contexts significantly influence your design decisions, they can shape the very nature of the design.

Inquiring Minds Want to Know ...

- What is the relationship between the performance context and the learning context, and how does each impact an instructional design?
- How does culture impact instruction?
- Why is it important to identify the assumptions about learning that are held by all stakeholders for the project, and how is that done?
- What should I remember and understand from this lesson?

  ⇒ The meaning for the terms "learning context," "performance context," "cultural context," "organizational climate," "theoretical context," "epistemology," "grounded design";
  ⇒ Factors to analyze in the performance and learning contexts;
  ⇒ The communication process and its impact on the design of instructional messages;
  ⇒ How to design instruction that reflects the applicable cultural context(s);
  ⇒ What it means to use an Instructivist, Constructivist, or Connectivist pedagogical approach to instruction; and
  ⇒ How to design instruction consistent with valid assumptions about how people learn.

Jargon Alert!

Performance context is a term that is derived from Human Performance Technology (HPT), a field closely related to Instructional Design and Technology. HPT is practiced primarily in business and industry career environments and it is in such environments that job performance is of paramount concern. However, *performance context* is really a generic term that applies to all settings. It refers to the environment where newly learned knowledge and skills are put to use, whether that is on the job, in the next school grade, in graduate school or the next course of a sequence, in the operating room, on the battlefield, or in everyday life situations.

Notable Non-Examples

So what happens when the contexts of instruction are ignored? Read on to find out how different contexts can impact the success of instructional designs:

Sensory Alignment of the Performance and Learning Contexts for Critical Trauma Training—The U.S. military has a long history of using simulations to train personnel to respond to traumatic situations with a "cool head." To do this effectively requires a high degree of sensory realism. Through a process of trial and error, military trainers have determined that when individuals are confronted by real-life crisis events their training is often compromised by an emotional response of fear brought on by the presence of sensory factors not included in training simulations. Research has shown that smells can often produce a strong and vivid response by stimulating the emotions and memory (Allen, Pike, Lacy, Jung, & Wiederhold, 2010). For example, in combat situations the smell of blood can trigger unanticipated emotions that hamper the individual's ability to perform critical medical response procedures. To address this problem, the U.S. Army's Simulation and Training Technology Center (STTC) uses advanced severe trauma simulation technologies that also include olfactory elements to better prepare medical personnel to deal with injuries encountered on the battlefield. Training medical personnel with technologies that simulate the full spectrum of sights, sounds, smells, and haptic (touch) sensations experienced on the battlefield leads to increased success through a closer alignment between the *learning context* and the performance context where the critical knowledge and skills must be used (Basdogan & Loftin, 2008).

Cultural Candy Conundrum—An academic faculty training team was tasked with providing a workshop on effective instructional design for a group of educators from a conservative university in the Middle East. When the foreign educators requested separate classrooms for their male and female faculty, the trainers realized that this was probably only the first of many cultural differences that could impact the success of their workshop. They prepared for their task by reading books and articles about the target learners' culture, they purchased copies of a CultureGram™ for the training team that addressed the culture and customs of the learners' country, and they hired graduate assistants who were natives of that and other Islamic countries. Weeks of preparation paid off and the first three days of the workshop were well received by the learners. On the morning of the fourth day of the workshop, the trainers tackled the topic of learner motivation and they handed out candy to the learners who provided input in the class discussions to illustrate the effectiveness of rewards as an external motivator. At the first break, one of the graduate assistants pulled the facilitator aside with an urgent message. It seems that some of the candy handed out contained gelatin made from pork, and Muslims abstain from pork products. The trainers hastily went through the remaining cache of candy and removed the offensive pieces, and then apologized to the learners, who graciously forgave them. Lesson learned? By their very nature, cultural differences can blindside the well-intentioned instructional designer, and therefore it's a good idea to check your design with as many natives of the target culture as humanly possible.

Conflicting Assumptions About Learning—When a new virtual high school was chartered for a northeastern U.S. state, the State Department of Education (DOE) provided funds to pay for an instructional designer to help the instructors produce the online courses needed for the first year of operation. The first year was a trial period for the school, and the administrators cautioned the designer that they would need solid evaluation data to justify the program to the state's DOE. The designer worked closely with the teaching staff to develop the courses, held several practice sessions so the teachers were comfortable with the delivery system, and made sure that the course formats, assessments, and interactions were compatible with each teacher's preferred pedagogical style. By the end of the summer, the designer felt confident that the program was ready and that the planned formative and summative evaluations would clearly indicate to the administrators what was working and what needed revision. Shortly before the start of the school year, one of the teachers resigned and took a face-to-face assignment in another state. A replacement with online experience was hastily hired and the designer spent a day with the new teacher to demonstrate the course she would be teaching. He emphasized that he would be available to help her in whatever way he could, even offering to sit in on virtual sessions to ensure that the course was going as planned. The designer was a little concerned when the new teacher failed to contact him, but the periodic student surveys showed no signs of trouble, so he assumed all was well. At the end of the year he accessed the grading system to collect and analyze the data for the evaluation reports needed by the administration. He was shocked to see that the new hire had not implemented any of the quizzes or other assessment measures designed to prepare the students for the state end-of-course tests. When questioned, the teacher brushed off the designer's concerns and firmly expressed her belief that traditional testing measures did not adequately assess a learner's true capabilities. Unfortunately, the instructor's assumptions about learning did not align with the course design and, rather than use the course assessments, she had based her grading on her own impressions of the students' progress. The designer's worst fears were confirmed when the end-of-course test results came in and three-fourths of the students in the course scored below the acceptable standard.

Caution!

A common mistake for both novice and experienced designers is neglecting to consider the *level of alignment* between the performance context and the learning context. Even if misalignment is inevitable, acknowledging that fact enables you to make adjustments to minimize the impact and maximize the transfer of learning for the target audience. You should also research cultural factors that could inform different aspects of your design, including the examples and motivators you use. Finally, consider your own assumptions about learning and how they align with those held by the learners and key stakeholders to improve the acceptability and effectiveness of the design.

So What's Involved? Analyzing Contexts

We recommend a five-step process for analyzing the contexts that influence your designs:

1. *Identify and analyze the performance context*—Identify where the knowledge and skills learned are to be used. Consider the physical characteristics of the context, elements of support, the social aspects, and the relevance of the targeted skills and knowledge to learner needs in the performance context.
2. *Define the learning context and compare it to the performance context*—You may be able to design the learning context from the ground up, but it is more typical that your client, employer, or circumstances will dictate certain aspects of the context. Regardless, seek to define its physical characteristics and any personnel or resource constraints that will influence its design. Consider strategies to match the learning environment more closely with the performance context, since a high degree of alignment between the two contexts improves the transfer of learning. Identify the type of learning assessments that authentically reflect how learners will use the knowledge and skills in the targeted performance context.

3. *Analyze the culture and climate of both the performance and learning contexts*—Consider if and how the social culture and/or organizational climate of the performance context should influence the design of the learning context and the instructional materials.

4. *Determine the assumptions about learning held by all key stakeholders*—Identify the assumptions about how people learn that are held by the major stakeholders, learners, and the instructor (if applicable). Compare these assumptions to your own beliefs about how learning occurs and consider the implications for your decision on a theory base for the instruction.

5. *Analyze the contextual relationships and compile recommendations*—Review all contextual factors and consider how they interact and align with the other analysis data collected (needs assessment, resource and constraints, learner needs and characteristics, and the demands of the content). What are the implications of the information you've identified? Determine whether you have enough information to make recommendations for the learning context and, if not, gather additional information. Once you have what you need, produce design recommendations for a learning environment that will best support the project goals.

Performance Contexts

Situated learning theory, first proposed by Jean Lave and Etienne Wenger (1991), emphasizes that the context in which learning occurs is very important. In fact, the most successful learning takes place in the same context in which it is applied (e.g., apprenticeships or on-the-job training). Since that is often not possible, you must carefully analyze and compare the performance context (where the learner will use the skills and knowledge after instruction) and the learning context (where the learner actually receives the instruction). How similar are these two contexts? The degree of similarity or alignment between the context of learning and the context of use (performance) will impact how easily the learner is able to transfer and apply the knowledge and skills learned in new environments. Note the examples of learning and performance contexts for different career environments in Table 4.1.

The more you know about the performance context, the easier it will be to create a relevant learning environment that increases learner motivation and aids in the transfer of new knowledge and skills to the work setting. Sometimes you must design for multiple performance contexts, especially in situations where there is a diverse learning audience or when the instruction serves as a basic foundation for a variety of future performance contexts. For example, learners enrolled in an introductory photography course may have a wide range of reasons for enrolling. They may be taking it to build foundational knowledge for a photographic arts degree, to develop a needed subskill for a different field (such as property sales, website design, or forensics), to satisfy elective requirements for a liberal arts degree, or some learners may be merely taking the course to satisfy their leisure interests.

Table 4.1 Sample Learning and Performance Contexts

Career Environment of the Instruction	Learner	Current Learning Context	Future Performance Context
K-12	Ninth grader	Introductory biology course	Advanced biology course
Business and industry	Employee	Technical training workshop	Job site
Higher education	College senior	Degree program courses	Graduate program
Military	New recruit	Basic training	Battlefield
Health care	Medical student	Residency program	Emergency surgery practice

The best way to find out about the performance context is to visit it. Interview individuals who currently operate in that environment or who have done so in the past, study available descriptions, images, and videos of the site(s), look up data about the site, and consult floor plans of physical facilities. If the performance context is virtual, thoroughly explore the applicable platforms, programs, and equipment prior to making final decisions on the nature of the learning context. There are several questions you will need to answer about the performance context and several factors to consider when analyzing it:

- *Physical Characteristics*—In what type of physical facility or program will the learner use the new knowledge and skills following the instruction? Is the performance context high risk, extremely variable, or an unknown environment? What type of distinguishing features may impact the learning context or their use of new knowledge and skills following the instruction? What type of equipment and resources will the learner use in that environment? Should those items be included in the learning context to promote transfer? Can they realistically be incorporated into the learning context or, if not, can they be adequately simulated? Will the learner be held accountable for knowing and using the new information? To whom will they be accountable? Will the learner's performance be observed and judged? If there are several performance contexts, are those contexts physically different or are there differences in what the learner must know for each context?
- *Support*—What support and rewards will the learners receive in the performance context for using the new knowledge and skills learned in the instruction? Will the learner's supervisor, school, instructor, and/or the market encourage and support the use of the new knowledge and skills with the necessary resources and equipment? What consequences will result if the learner does not use the new knowledge and skills?
- *Social Aspects*—What are the social aspects of the performance site? Will learners work alone or in groups? Will they be praised in front of peers for their performance or will their peers resist their use of new knowledge and skills? Who do they work with (type of customers, peers, instructors, employers, subordinates, etc.), and how might those relationships impact their ability or willingness to use the new knowledge and skills in the performance environment? What is the ethical climate of the performance context, and how might that impact the transfer of learning?
- *Relevance of Skills and Knowledge*—How relevant are the new skills and knowledge to the actual performance context? Are there physical, social, or motivational obstacles that make the use of the new skills impractical or irrelevant? Is the instruction being developed as part of a change initiative and if so, have the proposed changes been thoroughly researched and communicated to the learners? How long is the instruction likely to be relevant, and how critical is it to the learner's job satisfaction, effectiveness, and advancement?

As you observe and analyze the performance context and/or data about that context, revisit and confirm your understanding of the problem and the needs to be met by instruction and non-instructional interventions. What is or is not happening that should change, and what contextual factors are involved?

If you don't have access to the performance context, devise other ways to find out about it. Research similar environments and confirm the characteristics you find with those who have experienced the target environment. Conduct phone interviews with learners or individuals at the performance site, or consult documentation that reveals the nature of the performance context (e.g., the syllabus for the next course in a sequence, marketing information for graduate programs to which your students apply, job ads and descriptions, college entrance requirements, certification requirements, site plans and production reports).

Learning Contexts

The learning context is the setting where the learning experience will take place (Oblinger, 2006). It may be virtual or face to face, or a combination of the two (referred to as a *blended* or *hybrid* environment). If virtual, it could be delivered in any number of settings where the learner is accessing it using a computer, laptop, mobile phone, or tablet. It could even be a correspondence course that uses print-based instruction, CDs or DVDs, audio recordings, or other media. You may be in charge of determining the location and nature of the learning context, others may make those decisions for you (your employer, client, institution, etc.), or project constraints may dictate those decisions. Familiarize yourself with the proposed learning context to identify any limitations that might affect the design of the instruction. If a part or all of the instruction will be delivered in a face-to-face setting, the learning context will be a physical facility. If it will be a correspondence-type delivery, consider the location(s) of the learners and the equipment and facilities available to them. If the delivery is to be partially or fully online, familiarize yourself with the online platform and delivery environment and the tools that will be used to convey the instruction. Be sure to ask yourself: "What are my assumptions concerning the learning and performance contexts? How can I confirm those assumptions?" As always, you must identify and acknowledge your assumptions to ensure they are based in fact.

Visiting the proposed physical or virtual learning site can quickly confirm your assumptions or point out problems with your plans. You won't always have enough time to try out all the tool possibilities for a virtual learning environment, so when possible save time by consulting reviews or ask for advice from experienced co-workers or members of professional IDT organizations. When considering the learning context, ask questions like:

- *Physical Characteristics*—How many physical instruction sites are involved? If there are several, will the instruction be delivered to all sites simultaneously and require synchronous connections between sites? What are the characteristics of the available facilities, equipment, and resources? If an online environment will be used, will it be synchronous (learners experience the instruction simultaneously, in "real time") or asynchronous (learners access the instruction at their convenience, at different times and from different locations)? Are all the tools available that are necessary for meeting the instructional goal?
- *Personnel or Time Constraints*—Are there any limits in personnel resources or time of availability that characterize the learning context? Will learners be allowed to begin and complete the instruction at any time or must they adhere to a pre-established schedule? Will learners have to complete the instruction autonomously, or is interaction with others possible?
- *Compatibility with Learner Needs*—Is the site convenient to learners? If learners have special needs, will the physical or virtual site accommodate those needs? Is there adequate space and equipment for all learners? How well can the performance context be simulated by the learning context to facilitate learner transfer of new skills? What sort of distractions may challenge different learner's abilities to concentrate and engage with the instruction?

(Table 4.2 and the website for this chapter feature additional questions to consider.)

Decisions to Ponder Concerning the Learning Context

At this point in the process you can begin to make some decisions about the basic nature of the instruction. Some decisions will be dictated by clients, your employer, or by project circumstances (thus introducing project constraints). Some decisions can remain flexible as the project evolves, while others must be made early in the project. Carefully consider all early decisions because some may be easy to adjust later, while others may constrict later options (e.g., the decision to purchase and use a specific technology platform). We emphasize, again, that *the ADDIE process is not linear*. Design decisions evolve and change as you gather data, test prototypes, and find out more about the target learners, the demands of the content, and the expectations of the stakeholders. It is more efficient and effective to complete all the different analyses simultaneously, continuously revisiting and updating throughout the life of the project.

Table 4.2 provides examples of options available to the instructional designer and the type of questions you must answer to make decisions about those options. Many of these decisions are interrelated. For example, the Time/Place Access factor illustrated in Table 4.2 refers to when and where the instruction must take place. Examples of options available for this factor include:

- *Same time and same location instruction*—When your learners all live within a certain geographic area or work for the same company, you can design a traditional face-to-face classroom delivery, a workshop format, or a home-office corporate training course.
- *Same time and different location instruction*—When the learners live at a distance but are still within three time zones of each other, you can design synchronous televised expert lectures that are broadcast simultaneously to several locations, or online synchronous instruction using virtual conferencing software.
- *Different time and same location instruction*—Sometimes scalability is a problem and even though a large number of learners live close to the location of the hands-on instruction, that instruction can only be experienced by a few learners at a time. In this case, you may have several smaller sections of a laboratory course that accompanies a single, large science lecture course. Or you might design an apprenticeship experience that is completed by three different learners on the same piece of machinery but during three different work shifts.
- *Different times and different locations instruction*—Global instruction can often be accomplished with self-directed, self-paced, web-based instruction delivered asynchronously, or a correspondence course delivered via the postal service or email.

Choices for the learning context are informed by data from all your analyses. Learner analysis data, in particular, generally influences all the factors listed in Table 4.2. For example, the level of learner prior content knowledge should inform your decisions about a pedagogical approach. Choosing the Internet as the learning context and prompting learners to find and link to information (a Connectivist approach), when they are novices with respect to the content, can lead to what Andrew Keen (2007) calls "the cult of the amateur." Keen warns that Web 2.0 tools that allow everyone (even the ill-informed) to participate in creating and posting items to the Internet have resulted in an explosion of content—and not all of it is accurate. To avoid overwhelming novice learners with misinformation in virtual contexts and to ensure that they can build a network of valid resources (Hannafin, West, & Shepherd, 2009), you could first help them build a knowledge base of foundational information through direct instruction (more of an Instructivist approach). (Note that more detail is provided on pedagogical approaches under "Theoretical Contexts.")

We recommend that you read through Table 4.2 to get an idea of the type of context-related decisions to contemplate early in the life of an instructional project.

Table 4.2 Planning the Learning Context: Options to Consider

Factor	Options and Descriptions
Scope	What is the scope of the instruction? What content is to be addressed and how extensively? For what purpose?
Time/Place Access and Dispersion	Will the instruction be asynchronous and/or synchronous? Are the learners geographically dispersed or centrally located? Can the instruction be accessed anytime or only during specified times? How often will learners access the instruction? Will the nature of the materials prompt them to use it frequently as a reference?
Pedagogical Approach	*Instructivist, Constructivist, or Connectivist approach, or a combination? Formal or Informal? Static or Dynamic? Amount of Learner control vs. Instruction/Instructor control? Didactic or Experiential (or a combination of the two)?* **Instructivist** (aka instructionist, behaviorist, essentialist, traditional, or classical) The instruction or an instructor presents content, monitors, and guides learner performance in a practice environment and provides feedback, the learner performs the goal task, and their performance is assessed. Also described as a "directed" learning environment (Sharma, Oliver & Hannafin, 2007). **Constructivist** (based on Constructivist and some Cognitivist assumptions) a task goal is set and the learner constructs tangible objects (alone or collaboratively) in a public environment, benefiting from the feedback of peers, instructors, and/or the public. **Connectivist** The learner builds a network of information sources to consult as needed when completing a related task. **Formal or informal** Will the instruction be developed for an established educational system (K-12, university, technical or professional programs, etc.) with aligned outcomes and assessments? Or will it be accessed informally by the choice of individuals, as needed throughout their lives, when at work, play, and during conversational and exploratory activities? Will it be a closed experience, or allow open access? **Static or Dynamic** Static instruction is complete when released and doesn't change. Dynamic instruction evolves through contributions of learners and jointly "negotiated" goals and means, and may occur in authentic, case- or problem-based contexts. **Learner-controlled vs. Instruction/Instructor-controlled** A continuum of control given to the learner over the pacing and content. **Didactic vs. Experiential** A continuum of instructional strategy types that ranges from "telling" to "doing."
Type of Instruction	*Instructor-led? Personal Learning Environment? Tutored, Mentored, or Expert Access? Performance Support and Knowledge Management? Community of Learning/Practice? Individual or Collaborative?* The type of instruction ranges from instructor-led to learner-controlled Personal Learning Environments (PLE). It may also include tutoring, mentoring or access to experts. It may actually consist of job aids and reference materials in an Electronic Performance Support System (EPSS) or a Knowledge Management system. Some instruction is situated within a social community of learning or professional practice, where experts and novices interact to learn and grow. Often, different strategies and structures are required for instruction targeted for individual consumption, as opposed to that designed to foster collaboration between many learners.
Audience Type	*Individual Learners, Small Group, Large Group?* Is instruction designed for individual learners, small groups, or large groups of learners? What type of distractions will the learners have to contend with in virtual and non-virtual settings? What impact will the audience size have on the required facilities (size of physical location, size of infrastructure for virtual system, amount of required learner resources and equipment, etc.)? If demand for the instruction increases, is the instruction and the learning context scalable?
Learning Processes, Activities, and Outcomes	*Will learners read, consume, and apply content? Observe, think, exchange information, learn and practice skills, receive feedback? Solve novel, real-world problems? Construct knowledge and negotiate meaning? Develop interpersonal skills? Learn to use physical or virtual tools? Work collaboratively? Participate in role play, debates, simulations, and games? Participate in discussions (synchronous or asynchronous)?* What learning processes will yield the desired outcomes? What static and/or dynamic resources will be provided? How will learners interact with and use the content? Will learners interact with others (peers, experts, an instructor or grader, etc.) and, if so, how?

Assessment	*Graded or Ungraded?* Will learners be assessed and, if so, will the assessments be traditional (tests) or non-traditional (complete a paper, project, or process)? If graded, by whom (instructor, grader, graduate assistant, administrative assistant)? Will it be peer- and/or self-assessed? What type of feedback will be provided for the assessments (correct/incorrect only, rubrics, explanation, remediation)? If ungraded, will learner be sufficiently motivated to take the assessment? Will feedback be provided?
Delivery	*Face to Face, Virtual/Online, Correspondence, Blended/Hybrid, or Mobile?* What delivery mode best supports the desired learning outcomes? A face-to-face course, workshop, or presentation? Will it be print- or other media-based correspondence instruction (mailed, emailed, or downloaded)? Will it be delivered online or via mobile applications? Will it be a blend or hybrid of two or more of these modes? Examples of blended options include face-to-face sessions at the beginning and end of the instruction, with online activities between; regular face-to-face sessions coupled with online discussions and group work.
Instructional Technology	*Media Mix, Social Presence/Socialization, Learning Affordances, Functionality, Use by Learners* What media are needed to convey the instructional content, and what tools will learners use? What provisions do the media and tools make for fostering socialization among learners and reducing social and psychological distance between people? What are the learning affordances inherent in the proposed media mix (characteristics that support learning tasks)? What functionality is required of the media used (grade book, record-keeping, quizzing, analytics, do learners need to use it to create media objects)?
Delivery Method/ Technology	*Platform, Functionality, Usability, Reliability, Cost, Number of Learners, Supportability, Availability, and Access* How will the instruction be delivered? (Course management? Virtually through the web or a company intranet? Through the mail, email, or a download?) If designed for a virtual environment, on which platforms should the instruction be accessible (web, mobile phone, mobile tablet, etc.)? What type of functionality should the technology support (synchronous or asynchronous communication, blogs or wikis, multimedia delivery, grading and record-keeping, document posting, file sharing and submission, feedback, assessment tools, etc.)? What type of interface would work best for the level of technology-savvy of learners, facilitators, instructors, etc.? How reliable is the delivery technology? What does it cost? How many learners can it handle? Can it be adequately supported with the organization's current level of staffing? Is it available and accessible by the targeted learners?
Length and Lifespan	How long is the instruction (size and amount of time to complete)? What is its expected lifespan? Is it ongoing or a one-shot implementation? How many months/years will it be used? How stable is the content—will it require maintenance and updating? For how long?
Support	*Instruction usually includes support for designers, learners, and facilitators (exceptions: books and virtual stand-alone static instruction)* **Institutional support** Does the institution provide sufficient resources and manpower (designers, production assistants, instructors, graders, graduate assistants, program administrators) for development and implementation? Does it mandate the instruction or provide marketing support to advertise and recruit learners? Has it established supportive policies (on compensation, intellectual property, copyright, release time, promotion, and tenure)? Has the institution committed to short- *and* long-term support? **Instructional and Technical Support** What scaffolds (support) and content help will be available to learners? What will help learners feel more socially supported and connected? Is the infrastructure sufficient to support the current instruction, and to support future program expansion? Is there technical support for both development and implementation? Is there technical support for learners and instructor/facilitators?
Instructor	Is there a live instructor (content transmitter) or facilitator (learning activity enabler)? Is he/she a subject matter expert (SME)? Experienced in face-to-face and/or online instruction? What are his/her theoretical assumptions about learning and pedagogical bent? What is his/her motivation for instructing or facilitating the proposed instruction? Is he/she also course manager or providing technology support?

The Essential Nature of Good Communication

As noted in Chapter 1, communicating an effective message to the learner is an essential aspect of the instructional designer's job. In Chapter 3 you answered the question: Who is the learner? Yet, the learner is only one side (the receiving side) of the communication equation that facilitates instruction. At the other end of the process is the *source* or *sender*, which is determined by *you* (and your stakeholders, as discussed in Chapter 2). The source of the instructional message might be:

- A live instructor or experts on the topic;
- Stand-alone mediated content; or
- A community of learners.

Good communication enhances the learning context, and some would even argue that it *is* the learning context. Let's briefly outline the process of communication to highlight its importance to successful instruction. For any given instructional message, there is an initiating source for the message, the message itself, a channel through which the message is delivered, one or more receivers of the message, and feedback from the receivers that impacts the nature of the message (refer to Figure 4.1). Here's how these elements interact:

- *Source*—The initiating source operates from a frame of reference based on attitudes and social and cultural assumptions that impact the nature and *fidelity* (accuracy and dependability) of the instructional message. Message fidelity is also influenced by the source's level of knowledge about the subject and by the skill with which the source crafts and conveys the …
- *Instructional message*—The message consists of content and treatment (structure and presentation) that may or may not appeal, make sense, or be relevant to the learners. It is constructed of symbol systems (written or spoken language, icons and images, numerals and formulas, musical scores, performances, maps and graphs, etc.) that are facilitated by the …
- *Channel*—The channel, or media and media systems, deliver the message so it can be absorbed by the learner via one or more human senses (seeing, hearing, smelling, tasting, and touching). Different media (text, audio, video, etc.) possess specific attributes that help convey the message and impact its effectiveness and, ideally, they should be chosen on the basis of the demands of the message to be conveyed.
- *Noise*—Noise can obscure or confuse the fidelity of the message or interfere with its transmission or reception at any point in the process. It can also enhance the message by adding context (for example, facial expressions that convey meaning). Examples of source noise include transmission delays or technology problems, visual and aural factors that either distract or enhance (body language, odd mannerisms, random motions, images, or sounds that are incongruent with the message or that underscore its meaning), environmental factors that either distract or enhance (lighting, colors, and sounds), and interruptions. Examples of noise originating at the receiver's end of the process include power or technology problems, personal discomfort or stress, adequate or insufficient skills to handle the instruction (e.g., language skills, communication skills, amount of prerequisite knowledge), and interruptions that distract or add to the instruction (e.g., children, telephone, visitors, or construction noise).
- The *receiver* (learner) also operates from a frame of reference made up of social and cultural assumptions and learner attitudes about the topic, the instruction, and the sending source. Receipt of the message is impacted by the sufficiency of learner prior knowledge, the learner's communication and interpretive skills (especially if the message is not in their native

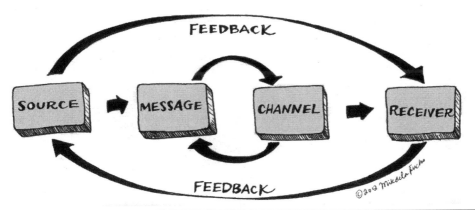

Source operates with certain ...	*Message* is encoded using specific ...	*Channel* used to convey the message ...	*Receiver* decodes the message based on ...
• Communication skills • Attitudes • Knowledge • Social assumptions • Cultural assumptions	• Content • Structure • Treatment • Symbol systems from noise	• Appeals to certain senses • Uses specific media that vary in richness • Is subject to interference from noise	• Communication skills • Attitudes • Prior knowledge/schema • Social assumptions • Cultural assumptions

Adapted from Berlo, 1960; Lengel & Daft, 1988; Salomon, 1979, 1981; Salomon, Perkins & Globerson, 1991.

Figure 4.1 The Communication Model

language), and any physical or mental challenges that may limit or prevent accurate message receipt.

- Well-designed learning experiences allow for *feedback* between the source and the receiver that allows both parties to gauge the success of the exchange throughout the communication process. Feedback also allows the learner to ask questions and it facilitates adjustments at either end of the communication process to improve the fidelity of the message.

Familiarity with this model provides you with a basis for fruitful conversations about the communication process with your stakeholders. Spector (2012) stresses, however, that this simple sender-receiver (or mechanistic) model of communication represents just one of many perspectives on the process. He identified these additional perspectives (pp. 80–81):

- *Psychological perspective*—focused on interpretation and feelings;
- *Social constructivist perspective*—focused on the creation of internal representations and interpretations;
- *Systemic perspective*—focused on throughput and efficiency; and
- *Critical theory perspective*—focused on values and challenging communication practices that seek to control individuals.

Knowing about the existence of these very different perspectives concerning the communication process can help you recognize when a key stakeholder may be viewing the process differently from you. So, assuming you are on the same wavelength with your stakeholders concerning the nature of the communication process, *what else might go wrong?* The following problems in the communication process can compromise the instructional message:

- *A mismatch of beliefs about the topic, or expectations for what the instruction will do, between the learners and those responsible for designing or funding it.* For example, learners may enroll for an online program that they believe will be convenient, flexible, and less time-consuming than a face-to-face program. However, if the sponsoring institution insists that students attend a face-to-face, day-long meeting once a semester and designs online courses with twice the amount of readings and assignments as the face-to-face counterparts, it is likely that enrollment will not meet the targeted goals.

- *A lack of feedback or a problem with the feedback process.* Feedback from and to the learners vastly improves the effectiveness of learning efforts. Designs that do not include a means for communicating performance feedback to the learner, or for collecting feedback from the learner, can severely impede learner mastery of the material.
- *A mismatch of social and cultural assumptions between the learners and those designing the instruction.* If the instruction reflects the social and cultural assumptions of the designer and/or key stakeholders, and those assumptions conflict with the assumptions of the learners, the effectiveness of the message will be negatively impacted (see the following section for examples).

Your job is to be thoroughly familiar with all the elements and contexts involved in the communication process so you can design to maximize the fidelity and effectiveness of the message and minimize noise and negative influences.

Cultural Contexts

Every country, ethnic group, business, and organization has a social culture or organizational climate that provides its members with a frame of reference that impacts learning. Culture has been defined in many ways, but in this book we define it as "the learned and shared behavior of a community of interacting human beings" (Useem, Useem, & Donoghue, 1963, p. 169). Cultures are distinguished by shared language/jargon, history, traditions, and values. Ideally, the learning context and instructional materials are aligned with the learners' cultural frame of reference to support their efforts to make sense of the instruction.

The second Notable Non-Example for this chapter illustrates why it is important to consider the cultural background of your learners and the climate of the sponsoring organization. Organizational climates can also impact the effectiveness of instruction. For example, suppose you must design transport safety training for a company that employs truckers who lift and load heavy products. Through your context analysis, you discover that the company keeps track of each trucker's accident-free miles, publishes exceptional records internally, and gives out awards at annual safety picnics. The annual picnics feature well-loved contests of strength between the truckers, and the results of these competitions are shared within the company all year long. In light of this information, you decide that the training will feature stories of stellar safety records, as well as tales of the physical handicaps resulting from bad safety practices like speeding, traveling with unbalanced loads, and failing to stop when tired. But what if the health risks of tobacco use are also to be included in the training, and you find out that suited company executives often attend meetings with an empty soda can for use in spitting out their chewing tobacco? How might this cultural information impact how you approach the topic of tobacco use among employees?

In addition to becoming familiar with your learners' cultural contexts, you must also be aware of *your own* cultural identity and frame of reference. This type of self-knowledge is important, because we all wear cultural "lenses" and see things with a perspective shaped by our values, assumptions, experiences, and worldview. Your views can infiltrate your design and subtly compromise its effectiveness, producing instruction that you find meaningful but that may not

Figure 4.2 Informal Learning: Cultural Context

make sense to other cultures. How can you determine whether your assumptions about life, the world, and people are universal or in line with the learner audience's assumptions? Do you identify with the culture of the sponsoring organization, or do you need to find out more about it to ensure that you do not inadvertently design instruction that is irrelevant or even offensive to the learners? Is your design *ethnocentric*—that is, based primarily on the values and standards of your own culture? Ponder these questions:

- Why do most Arabic websites have the scroll bar on the left side of the screen rather than on the right side?
- Do all cultures wear black to funerals? Does red always signal danger? Do brides in other cultures wear white?
- Would a button in the shape of a question mark guide learners to help in languages that doesn't use question marks?
- Why do you think translators find it difficult to translate some American time-related terms and idioms like "time-consuming," "multitasking," "getting to the point," "time is money," and "deadline" (Ferreira, 2011)?
- How should you adjust multimedia web instruction for use by learners in other countries where there are connectivity issues?

Questions like this should characterize your preparation when designing global training or instruction that will be consumed by multiple cultures. So how can you find out the answers to such questions and educate yourself about another culture for which you must design instruction?

- *Government and Commercial Resources*—Many world and U.S. government departments and institutions (e.g., the World Health Organization and the State Department) produce fact sheets on the demographics, culture, and economy of different countries. There are also many commercial resources available, such as the CultureGrams™ mentioned in the Notable Non-Example (http://www.culturegrams.com).
- *Personal Interviews*—It is always a good idea to interview natives of the target culture or those who study that culture for a living.
- *Sociological Shift*—You can also search the Internet for clues on how the target culture views *your* culture! Learner receptivity to the origin of the instruction can impact its success. (Such activities can also help you check your assumptions about learning, the learner, and the instruction.)

Research on culture has resulted in a variety of taxonomies that categorize societies, many of which are values-based. You can learn more about the topic of intercultural context and design by consulting Geert Hofstede's (1986) Cultural Dimensions Theory, as well as websites that address international business relations and political protocols (Hall, 1976).

Attempting to learn distinctions between cultures can take a lifetime, but as Ferreira (2011) emphasizes, "achieving effective intercultural communication is not about learning all the differences … but about developing mindfulness" (p. 11). It's about taking the time to research the target culture so that you know the prominent priorities that might differ from your own, and then being attentive to differences in perspectives to continually improve your intercultural competence (Copeland & Griggs, 1985). Once you've identified differences, there are several design factors that may be impacted by the target learners' culture:

- *Pedagogy*—The predominant epistemological beliefs in a culture, as well as the goal norms and the tolerance for ambiguity and uncertainty can impact whether learners prefer a more Instructivist (direct) approach based on an objective reality, or a more Constructivist approach based on convergent or even *divergent* realities.
- *Instructor versus Facilitator*—How a culture views authority can impact whether learners prefer a didactic instructor who transmits knowledge or a facilitator who works to guide exploratory learning without controlling the outcomes.
- *Group versus Individual Learning*—The amount of emphasis a culture places on collective achievements and relationships, versus individuality and individual rights, can influence learners' receptivity to group work and team-based learning experiences.
- *Accommodation*—Societies that emphasize the needs and rights of individual learners also tend to emphasize efforts to customize instruction to accommodate individual needs. In some societies, the instruction is presented in just one way with the expectation that learners will figure it out regardless of differing needs or learning challenges.
- *Learner Control*—A society's philosophy on the purpose of education and how it should be implemented can impact whether learners are comfortable with discovery activities that allow them to control the direction of their learning or if they prefer instruction with a predetermined, predictable path.
- *The Design Process*—Differences in culture can even impact the analysis and instructional design process itself, especially when time is involved. You may find it difficult to

complete a cultural analysis or subject matter research if those you wish to interview do not share your priorities concerning deadlines (Edmundson, 2007; Henderson, 1996; Reeves, 1994).

As noted, a business or institution also has a distinct culture, referred to as its *organizational culture* or *climate*. Richard W. Scholl of the University of Rhode Island claims that there is no single accepted definition of organizational culture, in part, because it is defined both in terms of its causes and effect (http://www.uri.edu/research/lrc/scholl/webnotes/Culture.htm). Deal and Kennedy (1982) define it as the behaviors and beliefs that guide an organization's actions. It includes the norms and shared values that are identifiable through its heroes, rituals and ceremonies, well-told company stories, and modes of communication (Sleezer, 1993).

King (1998) found that organizational culture frequently influences the success of training for management development, regulatory compliance, and technical skills. Sometimes the organizational culture is explicitly communicated and fostered, and sometimes it is unexplored and undocumented. King's recommendations of information to collect on an organization's culture also serve to provide details on the performance context:

- The organization's purpose, mission, vision, and goals;
- General business data such as efficiency indices, quality control reports, productivity reports, sales and customer satisfaction reports, and safety records;
- Available resources such as the equipment, financial and manpower resources available to perform tasks, absenteeism and turnover records, and demographic data about employees;
- Primary work functions of the organization and the people who perform it;
- Reward systems and forms of recognition;
- Leaders' expectations and support for training;
- Formal structures and policies;
- Willingness of management and employees to mentor new hires;
- Attitude of employees toward previous training;
- On-the-job reinforcement of previous training and other factors that might create barriers to successful transfer of new knowledge and skills;
- Attitudes toward/compliance with external regulating agencies and legal requirements; and
- Stated or unstated information on the organization's values (as described above) (adapted from King, 1998).

If possible, and if time allows, interview people at different levels of the organization to find out what they *say* they value. Then, compare that information to your observations of their actions and the organization's typical business practices to gauge the *real* values in the organization. Your investigation of the organization's culture may be more complicated if the learning effort is supported by a collaborative partnership between two different organizations with two very different cultures. In such cases, be sure to have your design plans approved by authoritative representatives from *both* cultures in the partnership.

Theoretical Contexts

One of the strengths of the field of Instructional Design and Technology is the priority placed on designing within a theoretical context, using a variety of valid assumptions about how people learn that are based on integrated research, theory, and practice (Rieber, 2009). You can speed up and, in some cases, simplify the task of crafting an effective and consistent instructional message by aligning your design with assumptions about learning from recognized learning theories. The caveat "in some cases" applies here because, if the design process is team-based or requires a consensus of key stakeholders, multiple pedagogical philosophies could complicate the task (Willis, 2009). However, communicating with your team or stakeholders about your ideas for the theoretical basis for your design will always result in a clarification of project scope, because it serves to highlight conflicts (in purposes and goals, philosophies and methods) earlier in the process so they can be acknowledged and resolved. The combination of your perspective and those of the major stakeholders for the project are reflected in the learning theories and assumptions chosen as the basis of a design, which forms the *theoretical context* for the instruction.

So what's a learning theory? The word "theory" has many definitions, but in brief, a *learning theory* is based on empirical research and assumptions about how people learn, it provides an explanation of the underlying processes involved in learning, and it is used to predict future learning behavior. *Assumptions* are beliefs or ideas that we hold to be true, with or without supportive evidence. Research studies are often designed to test specific assumptions about learning, and some assumptions have a significant amount of empirical support, while others remain largely unsubstantiated. Some assumptions about learning are unique to a specific theory, while others are shared between several theories. This has much to do with the way that research and theory concerning instruction has progressed, so that assumptions from previous theories are often adopted or expanded upon by new theories. As a result, the instructional designer's repertoire of theoretical tools continues to expand, and now includes assumptions and methods from Behavioral and Cognitivist theories, Situated and Sociocultural Learning theories, Constructivist theories, Distributed Cognition Theory, and more.

Learning theories include *principles* that describe how particular factors affect learning, and practitioners develop teaching and learning strategies based on those principles. These principles and strategies are supported by a large amount of research and are continually modified as new data emerge. Instructional designers also talk a lot about *models*. The term "model" has been used to mean many things, but in this book we use it to describe a symbolic representation of a process or concept related to instructional design.

Beliefs and assumptions about how people learn or come to know (*epistemology*) and the very nature of truth and reality (*ontology*) are the foundation of all learning theories. Your own beliefs and opinions on how people learn and acquire knowledge, how they should be taught or prepared to learn, and what actually constitutes knowledge and reality, represent your *epistemic perspective*, or *worldview*, which is reflected in the way you design instruction. However, *all* members of the communication process see things from their own perspective, and have opinions and make assumptions about how learning occurs (whether they've consciously articulated them or not), and your viewpoint may not be the only one influencing the foundation of the design. You should attempt to align the assumptions you use as the foundation for your instruction with the assumptions of the learners and those that may be facilitating the instruction. If this is not possible, be sure to explicitly state your assumptions in some way and acknowledge that they may be different from those using or taking the instruction.

A vast array of excellent resources are available on the topic of learning theories and the website for this chapter recommends several books, articles, and Internet links that do a good job of describing their use in instructional design. (See, for example, Driscoll, 2004; Richey, Klein, & Tracey, 2011.) To shorten the discussion and this chapter, we offer a gross simplification of the most common theories used in designing instruction. This information, along with the summary charts provided at the end of this chapter, can provide you with a reference point as you continue to learn more about learning theories.

Behaviorists focus on change in learning behaviors, believing that what goes on in the mind is immaterial, since it cannot be observed and verified. Behaviorists assert that knowledge is objective, or external to the learner, and that the goal of instruction is to effectively and efficiently communicate or transfer this knowledge to the learner (Ertmer & Newby, 1993). A key idea from Behavioral theory is the use of positive and negative *reinforcement* to shape learner behavior. Here is an example of a Behavioral assumption: *behavior that is positively reinforced will reoccur* (Skinner, 1969).

Cognitivists focus on the growth and change of mental knowledge structures. Cognitivists also believe that knowledge is objective, but unlike the Behaviorists they concentrate on what the learners know and how they come to know it. Knowing this, they believe the goal of the educator is to design instruction that helps the learner effectively process, code, retrieve, and transfer information (Ertmer & Newby, 1993). A key idea from Cognitivist theory is the concept of *schemas*, or mental models and frameworks that we use to organize our knowledge and help us interpret new information. When confronted by new information that is not consistent with our existing schemas, we experience *disequilibrium* and must do something to reach a balance mental state of *equilibrium*. We either *assimilate* new information into our existing schema, or we *accommodate* the new information by altering our existing schema or by creating new schema. An important Cognitivist assumption is that *learning is the linking of new information to prior knowledge* (Jones, Palincsar, Ogle, & Carr, 1987).

Sociocultural Theorists emphasize how social and cultural interaction impacts learning. Key ideas from Sociocultural theory include the idea that people learn through *observation* (Bandura, 1977) and how *self-efficacy* (learners' beliefs about their own ability to achieve learning goals) can impact how they approach a learning challenge (Bandura, 1997; Schunk, 1983). Another important concept contributed by Sociocultural theory is Vygotsky's (1978) *Zone of Proximal Development (ZPD)*. ZPD refers to the difference between the independent problem-solving abilities of the learner without help and what he or she can do with the support and guidance of more capable others. Educators should seek to determine the learner's ZPD, guiding and supporting the learner and gradually removing aid as he or she progresses. A key assumption of sociocultural theory is that *novices can complete challenging tasks when helped by more experienced others.*

Constructivists focus on how individuals and groups construct meaning. In contrast to the previously described theories, Constructivism asserts that knowledge is not objective, but rather subjective. It is individually and socially constructed through discovery, interactions, and negotiations with others, society, events, and objects, and since everyone has different social experiences, this process results in multiple interpretations of reality (Colliver, 2002; Jonassen, 1996b). There are many branches of Constructivism (Kanuka & Anderson, 1999), but the main ones that impact practice are *Cognitive Constructivism*, which concentrates on the design of instruction that helps *individuals* construct meaning, and *Social Constructivism*, which focuses on designing instruction to facilitate the construction of meaning by *groups*. A key idea emphasized by Constructivists is the importance of learning through *authentic real-world experiences* and *reflection* about those experiences. Along with Sociocultural theorists, the Constructivists embrace Vygotsky's (1978) emphasis on experts assisting novices or apprentices, something the Cognitive psychologist Bruner (1978; Wood, Bruner, & Ross, 1976) termed *scaffolding*.

Situated Theorists stress the influence of situational and contextual factors on learning. A key idea is the *community of practice*, people with similar interests, professions, or learning goals that share information and experiences within the group (Wenger, McDermott, & Snyder, 2002). These communities usually consist of individuals with varying degrees of expertise, and novice members gradually learn and develop personally and professionally as a result of participating alongside experienced members in the legitimate practices and activities of the group (Lave & Wenger, 1991). A related concept is learning by *cognitive apprenticeship*, whereby an individual explores and reflects to learn cognitive skills through interaction with a more experienced practitioner who models, coaches, scaffolds, and articulates his or her tacit knowledge. A major assumption undergirding Situated Theory is that *knowledge should be presented and applied in authentic contexts* (Brown, Collins, & Duguid, 1989).

Distributed Cognition states that *knowledge is distributed and resides, not just in the mind, but in the connections made by the individual to practices, processes, artifacts, symbols, and other people.* Those who advocate the theory focus on the connections that people make between information sources, contacts, and resources, for the purpose of applying them to solve real problems (Downes, 2012). A key idea is that large and global problems can be solved only when you connect the distributed brainpower of many.

Learning theories can be thought of as the blueprints or tools that guide and enable designers to build effective instruction. Say, for example, that you have a lot of car repair knowledge and have decided to replace the water pump in your car. However, if the only tool you have available in your toolkit is a hammer, you will be frustrated in your efforts to remove and replace the pump. In the same way, the more learning theory tools you have in your toolbox, the better equipped you'll be to design instruction that meets the needs of learners who differ with respect to motivations, prior knowledge, and intellectual capabilities. The bottom line: A repertoire of strategies from multiple theories enhances the design tools at your disposal and, when you are armed with knowledge of the many ways that people conceptualize learning, you can "choose more purposefully among techniques to accomplish specific goals" (Bransford, Brown, & Cocking, 2000, p. 22).

Many designers combine assumptions about learning from several theories to support a particular *pedagogical approach*. In this chapter, and throughout the rest of the book, we highlight three pedagogical approaches used in instructional designs:

- *Instructivist*—With an Instructivist approach (sometimes referred to as "direct instruction"), the instruction or instructor presents content, monitors, and guides learner performance in a practice environment, and provides feedback. In most Instructivist learning environments, learners are assessed on their performance of the stated outcome, objective, or goal (Sharma et al., 2007). The Instructivist approach pulls from both *Behaviorist* and *Cognitivist* assumptions about learning, and tends to see the design challenge as organizing and presenting information in a way to facilitate effective and efficient learner encoding, storage, and *retrieval.*

- *Constructivist*—A Constructivist approach is focused on authentic experiences that involve learners in activities carried out in the real world. It typically provides a goal for learners involving the construction of knowledge or a tangible object or public entity (alone or collaboratively, e.g., a robot or theory). This is generally done in a public forum, so that learners benefit from the feedback of peers, instructors, and/or the public. The Constructivist approach pulls from *Constructivist, Cognitivist*, and *Sociocultural* assumptions about learning. It views the design challenge as exposing learners to multiple problems and multiple perspectives, providing learning-rich activities and projects to be constructed, identifying appropriate contexts for learning, and providing sufficient cultural, pedagogical, and technical scaffolding/support for learners (Papert & Harel, 1991).

- *Connectivist*—Connectivist learning experiences are designed to support learners in building a network of relevant information sources to consult as needed for daily tasks and learning. According to Siemens (http://www.connectivism.ca/?p=116), Connectivism pulls from a broad array of theories and concepts, including: *Activity Theory, Sociocultural Theory, Social Learning Theory, Situated Learning, Complexity Theory, Network Theory, Distributed Cognition, Embodied Cognition, Media Theory, Affordance Theory,* and more. Design efforts for this type of approach are still evolving, but focus on facilitating the learner's ability to create and maintain connections to current, distributed knowledge sources (both human and mediated), fostering contextual interactions, and helping learners manage an abundance of information and diversity (Cook, 2012; Cormier, 2008; Downes, 2012; Siemens & Conole, 2011; Tschofen & Mackness, 2012).

Note

Connectivism has been promoted by some as a "learning theory for the digital age" (Siemens, 2004), while others argue that it does not qualify as a theory (Kop & Hill, 2008). What do you think? As you continue to build your knowledge base for different theories and pedagogical approaches, consider whether you think Connectivism qualifies as a theory, or if it is more accurately portrayed as a pedagogical approach to designing learning experiences that is based on assumptions from several learning theories.

You may decide to use all three pedagogical approaches for a particular instructional project. This is a viable plan, because many learning experiences include foundational content (often taught through an Instructivist approach) that learners need to use in constructing artifacts and meaning (Constructivist approach). As learners participate in real-world activities, they also make connections to current knowledge that is distributed and resident outside of their own brains (Connectivist). All three approaches use assumptions from different theories and theorists, so there is some overlap between the approaches (see Table 4.3 for a comparison and Tables 4.4–4.7 for more detail on individual learning theories). For example, practitioners and theorists alike continue to struggle with distinctions between Constructivism and Connectivism (see the blogs of George Siemens and Stephen Downes, and respondents' comments, e.g., Downes, 2006, 2007).

As a means to distinguish between Constructivism and Connectivism, blogger April Hayman (http://aprilhayman.wordpress.com/2009/09/16/deciphering-connectivism/) suggested a helpful visual metaphor involving two popular children's toys. Hayman compared Constructivism to LEGO™ and Connectivism to Magnetix™. She emphasized that, although both toys are resources for building, Magnetix™ enables interchangeable connections that, as a result of their magnetism, attract other connections. The comparison of all three pedagogies in Table 4.3 provides more material for distinguishing the similarities and differences between the approaches.

Hannafin and Hill (2002) contend that when designers "recognize the utility of various approaches and perspectives and understand key foundations and assumptions" (p. 74) related to learning theories, they will produce grounded instruction. In a *grounded instructional design*, the foundational assumptions about learning are reflected in the organization of the instruction, the teaching and learning strategies used, and the technology selections. We recommend you take a pragmatic approach and use what works best to address the problem you've identified. Your

Table 4.3 Contrasting Pedagogical Approaches

Factor	Instructivist Approach	Constructivist Approach	Connectivist Approach
Learning Definition and the ID Process	• **Learning:** Is a change in either the form or frequency of observable behavior, and/or discrete changes in internal mental associations and states of knowledge. Instruction is structured and organized; elaboration of new information is encouraged to foster formation of effective mental models for later retrieval and use. • **Knowledge:** Is a goal in itself. • **Theoretical bases:** Behaviorism and Cognitivism. Focus is individualized learning with learner freedom to determine the space and pace for learning, but learner typically attributes control of the learning process to the instructor or the instruction. • **Epistemology:** Objectivist, rationalist. • **Typical ID process:** Design is primarily systematic, systemic, and iterative. Analyze objective data to establish needs and define content; consult experts or SMEs; use objectives and assessments to guide success; use evaluation to gauge success of instruction. • **Scalability:** Usually easy to scale up to accommodate more learners.	• **Learning:** Occurs while engaged in solving problems, pursuing goals, performing work-related tasks, and constructing knowledge and artifacts. Meaningful instruction is embedded in authentic contexts, encourages mindful learning, and includes social experiences, and multiple perspectives and presentation modes. • **Knowledge:** Exists in the mind and is a tool to support inquiry and learning. • **Theoretical bases:** Constructivism and Sociocultural Learning Theories. • **Epistemology:** Interpretivist. • **Typical ID process:** Design is iterative and sometimes chaotic, reflective, and collaborative. Analyze contexts and subjective user data to establish needs and subjective user data to establish needs and define content; allow outcomes, content, and activities to emerge from processes; test prototypes; prepare learning resources and processes to facilitate meaning-making; and formatively test and evaluate to improve instruction. • **Scalability:** Usually difficult to scale up to accommodate more learners.	• **Learning:** Is the process of building current and flexible connections between information sources, contacts, and resources to apply to real problems. Learning, knowing, and cognition are distributed, social, and networked, and require learners to judge the utility of information, navigate, grow, and prune connections. • **Knowledge:** Exists in the world rather than in the mind and is a distributed resource. • **Theoretical bases:** Social Constructivism, and Situated and Sociocultural Theories (Communities of Practice). • **Epistemology:** Distributed Cognition. • **Typical ID process:** No established process yet. Context rather than content drives the design. Use primarily generative sources of knowledge with some declarative, expert sources of information, to support the idea that learning and knowledge rest in diversity of opinions. Promote the establishment and use of learning networks in formal, informal, and non-formal environments. Leverage technologies to mediate knowledge and enable learners to extend themselves through tools (language, technology; signals). Focus on the design of interactions between learners using those tools in groups, networks, and collectives. • **Scalability:** Moderately easy to scale up to accommodate more learners.
Use Approach When …	• There is limited time for development and/or delivery, there is high accountability for learning results, and/or when "life-and-death" skills are involved, and/or when domain-specific skills must be learned for certification, accreditation, or satisfaction of regulations. • Learners and/or stakeholders have a low tolerance for content ambiguity. • There are novice learners or cultures that prefer authoritative instruction. • Learners have low levels of prior knowledge/experience with the content.	• There are more flexible requirements for delivery and when there is relatively low accountability for learning results. • Learners are more experienced with the content. • The learners, culture, and/or organization prefer instruction that is embedded in real-world contexts.	• Learners are experienced, self-directed, autonomous, and prefer a loosely structured, flexible learning environment where they have a lot of control. • Learners prefer an abundance of interaction with content through a community of practice. • Learners are familiar with multiple technologies or have time to learn them, and are familiar with navigating cyberspace. • The facilitator has time to maintain the network. • You need to connect the distributed brainpower of many to brainstorm and solve global-type problems (e.g., organization-wide issues, epidemics).

Source: Compiled from Anderson and Dron (2011); Deubel (2003); Downes (2012); Siemens (2004); Smith and Ragan (2005); Willis (1995).

Example

You are designing an online program to train learners how to utilize a new software application in a way that is specific to your company's business. You support your **Constructivist** approach with the assumptions that individuals learn best when allowed to determine what and how they will learn, and when they are actively exploring and solving complex problems in authentic contexts. Your approach provides minimal guidance, a task goal and a help file for the learners to access if needed. This works for the learners who are experienced, confident, and like to jump in and explore a new online environment or solve an ill-structured problem. It also supports learners who have a task to complete and wish only to learn what is necessary to complete that task. However, you also agree with the **Cognitivist** assumption that learning involves building on prior knowledge, and some of your learners have insufficient prior knowledge or experience. For those learners, you add some **Instructivist** elements by providing more structure and optional guidance in the form of detailed directions. In addition, your learners need to keep current on software updates and be aware of new uses for the software developed by users around the globe. In response to this need for currency, you also incorporate a **Connectivist** approach through an online community that enables learners to share ideas, and link to the software company's news feed to access notifications on upgrades, enhancements, and user-submitted contributions.

---

decision on whether to use one approach or a combination depends on the nature of the content and proposed instruction, the contexts (Deubel, 2003), and whether different approaches are needed at different points in the learner's development.

There are several other specialized theories that are significant for the design of instruction, and that you may want to research as you become more familiar with the field:

- *Cognitive Load Theory* (referenced in Table 4.5) informs methods designed to reduce demand on learners' working memory.
- Keller's (1987) *ARCS Theory of Motivation* (described further in Chapter 8) provides guidance on adding motivational elements to instruction.
- Mayer's *Cognitive Theory of Multimedia Learning* (2009) is frequently used as justification for the design of instructional messages and media (referenced in Chapter 10).
- Moore's (1993) *Theory of Transactional Distance* describes the interaction of course structure, dialogue, and learner autonomy (self-directedness) and how that interaction impacts the amount of transactional (cognitive) distance between the learner and the instructor or instruction. Transactional distance refers to the amount of psychological and communication distance in a learning environment that has the potential to foster misunderstanding and reduce learning. The concept can be applied to all formats of instruction, but is particularly applicable to online and blended environments, where the goal is to assess learner autonomy and manipulate the amount of structure and dialogue necessary to minimize or reduce transactional distance (see Benson & Samarawickrema, 2009).

The theory charts in Tables 4.4–4.7 address the major topics that learning theories address, including how learning occurs, the role of memory, and the factors that influence learning (Janzen, Perry, & Edwards, 2011). You can use the theory charts provided in this chapter as a resource

Table 4.4 Behavioral Theory

Behaviorism

Learning is a change in behavior …

Ivan Pavlov (1927)—*Classical Conditioning*

Guthrie (1930)—*Contiguity Theory*

E. Thorndike (1911)—*Instrumental Conditioning, Law of Effect*

John Watson (1913, 1925)—*Early Behaviorism*

B.F. Skinner (1953, 1968)—*Operant Conditioning, stimulus generalization, contiguity, reinforcement schedules, extinguishing and shaping behaviors*

John Dewey (1896) and William James (1904)—*Philosophical Behaviorists*

Some Assumptions

- Knowledge is objective, absolute. Seek one reality.
- All behaviors are acquired through conditioning, which occurs through interaction with stimuli and consequences in the environment. We learn individually and socially.
- The learner is a receiver and receptacle (tabula rasa, or "blank slate") for presented content, and is reactive (as opposed to proactive) in this process (not passive, as some have claimed).
- Psychology is a natural science, and the study of learning should be objective and empirical.
- The mind cannot be read or observed, so observable behavior should be studied without consideration of the mental processes involved.
- Behavior that is positively reinforced will reoccur.

Description of Learning, Origins, Factors, Role of Memory, and How Transfer of Learning Occurs

Behaviorists define learning as a permanent change in the form or frequency of *observable*, measurable behaviors, focusing on external behavior or what learners can do, rather than on internal mental processes. Learners are *reactive* in this process, absorbing and reacting to stimuli.

Classical Conditioning says that environmental stimuli provoke or *elicit* certain behavioral responses and this stimulus-response relationship can be used to predict, condition, and control behavior.

Operant Conditioning says that organisms *emit* behaviors that operate on their environment to produce consequences, and these consequences then condition the organism's future behavior.

Origins of Behaviorism: Objectivism (Hannafin & Hill, 2002); Functionalism and Empiricism (Burton, Moore, & Magliaro, 1996).

Influential factors: Strength of the associations, interactions between the learner and stimuli in the environment, the learner's prior knowledge, and the consequences of actions.

Memory is fostered by repeated proper use of knowledge and the development of habits; forgetting results from insufficient use. Transfer occurs when learners generalize, or transfer learning in similar situations/contexts.

Principles

- Instruction should seek to transfer knowledge to learners in the most efficient, effective manner possible.
- Learning is facilitated by effective cues, prompts, and feedback.
- Several learned behaviors can be "chained" together to learn more complex behaviors.
- Consequences are either added or removed to maintain or increase desired behaviors or to decrease undesirable behaviors:
  - Positive reinforcement (add to maintain/increase)
  - Negative reinforcement (remove to maintain/increase)
  - Positive punishment (add to decrease)
  - Negative punishment (remove to decrease)

Design Guidelines

- Structure learning experiences around the presentation of instruction (a stimulus) with appropriate cues, and reinforce desired responses.
- Provide plenty of opportunities for learners to practice appropriate behaviors to habituation.
- Use repetition and consequences to impact performance and condition the learner.
- Gradually shape behavior to reach a terminal goal, by presenting material in small amounts, soliciting responses after each piece and providing immediate feedback to reinforce desired responses.
- Motivate through reinforcement. Manipulate the timing and schedule of reinforcement to foster learning. The most effective reinforcement is intermittent.

Behaviorally Based Instructional Theories, Programs, Methods, and Strategies

Programmed Instruction—gradually building knowledge and skills through progressive sequences of content, questions and feedback.

Direct Instruction, Mastery Learning, Behavior Modification, Competency Modeling, the use of pretests and *posttests*. Note: Behaviorism is prominent in the roots of a systematic approach to instructional design.

Use discriminations, generalizations, associations, drill and practice, shaping and chaining to help learners remember, understand, and apply knowledge.

Behavioral approaches are particularly effective for developing procedural skills, teaching novice learners, the design of practice and feedback, the design of all types of reinforcement, and for classroom management.

Source: Adapted from Burton, et al. (1996); Dooley, Lindner, and Dooley (2005); Driscoll (2004); Ertmer and Newby (1993); Hannafin and Hill (2002).

Table 4.5 Cognitive Theory

Cognitivism	Description of Learning, Origins, Factors, Role of Memory, and How Transfer of Learning Occurs
Learning is a change in knowledge … **Edward Tolman** (1932, 1948)—*Cognitive Learning, Cognitive Maps* **Jean Piaget** (1977)—*Cognitive Development, Cognitive Constructivism, Equilibration* **Lev Vygotsky** (1978)—*Zone of Proximal Development (ZPD), Scaffolding* **G.A. Miller** (1956)—*CIP, Chunking* **Jerome Bruner** (1962; Bruner, Goodnow, & Austin, 1956)—*Early Cognitivism, Discovery Learning, Cognitive Constructivism* **Kolb** (1984)—*Experiential Learning*	Cognitivists define learning as discrete changes in internal mental associations and states of knowledge. The learner is actively involved in acquiring knowledge and forming internal mental structures (schemas) by building on and adjusting prior knowledge. Cognitivists focus on what learners know and how they come to know it. Origins of Cognitivism: Functionalism (Burton, Moore, & Magliaro, 1996), Objectivism and Rationalism (Hannafin & Hill, 2002), Pragmatism (Driscoll, 2004). Influential factors: processing quality, how the learner links existing knowledge with new information, learner ability to encode, store, and retrieve information, the environment, and meaningful instruction. Memory is pivotal to learning and it consists of sensory memory, working memory, and long-term memory (Baddeley, 2003). It is fostered through meaningful associations to prior knowledge, and helpful organization of instruction that aids the processing and encoding of information. Improper information storage can interfere with recall. Transfer of learning occurs when learners effectively store information in memory and generalize its use in similar situations, as well as appropriately transfer it to different situations.

Some Assumptions	Principles	Design Guidelines
• Knowledge is objective, absolute, and organized. Seek convergent realities. • The mind processes information like a computer, building upon prior knowledge and creating mental structures. • Learning is the acquisition of knowledge and expertise. It involves relating new knowledge to prior knowledge. It occurs when mental models, maps, and frameworks are stored in long-term memory. • Instruction should seek to transfer knowledge to learners in the most efficient, effective manner possible.	• The brain perceives patterns, works by analogy and metaphor, and looks for similarities, differences, and relationships between concepts. • Some prior knowledge is always required for the learner to recognize a pattern for processing. • Meaningful organization of knowledge (hierarchical, chronological, etc.) enhances knowledge encoding and retrieval. • Schemas and scripts can become automated through practice, placing less load on working memory processing. • An awareness of how you learn best (metacognition) can help you retain, retrieve, and achieve. • Reflecting and elaborating on information increases retention, comprehension.	To facilitate learner encoding, storage, retrieval, and transfer: • Organize information from simple to complex, provide explanations, demonstrations, examples, comparisons, and practice with feedback, use strategies like analogies and metaphors, framing, outlining, *mnemonics*, concept mapping, and advance organizers (Ausubel, 1960, 1980). • Create bridges to help learners connect new knowledge to prior knowledge and existing schema, and move learners toward a definite goal or accepted knowledge base. • Guide with feedback, provide practice opportunities, motivate by giving learners choices and challenges. • Decrease extraneous cognitive load by eliminating confusing or competing instructional formats, and irrelevant or non-essential activities and information. • Chunk instruction into meaningful units or modules to reduce demand on the learner's working memory.

Cognitive Instructional Theories, Programs, Methods, and Strategies

Gestalt Theory (M. Wertheimer)—A precursor to Cognitive Theory. The whole is greater than the sum of its parts, producing a different meaning than the parts.

Cognitive Information Processing (CIP) (G.A. Miller)—The earliest expression of Cognitive Theory, which uses the analogy of the computer to describe how humans learn.

Cognitive Load Theory (G.A. Miller, John Sweller)—Design instruction that reduces cognitive load, or the processing demand placed on working memory.

Cognitive Constructivism (J. Piaget, J. Bruner, J. Dewey)—Describes individual acquisition and construction of knowledge through assimilation and accommodation.

Other: Gagné's *Conditions of Learning, Types of Learning, Nine Events of Instruction*; Merrill's *Component Display Theory*; Reigeluth's *Elaboration Theory*; Scandura's *Structural Learning Theory* (Scandura, 2001); Keller's ARCS Motivation Model; Mayer's *Cognitive Theory of Multimedia Learning (CTML)*; Bruner's *Discovery Learning, Guided Discovery.*

Strategies: Objectives, Criterion-Referenced Tests; Memorization Strategies; Cognitive Maps; Advance Organizers; Bloom's Taxonomy (Bloom et al., 1956); Graphic Organizers.

Source: Adapted from Bonk and Cunningham (1998); Burton et al. (1996); Dooley et al. (2005); Driscoll (2004); Ertmer and Newby (1993); Hannafin and Hill (2002).

Table 4.6 Sociocultural, Social, and Situated Theories of Learning

Sociocultural, Social, and Situated Theories of Learning	**Description of Learning, Origins, Factors, Role of Memory, and How Transfer of Learning Occurs**
Learning is participating socially and observing others	Sociocultural and Social Learning Theorists say learning occurs through observation and imitation of society. For Situated Theorists, knowledge is co-constructed and learning is situated in activities bound to the social, cultural, and physical contexts in which it occurs. Learners interact socially through "legitimate peripheral participation" (Lave & Wenger, 1991) in communities of practice that embody the beliefs and behaviors to be acquired. Designers focus on the types of social interactions and situations that foster the desired learning.
J. **Dewey** (1933)—*Reflective Inquiry and Discourse*	Origins of Situated and Sociocultural Learning Theories: Pragmatism and Interpretivism (Driscoll, 2004).
G.H. **Mead** (in Cook, 1993)—*Social Pragmatism*	Influential factors: interaction of *social factors in the environment* with an individual's own *personal factors* (cognitive, expectations, attitudes, biological events) and the *learning behaviors* (skills, practice, goal progress, motivation, learning, self-efficacy), which, in turn, interact with the other factors.
J. **Lave** (1988)—*Situated Learning*	
Wenger (1999)—*Communities of Practice (CoP)*	Memory enables the learner to recall and repeat observed behaviors, and it is dependent on attention, retention through effective coding and elaboration, and motivation.
Brown, Collins, and Duguid (1989)—*Cognitive Apprenticeship*	
A. **Bandura** (1986, 1991, 1997)—*Social Cognitive Theory, Self-Efficacy, Self-Directedness, Modeling*	Transfer is accomplished when learning is successfully generalized and applied to new situations, and is enhanced by the degree of similarity between the learning context and the new situation.
Lev **Vygotsky** (1978)—*Social Development Theory, Zone of Proximal Development (ZPD), Scaffolding*	

Some Assumptions	**Principles**
• Knowledge is not absolute but is individually and socially constructed through discovery and interactions with society, others (negotiations), events, and objects. Seek to accommodate divergent realities.	• Human learning occurs in contexts that include others, goals, artifacts and technologies, activities, and cultural, organizational, and societal influences.
• Learning is an active, social process (learning by doing), involving the learner, an object (task or activity), and tools or mediating artifacts. Learning is located in the minds of individuals and in contexts and relationships.	• Social and cultural factors are key to learning, since all knowledge is situated in activity bound to social, cultural, and physical contexts.
	• People learn by observing others' actions and the consequences of those actions. The instructor or designer models and guides learning activities and designs the learning environments.
• Learning occurs through direct and practical application of information, and through legitimate peripheral participation with experts in a community of practice (CoP).	• Scaffolding/support by more knowledgeable and experienced others can expand learners' Zone of Proximal Development (ZPD), helping them achieve more than they could alone.

	Design Guidelines
	• Situate content in authentic real-world contexts, integrate knowing and doing, foster in-depth learning and analysis.
	• Expose learners to authentic discourse in a community of practice to enhance reasoning and ability to learn.
	• Enhance transfer of learning with similarity between the learning and performance contexts.
	• Design CoPs to be flexible and support shifts in focus, provide for group dialogue and outside perspectives, foster different levels of participation, support both public and private communications, provide regular opportunities for group reflection and evolution.
	• Use authentic experiences, realistic stories, or case studies to facilitate learner interaction and to provide a context for learner goals and to form and test hypotheses.

Situated and Social Instructional Theories, Programs, Methods, and Strategies

Social Cognitive (Learning) Theory (Bandura)—We learn by observing and imitating others; we teach by modeling; self-efficacy and self-regulation are key to success.

Sociocultural Learning Theory and Constructivism (Vygotsky)—Seeks to explain how knowledge construction and meaning-making occurs in social groups and contexts. Both Cognitive (Individual) Constructivism and Social Constructivism emphasize designing with authentic real-world problems and contexts, social negotiation and multiple perspectives, joint responsibility for learning, and learner metacognition and ownership of the learning process.

Communities of Practice (CoP) (Wenger)—A theory, framework, or practice that advocates learning as community, identity, meaning, and practice.

Computer-Supported Collaborative Learning (CSCL)—Learning or interaction using a computer or through the Internet, face to face, or virtually.

Community of Inquiry Model (Garrison, Anderson, & Archer, 2000)—Meaningful online learning through community, with adequate social, cognitive, and teacher presence.

Major strategies: *Reciprocal Teaching*, Case-Based and Problem-Based Learning, Inquiry Learning, Cooperative learning, Dialogue, Discussion, Cognitive Apprenticeship.

Source: Adapted from Bonk and Cunningham (1998); Dooley et al. (2005); Driscoll (2004); Hannafin and Hill (2002); Hill, Song, and West (2009); Jonassen (2011); Jonassen and Land (2012).

Table 4.7 Constructivism

Constructivism	Description of Learning, Origins, Factors, Role of Memory, and How Transfer of Learning Occurs
We make meaning as we interact with our environment and with others … **John Dewey** (1933)—*Project-based learning* **Jean Piaget** (1985)—*Equilibration, Assimilation, and Accommodation* **Lev Vygotsky** (1978)—*Social Constructivism and Zone of Proximal Development* **Jerome Bruner** (1962; Bruner et al. 1956)—*Discovery Learning* **E. von Glasersfeld** (1995)—*Radical Constructivism* **David Jonassen** (2006)—*Mindtools, Guidelines for Constructivist Learning Environments* **Rand Spiro** (Spiro, Coulson, Feltovich, &Anderson, 1988) *Cognitive Flexibility Theory*	Individuals learn by constructing knowledge and making meaning from personal and group experiences, through accommodation (adjusting one's mental models to fit new experiences) and assimilation (fitting new experience into existing mental models). The mind filters input from the world to produce its own unique reality. The origins of Cognitive and Social Constructivism are disputed. Some say Pragmatism, some Interpretivism (Driscoll, 2004). Cognitive Constructivism "assumes that an individual attempts to reach coherence among the different pieces of knowledge … [Social Constructivism] sees consensus between different subjects as the ultimate criterion to judge knowledge. 'Truth' or 'reality' will be accorded only to those constructions on which most people of a social group agree" (Heylighen, 1993, paragraph 8). Influential factors: learner interactions with the environment and others, the prior knowledge the learner uses to interpret new situations, culture and context, and the instructional activities and type and amount of practice. Memory is a cumulative history of interactions, has a flexible organization, and is always under construction. Transfer occurs when learning experiences are authentic, meaningful, and appropriately contextualized so learners can build personal interpretations and understandings that can be used in novel real-world situations.

Some Assumptions	Principles	Design Guidelines
• Knowledge is not absolute but subjective and interpreted. Seek to accommodate divergent realities. • Knowledge and meaning is individually and socially constructed through discovery and interactions with society, others (negotiations), events, and objects. • Learning is facilitated when information can be directly and practically applied to solving a problem or filling an identified gap. • Instruction should assist the learner to construct and refine their individual or group representations and understandings. It should emphasize the process and learner goals, instead of a specific goal defined *for* the learner. • Individuals learn best when allowed to determine what and how they will learn, and when actively exploring and solving authentic complex problems.	• Learning results from a personal interpretation of one's experiences, and individuals store that interpretation rather than a mirror image of the experience. • Learners construct their knowledge through a process of active inquiry, enhanced by complex, authentic, and relevant situations. • Learning results from social negotiation and an exploration of multiple perspectives, and multiple modes of learning. • Learners are motivated by many choices in learning and when learning experiences relate to their personal goals. • Learning experiences should foster self-awareness of learning. • Collaboration and knowledge construction are effective for exploring subject matter that is ill-structured and still fluid and developing.	• Build constructivist learning environments around questions or issues, case studies, long-term projects, or problems. Facilitate learning by modeling, coaching, and scaffolding. Challenge learners' conceptions with questioning and activities that produce disequilibrium. • Promote collaboration and group work to expose learners to multiple perspectives, and facilitate social negotiation and joint knowledge construction. Encourage thoughtful reflection on experiences. When appropriate, allow learners to come to different conclusions. • Foster exploration through active, hands-on experiences in information-rich environments. • Engage learners in authentic experiences with experts, encouraging interaction to make tacit knowledge explicit. • Monitor learners' progress with frequent formative assessments; support their metacognitive development. • Scaffold learners with suggestions, comments, feedback, and increasing task complexity. Gradually "fade" or remove learning supports as students gain mastery.

Constructivist Instructional Theories, Programs, Methods, and Strategies

Cognitive Constructivism and Social Constructivism (described in Tables 4.5 and 4.6).

Major strategies: Case-Based Learning, Project-Based Learning, Anchored Instruction, Discovery Learning, Dialogue and Discussion, Reciprocal Teaching, Reflective Learning, and Cognitive Flexibility Hypertexts. Also Problem-Based Learning, Inquiry Learning, and Cognitive Apprenticeships (see Table 4.6 and Chapter 8).

Source: Adapted from Bonk and Cunningham (1998); Dooley et al. (2005); Driscoll (2004); Ertmer and Newby (1993); Hannafin and Hill (2002); Jonassen (2011); Richey et al. (2011).

to produce grounded and consistent instructional designs. Add to the charts as you continue to build a knowledge base of learning theories throughout your career. An internet search on any of the people or terms listed in the tables will lead you to articles and resources to build your understanding of different learning assumptions and guide you in implementing the programs, methods and strategies designed to support those assumptions.

Making Your Recommendations for the Learning Context

Once you have analyzed the performance and proposed learning contexts, and considered the implications of the cultural and theoretical contexts, *revisit your other analyses* to compare data and determine if you need to revise your plans or collect more data. Say, for example, that your context analysis reveals that the proposed learning site is accessed via a flight of stairs. You will need to consult data from your learner analysis to determine if all the learners can climb stairs, and if a learner is wheelchair-bound or unable to navigate the stairs you may need to find another learning site. The revision of previous versions of your design is all part of the iterative approach that characterizes the instructional design process.

Once you have the required supporting data, write up your recommendations for the learning context, incorporating information from your learner and needs analyses.

Thinking About Evaluation …

As you think about the contexts where the instruction will take place and where it will be used, *now* is the time to consider the logistics of end-of-project evaluations using Kirkpatrick's levels (Chapter 1). It's easy enough to distribute a *Level I Reaction* evaluation survey in almost any environment, but ensuring that you can measure learning, gauge behavioral change, and analyze results takes some forethought. For example:

- *Level II Learning*—Does the learning context feature software that collects assessment data and will provide analytics, or will you (or a grader) have to score assessments by hand and/ or aggregate and compile the results? If you are considering alternative, non-traditional assessments, who will evaluate the learners' work, and what grading guidelines will they use? Since some claim that alternative assessments are hard to grade objectively, will the credentials of the grader and the grading guidelines they use stand up to criticism or challenges from stakeholders or learners? If you develop instruction that features self-assessment or no assessment at all, how will you determine if any learning has taken place?
- *Level III Behavior*—If you wish to determine whether the learners are actually using the new skills on the job, how will you find out? Will you have access to the learners or others in the performance context (supervisors, customers, instructors, etc.)? How long after the training will you seek to determine if behavior change and transfer of training has occurred, and to whom will you go to obtain that information? If you have developed stand-alone instruction for a generic Internet audience and have no hope of ever directly contacting learners or observing their performance context, what other indicators might you build into the instruction to collect this type of data?
- *Level IV Results*—You may be asked to justify the expense of the development and implementation of your instruction by providing the results and demonstrating the impact on the organization's goals. If so, have you identified the goals you are expected to impact? Are there constraints or insufficient resources being provided for the learning context that will make it difficult to influence or track influence on those goals? Will you have access to the

performance context or to other organizational data so that you can adequately analyze the impact? It is notoriously difficult to measure impact and the return on investment (ROI) if you have not carefully recorded the current circumstances prior to instruction and isolated the factors against which the effects of training will be gauged. What benchmark measurements should you collect now for later comparisons? What aspects of the learning context will you need to arrange to enable you to identify the results later?

There's no time like the present to ponder what you must do now to secure a proper evaluation later. Begin now to lay the groundwork to justify, satisfy, and impress your funding stakeholders, accrediting agencies, future customers, or even the learners themselves.

Streamlining Context Analysis

So in what way can the process of analyzing the instructional contexts be streamlined? Here's a list of things you can do to make this process more efficient and effective:

- *Sustainable*—When designing the learning context, think about how the environment and instruction will be maintained over time. As you seek to align the learning and performance contexts, consider whether you've selected a design that can be easily adjusted if and when the performance environment changes. If an increase or decrease in demand or a change in the size or nature of the learner population is a valid possibility, think about how the instruction could be scaled up or down and make your technology and format choices accordingly. For example, if a company's home-office training program may eventually be used to train employees in its overseas offices, consider the potential differences in the performance and learning contexts and plan your design in a way that can be easily adjusted to fit the new contexts.
- *Optimized*—Flexibly designed instruction allows learners choice in matters of pacing, organization, order of content accessed, access location, and other structural and logistical elements, which accommodates the differing circumstances and abilities of learners. *Life happens*, and designing in flexibility is likely to keep learners and empower them to complete the instruction. It will also lead to a more positive and successful educational experience. That said, if your instruction allows learners this type of flexibility and choice, you should also give them some guidelines and a timetable to help them keep a regular schedule and make good progress. Another aspect of flexibility regards providing alternatives to ensure that all learners have access to your instruction. What alternative formats and access options for the facility and learning materials should be included to accommodate learners with special needs? Does the learning site require a wheelchair ramp or elevator? Can learners adjust the text size of content displayed, enter information with a variety of input devices (keyboard, joystick, mouse, or specialized accessibility hardware), or utilize a screen reader? Do you need to provide translations of the material for non-native language learners? Reflecting on the information from your learner analysis will help you make wise choices for the learning context and avoid placing obstacles in the way of some learners.
- *Redundant*—For the convenience of the learners and to save on travel costs, industry training programs are often delivered at remote job sites. These programs may be implemented in break rooms, conference rooms, or other locations that are not equipped for high-tech instruction. Or you may have to implement training in a location where the power supply or connectivity is unreliable, as is often the case in remote locations or

Third World countries. Be sure to have a backup plan for such situations and bring the materials in a redundant or alternate format (for example, paper copies of presentations or a DVD of a video that you had originally planned to stream via the Internet). As you research the performance context, be sure to ask about the facilities and infrastructure available for training if you suspect that this may be an issue, and design the instruction accordingly.

- *Right-Sized*—If the learning is to take place in multiple locations, each of which requires some customization of the instruction, establish the minimum requirements for all learning sites that will support the generic elements of the instruction. Then specify how the customization for each location might best be handled to maximize the return on the development and implementation efforts. For example, you may decide to deliver the common elements of instruction via an instructional video and provide handouts for the location-specific information. This customized approach will more effectively meet site-specific needs, as well as possibly save on development costs.
- *Continuously Improving*—If there is some question as to whether the plans for the learning context are realistic, put together a quick-and-dirty prototype system and test it out. Better to know early in the process that you have some logistical issues than to complete the instruction and have to return to the drawing board. Always remember that, as you progress through the design/development process, you will have to return time and again to your context analyses and plans and will probably need to adjust them to best meet the needs of the learners and the goals of the project.

Different Career Environments, Different Perspectives

- *Type of Instruction*—The difference in the performance contexts of career environments is reflected in the different types of instruction developed. For example, typical types of instruction developed in business and industry environments include basic skills training, specific job skill training, management and supervisory development training, specialized professional/scientific/engineering/technical skills training, quality training, executive education programs, sales and marketing training, customer service and maintenance/field service training, customer relations training, regulatory training and government-mandated training (e.g., Environmental Health and Safety requirements compliance, Equal Employment Opportunity and Affirmative Action requirements, and right-to-know), and other training, such as new hire orientation, ethics, communication, and supplier or dealership training (King, 1998).
- *Different Values and Goals*—Career environments not only differ with respect to performance and learning contexts, but due to basic differences in purpose, goals, and values environments they also differ in terms of organizational cultures. For example, a distinction has traditionally been made between the goals of a for-profit educational institution (educating learners for profit), and a non-profit educational institution (enhancing the quality of life for learners and society). However, as online learning has become more pervasive, the line between for-profit and non-profit educational institutions has become blurred. An increasing number of for-profit institutions have entered the marketplace alongside traditional not-for-profit institutions, intensifying the competition for market share (Rovai, Ponton, & Baker, 2008). For their online programs, many traditional non-profit institutions have adopted an approach that Slaughter and Leslie (1997) call academic capitalism. More differences in values and goals between career environments are highlighted on the website for this chapter.

- *Approach to Instructional Design*—In business and industry career environments, Human Performance Technology (HPT) is a commonly used framework for specifying and designing instruction. HPT is, in effect, a part of the culture of that environment (see the HPT model in van Tiem, 2004). In military career environments, the military Instructional Systems Design (ISD) model is often used for designing instruction. The ISD method was first developed in a military setting, and the current version used by the military training culture is referred to as the Interservice Procedures for Instructional Systems Development (approved by the Joint Chiefs of Staff in 1975 for all military education and training). You can view the model by searching the Internet for "military ISD model." K-12 designers are frequently also the instructors for the materials they design, and they tend to use discipline-specific or curriculum-driven models. In the health-care career environment, the learning and performance contexts are often well-aligned and a large amount of training is conducted in authentic settings with real patients or is conducted using elaborate simulations. Finally, it is impossible to generalize about approaches to design in higher education because practice varies across institutions, departments, and even amongst faculty. If you are responsible for helping faculty members move their instruction from a face-to-face format to an online format, it is a good idea to research the approaches taken in their discipline and in their department, and then also question them about their own preferred pedagogical approach.
- *Approach to Facilitating Learning for a Mix of Cultures*—A learning context that features a mix of cultures, if carefully fostered and managed, can result in a new social culture that enriches and deepens the learning of all participants. The specifics of how to foster and manage a mix of cultures in the learning context vary by career environment. McLoughlin (1999) stresses that, in K-12 classrooms, teachers must design activities that promote the type of participation, interaction, and power sharing that aligns with the learners' culture (although K-12 environments are often culturally diverse in themselves). Furthermore, what is right for one career environment may not be appropriate for another. Culture is a consideration in *all* career environments, in both virtual and physical settings, so plans for grouping and interactions must be carefully considered to minimize the strain on individuals as they seek to communicate and collaborate, and to optimize the benefits of multiple perspectives and varied prior knowledge and experiences. Design the learning context to align with the culture of the organization, but realize that for some governmental agencies, the military, and large non-profits, such cultural alignment may limit the portability of the instruction to other environments, even within the same sector (Spector, 2012).
- *Use of Asynchronous Activities for Second Language Learners*—In higher education career environments, courses are frequently populated by a significant number of international students. When making choices about the learning context for groups of learners that include those whose native language is different from that spoken by the majority of the group, remember that asynchronous learning activities like discussion board reflections can help such students become equal participants. Asynchronous activities allow students time to reflect on their assignments and more carefully craft a response. Such activities are also good for students who may have excellent language skills but are, for whatever reason, less likely to contribute verbally in a face-to-face or synchronous setting.

Test Your Understanding With a Bloom Stretch

Apply	Use the charts in this chapter to select a group of assumptions about learning and a pedagogical approach for your choice of an instructional project.
Analyze	Select an online unit of instruction and analyze it to determine its theoretical basis or the assumptions about learning that were used in the design. Compare your results to others who analyzed the same unit of instruction.
Evaluate	Conduct an Internet search to find examples of instruction for which the designer claims to have used a specific theoretical basis or assumptions about learning. Did the designer do a good job of producing instruction that reflects the theory or assumptions that he or she claimed were used?
Create	Using the tables in this chapter as a guide, pick one of the theories to research further. Imagine how a key theorist for that theory would react to the design of a unit of instruction with which you are familiar (or that you find online). Assume the identity of the theorist and compose a one-page reaction paper written from his or her point of view. Your reflection should include the assumptions about learning that you think the theorist would cite as the basis of criticism or praise for the unit of instruction under scrutiny. You should also comment on the strategies used in the instruction and whether the theorist would think they were appropriate for the instructional goal. Conclude by citing at least three resources that you found particularly helpful in researching your theory and theorist.

Diving Deeper

Want to know more? When time allows, we encourage you to research the different contexts that impact instruction. The website resources for this chapter can get you started:

- **Practical Exercises and Examples**—Worked examples and case studies for context analyses.
- **Job Aids**—Worksheets and questions to ask regarding the contexts of instruction.
- **Resources**—A wide range of recommended books, articles, and URLs on learning theories.

5
Analyzing the Content and Project Scope

THE COST OF FAILING TO IDENTIFY ESSENTIAL INFORMATION

The catchphrase "content is king" is not just a slogan—it truly conveys the prominence of content analysis in the process of instructional design. Of all the different analyses you conduct for a project, the examination of the content is pivotal and generally the most time-consuming. For most projects, a *content analysis* involves the definition and refining of instructional goals into the knowledge, subskills, and/or tasks that make up the substance of the learning experience. A thorough content analysis will identify the scope of the project by defining the prerequisites and priorities, and it can provide a basis for the structure and sequencing of learning experiences.

Inquiring Minds Want to Know …

- How do I gather information about the content and what methods are available for conducting a content analysis?

- Why is it necessary to classify, prioritize, and sequence your content?
- How can I integrate and communicate all the analysis data to produce a design plan?
- What should I remember and understand from this chapter?

> ⇒ The meaning of the terms "essential vs. non-essential content"; "cognitive domain," "psychomotor domain," "affective," and "interpersonal domain";
> ⇒ Different methods for analyzing content and identifying prerequisite skills and knowledge;
> ⇒ Methods for prioritizing content and sequencing it in a logical manner;
> ⇒ How to classify content by the knowledge, attitudes, skills, and interpersonal skills (KASI) desired, by Gagné's Five Learned Capabilities, and by Bloom's Revised Taxonomy; and
> ⇒ How to summarize content and project scope for stakeholder review.

The scope of a design project may change several times, as all parties involved collaborate to define just what is needed and how those needs will be met. An in-depth understanding of learning needs requires some type of content analysis, regardless of the theoretical or pedagogical basis of the instruction (Jonassen, Tessmer, & Hannum, 1999). Your job in this process is to closely examine the content, identify what's essential, organize it, and present it in a way that facilitates its review. Reviewing a summary of the content can prompt all stakeholders to think deeply about what it is that the learners must know and be able to do, and just what it will look like when they know and can do those things.

Figure 5.1 illustrates three main activities: needs and *goal analysis*, content analysis, and design. An analysis of needs and goals results in broad goals that you use to guide your exploration and analysis of the content. During content analysis you also identify types of learning; the *knowledge*, attitudes, skills and interpersonal skills required by the learner; and any prerequisites to the instruction. You also prioritize topics, *chunk* content into manageable units, and sequence the content during content analysis. Finally, the output from your content analysis enables you to move on from analysis activities to design activities. Design activities include identifying specific learning outcomes, the applicable teaching/learning strategies, and assessments for the instruction. Since different types of goals and content often require different types of analysis

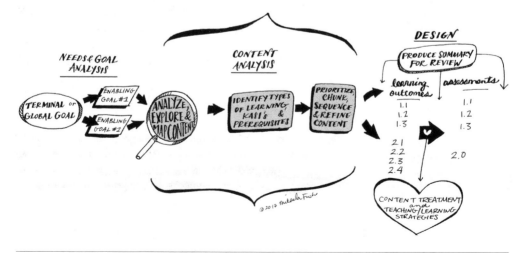

Figure 5.1 From Goals to Strategies and Assessments

Jargon Alert!

Due to the variety of instructional purposes and content and the lack of standardization in the content analysis process, there are many terms for this step in the ADDIE process. The most common are *content analysis, instructional analysis, **job analysis***, and *task analysis*. However, these terms are often used interchangeably so their definitions are confounded. Other terms and methods used include: *content domain analysis, content level analysis, performance analysis, procedural analysis, topic analysis, critical incident analysis, fault tree analysis*, and more. In addition, several taxonomies have been developed to classify the content for learning experiences, with the most well-known being Bloom's Taxonomy of Educational Objectives for the Cognitive Domain (Bloom et al., 1956), its 2001 revision by Anderson and Krathwohl, and Gagné's (1985) five learned capabilities (aka domains of learning). Explore the different possibilities and select a method and a classifying scheme that works best for your content!

methods, you should select an approach to the analysis that aligns with the goals you've identified for the project.

Notable Non-Example

Whether you are the content expert or you are working with one or more subject matter experts (SMEs) to identify the content, it's your job to ensure accuracy and limit the scope to the essentials. The following non-example illustrates what happens when these guidelines are disregarded.

> *Majoring on the Minor While Neglecting Essentials*—One of our graduate students shared that she had searched the Internet for instructions on how to replace the window regulator for the driver's door of her car. Finding a detailed description with plenty of photos online, she went out and bought the part and dedicated an evening to repairing the power window. After work, she set up her laptop in the garage and began to read and follow the instructions. The essential directives were interspersed with lots of nice-to-know information about hand-crank mechanisms that were previously used in car windows and advice on what to do if you couldn't find the right part. Halfway into the process, she discovered a problem. Step 15 in the instructions casually referred to the use of a special tool that was essential for making the repair. At that point, it was late at night, there were no auto-parts stores open that would have the tool, and her car door was disassembled (making the car undrivable anyway!). The person who posted the Internet instructions had neglected to include a list of all required tools upfront, to ensure that do-it-yourselfers would have everything they needed to successfully repair a power window.

Caution!

There are many online examples of poor instruction produced by individuals who haven't carefully distinguished between *need-to-know* and *nice-to-know* information. More formal types of instruction also fall prey to this common problem, and content "bloating" is common when you don't prioritize your content, have it reviewed by SMEs, or test and collect feedback on it. Read on to learn more about how to effectively analyze the content for your instruction and differentiate between essential and peripheral information.

Analyzing Content

Different types of learning experiences and instructional goals often require different types of content, which, in turn, must be identified using different methods of content analysis. The type of content that makes up instructional material ranges from objective, fact-based content, to more subjective learner contributions of personal stories and comments. The identification of content can be a very subjective process in itself, and it is particularly susceptible to personal bias. For these reasons, content analysis could be characterized as both an art and a science. Ultimately, you must base your selection of analysis and classification methods on what you think will work best for the type of content involved, the pedagogical approach you've selected, and what can most easily be communicated to the stakeholder audience reviewing the content.

Consequently, it is important to be clear about the questions that must be answered to identify the content. Answering questions like those listed in Table 5.1 will enable you to identify the content, as well as structure and organize it into a learning experience that addresses the goals of your instructional project.

So What's Involved?

Content analysis is very similar to the goal analysis process, with emphasis on defining the truly essential tasks down to the most basic level of specificity, and sequencing or ordering those tasks. It involves several basic steps that you can customize, based on the type of instruction and content for your project. Depending on the scope of the content, the project schedule, and your stakeholders, you may decide to have your work reviewed after each of the following steps, or at the end of your analysis. You may also choose to produce a design document, prototype, and/or storyboard for review.

1. *Gather and review the available content resources*—Revisit your overall (terminal) project goal to make sure you have identified any and all sub-goals (enabling goals). Your goals will provide a starting point for identifying the content to be included in the instruction. If you are not the content expert, this will involve working with SMEs or key stakeholders who can identify appropriate, authoritative content materials.

2. *Identify and classify what the learner must do, know, and believe to achieve each goal*—Analyze the content in light of your goals to identify what the learner must know and be able to do, and any desirable attitudes or interpersonal/social skills that should result from the learning experience. Select methods of analysis that are conducive to identifying the required details for the type of content involved in your project. Build a KASI (knowledge, attitudes, skills, and interpersonal skills) "map" for the goals and sub-goals.

3. *Isolate essential content and prioritize*—As you analyze the content and identify the knowledge, attitudes, skills, and social skills (KASI) to be communicated through the learning experience, isolate those that are *absolutely essential* to the learning goals. After distinguishing the need-to-know from the nice-to-know information, prioritize it and at an early point in the project, have those priorities approved by your stakeholders. This information will help you make decisions later if you run out of project funds, exceed schedule deadlines, and/or if there is too much content for the desired instructional length.

4. *Identify and map content dependencies and prerequisites*—Begin to map out a structure for your design by identifying the relationships between goals and the related skills,

Table 5.1 Content Analysis Questions for Different Pedagogical Approaches

Instructivist Approach	Constructivist Approach	Connectivist Approach
*Individuals learn **WHAT** by consuming content.* *Content is: objective, static, external*	*Individuals and groups learn **HOW** by constructing meaning, knowledge, and artifacts with content.* *Content is: objective and interpreted, static, internal*	*Individuals learn **WHERE** by making connections to external content.* *Content is: interpreted, constantly changing, external*

Content or Instructional Analysis
- What topics should be addressed?
- What does the learner need to know about each topic; what will he or she do with this information?
- What types of knowledge are involved (declarative, structural, and procedural knowledge), and what natural classifications exist in the content (themes, time, hierarchy, or chronology)?
- What topics should be prioritized over others in the instruction?
- What prior knowledge and/or skills should the learner possess prior to the learning experience?

Job/Performance and/or Task Analysis
- How is the job or function performed, and what is its difficulty and importance?
- In what type of environment and under what conditions is it performed?
- What tasks, responsibilities, and duties are involved?
- How frequently is it performed, and what resources/equipment are required?
- What knowledge, skills, and attitudes are necessary to effectively perform it?
- What decisions are made when performing it, and what type of problem solving is required?
- What quality standards apply, and what are the consequences of errors or poor performance?
- What factors and abilities contribute to making experts successful at this job or function?
- What prior knowledge and/or skills should the learner possess prior to the learning experience?

Content and Situational Analysis
- What meaningful situations, real-world tasks, authentic problems and projects, and questions will promote learning through engagement with the content and provide a bridge between old and new knowledge?
- Will learners construct an individual project or collaborate on a group project? How can they be scaffolded to facilitate effective teamwork?
- What content and expert resources should be made available for learners to use to hypothesize, predict, manipulate, and construct?
- What prior knowledge and experiences are necessary for learners to build upon?
- What social interactions and collaborations would best promote learning?
- What learner misconceptions should be challenged?
- How, and about what, should learners be prompted to reflect?
- What metacognitive and self-regulatory skills must learners possess, and how should learners be prompted to consider their learning process?
- What tools will the learner need to gather, analyze, and interpret information, and explain, predict, and communicate results?
- What goals and expectations should be communicated to learners?
- What scaffolds help learners effectively manage information and extract essential concepts and skills from examples and experiences?
- How can learners be supported in effective time management?

- For what topics should learners build a network of external knowledge sources?
- What connections should learners make and what meaningful underlying patterns should they recognize within distributed sets of information?
- What resources are required to support learners in self-organizing and managing their own personal learning network?
- To what type of relevant, current, high-quality information should they connect?
- How should learners be scaffolded to become effective at accessing, evaluating, constructing, managing, integrating, updating, and traversing their knowledge networks?
- What contextual information should the learner be given to help frame their connective activities?
- What guidelines will help the learner distinguish between important and peripheral information?
- What type of interactions with peers and experts will facilitate learning and knowledge connections?
- What case studies and examples will illustrate the utility and impact of the knowledge to which learners are connecting?
- What type of content should be included in corporate or institutional knowledge networks?

knowledge, and attitudes involved. Which goals or tasks are dependent on the learner's mastery of other goals, tasks, or knowledge? You will also identify any prerequisite knowledge or skills that the learner must possess prior to the learning experience you are designing. There are a variety of ways to accomplish this, and you should seek to streamline the process by selecting a method that can easily be adjusted for the next step in the process-content verification.

5. *Verify the content and scope*—Whether you are the content expert or you are working with SMEs, take time to have someone else review and verify your content analysis, both for accuracy and to ensure that you have included only the essential topics. Format the goals and content in a clear and concise manner to facilitate the process and to focus your reviewers on the content for which you particularly require feedback.

Gathering and Reviewing Content

As you collect and review the content, revisit your terminal instructional goal to ensure that you have identified all major enabling goals. If you find it difficult to write an overall goal under which all other goals fit, it is possible that the scope of your project would be more accurately characterized as an instructional program or curriculum rather than a single workshop, course, or unit of instruction.

Example

You are developing Hazard Communication (HAZCOM) training for company general maintenance staff. These staff members are rotated among four different job sites, based on varying needs at those sites. This training is intended to provide site-specific hazard training to protect your employees and to comply with the Department of Labor's OSHA HAZCOM standards. You have carefully reviewed content information about manufacturing processes, activities, and maintenance requirements at each site, as well as the governmental HAZCOM standards. You and your stakeholders have agreed upon an overall, or *terminal* goal, for the project, and you have identified at least three sub-goals or *enabling* goals:

Terminal Goal: The maintenance employees will competently and safely carry out assigned maintenance work at each of the four job sites, responding appropriately to any emergency situations to safeguard their own health and wellbeing and that of their co-workers.
Enabling Goals:

1. Safely and effectively maintain assigned equipment and facilities at each site.
2. Know and respect the danger represented by site-specific hazards.
3. Promptly and properly respond to site emergencies.

You can glean content related to your goals from a wide variety of sources, including content outlines, textbooks, audiovisual materials, previous versions of the proposed instruction, product documentation and users' guides, product specifications, job descriptions, websites, procedures manuals, industry best practices and guidelines, and information from personal interviews and observation. Applicable standards and regulations will also impact the content and should be reviewed; both those having to do with the content itself (for example, curriculum standards for

K-12 instruction or certification requirements for professional positions) and those related to the technology you are using (such as accessibility, usability, or universal design standards). Use the questions in Table 5.1 to guide the type of content you collect to address the demands of your instructional goals.

Identifying and Classifying Knowledge, Attitudes, Skills, and Interpersonal Skills

There are several factors to consider as you select methods to identify and analyze the content associated with the terminal and enabling goals for your instruction:

- Is the instruction for learners with a low or high level of prior content knowledge and experience? (experts vs. novices)
- Does the content consist of overt, step-by-step instructions, or more complex *procedures* requiring decision making and problem solving based on situational factors?
- Do you have to identify required learner actions, decision points, needed resources, and outputs for completing a job or task?
- Do you have to identify decision-making processes, troubleshooting or problem-solving processes, or define how experts combine complex processes to accomplish a goal?
- Are you providing heuristics (guidelines or "rules of thumb") to guide learners as they solve complex problems, or algorithms (set of rules) to direct learners in solving a straightforward problem?
- If providing instruction for problem solving, are the problems generally well-structured (where the beginning state, actions, end state, and constraints are well-defined) or ill-structured (where only the beginning state is well-defined, the actions and end state are undefined, and the constraints are frequently poorly defined)?
- Do the learners need to recall or recognize content? Do they need to merely remember and understand the content or do they need to be able to apply, analyze, evaluate, and/or create using the content? Do the learners need to come up with (construct) the content themselves? Do the learners need to find the content themselves (connect to content)?
- Can the content be characterized as "what" (for Instructivist instruction), "how" (for process-oriented Constructivist instruction), or "where" (for Connectivist instruction)?

For example, you would probably find a traditional Job or Performance Analysis sufficient for determining the content on how to bake a strawberry cake from scratch. However, if you were developing heuristics or guidelines for company experts tasked with creating a new product, you might want to use a Cognitive Task Analysis (see descriptions in Table 5.2). A good resource for different approaches to content analysis is *Task Analysis Methods for Instructional Design* by Jonassen et al. (1999), which describes five basic types of analyses and provides recommended methods for each. Their conceptualization informs Table 5.2. Remember that, as you gather and analyze data to identify content, you should also be distinguishing between what *is* and what *should be*, and between what *is* happening and what *should be* happening.

As you analyze content, identify the different knowledge, attitudes, skills, and interpersonal skills (KASI) required to enable the learner to competently complete the goals. We advocate using the KASI acronym even though the term *KSA*—knowledge, skills, and attitudes—is more common in the field. This is because the current increased prominence of social learning communities and collaborative learning experiences justifies additional emphasis on interpersonal and social skills. This classification of content types also aligns well with UNESCO's four pillars of

Table 5.2 Methods for Analyzing Content

Analysis Type	Focus and Applications	Appropriate Methods and Tools
Data-gathering techniques for all types: Document/Artifact Analysis, Observations and Field Notes, Surveys, Delphi Technique, Individual/Group Interviews, Think-Aloud Protocols		
Job or Performance Analysis	How jobs are performed, and the tasks, actions, behaviors, and resources involved. Used for technical and procedural training.	Job/task analysis; functional job analysis; procedural analysis; methods analysis; task descriptions; action mapping; observation. Hierarchical chart, flow chart, action map, procedure list, equipment and materials lists, scenario generation instrument, interview protocol, skill and cognitive skill taxonomies.
Subject Matter Analysis or Content Analysis	The structure of subject matter, the concepts and their relationships. Used for curriculum planning and for subject- or topic-oriented instruction. (*Note that the term "Content Analysis" is also used to refer to a specific research methodology for analyzing human communication.*)	Conceptual graph analysis; master design chart; matrix analysis; repertory grid technique; fault tree analysis; cluster analysis. Hierarchical chart, flow chart, concept diagram, outline, integration ladder, concept and mind maps, web, templates for lesson and differentiation plans, procedure list, equipment and materials lists, cognitive skill taxonomies.
Learning or Mental Processing Analysis	How learners mentally process information while performing tasks. Used for direct forms of instruction.	*Learning hierarchy analysis*; learning contingency analysis; information processing analysis; path analysis, interview protocol, cognitive skill taxonomies.
Cognitive Task Analysis	Performances and their associated knowledge states. The actions, knowledge, and thinking skills used when performing tasks. Tacit and explicit knowledge of experts. Used for developing instruction for problem-solving, troubleshooting and guided instruction.	Cognitive simulations; case-based reasoning; topic analysis; GOMS (identifies Goals, the Operator, Methods and Selection rules); PARI (identifies troubleshooter Actions, Precursors to the actions, Results and Interpretations); DNA (Decompose, Network, Assess). Hierarchical chart, scenario generation instrument, interview protocol, cognitive skill taxonomies.
Activity Analysis	Human activity and understanding in context. How people perform in natural, real-world situations, and the impact of social and contextual values on their activities. Used to identify content related to interpersonal skills and attitudes (e.g., classroom management), and to define complex tasks (e.g., predicting weather).	Activity system analysis; critical incident/critical decision analysis; syntactic analysis; task knowledge structures; social network analysis; Interaction Analysis Model (IAM); cognitive ethnographic analysis; discourse analysis; microethnographic analysis; interaction analysis; CSCL scaffolding research; qualitative thematic analysis. Survey, hierarchical chart, scenario generation instrument, interview protocol, skill and cognitive skill taxonomies, data mining and learning analytics tools, recommender systems, participation and contribution measures, reputation measures, information flow.

Table 5.3 Portion of the KASI Map for a Furniture Refinishing Course

Furniture Refinishing						
Terminal Goal: *Students enrolled in WW150 Fundamentals of Furniture Refinishing will acquire a detailed, working knowledge of the refinishing process and the advantages and disadvantages of different finishes, and will refinish a small piece of furniture.*						
Module 4	**Module Title: Selecting Appropriate Methods, Tools, and Materials** **Enabling Goal 4.1:** *The learner will competently complete a small-scale refinishing job.*					
	Lesson 4.1	*How do you competently refinish furniture?*				
	Knowledge	Attitudes	Interpersonal Skills	Skills	Frequency/Difficulty*/Priority**		
	Procedures for refinishing tasks. Refinishing best practices.	Choose to provide quality work to customer.	Effective customer service and relations.	Identify the type of wood to be finished.	1 x	M	E
				Select appropriate solvent for paint or finish.	1 x	E	E
				Remove old finish.	1 x	D	E
				Sand and fill if necessary.	2–3	M	E
				Apply stain or sealer.	2–3	M	E
				Apply finish coat(s).	2–3	D	E

* Difficulty: E = Easy; M = Moderately Difficult; D = Difficult
** Priority: E = Essential; I = Important; N = Nice to know

education: learning to know, learning to do, learning to be, and learning to live together (Delors et al., 1996; Draxler & Carneiro, 2008). The website for this chapter provides a detailed example of what a KASI map might look like for a course or workshop on furniture refinishing. A *portion* of that KASI map is reproduced in Table 5.3. This form is just one of a variety of tools and formats you can use to map out the KASI applicable to your instruction (others include hierarchies, flow charts, mind maps, etc.; see Table 5.2 for more).

So how can content analysis support different pedagogical approaches? The previous hazard training example and the furniture refinishing course would likely benefit from a primarily *Instructivist* approach, since both involve set content and procedures that learners must know to either satisfy regulations, maintain a safe environment, or meet quality standards. As a result, the methods you use to identify content would probably include a Job and/or Task Analysis. You might also find it necessary to conduct a Cognitive Task Analysis to identify the more complex actions, knowledge, and thinking and problem-solving skills that learners engage in when performing some of the tasks, such as assessing and responding to emergency situations (Jonassen et al., 1999, p. 6).

The furniture refinishing course also includes elements of a *Constructivist* approach, since the terminal goal indicates that participants will actually carry out the process of refinishing a piece of furniture. For that aspect of the instruction, your content analysis should identify what learners need in the way of content, job aids, and expert resources to support their efforts to complete the refinishing job and, if they are working collaboratively, to support effective teamwork. Finally, you may also decide to add a *Connectivist* aspect to the course by encouraging the participants to jointly develop into a community of practice and to develop a network of resources to help them in their future refinishing work. For this aspect of the course, your content analysis should identify sources of refinishing information, supplies, and equipment; a range of websites and professional organizations that would provide job opportunities and guidance from experts; the type of online interactions that would encourage them to participate in a community of practice both during the course and after; and the social and professional network-based tools and scaffolds that will support them in accessing, evaluating, constructing, managing, integrating, updating, and traversing their personal knowledge networks.

For each method of analysis, designers have developed tools and graphic organizers that you can use to guide the collection and classification of the content. A simple search on any of the methods listed in Table 5.2 will yield examples that you can customize to meet your needs, and there are many online tools you can use to visually represent your results.

Example

IDT blogger Cathy Moore developed the *Action Mapping* method that streamlines the process of job and task analysis. It is popular in business and industry, government and military settings where there is an emphasis on performance improvement. Action Mapping does a good job of helping designers and stakeholders work together to connect learning experiences to organizational goals through a visual process. The process begins with the identification of employee *actions* that will lead to realizing the project goals, followed by the design of *practice activities* that reflect those actions. Only then does the process identify the *essential information* that employees need to know to support the desired actions and activities. Moore claims that Action Mapping's graphic representation and method of "backwards design" helps focus everyone on "the business reason for the project and keeps extraneous information out—it provides discipline [for the designer]." (Moore, 2008, *Why use the map?* paragraph 1)

Once you have identified the KASIs, you will *classify* the content as to the type of learning involved using a classification system (taxonomy) of your choice. This, in turn, prepares you to identify more detailed statements of learning outcomes or objectives (covered in Chapter 6). According to Jonassen et al. (1999, p. 11), classifying the KASI helps you produce aligned instruction by helping you identify valid assessments that are congruent with the learning outcomes, define appropriate activities and practice exercises to support learning, and properly sequence the instruction and identify *prerequisite entry skills* and knowledge.

There are several taxonomies that have been developed to classify tasks and content for instruction. You should select a classification that you understand, that works for the content and pedagogical approach you've chosen, and that clearly communicates the content to your stakeholders, reviewers, and/or co-developers. The following discussion of classifying outcomes will use two of the more commonly used taxonomies: Bloom's Revised Taxonomy of Educational Objectives for the Cognitive Domain (Bloom et al., 1956; Anderson & Krathwohl, 2001), and Gagné's (1985) five learned capabilities or domains of learning. You should also use the online sources referenced on the website for this chapter to consider how Churches' Digital Bloom's Taxonomy (2009) applies the revised Bloom classifications to new learning processes and actions afforded by 21st-century technologies. The Digital Bloom's Taxonomy can be applied to all three pedagogical approaches, but it is particularly helpful in identifying the type of learning outcomes required for Constructivist and Connectivist approaches to instruction. Depending on your content, you may also wish to investigate some of the following taxonomies:

Global Taxonomies:

- Jonassen and Tessmer's Outcomes-Based Taxonomy (1996/7);
- Marzano and Kendall's (2007, 2008) New Taxonomy of Educational Objectives;
- David Merrill's Instructional Components (Merrill, 1983; Merrill, Li, & Jones, 1991);
- Siemens' (2005–2012) Connectivist Taxonomy;
- Fink's Taxonomy of Significant Learning (2003).

Single-Domain Taxonomies:

- Krathwohl, Bloom, and Masia's (1973) Taxonomy of the Affective Domain;
- Simpson's (1972) Psychomotor Taxonomy;
- Harrow's (1972) Psychomotor Taxonomy;
- Dave's (1970) Psychomotor Taxonomy.

Bloom's Revised Taxonomy of Cognitive Outcomes

For over fifty years, educators have been using a classification system for thinking skills developed by the psychologist Benjamin Bloom and his colleagues (1956). Bloom identified three domains of learning—cognitive (knowledge), affective (values and attitudes), and *psychomotor* (physical skills)—and developed a *taxonomy of learning outcomes* for the cognitive domain. His taxonomy is widely used to define the progression of thinking skills that learners should master. A revision by Anderson and Krathwohl in 2001 uses verbs to define the lower-order thinking skills (LOTS) of *Remembering, Understanding,* and *Applying,* which are prerequisites for the higher-order thinking skills (HOTS) of *Analyzing, Evaluating,* and *Creating.* Higher-order thinking is defined as the ability to consider information to solve problems, analyze arguments, negotiate issues, or make predications (Underbakke, Borg, & Peterson, 1993; Wenglinsky, 2002), and these skills are sometimes referred to as *critical and creative thinking skills.* When you inform learners that the instruction is intended to foster specific higher-order thinking skills, it encourages and guides them to move beyond simple recall of facts and develop their abilities to think analytically, write critically, and use knowledge to create something new. Furthermore, "instructional strategies that use higher order thinking as a means to achieve active student engagement and metacognitive thinking show the strongest relationship to improved student achievement" (Richards, 2005). Chapter 6 more thoroughly covers *Bloom's taxonomy* and provides examples of how to specify outcomes for each of Bloom's levels for the content identified.

Gagné's Five Types of Learning Outcomes

Robert Gagné, an influential theorist in the field of instructional design, developed a classification consisting of five *types of learner outcomes* (also known as *learned capabilities*). His work is based on the assumption that there are different types of learning and that different instructional conditions are most likely to bring about these different types of learning. Gagné's five types of learning outcomes include: verbal information skills, intellectual skills (including *discriminations, concept formation,* and rule use), cognitive strategies, motor skills, and attitudes (refer to Table 5.4). He also identified the internal and external *conditions* that provide a meaningful context for learning each type of outcome (covered in Chapter 6) and a set of *Nine Events of Instruction* that can be used as a framework for designing learning experiences (covered in Chapter 8).

There is some commonality between the Bloom and Gagné taxonomies, but using both will enable you to make finer distinctions in your analysis, resulting in a better design. The first three of Gagné's categories (verbal information skills, intellectual skills, and cognitive strategies) would fall under Bloom's Cognitive domain, but they enable the designer to more specifically identify the type of mental functions involved in learning. Verbal information skills are used by the learner with *declarative* knowledge (facts, lists, names, etc.) and roughly correspond to Bloom's *Remember* level of thinking skills. There is also some overlap between Gagné's Intellectual Skills of Discrimination and Concept Formation with Bloom's *Understand, Apply,* and *Analyze* skill levels. The Rule Application and Higher-Order Rules categories of Gagné's Intellectual Skills are less directly aligned to Bloom's taxonomy, with some overlap at the *Apply* level and more clear correspondence to the higher-order thinking skills of *Analyze, Evaluate,* and *Create.* Gagné's Cognitive Strategies category is an important tool for identifying learning outcomes for all designs, but is particularly helpful for Constructivist and Connectivist pedagogical approaches.

Gagné's fourth and fifth categories (Attitudes and Motor Skills) align with Bloom's Affective and Psychomotor domains and content identified for both categories can be used in conjunction with verbs at all of Bloom's thinking skill levels to specify learning outcomes. Table 5.4 details Gagné's taxonomy and adds an Interpersonal domain to address the increasing need for instruction to help learners develop social skills. Tables 5.5 and 5.6 provide examples of categorized goals for both Gagné's and Bloom's taxonomies. You can conduct a web search to locate more on the taxonomies, along with lists of verbs that can be used for each level of Bloom's thinking skills. You'll want to remember that *the verb used for a learning goal or outcome provides a clue as to the type of learning involved* and, thus, to its classification. Therefore, make sure your instructional goals and outcomes use verbs that reflect what the learner must be able to know, do, and believe, and how they must interact with others, following the instruction!

Isolating Essential Content and Prioritizing

Today's learner is bombarded with information, and not all of it is helpful. In the same way, you may find yourself engulfed by an overwhelming amount of content material. But does it all have to be included in the instruction? *No!* The available content often represents much more than the learner needs to know, and it is your job to identify the *essential* knowledge, attitudes, skills, and interpersonal skills (KASI) related to the project goals. As illustrated in the notable non-example for this chapter, this is a common problem and represents one of the biggest challenges you will encounter when designing instruction: limiting the content scope to the essentials. You must ask what the learner *needs to know*, as opposed to what would be *nice to know*, because learners resent, and typically do not learn from, instruction that appears irrelevant or inaccurate. Of course, there will be times when you find it difficult to cut material because it *all* seems important. You can minimize this type of dilemma by prioritizing your content and having those priorities approved by stakeholders and reviewers.

In K-12 education, *essential knowledge, skills, and attitudes* are those learning outcomes that represent what students must know, be able to do, and understand. Larry Ainsworth of the Center for Performance Assessment, and author of *Power Standards: Identifying the Standards that Matter the Most* (Ainsworth, 2003), recommends that teachers consider the critical intersection of three things when determining essential knowledge and skills:

1. Subject-area standards;
2. Life skills; and
3. State tests.

Of course, many of the standardized tests *still* dictate too much material, so designers and instructors must ask themselves questions like:

- *Why must individuals know this, and what need is there for this learning across time (a lifetime) and applications (all areas of life)?*
- *What might the demonstration of learning (the assessment) for this information look like?*
- *What deeper levels of thinking are needed to truly demonstrate the standards included in the unit?* (This relates, again, to the thinking skills highlighted in Bloom's taxonomy.)
- *How can I incorporate the demonstration of those levels of thinking into the assessment?*
- *How can I translate the standards into meaningful questions for learners?*
- *How can I "chunk" the content in the instruction to aid learning?*

Example

Imagine that you are a community college physics instructor who meets a former student (Amanda) three years after her graduation. Amanda shares that she is pursuing a career in artistic sculpture. She has likely forgotten much of the information covered in your class. But what is it that she *should* remember? What physics concepts or facts should a literate individual retain over time to enable them to function effectively in life and society? A foundational understanding and the ability to apply the principles of simple machines (wheels, levels, inclined planes, etc.) would probably be helpful to Amanda, if only to enable her to move a large stone sculpture from her backyard to a customer's house!

Of course, if in the previous example you taught a *high school* physics course, your instructional planning would likely have revolved around your state learning standards for

Table 5.4 Gagné's Taxonomy and Interpersonal Dimension

Learning Domain	Gagné's Five Types of Learning Outcomes		Detail
Cognitive	**Verbal information:** Declarative knowledge such as facts, lists, names, or organized information that the learner must recall verbatim, recall with aids, *paraphrase*, summarize, or recognize. The learner engages with this material using thinking skills at the first two levels of Bloom's taxonomy.		Frequently, this category refers to the basic information or "grammar" of a subject that provides a foundation for more advanced learning. Common verbs used for this category require the learner to "state," "list," "find," or "describe" something, and require that the learner store information in memory and remember it (*recall* from memory or with aids, or *recognize* it from a collection) for manipulation and use.
	Intellectual skills: Unique cognitive activities that range from simple discriminations to complex problem solving. There are five subcategories at right that are hierarchical: you must first discriminate between objects before you can classify them as concepts; you must know the concepts used in rules before you can apply those rules; and you must know the rules before you can select those to use in problem solving. When analyzing learning tasks that involve intellectual skills, examine the task to identify the hierarchical elements (e.g., examine a procedure to identify concepts that the learner must understand).	☞	1. **Discriminations:** Recognizing differences between two things. Distinguishing variances that are visual, auditory, tactile, olfactory, and/or gustatory, to identify whether they are alike or different. 2. **Concrete Concept Formation:** The ability to classify things into categories by physical characteristics or relationships between objects. 3. **Defined Concept Formation:** The ability to classify an abstract idea by its functions, determining whether it matches a definition or list of characteristics. 4. **Rule Application:** Applying principles and procedures to solve a problem or accomplish a task. Principles are relational rules that enable the learner to predict, explain, or control circumstances in the environment. Principles are often expressed as "if-then" statements. Procedures are rules that provide a step-by-step description of the sequence of actions to be followed to complete a task. 5. **Higher-Order Rules:** Selecting and applying complex principles and procedures (or multiple simple procedures) to solve a new problem or accomplish a task.
	Cognitive strategies: Thinking skills and strategies used by individuals to manage their own learning and that support learning in other domains. There are five major categories of these strategies:	☞	• *Rehearsal* Strategies—Practicing information to be retained and recalled, by repeating, highlighting, visual associations, using flash cards, chaining, and using rhymes and mnemonics. • *Elaboration Strategies*—Building on and tying new information to old, by paraphrasing, summarizing, and generating examples and non-examples. • *Organizational Strategies*—Ordering information to be personally meaningful by clustering, outlining, drawing analogies, representing it graphically, and connecting it to personal experiences. • *Metacognitive Strategies*—Internally controlling what and how one learns, through being aware, focusing attention, employing learning strategies, self-monitoring, self-regulating, and reflecting on one's own learning process. • *Affective Strategies*—Managing emotions, attitudes, and motivation through anxiety reduction, self-encouragement, and self-rewards.
Affective	**Attitudes:** An internal state of understanding or feeling related to values, beliefs, motivations, and ideas that exerts influence over a learner's choice of action, and plays a role in learning motivation and persistence (Gagné & Medsker, 1996). Affective learning is confirmable when external behaviors reflect internal states (so identify comments or actions that reflect the attitude).		**Krathwohl, Bloom, and Masia's Affective Taxonomy (1973)** • Receiving/attending to • Responding to • Valuing • Organizing/prioritizing values • Internalizing and being characterized by values

Psychomotor	Motor skills: A progression of physical movements from basic involuntary reactions to complex and coordinated movements that reflect the relationship between body and a cognitive component such as intention to carry out a sequence of physical actions or manipulate an object.	Detail from three Psychomotor Taxonomies		
		Dave (1970) • Imitation • Manipulation • Precision • Articulation • Naturalization	**Harrow (1972)** • Reflex movements • Fundamental movements (walking, grasping, etc.) • Perceptual responses and interpretations • Physical abilities (stamina) • Skilled movements • Non-discursive communication/ body language	**Simpson (1972)** • Ability to perceive • Readiness to act • Guided response via imitation, trial, and error • Mechanization of learned responses (habit) • Performing complex skills • Ability to adapt skills to special requirements • Ability to originate new movements to fit situations
Interpersonal Skills	Interpersonal skills: Related to communication, teamwork, relating to and working with other cultures, management of others, leadership, and self-awareness.	• Effective communicator (writing, speaking, presenting, listening) • Effective contributor (commitment, cooperation, collaboration, teamwork, follow-up, acknowledging contributions of others) • Effective global citizen (relating, communicating interculturally) • Effective manager, mentor, and leader of others • Self-aware and reflective (about behavior, appearance, identity, goals, stress, wellbeing, commitments, relationships, learning, growth)		

Table 5.5 Content Examples for Gagné's Categories

Examples of Gagné's Types of Learning

Verbal Information
- List the capital cities for each state in the United States.
- State the requirements for passing the written driver's test in a specific state.
- Recall and recite the major bones in the human body.
- Describe the warning signs of shock.
- List the rules for an international soccer match.

Intellectual Skills

Discrimination
- Distinguish between two notes played on an instrument.
- Distinguish between colors by selecting two matching socks from a drawer.
- Distinguish between the symbols used for an addition and a subtraction problem.

Concrete Concepts
- Arrange objects by size, color, and shape.
- Arrange musical notes from highest to lowest.
- Mark triangular architectural features in a photo.
- Identify the middle object in a line of objects.
- Distinguish healthy cells from cancerous cells.

Defined Concepts
- Identify instances of discrimination in a case study.
- Recognize satire.
- Distinguish between democratic and autocratic practices.

Rules
- Calculate the miles per gallon achieved with your car on a family trip.
- Convert a recipe from American to European measurements.
- Create a sentence with a subject, verb, and direct object.

Higher-Order Rules
- Prepare a report of the projected return on investment (ROI) of a training effort for your company.
- Differentiate an instructional lesson for a class of students with a variety of learning disabilities.
- Translate a technical specifications manual into an online job aid.

Cognitive Strategies
- Use earplugs to block out noise when concentrating on a reading selection.
- Use alliteration or develop a mnemonic to memorize concepts.
- Repeat the lines of your part in a play to memorize it prior to a performance.
- Search the web for examples and non-examples of a difficult concept you are trying to learn.
- Organize items on a grocery list in order by the sections of the store to help you remember items and to speed up the process of shopping.
- Reflect on your academic efforts and identify learning strategies that work well for you.

Psychomotor Skills
- Perform a back-flip dismount from a balance beam.
- Create a sign using calligraphy.
- Change the filter in a heating and air-conditioning system.
- Draw a three-dimensional figure.
- Safely drive a car during inclement weather.

Attitudes
- Choose to eat healthy foods.
- Appreciate the contributions of Vietnamese immigrants to the U.S. culture.
- Value diversity in government.
- Demonstrate concern for the welfare of other students.

physics. In this case, you could use a strategy for determining essential information referred to as *unpacking standards*. While this tactic originated in K-12 environments, it can be used in any career environment to identify the implications of established standards or requirements. The term "unpack" or "unwrap" refers to analyzing the standards or requirements to get at the essential knowledge. When looking at standards and requirements, ask: What specific embed-

Table 5.6 Sample Goals Categorized Using Both Bloom's and Gagné's Taxonomies

Knowledge	Attitudes	Skills	Interpersonal Skills
Learning to Know	*Learning to Be*	*Learning to Do*	*Learning to Live Together*
Cognitive	Affective	Psychomotor	Social Skills
• (*Terminal goal in Gagné's Intellectual Skills, Higher Order Rules category, Bloom's HOTS categories*) The pharmacy technician will successfully pass either the Pharmacy Technician Certification Exam (PTCE) or the Exam for the Certification of Pharmacy Technicians (ExCPT). • (*Enabling goal in Gagné's Verbal Information category, Bloom's LOTS categories*) The learner will recall the pharmacy laws and regulations that apply to maintaining medication and inventory control. • (*Enabling goal in Gagné's Cognitive Strategies category*) The learner will self-monitor their progress on the test and make adjustments to complete the test within the time limit. • (*Enabling goal in Gagné's Intellectual Skills, Rule Application category*) The learner will solve allegation problems similar to those given on the PTCE or ExCPT exam.	• (*Terminal goal in Gagné's Affective category, and Krathwohl et al. Characterized by Value category*) The participant in the Global Awareness Workshop will pursue a lifelong pattern of interest, participation, and advocation consistent with valuing citizen involvement in U.S. Middle East policy. • (*Enabling goal in Gagné's Affective category, Krathwohl et al. Valuing category, and Bloom's Evaluate category*) The individual will participate in value-based discussions about U.S. Middle East policies, evaluating the arguments of others and willingly sharing his or her own ideas.	• (*Terminal goal in Gagné's Psychomotor Skills, Harrow's Nondiscursive Communication, and Bloom's Create categories*) The dance major enrolled in EDHP 2204 will choreograph and perform an interpretive dance using learned movements from the semester. • (*Enabling goal in Gagné's Psychomotor Skills and Verbal Information categories, and Bloom's Remember category*) The learner will recall and perform basic movements from the semester, including the arabesque, chaîne turns, pas de bourrée, and pirouette.	• (*Terminal goal in Interpersonal Effective Global citizen, Krathwohl's Responding, and Bloom's Analyzing categories*) The employee actively relates to and communicates with his or her international counterparts to identify their underlying assumptions concerning company operations that differ from his or her own. • (*Enabling goal in Interpersonal Effective Global Citizen and Gagné's Defined Concept categories*) Learner will classify comments as reflecting an American or European worldview.

ded knowledge and skills are required, and what specific procedures must be performed? Again, a *know/do/be* framework (like KASI) can be helpful for isolating and emphasizing the essential or significant tasks suggested by the standards. This method may help you identify elements that are common across several standards that can then be taught together using strategies that provide a more authentic learning context for your students (e.g., through a problem-based learning experience).

A study of practitioner perceptions by King (1998) identified the essential or critical content and factors to consider when designing regulatory training, technical training, and management development training (each of which require a different ratio of skills- and knowledge-based content). King found that there were critical factors common to all three types of training that designers should consider, including the support and expectations of the sponsoring organization's leadership, barriers to the transfer of training, and obtaining an accurate description of mastery performance. Content judged particularly critical for regulatory training included those items related to the legal guidelines and the risks involved in the regulated process. Practitioners identified specific task characteristics as most critical for technical training, including things like the steps and sequence of the task, job conditions for performing the task, the knowledge and skills required, critical actions or incidents related to the task, and the risks involved for incorrect performance. Finally, content related to the culture and structure of the organization was found to be most critical for management development training.

The priority of content is determined by factors that are content-specific and vary by project. You will note that the previous KASI lists the frequency, difficulty, and priority of each task required for refinishing furniture. These are commonly used factors, but there may be others that are appropriate, and it is wise to consult with stakeholders to determine those by which to judge content. You may need to develop a separate form for analyzing individual job tasks or content if your list of factors is long. As you develop a tool for recording information about the content, seek to identify both the factors and the variables associated with those factors (e.g., Factor: difficulty; Variables: difficult, moderately difficult, easy). As you interview SMEs concerning the content, ask questions to determine other factors to use in prioritizing content:

- How universal or unique is the task/content?
- How standard is the performance of the task across contexts, or how global is the content?
- What and how many other tasks are dependent on this task, or how many other topics depend on knowledge of this topic?
- How difficult is the task/content to perform or learn?
- How crucial is the task/content to the instructional goals or the organization's goals?
- How frequently is the task performed, or how frequently would the content be accessed?
- How critical is the task or content to the personal wellbeing of the learner?
- How practical/possible would it be to learn the task/content?
- What level of mastery and quality is required for learning the task/content?

Take a moment to consider the factors of frequency and criticality and how they might impact the priority of a topic or skill to be covered in the instruction. At first glance, tasks that are infrequently performed, knowledge that is rarely accessed, or skills that are seldom used may appear to deserve a low priority rating. However, if the nature of the task, knowledge, or skill is critical, you may need to give it higher priority. Content is considered critical if life-and-death consequences are involved, or if the task, skill, or knowledge would significantly impact the learner's career, academic or social success, or ability to contribute to the organization. For example, a small business owner would complete and submit once-a-year or quarterly tax payments much less frequently than she would do daily bookkeeping tasks. However, the repercussions of neglecting to complete and submit (or erroneously completing) a tax payment would be critical to the survival of the business. As a result, the task, "Correctly complete and submit tax payments," would likely be prioritized as essential.

Identifying and Mapping Dependencies and Prerequisites

At this point, you begin to map out a structure for the instruction by identifying the relationships between goals and the related skills, knowledge, and attitudes involved. Identify dependencies and other associations that influence the order in which they should be addressed in the instruction (sequential, chronological, procedural, topical, hierarchical, etc.). Are some of them dependent on others? Is there a sequence or procedure? Can you cluster them and represent them in a hierarchy or flow diagram? Should the more general ones be presented first, followed by the more specific ones (or vice versa)? Or should they be presented from less complex to more complex (or vice versa)? If there is no logical order, are there clusters or categories of information that are related? Here are a few sequencing options to consider:

- *Task sequence*—Present tasks in the order in which they should be performed.
- *Most critical point or task*—Teach the most critical task or content first and then keep returning to it as you address the other tasks or topics.
- *Whole, parts, whole*—Present an overview of the entire topic, then focus on each part, and finish by elaborating on the whole topic.
- *Simplest to most complex*—Begin with the most simple components.
- *Known to unknown*—Build on what the learner knows to teach the unknown.
- *Center of interest*—Organize the instruction around a main point or activity and address the other topics as they relate to that main point.

In addition to determining a sequence or arrangement for organizing the instruction, analyze each goal to identify any *prerequisite* knowledge, attitudes, skills, interpersonal skills (KASIs), or certifications that the learner should possess *prior* to the instruction. For example, before you learn to read a language, you must learn the alphabet for that language; before you take an advanced chemistry course, you must take a basic chemistry course; and before you can become an underwater welder, you must be a certified commercial diver. In addition to the content itself, the characteristics and prior knowledge of your learners influences what you define as a prerequisite. For example, suppose the majority of your learners possess the necessary knowledge they will need to learn the new content, but about 5% of the audience does not. If you classify that knowledge as a prerequisite, you will need to either find a way to provide the 5% with the necessary knowledge or use an administrative solution to prevent that 5% from taking the instruction until they obtain the required knowledge on their own.

Once you've conceived of a sequence or arrangement and have identified prerequisites, consider how you might graphically represent or "map" the concepts. The dependencies and relationships between the goals and/or KASIs will dictate the way you *illustrate the content graphically*. There are a variety of formats that you can use to summarize and visually represent the content. The format you choose should clearly indicate how the content should be structured and/or sequenced and should illustrate the learning options that will be presented to learners. You can produce a content outline, a flow chart, hierarchical map, mind map, an action map, or even a detailed design document. If you are attempting to streamline the process substantially, you can produce an interim stage artifact for review by the stakeholders or SMEs. For a multimedia project, you can produce an interim script of the audio or a storyboard that includes an audio script and sketches of visual information. For web-based instruction or a learning product, you can produce a prototype.

A *prototype*, or rough model of all or a representative portion of the instruction you plan to produce, helps your reviewers and stakeholders envision what the learning experience will look like and how it will progress. Prototypes can be as low tech or high tech as necessary to fit the demands of your schedule and the level of detail required to meet the requirements of your reviewers. Designers can have stakeholders review an early prototype (paper- or web-based) to test their design concepts. The advantages of this approach:

1. Allow stakeholders to review the content for accuracy.
2. Enable all parties to evaluate the look and feel of the product and suggest changes before expending significant time and resources.

3. Enable the designer and stakeholders to evaluate learner interaction with the instruction, and make modifications to improve the product and increase learner satisfaction.

4. Enable the designer to experiment with alternative approaches and media, and to develop a consistent approach and look that best accomplishes project goals.

5. Provide stakeholders with an immediate impression of the proposed instruction and encourages reflection on essential content and desirable instructional features.

6. Provide the opportunity to iteratively improve the product while reducing the possibility of producing instruction that fails to meet project goals.

These advantages can be summed up with an old Welsh proverb: "An early stumble saves a later fall" (Lamancusa & Pauley, 2011). Figure 5.2 provides an example of a paper prototype for a scenario-based unit of instruction. In the portion of the prototype illustrated, the left side shows the choices available to the learner and the right side illustrates the feedback resulting from each choice. The right column can even be cut at the zigzag line and folded to hide the feedback, so that, as the reviewer uses the prototype, they can simulate how the feedback would be displayed as a result of different learner response choices (A or B). This paper prototype also included a flow chart of all the screens and branching possibilities in the instruction to provide reviewers with an overall summary of the design.

Whatever format you choose, be sure to place the final or culminating goal for the instruction in a prominent position. Break down the content into clusters of topics or tasks that make sense and represent manageable "chunks" for the learners. If the content is complex, it is also helpful to use a numbering system that reflects the priorities and relationships between goals and KASIs.

Getting All the Facts

It's your first day to pick up food donations for the Caring Aid Agency. As you head out the door, you get a phone call:

"Hello, this is June at the Caring Aid Agency. I'm just calling to see if you have any questions about the food pick up today at the Tasty Toadstool Café."

Choose your reply:

A. Hi June. No, no questions. I was just heading out.

B. Hi June. Yes, I have a small compact car. How much am I picking up and what do I need to take along?

Feedback for Learner Choices

Feedback for Choice A:

Hold it. You are in a small compact car – you'd better ask how much food you're picking up and what you need to take along.

How much am I picking up and what do I need to take along?

<This link goes to feedback below>

Feedback for Choice B:

June answers: "You'll be picking up about six frozen quart bags of mushroom sauce, so take a container to carry it. They'll probably ask to see your I.D. and want you to sign for the food. Remember that the food must be kept at or below 40 degrees Fahrenheit during transport to avoid harmful bacterial growth, so after you pick it up, come straight here!"

Sounds good! I'll get a container.

Figure 5.2 Paper Prototype Example: Portion of Safe Food Transport Training

Returning to the example of the Hazard Communication (HAZCOM) training for company general maintenance staff, you could illustrate the terminal goal, enabling goals, KASI and prerequisites as follows:

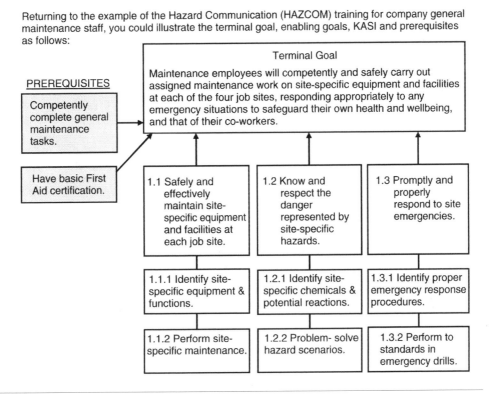

Figure 5.3 Diagram of Instructional Goals and Prerequisites

Use a dotted line, shading or some other visual signal to indicate which items are to be included in the instruction and which are prerequisites to it. As you consider how to visually represent the organization and granularity of the content, seek to streamline the process by selecting a format that can easily be adjusted for the next step in this process: content verification. There are many free concept mapping and flow-charting programs online that you can use to develop a visual representation of your content. Once you've settled on a format, continue to expand your visualization of the content throughout the design process, adding learning outcomes as your plan for the instruction becomes more and more detailed. (See the example in Figure 5.3.)

Verifying Content Scope

As stated, a content analysis provides an in-depth understanding of the learning that should take place, and when you involve all stakeholders in the process of reviewing the analysis it ensures "buy-in" and agreement on the direction of the design project. If you are working with a client, the content analysis is definitely something that you should have the client review and "sign off" on. The content analysis starts where the goal analysis leaves off and serves to further refine the statements of instructional intent. Each task identified in this process will eventually become a formal learning objective for your instruction. Provide reviewers with an easy and convenient means to comment on your content conceptualization. If you need detailed feedback on the specific content to retain or cut, or if a formal "sign off" is necessary, you may need to list items separately in a chart and ask reviewers to sign off on each item.

Next Steps

Generally, the process of identifying and analyzing content to support the goals and breaking it down into successively more distinct elements flows quite automatically and naturally into the identification of detailed learning outcomes and objectives (Chapter 6), assessments to test mastery of those outcomes (Chapter 7), and the strategies and activities to facilitate those outcomes (Chapters 8 and 9). Those topics are addressed in future chapters because we're "chunking" the content to aid your understanding.

Thinking About Evaluation …

How should you address Kirkpatrick's evaluation levels (Chapter 1) at this point in the process?

- *Level I Reaction*—Ideally, your content analysis will yield indisputable results concerning what should be covered in the instruction, but part of your evaluation effort should be designed to verify that fact. What type of measures will you employ to determine whether the learners are satisfied with the content of the instruction and feel that it addresses what they need to know and do? Thinking about this during the content analysis should prompt you to think carefully about the type of examples you use to help learners perceive the relevance of the instruction.
- *Level II Learning*—As you analyze the content, think about how you will determine if the desired learning has taken place. What assessments will accurately measure the goals you've identified? Work backward from the assessments you anticipate using to identify the content (skills, knowledge, attitudes, etc.) that the learner will need to master to pass the assessment (and therefore satisfy the demands of a Level II evaluation).
- *Level III Behavior*—Measuring a change in behavior or transfer involves determining whether your learners are actually implementing the new knowledge or skills several months or more after the instruction. If transfer of learning is a goal for your instructional project, think about how you will measure transfer as you investigate the content. Your analysis of the content should seek to identify meaningful situations, real-world tasks, authentic problems and projects, and questions that will help learners connect to the new content and enhance their ability to change their behavior and transfer their learning following the instruction.
- *Level IV Results*—Measuring the results and impact of an instructional effort on organizational goals can be difficult if you have not planned how you will isolate the different factors that might contribute to a gain or decline in the targeted organizational goal. For example, suppose you develop and implement a training unit on effective Internet marketing for employees and plan to gauge the impact of that program by measuring the number of successful Internet sales made by employees during a four-month period following the training. You later discover, however, that some of the employees had substantial prior knowledge about Internet marketing. Since you did not anticipate this and measure learner prior knowledge of the content before the training, you have no way of knowing how many of the sales were a result of your training program. As you gather and analyze content, consider how it might impact organizational goals and how you might benchmark the factors you intend to measure.

Streamlining Content Analysis

So in what way can the process of analyzing the content be streamlined? Here's a list of ways to make this process more efficient and effective:

- *Sustained*—Design instruction around the use of content-laden job aids that either already exist or can be utilized by the learner beyond the learning experience. This will ensure that the content will be frequently viewed and used, and it is likely that those using the aids will be willing and able to contribute to any necessary maintenance and updating. Educate and prepare your subject matter experts (SMEs) concerning the design/development process. This will speed up content analysis and review processes for both the current and future projects.
- *Optimized*—If you are unfamiliar with the content and your SME is too busy to meet or an SME has not been identified, use existing documents, records, and statistics to identify content and then produce interim documents (scripts, storyboards, action maps, scenarios, etc.) for review. This will speed up the process and yield feedback on your initial plans for content treatment. You can also incorporate and revise existing materials and activities rather than starting over.
- *Continuously Improving*—Use paper or interim prototypes to gain feedback from reviewers, and/or have individuals who are representative of your target audience test the prototypes to provide feedback on content that is unclear, does not appear to be relevant to their needs, or that is incomplete. In the long run this will result in more effective instruction.
- *Right-Sized*—Be careful to restrict your coverage of the content to the essentials, designating any nice-to-know material as supplemental and working collaboratively with your SMEs to prevent content "creep," or expansion.

Different Career Environments, Different Perspectives

- *Type of Content*—Content differs between *and* within career environments. Some environments have content that is fact-based and straightforward (e.g., scientific fields, finance), and others are characterized by content that is evolving, social, and context-dependent (e.g., politics, social services, religion). Different kinds of content require different kinds of analysis, collection techniques, and treatments. For example, both government agencies and private industries are often subject to federal legal regulations that impact their day-to-day operations or that dictate the training requirements for performing those operations. Such regulations are written up in the Code of the Federal Register (CFR), and you can consult this source to obtain applicable content or standards for projects that involve regulatory compliance or technical training. Health-care environments feature a large volume of knowledge that medical and nursing students must consume and retain, on a broad range of topics that are heavily science-based. While students do not need to know as much as specialists in those scientific fields need to know, they do need to be able to apply the knowledge and make interdisciplinary linkages to connect relevant content from several different fields.
- *Type of Content Analysis Methods*—Different career environments have different values, needs, and types of instruction. As a result, some content analysis methods are more common in certain career environments, although you can find examples of the use of each method in all environments. For example, subject matter analysis is frequently used in higher education and K-12 environments, and job and performance analyses are frequently used in business and industry, government, and the military.

Test Your Understanding With a Bloom Stretch

Apply	Select a content analysis method and use it to identify need-to-know versus nice-to-know content for your choice of a topic. Have several SMEs check your work and see if they agree with you (and with each other) on the essential content.
Analyze	Choose a topic and analyze the content to identify portions that might require an Instructivist approach, a Constructivist approach, and a Connectivist approach. Describe how all three approaches combine to holistically cover the entire topic.
Evaluate	Select a hypothetical instructional project and a stakeholder reviewer, and compare at least two different formats that could be used for stakeholder content review (concept map, outline, paper prototype, etc.). Provide a brief justification of your choice of the best format to use for your project and stakeholder.
Create	Select a specific content analysis method and create a list of resources that includes instructions on how to use the method, examples of its application to different types of content, and weblinks for related books, websites and experts.

Diving Deeper

Want to know more? When time allows, we encourage you to go deeper to learn more about the different contexts that impact instruction. The website for this chapter provides exercises and resources for further study on the following topics:

- **Practical Exercises and Examples**—Worked examples and case studies for content analysis.
- **Job Aids**—Sample content analysis and questions to ask SMEs about content.
- **Resources**—Resources on different approaches and types of content analysis and tools to use to format content for review and testing.

6

Identifying the Outcomes and Aligning Instruction

THE CONSEQUENCES OF NEGLECTING TO PROPERLY ORIENT THE LEARNER.

One of the most critical activities you tackle when designing instruction is the definition of the *learning outcomes*. Learning outcomes evolve from the identified goals and KASIs, are written from the viewpoint of the learner, and communicate precisely what the learner should know, feel, and/or be able to do following the learning experience. Since they specify what should "come out" of the learning experience, outcomes indicate how the learner will be assessed and provide guidance on the strategies to use for the learning experience. As a result, the outcomes, assessments, and teaching/learning strategies in your design should reflect each other or be *aligned*, so that they support the learner in mastering the required knowledge and skills. Outcomes also provide accountability and a way to measure the success of your instruction. A list of all the aligned outcomes, assessments, and strategies provides your stakeholders with the essence of your instructional plan and, when approved, these aligned elements help you organize your design and ensure that you cover all that is essential in the instruction.

Inquiring Minds Want to Know …

- What does it mean to align outcomes, assessments, and strategies?
- What's the difference between outcomes and activities?
- How does Bloom's Revised Taxonomy help in the classification of outcomes?
- What do I need to remember and understand from this chapter?

   ⇒ The meaning of the terms "learning outcomes," "learning objectives," "SMART outcomes," "competencies," "metacognition," and "backwards design";

   ⇒ How to write specific outcomes that communicate the applicable ABCDs: audience, behavior, conditions, and degree;

   ⇒ How to motivate learners to accomplish the learning outcomes by communicating relevance; and

   ⇒ How to illustrate dependencies and relationships between learning outcomes by using a numbering system and a flow chart.

Jargon Alert!

Learning outcomes are frequently referred to as *learning objectives*. In addition to the adjective *learning*, outcomes and objectives are described using many other modifiers, including *instructional, behavioral, performance, operational, tactical, strategic, primary, secondary, terminal,* and *enabling.* We use the terms *learning objectives* and *learning outcomes* interchangeably in this book.

Notable Non-Example

One of the first tasks you tackle when designing instruction is to identify the intended learning outcomes. Unfortunately, not everyone understands the pivotal role that learning outcomes play in successful instruction. Clear outcomes not only benefit the designer, but they also support the efforts of the learners and any instructors or facilitators.

> *Missing the Target*—At a recent development workshop for community college faculty, an instructional designer handed out marshmallows to the participants and instructed them to throw them into a waste basket. The participants looked a bit confused and one person finally spoke up to say that there was no waste basket in the room. The designer smiled, brought a waste basket into the room, and then proceeded to walk around quickly with it while exhorting the participants to throw their marshmallows into it. Another participant commented that the waste basket had become a moving target and that the assigned task was too difficult for most participants to accomplish. The designer once again smiled and placed the basket on the floor, saying, "Oh! So you want me to provide you with a stable target!" After several tries, most of the participants were able to toss their marshmallows into the basket, and the designer then said, "Would you want me to grade you on your first attempt to throw the marshmallow into the basket?" Most of the participants felt that a grade on their first attempt would be unfair, since they had not had time to practice the throw. The designer summarized the activity by saying, "So for this activity, we've agreed that it was necessary to have a target, that the target should remain constant and not move, and that the task required opportunities to practice prior to assessment. That's a little like designing successful instruction, isn't it?!" She went on to emphasize the importance of informing students of the intended outcomes for the instruction prior to teaching them

the content. She also stressed that any assessments should clearly reflect the originally stated outcomes, so that students have a clear picture of the expectations for the course. One of the more seasoned faculty participants was clearly perplexed and asked: "If you tell them exactly what they're going to be tested on, won't that make it too easy to get an 'A' in the course? How will you ever get a bell curve for the course grades using that method?!" Seeing that the professor wasn't quite getting her point, the designer took a deep breath and chose her words carefully: "Well, if your goal is for the students to actually *learn* the content, a sure way to accomplish that goal is to establish clear expectations for what students will learn, and design experiences and assessments that reflect those expectations."

Caution!

Providing instruction without informing the learner of the expected outcomes is a bit like placing someone on a road without a clear idea of where they are to go or how they are to get there. If you compound the problem by assessing your learners in an unexpected way or in a way for which the instruction did not prepare them, you not only hamper their ability to master the material, but you risk frustrating and angering them (which, in turn, damages their motivation to learn). Learners need a clear picture of the targeted outcomes before they can be expected to work toward achieving them. The designer in this example was attempting to give the faculty members a taste of what their students might experience when goals and expectations are not clearly stated and activities are not aligned to outcomes and assessments, but at least one of the participants was so focused on previous departmental pass/fail expectations that he had failed to focus on the bigger goal: ensuring that students learn the content.

So What's Involved? Defining Outcomes

Defining learning outcomes is a refinement and continuation of the content analysis process described in Chapter 5. It requires that you have a clear picture of the instructional goals, and the knowledge, attitudes, skills, and interpersonal skills (KASIs) that the learner must possess following the instruction. Here are a few basic tips on defining outcomes that can be customized for the type of content and the approach you've chosen for your design:

1. Define the type of outcomes to be identified and the level of detail to be assessed.
2. Write outcomes that communicate the desired behavior, conditions, and standards.
3. Align outcomes to assessments and strategies.
4. Plan how to convey the outcomes and communicate their relevance to learners.

Defining Outcome Types and Level of Detail

Not all outcomes and *objectives* communicate the same level of specificity or even the same type of KASIs or content. As with design in general, different assumptions about learning result in different outcomes to be fostered through the instruction. Behavioral objectives (frequently cited as an important contribution of Behaviorism to the field of ID) emphasize performance and competencies. Cognitivist learning objectives often focus on the way knowledge is acquired, *encoded*, and retrieved. As a result, an Instructivist approach (based in Behaviorist and Cognitivist assumptions), typically:

- Presents clear goals and mastery-based objectives at the beginning of the instruction to facilitate the learning process;

- Addresses discrete *"chunks" of learning* that represent degrees of growth in skills and thinking, and incrementally assesses learners on each chunk; and
- Elaborates on the *relevance* of the outcomes to learners, and makes a distinction between "need-to-know" and "nice-to-know" information and skills.

According to Sullivan and Higgins (1983), the outcomes for instruction should always reflect learning that is *worthwhile* and *measurable*. *Worthwhile* outcomes are those that are relevant to the learners, preparing them with a skill they will use in "real life," or providing knowledge or a skill that they must possess to learn other knowledge or skills. For example, which of the following outcomes describes a learning experience that you would rate as more worthwhile?

1. The learner will list the steps involved in changing a car's engine oil.
2. Given fresh engine oil, a new oil filter, appropriate wrenches, a pan, and a funnel, the learner will change the oil in their car.

Recalling the steps involved (outcome #1) doesn't guarantee that you will be able to physically change your oil in the future. While knowledge of the procedure is important, a job aid could provide that information. Rather than just listing the steps, a better way to prepare learners for changing their oil is to actually have them practice the skill (outcome #2).

Instructivist outcomes are also characterized as being *SMART*: Specific, Measurable, Action-oriented, Realistic, and Timely (Smith, 1994). They consist of precise statements of observable competencies that learners will demonstrate after the instruction, stated in a way that indicates how the learning will be measured or assessed. SMART outcomes use *action verbs* to indicate the observable behaviors that learners will exhibit, they are realistic given the time and resources available for implementing the instruction, and they define reasonable time boundaries for completion. Robert F. Mager's (1975) popular book *Preparing Instructional Objectives* is probably the best-known and most frequently cited material on developing learning outcomes for Instructivist approaches. Mager states that learning objectives should include: a specific and observable performance or behavior, the conditions under which the behavior is to be exhibited, and the desired criterion, level, or standard of acceptable performance. You can remember these elements by using the acronym *ABCD*: Audience, Behavior, Conditions, and Degree (see Table 6.1).

With Instructivist approaches, the instructional *goals* tend to be very broad and you use relatively few of them to convey the overall purpose of the instruction. In contrast, Instructivist approaches tend to include an abundance of learning *outcomes* (or objectives) which are defined to the level of detail required for adequate learner assessment. As a result, you will define as many outcomes as required to address all the identified KASIs. As mentioned in Chapter 5, it is helpful to use a numbering system that shows the relationships between goals and outcomes. Figure 6.1 illustrates how this can be done. The prerequisites are listed at the left and bottom of the diagram, separated from the instructional outcomes by a dotted line. The arrows indicate dependencies between outcomes, illustrating that the learner must master cognitive outcome 1.1 prior to 1.0, and both 1.1 and 1.0 prior to accomplishing cognitive outcome 2.0. The psychomotor outcomes of 3.0 and 4.0 are similarly related, with several enabling outcomes contributing to the accomplishment of outcome 4.0 (including outcomes 4.1.1 and 4.1, 4.2.1 and 4.2, and 4.3.1 and 4.3).

Conversely, outcomes identified for Constructivist and Connectivist instructional designs are often more general statements of the processes or interactions that learners are to engage in rather than on a final product or test of knowledge. For example, a common goal of Constructivist and Connectivist learning experiences is to foster autonomous, self-directed individuals who are responsible for their own learning. Autonomous, self-directed learners make good lifelong

Table 6.1 ABCDs of Outcomes

	Description	Examples
Audience	The intended target audience for the outcome is typically identified once for all the learning outcomes, unless the instruction targets multiple learners and groups with different characteristics.	• The student will be able to … (aka SWBAT) • The senior enrolled in EPD-9001 … • The team of Navy recruits will … • X-ray technician trainees will … • Social network members will …
Behavior	The desired behavior to be exhibited by the learner is described using action verbs to clearly communicate expectations and avoid ambiguity. The behavior should be specific and observable. Attitudinal outcomes should be operationalized by specifying an observable behavior, e.g., "display an appreciation for democracy by voting …"	***Ambiguous performance statements*** • Really understand the … • Appreciate the contributions of … • Grasp the significance of … • Become aware of … • Become familiar with … • Learn about … ***Clear performance statements*** • Build/construct a model of … • Recite a poem from the … • Interact with team members to design … • Contribute practical feedback on peer posts … • Compare and contrast the … • Show appreciation for X by choosing to … • Demonstrate understanding of X by classifying …
Conditions	Outcomes should include the conditions, or resources, circumstances, or *givens* under which the behavior is to occur (including the tools or assistance to be provided). Conditions are often stated at the beginning of an outcome, e.g., "Given a bat and a ball …," "Given a case study and spending parameters …," "Given the opportunity to vote …," or "Given a model kit …"	***"Givens"*** • Given a database of resources … • Given a description of symptoms … • With a calculator, ruler or scale … • Using notes and a dictionary … • From memory without any aids … ***Setting or situation*** • In front of an audience … • When provided with a general goal … • When corrected … • When working with a team of peers … ***Behavior plus conditions*** • The learner will compute measurement equivalents *while following a recipe* … • The learner will correct punctuation errors *while proofreading an essay* … • The learner will correctly pronounce German words *when shown flashcards* … • The team will construct a model *from the provided materials* … • The participant will select applicable resources *when provided with a list of URLs* …
Degree	Set clear expectations by specifying the degree or level of performance mastery expected of the learner. Degree criteria can include an acceptable range of answers, a statement of accuracy or frequency, or a qualitative description. For example, "nine times out of ten," "staying within the acceptable range stated," and "80% or more of the parts."	***As a description of the result*** • Until the liquid disappears … • Until a consensus is reached … • Until a reservoir of resources is amassed … • Story includes a conflict and a resolution … • Solves the problem in the fewest steps … • Backing up opinion with data from three relevant research studies … • Paragraphs include topic sentences … ***Total number, proportion, time, or measurement*** • Comparing four key elements … • Five paragraphs in length … • In three out of four posts … • Within ten minutes …/Within plus or minus ten … • The first time … • Prior to graduating … • To the nearest mile … • 90% of the comments …

learners, and in this rapidly changing world everyone needs the skills necessary to continue learning on their own. Rather than test your learners on specific declarative content, you may, instead, assess them on the use of that content to construct a project or solve a problem, or on the ability to find and connect to quality content sources.

To clarify the outcomes for such learning experiences, determine whether learners should be able to recall detailed content from memory, if they must merely recognize applicable content in a provided reference, if they must glean applicable content from the context of a situation, or if they need guidance to discover the content on their own. When learners must glean or discover the content, the outcomes place less emphasis on what the learner should memorize and recall, and more emphasis on what the learner will analyze, investigate, share, build, and generate. Such outcomes emphasize exploration and selection of resources, peer interactions to observe and model thinking skills, and participation in social interaction and knowledge creation. Remember that, while you may not always be able to identify an observable behavior, learning conditions, and criteria for your Constructivist or Connectivist outcomes (à la Mager), the process of contemplating those elements will help you design a better learning experience.

Many Connectivist outcomes evolve from the learning experiences themselves and may be verbalized by the participants, or jointly by the designer/instructor/facilitator and the learners. As a result, the outcomes are difficult to articulate during design. As George Siemens (2010) ponders, "How do you create a centralized outcome through a decentralized, distributed process?" One solution is to allow learners to customize the outcomes for themselves by involving them in the learning process, thus building their "buy-in" and ownership in the process. You can encourage learners to develop their own learning outcomes by providing them with a small, set number of learning areas or goals for which they develop more specific, personalized objectives. The metaphor of a tree aptly conveys this type of approach, with the overall learning goal represented by

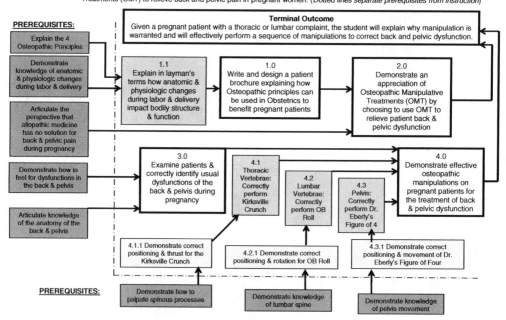

INSTRUCTIONAL GOAL: An Osteopathic Obstetrics course will provide osteopathic medical students with an understanding and appreciation for the critical role of osteopathic philosophy in the practice of Obstetrics, and will teach students to use Osteopathic Manipulative Treatments (OMT) to relieve back and pelvic pain in pregnant women. (*Dotted lines separate prerequisites from instruction*)

Figure 6.1 Numbered Flow Diagram for a Third-World Community Health Program on Osteopathic Obstetrics

Source: Contributed by Amy Keurentjes, 2008. Used with permission.

Table 6.2 Sample Instructivist, Constructivist, and Connectivist Learning Outcomes

Instructivist Outcomes (Learner needs direct guidance)	Constructivist Outcomes (Learner explores and develops ideas)	Connectivist Outcomes (Learner builds connections to support activities)
1. Given a one-day workshop on the Company's social networking software, employees will make effective use of the software to answer customer questions.	1. Employees will work in teams to explore social networking technology and produce guidelines for its use in addressing customer questions and problems.	1. Employees will cooperatively participate in the Company Intranet, sharing resources and ideas to build a personal network of sources for addressing customer questions and problems.
2. Upon completion of the unit on culture, the learner will identify elements of Hispanic and indigenous cultures in the customs, traditions, and institutions of Central American countries.	2. Given a range of resources on Hispanic and indigenous cultures in Central American countries, and open-source publishing software, the learner will explore the content to produce a trifold brochure on the culture of (their choice of) a country.	2. The self-directed learner will locate and create resources to share on Hispanic and indigenous cultures in Central America, linking to diverse groups (interest groups, experts, native social groups, and cultural institutions) to increase knowledge of Central American cultures and pursue personal interests.
3. After completing the Patent Department's online invention module, learners will write a paper citing three ways it informed their own efforts to invent something from a half-gallon milk carton.	3. After exploring resources on inventions and patents, teams will collaborate to design and construct an original invention.	3. Innovation teams will use technological research tools to locate, evaluate, and collect quality information on inventing and inventions from a range of sources to support creative work.
4. Learning teams will write a two-page summary about the properties of water, using the results of class lab experiments to justify their conclusions.	4. Learner teams will develop a hypothesis about the properties of water, perform experiments to test it, and use feedback from the experiments to produce final conclusions.	4. After using a WebQuest designed to frame and guide exploration of resources on the properties of water, learners will locate and submit additional resources, and review and rate resources submitted by others.
5. Learners will debate the relative merits of the five problem-solving methods used in a series of forensic case studies, justifying the choice of a preferred method on the basis of its general and specific applicability.	5. Given a set of forensic case studies that feature contextual variations of key elements to be investigated, students will develop a procedure for solving forensics problems and identify the important structural features and sources of variability in the problems.	5. Group members will cooperate through the network to observe and model appropriate forensic problem-solving methods, providing feedback concerning the appropriateness of the methods with regards to personal competencies and knowledge, work-flow, job role, working styles, performance goals, and case context.
6. After completing the instruction on sales trend analysis, sales associates will review market trend reports for personal care products and will present their conclusions virtually during a web conference.	6. Sales associates will explore the use of various marketing and trend analysis tools to produce a development and proposal for personal care products.	6. Sales associates will use word clouds, tags, and analytics to discover online search patterns and trends reflecting personal-care product interests, and create and share visualizations of the data with the network.

the trunk of the tree and the learning areas as major limbs. Each individual's specific learning outcomes are the smaller branches or leaves on the limbs and these vary with the needs of each learner. To extend the metaphor, when learners share their input and interact with other learners, as in a Connectivist environment, each individual's outcomes enrich the learning experience for all participants. Question "stems" or prompts can be used to aide learners in their attempts to develop their own personalized learning outcomes.

Finally, it's important to note that, while very *specific* learning objectives help you design a more complete learning experience, they may not always produce the expected benefits for your learners. Research suggests that specific outcomes improve intentional learning, but can lead to a decrease in incidental learning (Biehler & Snowman, 1993). So, for instruction meant to foster exploration of a topic, specific objectives might narrow the learner's focus and limit their learning (Marzano et al., 2001). For this type of instruction, researchers recommend that you provide learners with more general goals to set the direction for their learning, and then encourage them to personalize those goals or define related learning outcomes that address their specific interests (Bandura & Schunk, 1981; Marzano et al., 2001; Morgan, 1985). Table 6.2 illustrates how different instructional purposes are reflected in Instructivist, Constructivist, and Connectivist versions of learning outcomes.

Writing Outcomes that Communicate to the Learner

Outcomes communicate the purposes of the instruction to learners, as well as expectations for their post-instruction performance. Therefore, write outcomes from the viewpoint of the learner and use action verbs to provide a clear picture of what the learner should know and be able to do following the instruction. In the classic book *Teaching for Competence*, Howard Sullivan and Norman Higgins (1983) emphasize that novice instructional designers commonly confuse learning *outcomes* with learning *activities* (or strategies). Well-designed Instructivist learning objectives define the *competencies* (or capably performed skills) that your learners should possess after they receive instruction. In contrast, learning *activities* are the things the instructor or the instruction does, or the events that learners participate in during the learning experience.

Table 6.3 illustrates the distinction between learning activities and learning outcomes. In each row, the first statement is an activity that describes what the instruction or instructor will do, or the events in which the learner will participate. The second statement is a *learner-oriented* outcome that reflects a subtle but important shift to adopt the viewpoint of the learner; defining what the learner will *know* and *be able to do* following the instruction (Sullivan & Higgins, 1983).

At times you may find it difficult to distinguish between learning outcomes and your *instructional intentions*, or the learning tasks and mental processing you are trying to facilitate through the structure and flow of your instruction. In such cases, you may have to work backwards from your instructional intentions to identify the learning outcomes that those intentions would foster. Table 6.4 provides examples of common instructional intentions and the learning outcomes

Table 6.3 Contrasting Learning Activities and Learning Outcomes

Non-Examples (Activities)	Examples (Outcomes)
I will use video examples to train employees to use persuasive sales techniques.	The employees will use persuasive techniques to make a sale following the instruction.
The instruction will teach the learner how to calculate the time required to travel a distance of X miles.	Given the miles per hour and the distance, the learner will correctly calculate the time required to travel from point A to point B.
The learner will watch a video about different land formations and the tectonic plate movements that are believed to have produced those formations.	The learner will draw and describe three different land formations and the tectonic plate movements that are believed to have produced them.

Table 6.4 Working Backwards from Instructional Intentions to Identify Learning Outcomes

Motivate learners to engage in learning processes	Present content and communicate expectations	Organize content to aid mental processing	Prompt knowledge/content creation
Attend to and continue to focus on learning tasks. Demonstrate a favorable attitude toward learning. Communicate effectively with peers and instructor. Demonstrate self-directedness and autonomy. Express satisfaction with the learning experience and confidence in personal competence. Reflect on personal needs and goals to produce learning outcomes for the content.	Consume or absorb content by reading, viewing, calculating, etc. Explore and discover new content. Activate and reflect on prior knowledge and experiences, relating new content to existing mental schema. Relate stated instructional goals (expectations) to personal learning goals. Reflect on the content to relate it to personal needs and goals. Monitor personal learning progress and compare it to instructional goals/expectations.	Activate prior knowledge and make new content meaningful by relating it to existing knowledge and experiences. Focus on and identify relevant points. Learn and remember content (recall from memory, recall using memory aids, and/or recognize content). Explore or search for content using the provided scaffold (e.g., study guide, WebQuest, guiding questions, etc.). Study the worked examples. Use scenario facts to solve the problem. Locate trusted information sources and organize content from those sources in a personally meaningful way.	Use the resources provided to construct an artifact (a procedure, process, structure). Use the information provided in the case study to solve the problem. Identify the problem and solve it (individual)/negotiate a process to solve it (group). Create, mix, or remix to produce an artifact that represents your interpretation of the content. Select a tool to create or collaboratively create a [description of desired product or process]. Submit questions to the network group/community to build your understanding of _____. Answer submitted questions to contribute to the network/community knowledge.

Scaffold and guide, provide practice and feedback, differentiate and transfer	Promote cooperation and collaboration	Build autonomy, metacognitive skills, and personal knowledge management
Complete the task using the provided aids (references, job aids, procedures, processes, guidelines, peer or instructor help). Complete the incremental learning units; skip levels by taking and passing the mastery tests. Complete the simulation tasks, using the hints until you can do the tasks without help. Access the tutorials for help on finding, filtering, and managing content resources. Read the chapter, solve the practice exercises, and check your work with the answer key. Consult the feedback on your test results and use the recommended remedial materials. Access accommodations that meet your needs. Select the version of the lesson that matches your prior knowledge pretest results. Transfer learning to solve a new problem.	Cooperate with your team to [accomplish a goal, solve a problem, complete a project]. Participate in the teamwork skills exercises to build a cooperative and effective team. Consider the opinions of network members and state how each point of view contributed to your understanding of the topic. After participating in the [role play, debate, panel discussion], describe how it changed or supported your opinion on the issue. Teach [your partner, your small group, the class] about the topic you researched. Cooperatively develop a project schedule, identify responsibilities, develop a communication plan, and monitor project progress. Individually brainstorm ideas, then collaborate with your team to produce an integrated list of ideas.	Tackle the task by identifying the steps to take, developing a schedule, and monitoring your progress (builds autonomy by fostering self-directedness and self-regulation). Monitor your learning progress and reflect on the success of the cognitive strategies you used and the level of effort expended. Use the self-check to assess your comprehension and learning progress, and try new cognitive learning strategies to improve. Use the quick reference aids, as necessary, to gather, filter and organize information. Access the tutorials to learn how to use the software to develop an artifact for your portfolio. Pull content, annotate it, and organize it for future use in your personal learning environment.

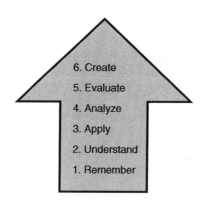

Figure 6.2 Bloom's Thinking Skills Progression

that those intentions support. Which pedagogical approaches do you think you could support by rewriting the outcomes in Table 6.4 to relate specifically to your instruction? (Note that Table 8.4 in Chapter 8 elaborates on Table 6.4 by identifying strategies that can be used to foster the instructional intentions.)

As referenced in Chapter 5, Bloom's Taxonomy for Cognitive Objectives is a helpful tool for writing outcomes that effectively communicate expectations to learners and stakeholders. It is often referred to as a sequence of *thinking skills* (Anderson & Krathwohl, 2001) that progresses from the lower-order thinking skills (LOTS) of remembering, understanding, and applying content, to higher-order thinking skills (HOTS) that build on those lower-order skills (refer to Figure 6.2). In other words, you must be able to remember, understand, and apply the content before

	Outcome Examples for Credit Union Employees
Terminal Goal:	The learner will develop customized savings plans for credit union customers based on current income, years to retirement, anticipated retirement needs, cost of living adjustments, and rate of inflation.
Enabling Goal:	The learner will evaluate investments that vary with respect to interest rates, investment length, and compounding to select appropriate plans for customers.
Remember:	Recall from memory the definition of compound interest.
Understand:	Classify sample case studies into two groups: those that illustrate the application of compound interest and those that illustrate the application of simple interest.
Apply:	Given a beginning account balance and an interest rate, calculate the interest earned for a year when compounded daily, and the total account balance.
Analyze:	Compare the difference in results when interest is compounded daily and monthly, and identify the conditions required to meet a specific monetary goal.
Evaluate:	Review potential investments and evaluate them based on interest rates, length of investment, and compounding schedule, to select the best option for customers.
Create:	Develop a savings plan for a customer that takes into account current income, cost-of-living adjustments, the rate of inflation, and needs at retirement.

you can perform higher-order skills with that content, including problem solving, analyzing arguments, negotiating issues, and making predictions. Effective use of HOTS involves considering *how best* to employ these skills. It requires that you use *metacognition* (thinking about how you think and learn best) to successfully analyze, evaluate, and create with content (Brown, 1987). Contemplating the progression of thinking skills required of the learner helps you identify action verbs to use in learning outcomes, as well as the dependencies between outcomes and the proper sequencing for your instruction.

Table 6.5 provides a description of Bloom's thinking levels, along with sample verbs to use when writing outcomes, and ideas for assessments that require learners to use each thinking skill. Table 6.6 features outcomes developed using both Bloom's and Gagné's taxonomies.

The second level of Bloom's taxonomy emphasizes understanding. The word "understand" is one of those ambiguous verbs that you should avoid when writing outcomes, since it doesn't provide much guidance for determining whether your learners really understand the content they are supposed to know. Instead, consider some of the verbs used by Grant Wiggins and Jay McTighe (2005) to elaborate on what it means to understand. In their book *Understanding by Design*, Wiggins and McTighe define *six facets* of understanding: explanation, interpretation, application, perspective, empathy, and self-knowledge. To elaborate, when a learner truly understands something, he or she can:

- *Explain* it—providing complete facts and data to support the explanation;
- *Interpret* it—showing through examples, meaningful stories and analogies that he or she has a grasp of the essence of the topic;
- *Apply* it—effectively using it and adapting it to new situations;
- *Demonstrate Perspective*—including knowledge of the big picture and an informed and critical eye;
- *Empathize*—finding value in something that mere observers might not perceive; and
- *Exhibit self-knowledge*—about what is understood or not and why, so that he or she can direct his or her own learning on the topic.

When you fully understand, you realize that you are viewing a topic from your own narrow perspective and probably have certain biases and prejudices concerning it. You are also aware of the role that your *prior knowledge* and experiences play in how you understand a topic. This type of self-knowledge is also referred to as metacognition.

Breaking down understanding in this way enables you to develop more specific outcomes. Wiggins and McTighe call this "beginning with the end in mind," quoting author Steven R. Covey:

> To begin with the end in mind means to start with a clear understanding of your destination. It means to know where you're going so that you better understand where you are now so that the steps you take are always in the right direction.
>
> (Covey, 1989, p. 98)

In other words, instructional designers should have a clear understanding of where their learners need to end up. To plan instruction based on the end goals, designers begin at the end to:

1. Identify the desired results;
2. Determine what constitutes acceptable evidence of those results; and
3. Plan learning experiences and instruction that are geared toward producing those results.

Table 6.5 Using Bloom's Levels to Define Outcomes

	Thinking Level	Description	Verbs for Associated Outcomes	Assessment Ideas that Address this Thinking Level
Higher Levels	Creating	Putting elements together to form a coherent or functional whole; reorganizing elements into a new pattern or structure through generating, planning, or producing.	Change, combine, compose, create, design, construct, plan, formulate, devise, blog, mix/remix, publish, direct, produce, compile, make, program, film, animate, predict, hypothesize, improve, invent.	Model, role play or skit, poem, cartoon, book cover, multimedia artifact, new game, process, product, hypothesis, invented experiment, invention, presentation, report, software program, plan of action, design, song, model, etc.
	Evaluating	Making judgments based on criteria and standards through checking and critiquing.	Appraise, defend, dispute, check, detect, monitor, moderate, collaborate, network, comment, editorialize, judge, justify, hypothesize, experiment, critique, review, reflect, prioritize, rate, test, select, support, verify, validate.	Critique, judgment, opinion, recommendation, report, self-evaluation, essay questions, debate arguments, blog or mediated commentary, discussion points, editorial comments, persuasive speech, collaborative projects, investigation, product or process review, etc.
	Analyzing	Breaking material into constituent parts, determining how the parts relate to one another and to an overall structure or purpose through differentiating, organizing, and attributing.	Appraise, compare, contrast, differentiate, distinguish, structure, deconstruct, examine, infer, outline, sequence, organize, integrate, link, reverse-engineer, mash up, mind map, attribute, test.	Chart, plan, questionnaire or survey, spreadsheet breakdown and/or data analytics, summary, multiple choice and essay questions, database structure, article abstract or summary, relational graphic mind map or diagram, report, graph, checklist, outline, comparison chart, etc.
	Applying	Carrying out or using a procedure through executing, or implementing.	Implement, carry out, share, execute, load, play, produce, edit, classify, use, demonstrate, illustrate, dramatize, practice, solve, operate, upload, hack.	Collection, interview, model building, presentation, role play, scrapbook, simulation, multiple choice questions, essay and short answer questions, software hack, graphic representation, performance, edit, etc.
Lower Levels	Understanding	Constructing meaning from oral, written, and graphic messages through interpreting, *exemplifying*, classifying, summarizing, *inferring*, comparing and explaining.	Calculate, describe, discuss, expand, explain, infer, identify, locate, outline, report, restate, paraphrase, tag, post, annotate, comment, compare, classify, compare, summarize, exemplify, reflect, and journal.	Drawing, paraphrase, peer teaching, show and tell, story problems, summaries, multiple choice questions, T/F and matching questions, short answer and essay questions, blog or vlog journal posts, explanations, advanced and boolean Internet searches, aggregations, annotations, tags, commenting, etc.
	Remembering	Retrieving, recalling, or recognizing relevant information from long-term memory.	Define, describe, identify, locate, find, highlight, bookmark, duplicate, list, name, recall, recognize, reproduce, tell, underline.	Definitions, fact charts, lists, recitations, worksheets, multiple choice questions, T/F and matching questions, short answer and essay questions, flashcards, bookmarks, tags, basic Internet searches.

Source: Adapted from Anderson and Krathwohl (2001); Churches (2009).

Table 6.6 Using Gagné's and Bloom's Taxonomies to Identify Outcomes

Subject: Earth Science **Topics:** Mohs Scale for Mineral Classification, the Rock Cycle, Earthquakes, the Water Cycle

Gagné's Learning Types	Bloom's Thinking Skills (*these build in complexity from left to right*)					
	Remember	Understand	Apply	Analyze	Evaluate	Create
Verbal Information	List the minerals at each level of the Mohs hardness scale.		✕	✕	✕	✕
Intellectual Skills: Discriminations	✕	Use spreadsheet software to classify minerals by hardness, luster, color, and streak.	Use the Mohs hardness scale to identify unknown minerals.	Compare two minerals on the basis of hardness and luster.	Appraise the qualities of two gemstones, selecting the best for a stated purpose.	✕
Intellectual Skills: Concepts	Label the phases of the rock cycle.	Given a description of a rock, identify where it would be placed in the rock cycle.	Use the rock cycle to describe the formation of rocks in a certain region.	Use a concept map to illustrate rock-type relationships.	Select the best of two possible hypotheses for the history of rocks in a region.	Create a picture book to illustrate and explain the rock cycle.
Intellectual Skills: Rule Application	Explain to a peer how to follow the procedure for calculating the epicenter of an earthquake.	Describe why it is important to consider a building structure as a whole when carrying out earthquake rescue operations.	Calculate the epicenter of an earthquake.	Identify regional patterns in earthquakes.	Given damage reports, rate the intensity of an earthquake.	Using historical data on the U.S. New Madrid region, create a news report for a fictional 2015 earthquake.
Intellectual Skills: Higher-Order Rules	When designing a custom mineral, recall from memory the characteristics used to classify minerals.	Demonstrate an understanding of special mineral qualities by explaining how they contribute to the utility of your custom mineral.	Accurately apply the Mohs scale to describe the hardness characteristics of your custom mineral.	Provide a description of how characteristics of your custom mineral combine to produce a useful mineral.	Evaluate the custom mineral produced by two course peers to judge the appropriateness of the defined qualities to the stated purpose.	Design a custom mineral for a specific purpose; include how its qualities contribute to its utility.
Cognitive Strategies	Devise a memory aid to help you remember the water cycle.	Use a concept map to show the relationship between the water cycle and sources and impacts of pollution.	Use before, during, and after reading strategies to optimize use of an article on storm water pollution.	Use a classification chart to analyze and categorize the invertebrates found in a stream sample.	Try out three different methods for analyzing water-quality samples and select the one that works best for you.	Create a checklist to use for water-quality testing.
Motor Skills	Use appropriate machines and safety equipment to produce thin sections of rock for microscopic analysis.					
Attitudes	Demonstrate a respect for scientific evidence by evaluating both sides of a scientific debate, and use the scientific method to outline and identify justified and unjustified arguments.					

This type of backwards approach is employed in many other creative design fields, as well, including creative writing, software design, and even in proofreading. It represents a reliable method for improving the integrity and accuracy of the final product.

Yet another helpful tool for defining outcomes is Gagné's Conditions of Learning (1985), which describes internal and external conditions necessary for learning. The combination of Gagné's conditions and his Nine Events of Instruction is frequently used as a framework for selecting strategies and learning activities. A framework that includes both of these tools is provided in Chapter 8.

Aligning Outcomes to Assessments and Strategies

Practically speaking, beginning with the end in mind means that you *develop your assessments at the same time that you develop your learning outcomes*. In fact, your outcomes and assessments will sound very similar because they will be *aligned*, and they will then guide you in the selection of teaching and learning strategies that reflect the outcomes and prepare the learner for the assessments. As emphasized in an earlier chapter, when you use aligned outcomes, assessments, and teaching/learning strategies, the resulting instruction will:

> Tell them what they need to know and do, instruct them on what they need to know and do, and test them on what they need to know and do.

Aligned instruction helps you design better instruction, and enables you to *scaffold*, or support, the learner. You'll read more about alignment in Chapters 7 and 8.

Communicating Relevant Outcomes

Learning outcomes provide the most benefit when learners are aware of them and understand that they are meant to provide direction for learning specific material (Biehler & Snowman, 1993). If the content you've identified is truly essential and the outcomes reflect how individuals and groups will use the learned KASIs, consider how you can convey the relevance of learning outcomes in a way that will motivate learners to accomplish them. Communicate relevance by:

- Illustrating how concepts and skills relate to the learner's current or future needs or goals;
- Describing how the new material might relate to the learner's past experiences, or how others have used the information in their lives; and
- Providing guidance on how the learner can customize the experience to self-motivate.

In addition, you can format the outcomes in different ways, communicating them as originally written for the design, as questions the learner might ask about the content, or through a compelling story that illustrates the importance of the outcomes. Robin Neidorf (2006) claims that the key to communicating objectives is to connect with "the learner's emotional commitment to learning" (p. 97) without boring them, as with a scenario that illustrates their need for the skills your instruction is addressing. Ideally, you should present the outcomes to learners at the beginning of the instruction, and then provide frequent checks for understanding (or self-assessments), along with feedback on the results of those assessments. This strategy enables learners to monitor and track their own progress against the outcomes and, if their progress is not satisfactory, to access remedial materials or ask for help. Ultimately, this approach develops more autonomous and self-directed learners.

Finally, learning outcomes should be reviewed and approved by your key stakeholders. You can do this at any time, but a table of aligned outcomes, assessments, and strategies more fully communicates your plans to stakeholders and will yield more constructive feedback (examples of aligned outcomes, assessments, and strategies are provided in Chapters 7 and 8).

Thinking About Evaluation ...

Defining learner outcomes relates directly to evaluating the success of your instruction. This is because you define learner assessments along with the outcomes and, of course, if the learners don't pass the assessments, it's likely they didn't learn what you intended for them to learn (remember that assessments are the metrics for Kirkpatrick's Level II Learning evaluation). Since outcomes and assessments are so closely aligned (or at least they *should be*), Chapter 7 will address the related evaluation measures that can be implemented during this portion of the design process.

Streamlining Outcomes

So in what way can this portion of the design process be streamlined?

- *Sustainable*—If revising or updating existing instructional materials, use or revise the old outcomes, if applicable. If designing performance-based instruction, speed up the process and link outcomes more closely to organizational goals by using Cathy Moore's (2008) *Action Mapping* technique. The technique makes writing outcomes easier by identifying the actions (behaviors), practice activities (which give clues to conditions and degree), and information (the "givens" or conditions required to perform the desired behaviors) that the instruction needs to address.
- *Optimized*—Speed up the design review process by producing a single table of aligned outcomes, assessments, and teaching/learning strategies for your instruction. The combination will give your stakeholders a better idea of your overall plans for the instruction. You can also optimize by organizing the outcomes into "chunks" of stand-alone content that can be reused by other training programs or for other instructional purposes. Optimize with formatting by informing learners of outcomes at the beginning of the instruction and then using them again as section headings. As a result, your first reference to the outcomes will also serve as an "advance organizer" or outline, informing learners of the structure for the instruction.
- *Right-Sized*—You may need to have stakeholders or SMEs approve all of a large number of detailed outcomes to verify the direction of the instruction. However, your learners often don't need to know all of those outcomes, so avoid overwhelming them by limiting the number you communicate to about three to five outcomes per unit of instruction. Alternatively, identify a culminating or "capstone" task that would enable learners to demonstrate mastery of most, or all, of the outcomes and write a single outcome that addresses that final task.
- *Continuous Improvement*—Check the outcomes early in the design process with a representative sample of learners to ensure that you've identified outcomes that are truly relevant to your target audience. *Quality Checks for Continuous Improvement*:
  - ✓ Does each outcome clearly state an observable behavior, the conditions or givens to be provided, and the degree of mastery targeted?
  - ✓ Does the language of each outcome reflect the identified pedagogical approach?
  - ✓ Is each outcome reasonable given the scope of the content, the learners, and the time available?

Different Career Environments, Different Perspectives

- Business and industry and private sector career environments are typically driven by the need to turn a profit. The focus is usually on performance improvement, defined by SMART, performance-based objectives that specify criteria for measurement and are designed to yield a better profit margin. Outcomes are also shaped by industry standards and best practices, regulations, and applicable certification requirements.

- By 2012, forty-eight U.S. states, two territories, and the District of Columbia had adopted the Common Core State Standards for K-12 education, designed to provide a nationally consistent framework to prepare students for college and the workforce. The standards address English language arts and mathematics, but also require teachers to incorporate 4Cs into their teaching: critical thinking, collaboration, creativity, and communication. Learning outcomes for K-12 education must therefore be aligned to the common core standards, which reflect Instructivist, Constructivist, *and* Connectivist pedagogical approaches.
- Most learning outcomes in health-care settings are behaviorally based and mastery-oriented. There are also outcomes that address desirable attitudes and ethical beliefs and behaviors.

Test Your Understanding With a Bloom Stretch

Apply	Apply the information from this chapter to identify both good and bad examples of learning outcomes on the Internet.
Analyze	Conduct an Internet search to find examples of outcomes and mark each to identify the A—Audience, B—Behavior, C—Conditions, and D—Degree.
Evaluate	Rate the contents of Table 6.5 based on how easy you think it would be to develop an aligned assessment to test each outcome.
Create	Create Instructivist, Constructivist, and Connectivist learning outcomes for your choice of an instructional goal.

Diving Deeper

Want to know more? When time allows, we encourage you to go deeper to learn more about defining outcomes for different instructional approaches. On the website for this chapter you'll find things like:

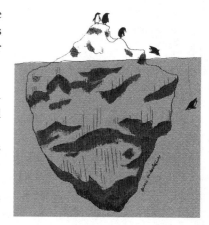

- **Practical Exercises and Examples**—Worked examples and exercises on outcomes and objectives, and activities.
- **Job Aids**—Worksheets for identifying outcomes for each level of Bloom's Taxonomy and for different types of knowledge.
- **Resources**—Links to lists of verbs for outcomes and other resources related to writing objectives.

7
Assessing Learning

THE DANGERS OF MISALIGNED OUTCOMES AND ASSESSMENTS

Determining whether your target audience has learned what they were supposed to learn goes hand in hand with identifying the outcomes. Identifying aligned outcomes and assessments provides the "bookends" for a design. Taken together, the outcomes and assessments clearly indicate the KASIs to be learned and how learners will be tested to determine if they have mastered those desired learning outcomes. Ultimately, the success of the target audience in mastering the outcomes and passing the assessments is a critical indicator of the success of your instruction.

Inquiring Minds Want to Know …

- What is the difference between assessment and evaluation?
- What is the difference in assessment *of* learning, assessment *for* learning, and assessment *as* learning?
- What types of traditional and non-traditional assessments would work for my instruction?
- What are the advantages to using peer and self-assessments?
- What do I need to remember and understand from this chapter?

⇒ How to develop assessments that are aligned to learning outcomes;

⇒ The meaning of the terms "formative assessment," "norm-referenced" and "criterion-referenced tests," "rubrics," "alignment," "data-driven decision making," and "differentiated instruction."

Jargon Alert!

Learning assessments are known by many names. Here are a few terms you may encounter in different career environments and settings: *objective* and *subjective assessments, formal* and *informal assessments, criterion-referenced* and *norm-referenced assessments, summative* and *formative* (aka *educative*) *assessments, traditional* and *non-traditional assessments, self-assessments* and *peer assessments, standardized* or *standards-based assessments, performance* and *product assessments, diagnostic assessment, mastery tests, end-of-course tests, capstone experiences, job evaluations, accountability measures, progress checks, ability inventories, examinations, quizzes, clinical trials, design juries, pin-up critiques,* and *performance-based evaluations, assessments, appraisals, analyses,* and *audits.* Ultimately, all types of assessment are intended to provide feedback on progress toward learning and performance goals.

Notable Non-Example

A critical aspect of assessment relates to its relevance to both the stated learning outcomes and learners' goals. What happens when the outcomes and assessments are misaligned?

> *Confusing the Focus*—The administration at a Midwest medical school noted a disproportionate number of requests from medical students to specialize in four areas, Radiology, Ophthalmology, Anesthetics, and Dermatology. They suspected that this was a result of a popular belief that these specialties constituted the "ROAD to success" in medical practice. Wishing to avoid exceeding the demand for graduates in those specialties while failing to meet the need in other areas, the administration conceived of a workshop on choosing a specialization. The goal was to stimulate interest in other specializations, including obstetrics, surgery, neurology, urology, pediatrics, and emergency room practice. Faculty members in those departments were asked to develop the workshop, and they were tasked with encouraging more interest in their specialties, while maintaining the students' sense of autonomy and self-directedness. The faculty came up with a learning outcome that stated that *Students will identify options for a future specialization.* They designed a capstone assessment that required the students to *Prepare a personal learning plan with action items for professional development in your chosen area of specialization.* The resulting workshop did stimulate interest in the targeted specializations, but the professional development plans produced by the students were shallow and characterized by a lack of realistic action items for attaining their goals. A

summative evaluation of the workshop revealed that the outcome and capstone assessment were misaligned. The developers had placed more emphasis on the learning outcome when planning the workshop experiences rather than the assessment. Since the outcome emphasized knowledge retention and was geared to the lower-order levels of Bloom's Thinking Skills Taxonomy, they provided an abundance of information on the possible specializations and the kind of work students could expect to do in each of those areas. However, the capstone assessment emphasized knowledge *application*, and required the use of higher-order thinking skills to evaluate their options and synthesize the information to develop a plan for professional development. Not only did the workshop omit information that students needed to develop a complete plan (applicable courses, length of training required, and the type of residency programs desirable), but it also lacked activities that would have given students practice in defining a plan of action to accomplish their career goals. As a result, the students' professional development plans lacked sufficient detail and failed to provide them with a realistic picture of what was involved in their chosen area of specialization.

Caution!

When there is misalignment between the assessments and either the learning outcomes or the learners' expectations and personal learning goals, the integrity and success of the instruction will be compromised. In this case, identifying options for specialization was *necessary* for medical students' future professional development, but *insufficient* to enable them to identify a solid plan for accomplishing their goals for future professional practice. While the assessment was realistic, the instruction failed to adequately prepare the students and they were frustrated in their attempts to complete the plan. It is also possible to err on the other side of this issue. Learners typically view the assessments as reflective of what they will be expected to know in future situations. Assessments that are designed to test lower-order skills rather than the higher-order skills defined by the outcome do not accurately communicate the skills required in future performance environments. For example, designers sometimes make the mistake of using a verbal-information-based multiple choice test to assess problem-solving abilities or other higher-order thinking skills. As a result, learner expectations do not match the requirements of the performance environment.

Assessment vs. Evaluation

In this book, we use the term "assessment" to refer to the measurement of student learning, and the term "evaluation" to refer to the appraisal of the success of the instruction itself. It is common to confuse assessment with evaluation, since the words are often used interchangeably in the IDT field as well as in other fields. There is, however, an important distinction between the two words. *Assessment* involves determining what has been learned and it is carried out both formatively (during the course of the instruction) and summatively (after the completion of the instruction). The results of assessment allow everyone involved—the designer, stakeholders, and learners themselves—to gauge the progress of the learner toward reaching the identified outcomes. *Evaluation* is the process of determining whether something (in this case, the instruction) fulfills what it was designed to do. It is important to note, though, that assessment can be part of your overall evaluation plan. The results of learning assessments can also contribute to the evaluation of the instruction itself, as reflected by the fact that assessments are the measurement instruments used at the second level of Kirkpatrick's evaluation model (i.e., Level II Learning evaluation).

Therefore, well-designed, -implemented, and -analyzed learning assessments can help you continuously evaluate your instruction during and after the design/development process to improve its ability to increase understanding and achievement for all learners.

So What's Involved? Defining Assessments

Assessments should be aligned to outcomes, but, as with outcomes, different assumptions about learning result in different types of assessments. The basic guidelines outlined below can help you define the assessments for your instruction:

1. *Design different types of assessments for specific purposes*—Design a variety of measurements to address both formative and summative assessment, and to reflect the level of accountability required for the instruction. Make sure to clearly indicate the purpose of your assessments.
2. *Align assessments to the learning outcomes*—Assessments should clearly state the type of evidence that is sufficient to indicate that learners have attained the desired understandings and proficiencies outlined in the outcomes.
3. *Design assessments that reflect the chosen pedagogical approach*—Be sure that both the outcomes and the assessments are appropriate for the type of pedagogical approach you have selected.
4. *Plan for effective practice and feedback*—Practice activities and feedback are typically classified in the ID literature as teaching/learning strategies, but they should really be considered when you design your assessments, and both are, in fact, an integral part of formative assessment, or assessment *for* learning.
5. *Use assessment data to evaluate your instruction*—Design assessments that provide data on learner progress that can be used to evaluate the success of your instruction (see "Thinking About Evaluation").

Designing Different Types of Assessments for Different Purposes

There are three basic purposes that assessments address: appraisal (assessment *of* learning), diagnosis and guidance (assessment *for* learning), and/or fostering the learner's metacognition (assessment *as* learning). Earl and Katz (2006) make a helpful distinction between assessment *of*, *for*, and *as* learning. Assessment *of* learning is what we traditionally think of as *summative* assessment, carried out following the completion of the instruction to judge learner performance and measure their mastery of the learning outcomes.

Assessment *for* learning refers to collecting learning data from learners *before* instruction (*diagnostic* assessment) or during instruction (*formative* assessment). *Pre-assessment* of learner prior knowledge provides data before instruction that helps designers and instructors produce relevant materials that are aimed at a level that is challenging and yet attainable for the learners. Since pre-assessments are diagnostic in nature or are carried out to field-test the design of instructional assessments, they are typically not graded because this could discourage learners who do not know the material. This type of content test at the beginning of the instruction will tell you whether there is a wide range of prior knowledge among the learners and whether you must develop more challenging materials for some learners and remedial material for others. Formative assessment consists of quizzes and checks for understanding administered *during* the instruction, as well as direct feedback from learners on their understanding and satisfaction with their learning pace. These assessments provide a means for both learners and instructors (or the instruction) to monitor and gauge learner progress (Marzano, 2006). The results provide guidance for redirection or remediation during instruction, and help direct learner efforts to improve their ability to meet the instructional outcomes. If done correctly, formative assessment provides an opportunity to learn because a good assessment points out gaps in knowledge and skills that need to be filled.

Finally, assessment *as* learning is designed to help learners develop their metacognitive abilities and their skill at self-assessment. It assesses "each student's thinking about his or her learning, what strategies he or she uses to support or challenge that learning, and the mechanisms he or she uses to adjust and advance his or her learning" (Earl & Katz, 2006, p. 54). In addition, this type of assessment prompts learners to develop their own learning goals, and to track and reflect on their own learning. Lastly, you can empower learners for effective lifelong learning and improve their metacognition by suggesting strategies to use for improvement. The goal in creating assessments for any of these purposes is to design an appropriate level of challenge that motivates the learner, while avoiding excessive difficulty that could produce anxiety, and instruction that is below the learner's skill level and causes boredom.

In addition to formative and summative assessments, there are many other *types of assessments* that a designer can use for the purposes outlined previously. Common categories include norm-referenced and criterion-referenced assessments, formal and informal assessments, and traditional and *alternative assessments*. There is some overlap between these categories.

Norm-referenced tests measure the performance of a learner against others in the same learner group. Average scores for the group as a whole are used to establish what is a *normal* score. Norms are based on a bell curve, so the same percentage of students will score in the 90th percentile (above average) as will score in the 10th percentile (below average). Norm-referenced scores are thus typically reported in percentiles, and examples include the SAT and ACT tests (e.g., "Suzanne scored in the 96th percentile on the ACT"). Norm-referenced tests, such as standardized achievement tests, are typically administered on a yearly basis, are intended for large-scale assessment of the curriculum, and are thus used as the basis for "accountability" (such as that dictated by the No Child Left Behind Act; Gottlieb, 2003). They typically do not provide feedback on the specific weaknesses or strengths of instruction, since there are rarely enough questions on a specific learning objective to judge whether the student has a firm grasp of the concept. With regard to this aspect of norm-referenced tests, Chase (1999) claims that for test results to adequately inform instruction, an assessment should include at least ten test items for any one learning objective (such as an aspect of grammar structure). However, if standardized tests were to devote ten questions to every specific objective, they would require many weeks to complete!

Criterion-referenced tests are absolute measures of a student's performance based on specific criteria (e.g., learning outcomes). The number of correct or incorrect answers on the test determines whether students pass or fail the test. Criterion-referenced tests can show a learner's progress over time and, as such, they are valuable tools for educators to use in designing and revising instruction to meet individual student needs.

Formal assessments are administered and graded using established scoring and interpretation rules. Examples include standardized tests, certification tests, examinations and quizzes, benchmark assessments, end-of-course exams, and performance tests given in a formal educational setting (either physical or virtual). *Informal* assessments are carried out to gauge and improve learning through more unofficial practices such as questioning, discussions, observations of individuals or group processes, or via peer or self-assessment. This category would include ungraded *pretests* given to learners prior to instruction, mind-map exercises designed to expose learner misconceptions, minute papers and muddiest points designed to collect feedback on learner understanding, and impromptu checks for understanding during lectures using clicker technologies (hand-held audience response devices) or smartphones.

Designers often characterize assessments as traditional or alternative, and you will likely use both types to provide assessment during and after instruction. There are a wide variety of definitions for what constitutes traditional assessment. The educational lab NCREL (2004) defines *traditional assessments* as those for which learners *choose* a response from a given list, such as a multiple choice, true/false, matching tasks, and short answer or labeling tasks where the terms are provided. Traditional assessments typically test learner rote memory of declarative facts and therefore also include short answer or fill-in-the-blank tests.

When designing such assessments, you should define the question stems that will be used to prompt the learner to demonstrate their knowledge, the answer options (for multiple choice tests), and the type of feedback to be provided. Decide whether the learner must *recall* information from memory or if they should merely *recognize* the information. For example, if learners are studying to become hospital emergency room doctors, they must be able to *recall* the procedure for cardio-pulmonary resuscitation (CPR) from memory, and an appropriate assessment would require them to do so. However, since it is likely that they will have time to look up contagious disease descriptions on the Centers for Disease Control's (CDC) website, they would merely need to *recognize* that information to diagnose and treat a patient. Therefore, an assessment for flu diagnosis would require the learner to *recognize* where to go and how to search for flu symptoms from a list of possible options on a multiple choice test.

Effective assessments provide an accurate picture of the learner's knowledge and should therefore be designed so that the answers are not easily guessed without adequate study and engagement with the material. If a learner has not effectively engaged with the content, he or she likely does not have a firm grasp of the material. Avoid using test items with obvious answers, and design your tests to defeat the common strategies that students typically use to guess correct answers. When such easily guessed test items are eliminated, actually *learning the material* becomes the easiest way to pass a test. The website for this chapter includes a list of guidelines for designing traditional assessment items. Designers can use a wide range of available online tools to create effective traditional assessments, and some even allow for the use of question pools to enable learners to retake versions of the tests until they master the material.

Changing workforce needs in the 21st century demand that instruction and assessments build learner abilities such as expert thinking and complex communications, defined by Willis (2006) as "recognizing and organizing patterns and relationships and identifying and solving new problems as they arise" and "careful listening and observing to elicit, interpret, and convey critical information," respectively (p. 76). These are the type of skills that are more easily appraised through more non-traditional means. *Alternative* or non-traditional assessments are those for which learners must *create* a response to a question or task (NCREL, 2004). Alternative assessments are also characterized as *authentic, holistic,* and *integrative*. They are referred to as authentic because they require actions on the part of the learner that are closer to the performance that will be required of them in the real world. They represent an alternative to traditional assessments and they often test a holistic combination or integration of several learning outcomes. Examples of alternative approaches to assessment include:

- Lengthy descriptive responses to open-ended questions;
- Construction of a project or writing of a paper;
- A performance or demonstration of a skill;
- Problem solving a case study or scenario;
- Production of a concept map or mind map;
- Collection of learner work samples and self-reflections in a portfolio (paper-based, project-based, and/or electronic);
- Games;

- Badges and points;
- ePortfolios (Nielsen, 2012).

In addition to providing an indicator of what has been learned, alternative assessments are used to encourage self-reflection and meaning making. Technologies such as wikis, blogs, multimedia production tools, online surveys and discussion forums, self-assessment instruments, and social networking technologies can be used for alternative assessments. A good resource on ideas for using technology for assessing cognitive skills is Churches' (2009) Bloom's Digital Taxonomy.

The nature of alternative assessments often makes them more difficult to grade. There are several options available for grading, but in all cases you should provide clearly stated judgment standards to learners in advance of the assessment. Options for guiding and grading alternative assessments include rubrics, self-assessments, and peer assessments.

A *rubric* is a checklist that provides a uniform set of precisely defined criteria or guidelines for judging student work, intended to simplify and making grading more fair. Willis (2006) identifies the condition of *predictability* as a critical element in a positive learning environment, and if a rubric is given to students in advance for use in completing an assignment, it can provide guidance by making students aware of evaluation criteria and grading standards. Therefore, rubrics should always specify the criteria for judgment and provide descriptions of levels of performance. While rubrics are commonly used to provide feedback on alternative assessments, they can aid learners in their efforts to prepare for more traditional assessments. Effective rubrics provide additional benefits. They:

- Provide specific feedback to learners, identifying and explaining the various levels of information, processes, and skills to be achieved;
- Communicate goals, expectations for excellence, and results;
- Teach students how to break down a large task into manageable pieces, and to evaluate their own work;
- Promote consistent, accurate, and unbiased scoring;
- Document important judgments about students; and
- Provide a way to distinguish and convey the importance of effort, organization, priorities, judgment, analysis, cooperation, proper use of resources, focus, and metacognition (Willis, 2006, pp. 78–80).

In their book *Learning to Solve Problems with Technology: A Constructivist Perspective*, Jonassen, Howland, Moore, and Marra (2002) provide a rubric for assessing the effectiveness of rubrics. The criteria they suggest for rating rubrics provide helpful guidance on developing rubrics, and include comprehensiveness of elements, distinctiveness of ratings, comprehensiveness of ratings, descriptiveness of ratings, clarity, quality of scales used, and more. The website for this chapter provides rubric examples and instructions on developing rubrics, and there are many websites that provide free rubric creation tools.

Non-graded *self-assessments* represent an effective way to prompt students to self-reflect and set personal goals for learning and development. They provide a means of improving learners' metacognitive skills and are thus used for assessment as learning. The website for this chapter provides an example of a self-assessment on assessment practices, and you can find many other examples via an Internet search. Self-assessments can be provided as a rubric, developed to require learners to rate their level of agreement on items in a list of qualitative statements concerning a topic, or they can require a response to reflective prompts. Teams of learners should also be encouraged to self-assess their group learning processes. Take note of the prompt examples for both individuals and groups in Table 7.1.

Table 7.1 Example Self-Assessment Prompts for Individuals and Groups

Self-Assessment Prompts for Individuals	Self-Assessment Prompts for Groups
• My successes today included … • I need a better understanding of … • To improve, I should … • My top-priority learning goal is … • I learn best when I … • When studying, it helps me to …	• Did our team concentrate on the required tasks and accomplish the goal? • Did we work together effectively? • Did everyone have an opportunity to voice their opinions or share their ideas, and did we actively listen to each other?

Peer assessments require learners to review each other's work and assess or comment on it. It can be used to provide preliminary feedback or as part of a final assessment. If you use peer assessment prior to an assignment due date, it is a good idea to require learners to address the concerns raised by their peer evaluators and either revise their work accordingly or justify why they have chosen to ignore the feedback provided. Peer assessment can be accomplished through virtual or face-to-face observations of presentations, synchronous or asynchronous discussions and conversations, or by reading and commenting on written reflections or projects. You should provide learners with guidelines for peer assessments to ensure constructive criticism and effective communication.

In addition to types of assessments, you can communicate your instructional plans to stakeholders by describing different *assessment formats*, including quizzes and test items, academic prompts (questions or cues), and performance tasks and projects. *Quizzes and test items* assess learner knowledge of facts, procedures, and concepts (declarative knowledge). They usually have a single, best answer and can be easily scored.

Academic prompts are typically open-ended questions or problems that prompt students to go beyond mere recall of information to think critically about the topic. Academic prompts can be used for individual or group instruction, and are helpful to promote the use of higher-order thinking skills for solving ill-structured problems, which require students to form a strategy and analyze, synthesize, or evaluate information. Prompts should be used with a scoring system such as a rubric that provides established criteria and standards of performance. *Self-assessments* are a type of academic prompt that requires the learner to reflect on his or her own progress in relation to an overall goal or to personal learning goals. The website for this chapter provides a self-assessment on your own assessment practices.

Performance tasks and projects are authentic assessments that require students to perform a real-life task or develop a product similar to those used in the "real world." They generally feature a real or simulated setting (sometimes in the form of a case study), require students to address an identified audience, are based on a purpose that relates to that audience, and should, again, be judged based on criteria and standards of performance. Examples include reports, portfolio collections, problem-solving exercises, and simulations.

Aligning Assessments to Learning Outcomes

An assessment should either restate the learning outcome or elaborate on it. The two should, in other words, be *aligned*. At the risk of sounding redundant, we repeat: alignment of assessments and outcomes is important! If you have read Lewis Carroll's 1871 classic, *Through the Looking Glass*, you will recall that the protagonist Alice met many interesting characters in the course of her adventures. When walking through the woods, she met two comical, childish twins named Tweedledum and Tweedledee. The two brothers were a mirror image of each other in almost every way, except that Tweedledum had a new toy rattle. They got along quite fine until Tweedledum discovered that Tweedledee had spoiled his nice new rattle. At that point, they decided to do battle, and enlisted Alice's help in preparing for the fight.

Tweedledum and Tweedledee agreed to have a battle!
For Tweedledum said Tweedledee had spoiled his nice new rattle.

(Carroll, 1871)

WARRING OUTCOMES & ASSESSMENTS

Figure 7.1 Outcome and Assessment Alignment

Tweedledum and Tweedledee are very much like the learning outcomes and assessments used in an instructional design. As long as the outcomes and assessments mirror each other, they will function well to guide the instructional design. They will also provide learners with a clear picture of what they are expected to learn and how they will be assessed. However, if one has something the other does not have, the outcomes and assessments will "war" against each other, confusing the instructional design, as well as the learner! Instead, effective assessments should:

- *Align with the learning outcomes* defined for the instruction, and should therefore also be linked to any applicable standards or institutional learning criteria;
- *Be a learning experience* for both the *learner* (who continues to learn through the assessment process) and the *designer* (who learns about the effectiveness of the instruction);
- *Be known in advance by the learners* (i.e., "tell them what content they will learn, teach them the content, and then test them on the content").

These elements are all related: to be an effective learning experience, the learner needs to know how they will be tested and, for that to happen, you need to inform them of the expected outcomes. If the assessments are aligned to the outcomes, then knowing the outcomes should tell them how to prepare for the assessment. Proper alignment means that the assessment will *look* similar to the outcomes, using similar action verbs and describing almost identical conditions.

You may have to address alignment at multiple levels: aligning elements within the instruction and aligning the instruction to institutional factors. *Strategic alignment* (a private sector term) and *curricular alignment* (a term used in K-12 and higher education) refer to synchronizing the key goals of the instruction with institutional goals. Misalignment of instructional and institutional goals results in ambiguous outcomes, a lack of support for learning initiatives, and, ultimately, mission drift for the entire organization. For example, in a business environment, strategic misalignment is characterized by instruction that fails to support the company's productivity goals, mission, and attempts to meet industry standards, as well as by business structures that fail to provide motivation and resource support for the instruction. In K-12 environments, curricular misalignment produces instruction that does not meet state and national standards, or that fails to effectively prepare students for the next performance context. As a result, students experience low rates of academic success, schools fail to meet Adequate Yearly Progress (AYP), and graduates fail to meet expectations in post-secondary institutions and in the workplace.

Strategic alignment and curricular alignment are foundational to a design and should be addressed when developing the overall goals for instruction. As you refine your goals into more detailed outcomes, you must address a second type of alignment that is, in some ways, a subset of strategic and curricular alignment: *instructional alignment*. This alignment is internal to the instruction and involves synchronizing:

- *Learning outcomes* (what you tell the audience they will learn);
- *Assessments* (how you will determine whether the audience learned); and
- *Teaching/learning strategies* (experiences designed to improve mastery of the outcomes).

To improve alignment, write the outcomes and assessments concurrently, making sure the assessments *mirror* the outcomes. Start with the end in mind, using a backward design method, and identify exactly what the learners should be able to do, know, and feel, and how they should interact (the KASIs) following the instruction. Assessments should clearly state the type of evidence that is sufficient to indicate that learners have attained the desired understandings and proficiencies in the outcomes. They should include indicators and instruments to accurately measure the rate of progress defined in the outcomes. Finally, they should clearly communicate the specific conditions of the assessment, the resources and/or scaffolding that will be available to the learner, and the standards for performance.

Assessments should reflect the type of learning task described in the outcome, as well (i.e., cognitive, psychomotor, or affective learning tasks). Any of the assessment types mentioned previously can be used to assess the acquisition of cognitive outcomes. Psychomotor outcomes are most commonly assessed through observation of a performance test using checklists, rating scales, or rubrics for scoring. The assessment of affective learning outcomes is often more challenging.

Since affective outcomes address personal attitudes, interests, motivations, and self-efficacy, they are typically assessed using either observations of learner behavior or self-report questionnaires that feature rating scales and semantic differential scales. Observations of learner behavior (either formatively, summatively, or much later in the performance context) often make use of checklists to note the absence or presence of behaviors that have been identified as being indicative of the desired attitude, interest, motivation, values, etc. Self-report measures require learners to either provide their reaction to a topic through a written or oral reflection, or require them to indicate their degree of agreement with statements about the topic using a Likert rating scale. Semantic differential scales require learners to indicate their reaction to ideas, concepts, or topics along continua that feature contrasting adjectives at either end (good/bad, enjoyable/boring, difficult/easy, valuable/waste of time, etc.). If self-report measures are collected anonymously, the results reflect a group's response rather than an individual's response. Affective assessment may also involve a cognitive dimension if you need to assess the learners' knowledge of a situation in which they would display an attitude or a behavior that reflects that attitude. However, it is important to make a distinction between assessing knowledge *about an attitude* from assessment *of the attitude itself* (Reiser & Dick, 1996, p. 90).

Defining assessments can provide a clearer picture of the design and it is likely that you will find it necessary to revisit and revise your outcomes. Table 7.2 provides examples of aligned outcomes and assessments.

Designing Assessments that Reflect Pedagogy

The outcomes and aligned assessments should be appropriate for the type of pedagogical approach you have selected. *Instructivist assessments* can be used for all three purposes described: assessment of learning, assessment for learning, and assessment as learning. They can be traditional or alternative, and can be used to appraise lower or higher thinking skills. As a result of an emphasis on direct instruction, when compared to Constructivist or Connectivist assessments, Instructivist assessments are usually the most complete, providing specific guidance to the learner and the assessor on the expectations and standards to be met. For online instruction, they work well with learning objects that provide pre-packaged content designed to teach specific KASIs.

Constructivist outcomes and assessments are particularly applicable to domains for which the content is less structured, still emerging, and unstable. According to Schwartz, Lindgren, and Lewis (2009), Constructivist assessments should allow for learning *during the test itself.* Therefore, alternative assessments are particularly appropriate for a Constructivist approach because, when students construct a portfolio, work on a group project, negotiate meaning, or participate in role play or debate, there is great potential for learning during the process. Peer and self-assessments are particularly helpful in fostering the reflection typically emphasized in Constructivist outcomes, since they prompt learners to examine and measure their learning progress. Table 7.2 features two Constructivist outcomes with matching assessments that are designed to prompt reflection and are socially oriented and contextually bound. The second example also requires the learner to process multiple perspectives and utilizes a more traditional assessment to accomplish Constructivist goals. Constructivist assessments can be used to accomplish all three assessment purposes, but are particularly valuable for assessment *for* learning and assessment *as* learning, due to their emphasis on reflection, meaning making, and personal growth.

Connectivist assessments are difficult to define. Prominent Connectivists reject the idea that there is a specific body of content that should be acquired or remembered and emphasize that the responsibility for selecting, repurposing, creating, and verifying content is increasingly being delegated to individuals in distributed informal networks (Downes, 2012; Siemens, 2005–2012). This is a realization of Lave and Wenger's (1991) *legitimate peripheral participation* of novices alongside experts in a community of practice. According to Wiley and Edwards (2002), in these online self-organizing social systems (OSOSS), "learners do not sit through … resources and assessments linked to decontextualized instructional objectives. They employ resources provided by peers … in the solution of a self-selected problem or accomplishment of another self-selected goal" (p. 11). Siemens (2005–2012) claims that, even when we give learners structured content to learn, they will still learn only what they value and find useful in their lives. Downes (2012) succinctly summarized the Connectivist approach to learning by stating, "to teach is to model and demonstrate, to learn is to practice and reflect" (p. 17).

As a result, Connectivist instruction stresses the immersion of learners in a community of practice to learn by example from more experienced peers and experts, and to learn by doing, through iterative and scaffolded practice and experimentation. Learners typically record their experiences and analyze them to find and recognize patterns, and to enable them to make connections and see the big picture as it emerges (Downes, 2012). A Connectivist assessor also seeks to recognize patterns to gauge learning, seeking to find it in the learners' activities, the resources they access, the connections they make between resources, the analyses they conduct to make meaning, and the conclusions they make. Consequently, opportunities to practice making and refining

Table 7.2 Examples of Aligned Outcomes and Assessments

Outcome Type	Outcomes	Assessments
Psychomotor Outcome (*Instructivist*)	Given strips of white oak and appropriate weaving supplies, the learner will construct a basket of a specific size within three hours.	Given three hours, produce a basket (around 12" diameter, 6" deep), using: white oak strips, a spray water bottle, measuring tape, clothespins, clamps, a metal awl, scissors, a spoke weight, and a 1/4" and a 1/8" packer.
Cognitive Outcomes Categorized By Bloom's Thinking Skills (*Instructivist*)	**Remember**—Recall the definition of compound interest. **Understand**—Identify whether sample case studies illustrate the application of compound or simple interest. **Apply**—Given a beginning account balance and an interest rate, calculate the interest earned for a year when compounded daily, and the total account balance. **Analyze**—Compare the difference in results when interest is compounded daily and monthly, and identify the conditions required to meet a specific monetary goal. **Evaluate**—Review and evaluate potential investments on the basis of interest rates, investment length, and compounding schedule, to select the best option. **Create**—Develop savings plans for customers that take into account current income, cost-of-living adjustments, the rate of inflation, and needs at retirement.	**Remember**—Use the space below to define compound interest. **Understand**—Indicate whether each sample case illustrates the application of compound interest or simple interest. **Apply**—If interest on $100 is compounded daily for fourteen months at 10%, calculate the total amount of interest earned. **Analyze**—Using the previous example, if interest were compounded monthly instead of daily, what would the difference in interest be? What interest rate is required for $100 to grow to $125 in six months, compounded daily? **Evaluate**—Given a list of three potential investments with the respective interest rate, length of investment, and compounding schedule, select the best option, and defend your decision. **Create**—Given a consumer profile, develop a savings plan within four hours that takes into account the customer's current income, cost-of-living adjustments, the rate of inflation, and his or her needs at retirement.
Cognitive Outcomes (*Constructivist*)	1) The learner will reflect on and self-assess his or her own interpersonal communication skills and identify areas needing improvement and strategies to improve. 2) Following a group discussion of the environmental case study, learners will reflect on whether, and how, the discussion impacted their conclusions, and will write a one-page essay to describe the impact.	1) Following the group role play, reflect on the quality of your interpersonal communication, then complete the self-assessment to identify areas of skill deficiency and strategies you might use to improve your interpersonal communication. 2) Following the group discussion of the case, reflect on peer comments and arguments. Write a one-page essay on how others' arguments changed and/or supported your original conclusions.
Cognitive Outcomes (*Connectivist*)	1) Use a blog to describe and reflect on your experiences in the online community, showing evidence of regular connections to resources, sharing and review of peer contributions, and effective management. 2) Keep a record of, and reflect on, the resources and information you accessed during the course, and create a visual representation of how you think the resources and knowledge bits are related with respect to your own learning experience.	1) Describe and reflect on your experiences in the online community in a blog that shows evidence of weekly connections to a variety of human and non-human resources, consumption, analysis, sharing and review of peer contributions, and effective management of information and your personal learning environment. 2) Using a tool of your choice (concept map, Venn diagram, word cloud, etc.), create a visualization of the resources you accessed during the course, illustrating how you think those resources are interrelated, and communicating your reflections on the learning experiences of most value to you.

connections and frequent feedback are essential in Connectivist environments. Assessment can be accomplished via peer critique, the analysis of user-generated content, the quality of content aggregation, and the relevance of personalized learning environments to the learner's stated personal goals (Conole, Galley, & Culver, 2011). (See example in Table 7.2.) Siemens (2005–2012) and Downes (2012) suggest some metrics for Connectivist assessments:

- *Participation/Interaction*—A learner's participation in the network activities compared to average learner activity, measured as number of contributions, depth of engagement, or response rate;
- *Clarity of Communication*—A learner's efforts to communicate in a manner that avoids confusing less knowledgeable members of the community;
- *Contributions*—The number or quality of positive contributions to the community that result in problems solved, disputes adjudicated, concepts clarified, etc.;
- *Peer Ratings*—The relative standing or reputation of an individual within the community based on peer ratings;
- *Development of an Effective Network*—A learner's success in setting up a network of resources, filtering and analyzing large amounts of information to extract useful resources, and effectively managing information and connections; and
- *Growth of Capacities and Aptitudes*—A growth in the ability to recognize and analyze patterns and trends, find personal relevance in the environment, predict consequences, develop core values and principles, effectively communicate with the language of the community, aggregate and repurpose resources, and create and share resources that others find helpful.

Downes and Siemens advocate an eventual move toward openness in assessment (Downes, 2012, p. 465). How this will look is yet to be determined. Table 7.2 provides two examples of Connectivist outcomes and matching assessments.

Planning for Effective Practice and Feedback

Effective practice and feedback are important aspects of assessment. Robert Marzano (1998; Marzano et al., 2001) conducted a meta-analysis of research studies to identify effective instructional strategies that were successful in increasing learner achievement across student populations, content areas, and grade levels. Two of the nine categories of effective strategies they identified were *practice* (in the category of "Homework and practice") and *feedback* (in the "Set objectives and provide feedback" category).

Formative assessments and homework are both forms of practice for learners. Marzano's (1998) meta-analysis showed that homework and practice have an average effect size of .77 and a 28-point percentile gain. Most learners are able to see the value of formative practice and homework when they are told that it can be responsible for the difference between a grade of 70% and 98%! When using practice and homework, be sure to inform the learner of its importance and effect, emphasizing that the internalization of concepts and processes cannot (for the majority of learners) be accomplished just by listening to a lecture. Rather, learners must interact with the material many times before they gain the proficiency required.

Feedback is evaluative or corrective information provided to a student about how they did in light of the learning outcome. Over many decades, a wide range of research indicates that immediate feedback in the form of knowledge of results significantly enhances both short-term and long-term learning (Cassidy, 1950; Cawelti, 2004; Makin, White, & Owen, 1996; Peterson, 1931).

Effective feedback is specific, frequent, and timely (preferably immediate), and the more detailed the feedback, the better. You can provide feedback directly to the student, provide opportunities for peer feedback, or enable the student to self-evaluate for feedback. The level of feedback provided varies from an overall grade or percentage of correct responses, to knowledge of which responses were correct and which were incorrect, to knowledge of the correct answers for all incorrect responses, to a detailed explanation of why incorrect responses were wrong.

Prompting learners to set learning goals and keep track of their own learning progress on formative assessments promotes learner autonomy and has also been shown to improve achievement. It also "helps them develop clarity regarding goals, assignments and their progress; assists them in metacognition or thinking about what goes on around them in the classroom [or learning environment]; and provides them with skills of organization that serve them well in many settings" (Tomlinson, 2001, p. 95). The website for this chapter provides samples of forms that can be used to help students self-reflect and keep track of their learning, and Chapter 8 provides information on all of the effective instructional strategies identified by Marzano (1998).

The Challenges of Verification and Plagiarism

Advancements in technology usually make things easier and solve problems, but there are two issues related to assessment that have become more complicated in our technological world. With the availability of massive amounts of information at the learner's fingertips and the ease with which he or she can copy and claim someone else's work as their own, *plagiarism* has become easier than ever before in history. In addition to becoming informed on the nature of plagiarism and its causes (see http://www.plagiarism.org), you should keep current on the range of plagiarism prevention and detection tools available. (The website for Chapter 9 provides a list of tools you may want to consult.) The other challenge is *verifying the identity and work* of online learners. In the past, institutions proctored examinations at the learner's location. While this is still used in some settings, it is no longer possible with the global distribution of learners and instructors. Verification remains an issue, and technologies like eye recognition systems or fingerprint detection systems may some day solve the problem. In the meantime, however, some are calling for a whole new mode of assessment that focuses on competencies using a badge system in place of grades, verifying that an individual has mastered certain skills and knowledge (see http://chronicle.com/article/Badges-Earned-Online-Pose/130241/). Some see this as a move toward more individualized instruction that would foster the pursuit of lifelong learning and prompt individuals to take responsibility for and to direct their own education. Others label these ideas as just another fad. It is likely that the debate will be ongoing for some time to come. The website for this chapter provides recommendations for current resources on the topic of assessment and issues related to these challenges.

Thinking About Evaluation ...

Developing appropriate assessments helps you determine whether your target audience has mastered the intended outcomes, but it also enables you to figure out if your instruction was successful, since it addresses the second level of Kirkpatrick's evaluation model (Level II—Learning, described in Chapter 1). Learning assessment data provides a valuable indicator of overall instructional effectiveness and it is used in both public and private sectors for continuous improvement. In the private sector, stakeholders have always held designers and trainers accountable for results from training initiatives. However, bottom-line accountability for results has been more difficult to ascertain in K-12 and higher education career environments, and nowhere is the push to collect learner data more controversial than in the K-12 educational sector.

Due to the current emphasis on accountability in education and resulting legislation, the focus in K-12 education has shifted to *data-driven decision making*, a powerful tool that teachers and schools are using to meet the federal mandates and promote continuous instructional improvement. As defined by the National Education Association, it is the "process of making educational decisions based on the analysis of classroom data and standardized test data … [and it] uses data on function, quantity and quality of inputs, and how students learn, to suggest educational solutions" (National Education Association, 2011, p. 35). To implement the method, teachers and administrators collect and analyze learner data and use it as the basis of decisions on school and classroom practices. The information is also communicated to individual learners, parents, administrators, communities, employers, and other interested stakeholders. In a K-12 environment, such data can be used on a school-wide basis to:

- Measure student progress;
- Make sure students don't fall through the cracks;
- Measure program effectiveness;
- Guide curriculum development;
- Allocate resources wisely;
- Promote accountability;
- Report to the community;
- Meet state and federal reporting requirements;
- Maintain educational focus;
- Show trends (but not necessarily solutions) (American Association of School Administrators, 2002, p. 2).

At a classroom level, data enables the educator to track each student's progress and to customize instruction to maximize learning. In addition to pre-assessments and formative assessment results, learner data can be obtained from a variety of student performance measures compiled at the school, district, state, and national levels. These performance measures can be compared to the student's current class scores to diagnose learning needs and judge whether the student has developed the required knowledge and skills to keep pace with the demands of the content being taught. Ideally, the instructor would use the data to determine how to *differentiate instruction* to meet the needs of individual students. While this type of individualized instruction has traditionally been considered an unrealistic goal in education, the advent of new technologies and more sophisticated artificial intelligence holds great promise for diagnosing and meeting the learning needs of each diverse learner.

The type of performance measures used by K-12 educators are similar to those used to analyze learning in private sector businesses, health-care and other professions, and in government and military learning environments. Collecting data to determine the beginning status and progress of learner KASIs is an important task for *all* instructional designers, regardless of the educational level or sector involved. As noted, this data not only helps learners, but also provides a valuable indicator of the effectiveness of instruction. For example:

- Corporate trainers can compare the before- and after-training production rates for employees to judge whether current training efforts are improving performance;
- Individual teachers can compare their school's pass/fail figures to their own course pass/fail rates to obtain a picture of the success of their instruction;
- High school instructors can keep track of the percentage of their students gaining admittance to college and can seek to improve that percentage through learning activities that encourage students to acquire honors and awards to secure college admittance and scholarships;
- Teachers can note whether specific sub-groups in their school typically fail to meet the standardized testing goals, and can seek to improve the performance of that sub-group through individualized attention for sub-group members who are students in their classes;

- College professors can analyze end-of-course evaluations completed by students, and can make changes that address the concerns expressed by students;
- A community college administrator can analyze deficiencies in the skills of new freshmen, and can communicate those findings and the college's expectations for incoming freshmen to local high school administrators;
- A local employer who discovers that a training program is failing to improve quality control data can initiate a needs assessment or evaluation to determine the source of the problem; and
- Instructional designers who note that learner assessments are below the acceptable level can revisit their design to determine where there is a misalignment of outcomes, assessments, and/or strategies.

As you develop your assessments, contemplate how learner progress and achievement data can inform the design and revision of your instruction. The thought process will produce a valuable indicator for a Level II evaluation of your instruction.

Streamlining Assessments

So in what way can this portion of the design process be streamlined?

- *Sustainable*—Build the assessments around the use of existing job aids or job aids that you intend to develop. This will ensure that the job aids will be used in practice and will be viewed frequently so that updates and/or errors can be identified by learners and users and maintenance/updating will become a natural part of the work-flow. Ask your SMEs to help develop the observational checklists for performance assessments and consider asking them to take on the role of actually observing and assessing learner performance. This will do two things: it will enlist their help for the time-intensive assessment activities and it will ensure that they experience the use of their own checklists so they can catch errors and improve future attempts to design checklists.
- *Optimized #1*—It may be appropriate to start backwards by designing and gaining approval for the assessments prior to defining the learning outcomes. If stakeholders approve of how the learners will be assessed and if they commit to the assessment procedure, resources, and timeline required, you can then go back and articulate the learning outcomes based on the assessments.
- *Optimized #2*—Speed up the design review process by producing a single table of aligned outcomes, assessments, and teaching/learning strategies to be reviewed for the instruction. The combination will give your stakeholders a better idea of your overall plans for the instruction.
- *Appropriately Redundant*—Your assessments should be designed to provide alternatives to allow for the accommodation of learners with disabilities. Use multiple forms of representation to provide options for perceiving and completing the assessments through different senses. Allow for learners to choose among options for alternative assessments, to optimize the value and relevance of the assignment and minimize barriers and distractions.
- *Right-Sized*—Consider whether the assignments and assessments are of an appropriate length and level of complexity for the target learners.
- *Continuous Improvement #1*—Field-test your assessments with stakeholders, SMEs, and individuals who are representative of the target learner population but who already know the instructional content. If these knowledgeable test subjects perform well on the assessments, your assessment plan is probably well-designed. However, if they fail or have difficulty with the assessment, find it confusing or inaccurate, or point out that they didn't have

everything they needed to accurately complete the assessment, you should revisit and revise your assessment plans. In the long run, the field test will ultimately save you time and will help you create more effective instruction.

- *Continuous Improvement #2*—Obtain SME and stakeholder approval of your matched outcomes and assessments to make sure you have identified reasonable and feasible assessments. *Quality Checks for Continuous Improvement*:

  ✓ Are the outcomes and assessments appropriately aligned? Are they written with regard to the prerequisites identified for the instruction?
  ✓ Does the language of each assessment reflect the identified pedagogical approach?
  ✓ Is each assessment reasonable given the scope of the content, the learners, the nature of the learning context, and the time available?
  ✓ Is the quantity and scope of all graded assignments appropriate and reasonable?
  ✓ Are the alternative assessments adequately authentic?
  ✓ Do the alternative assessments allow for learner choice to accommodate different needs, interests, backgrounds, and abilities?
  ✓ Can the assessments be adjusted to accommodate learner physical and cognitive disabilities?

Different Career Environments, Different Perspectives

- As mentioned previously, different organizational values often result in different types of assessment measures. While there increasingly are exceptions, most business and industry and other private sector environments typically use Instructivist methods and assessments to provide clear measures to justify the expense of training efforts. In public and private educational environments, the pressure for accountability from stakeholders (parents, alumni, investors, and state and federal watchdogs), coupled with the strong desire to foster productive and creative citizens, has resulted in a mix of assessment types, from high-stakes state comprehensive achievement tests and end-of-course exams to formative traditional and alternative assessments.
- Medical education is characterized by frequent formative assessments and comprehensive summative assessments. These tests range from multiple choice electronic and/or paper-based tests, to problem-based assessments, oral exams, preceptors, and case studies. Some institutions make use of Immediate Feedback Assessment Technique (IF-AT) scratch-off tests that provide students with immediate knowledge of results. Students are also assessed using Objectively Structured Clinical Examinations (OSCE) that feature authentic care simulations that test student ability to communicate and problem-solve patient issues. Simulation-based exams are also common, as well as practical exams that feature mannequins to test emergency skills. Hospitals regularly rehearse "Code Blue" situations to foster peak performance levels for medical staff and conduct disaster drills in conjunction with local emergency services that simulate community catastrophes like tornados, train wrecks, and fires.
- The U.S. military has standard assessments that are administered at different levels of service by the various branches (Army, Air Force, Navy, Marine Corps, and Coast Guard). For example, the Armed Services Vocational Aptitude Battery (ASVAB) is a multiple-aptitude assessment that measures developed abilities and helps predict future academic and occupational success in the military. It is administered to all enlisted military personnel. Other tests are used for officer training programs or for placement in specific jobs and vary by the branch of the service and the area of specialization. Examples include the Air Force Officer Qualifying Test (AFOQT), the Navy and Marine Corps Aviation Selection Test Battery

(ASTB), the Navy Challenge Physical Standards Test (PST), and the Computerized Special Operations Resilience Test (C-SORT). Subject-specific training programs within the branches of the military are followed by traditional assessments and performance tests.

Test Your Understanding With a Bloom Stretch

Apply	Apply what you have learned about developing assessments to produce a pair of aligned outcomes and assessments for psychomotor, cognitive, and affective outcomes.
Analyze	Provide a list of at least three assessments that you experienced in your lifetime. Identify whether the assessments were clearly aligned to the stated goals or outcomes of the instruction. Note whether they were part of a multi-assessment approach to appraising your learning or if they represented a mastery test or a capstone-type experience that tested several outcomes. Identify how they would be classified with respect to the categories discussed in this chapter (traditional or alternative, formal or informal, etc.). Comment on the appropriateness and effectiveness of the assessments for both the stated instructional outcomes and your own personal learning goals.
Evaluate	Compare and evaluate two of the outcome/assessment pairs from the examples in this chapter. Identify whether you think one pair is superior to the other pair and why.
Create	Choose an outcome from either this chapter or Chapter 6, or create your own. Design an alternative assessment to test the outcome and develop an accompanying rubric to guide and grade learners.

Diving Deeper

When time allows, we encourage you to go deeper to learn more about defining assessments that match your outcomes. The website for this chapter provides the following exercises and resources for further study:

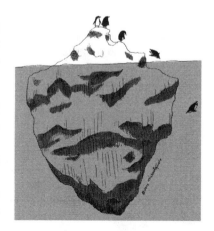

- **Practical Exercises and Examples**—Worked examples and exercises on assessment, and examples of different assessment types.
- **Job Aids**—Development guidelines and examples of rubrics and other assessment measures.
- **Resources**—Resources for assessment development, and links to current trends and issues in educational assessment.

8
Selecting Strategies
The Heart of Instructional Design

DR. SMITH TRIES OUT NEW CLINICAL TEACHING TECHNIQUES.

Instructional strategies are the very heart of an instructional design and serve to "foster student learning including pre-instructional activities, presentation of content, learner participation, assessment, and follow-through activities" (Dick, Carey, & Carey, 2005, p. 7). As you select strategies, be sure to consider both teaching strategies and learning strategies. *Teaching strategies* are the techniques used by an instructor or the instruction to bring about a specific learning outcome, and *learning strategies* are "those steps taken by the learner to … make learning more efficient and effective" (Lockee, 1996, p. 5). Both types of strategies are important to an effective design. The terminology used for Connectivist and some Constructivist designs is slightly different. These approaches emphasize planning *learning activities* and building *learning environments* to encourage specific learning outcomes, foster the use of higher-order thinking skills, and prompt interaction with content and between groups and individuals. To reflect these different approaches, we'll use the terms "strategies" and "activities" interchangeably.

As you design instruction, consider the effects on learning that result from the interaction of the strategies you choose and the technologies you select to support those strategies. To avoid a 100-page chapter, the selection and design of instructional and delivery technologies are covered in Chapter 9, but keep in mind that you consider both strategies and technologies concurrently.

Inquiring Minds Want to Know ...

- What factors should I consider when defining a delivery mode and selecting strategies?
- What categories are helpful to consider when selecting strategies to foster learning?
- What design guidelines should be used to create Instructivist, Constructivist, and Connectivist learning experiences?
- What learning outcomes are fostered by interaction in instruction?
- What frameworks, models, and guidelines exist to help me select strategies and design learning environments?
- What do I need to remember and understand from this chapter?

  ⇒ The meaning of these terms: "organizing strategies," "interaction strategies," "scaffolding," "supplantive strategies," and "generative strategies";
  ⇒ How to use Gagné's Nine Events of Instruction framework for planning Instructivist learning experiences;
  ⇒ The range of frameworks and models available for Constructivist learning experiences;
  ⇒ Guidelines to keep in mind when designing Connectivist learning experiences;
  ⇒ Marzano's nine categories of effective strategies.

Jargon Alert!

Teaching and learning strategies are also referred to as *methods, techniques, learning activities,* and *learning experiences.* Different sources provide a variety of categorizations for strategies, as well, including *organizational and management strategies, teaching and learning strategies, engagement strategies, interaction strategies, technology strategies, Web 1.0* and *2.0 strategies, direct* and *indirect methods, experiential strategies, self-paced methods, information processing* and *behavioral strategies, personal* and *social strategies, supplantive* and *generative strategies, student-centered* and *teacher-centered strategies,* and more. Knowing that the terms used by different sources sometimes overlap in meaning and in what type of strategies they encompass can help you determine which terms you will use in your professional practice.

Notable Non-Example

The selection of strategies is influenced by all other elements in the design, but most notably by learner characteristics, interests, and needs. Strategies shape the learning experience and should appeal to and meet the needs of the learner to ensure learner satisfaction. Here's a case in point:

> *Peeved Patrons*—One of the authors (Miriam) recently signed up for complimentary software instruction at a computer retail store. She had been given professional video footage

shot with a $60,000 camera and asked to edit it to produce five videos for a non-profit. She had very little time to learn the complicated professional editing program they had purchased for her use, so she took her equipment and footage with her to the retail store, hoping to speed up the process with some professional advice. She explained her needs to the retail store trainer and asked him about editing procedures for accomplishing some specific effects. The retail trainer did not answer her questions directly, and instead of providing clear direction on how to complete the desired tasks he questioned her intentions, as if to suggest that she really didn't know what she wanted and needed to explore the program on her own for a while. Thinking she recognized the trainer's comments as an attempt to force her into a Discovery Learning experience, she made a supreme effort to resist telling him off, kept her mouth shut, and decided to accomplish what she could while the trainer moved on to other clients. She had just about convinced herself that she was imagining it and shouldn't be getting so annoyed when she overheard another customer's voice rise and crack with emotion as she said to the trainer: "This is the *third time* I've been here and every time you answer my questions with more questions! I'm *so* frustrated! All I want to know how to do is get this video done. It's due in a week and I haven't made any headway at all on it! Why won't you just tell me how to do this???!!!"

Caution!

Teaching and learning strategies should be selected to meet learner needs rather than because those strategies are trendy, have worked well in the past, or can be quickly and cheaply implemented. Learner needs dictate the outcomes for instruction, and in some informal instructional situations or Connectivist learning environments those needs and outcomes are actually in the learner's head and not explicitly stated. In such cases, you must provide a way to enable learners to articulate their needs and try to help them satisfy their goals. As always, be sure to use the intelligence gathered from your learner analysis and test your instruction to ensure you are meeting learner needs, producing something relevant, and avoiding the label of Notable Non-Example!

You can visualize your instruction as a stool that supports learning experiences with three legs: the learning outcomes, the assessments, and the strategies (or learning *activities*). If a leg is out of alignment (longer than the others), the integrity of your design is compromised and the stool won't support the learner adequately. If instructional activities lack a clear purpose they often won't engage or motivate learners. When assessments fail to match the outcomes and learning activities, learners are unprepared to transfer and use the new information. Finally, the Notable Non-Example illustrates that when learner needs and desired outcomes are not supported by the instructional activities, learners can become frustrated and dissatisfied with the experience. You will, of course, have guessed the bottom line here: learning outcomes, assessments, and strategies must all be appropriately aligned and must match the needs of the learner.

So What's Involved? Selecting Strategies

Strategies designed to instruct and foster learning date back to Socrates in ancient Greece, and as a result there are literally *thousands* of strategies available, with more being developed every day. Strategies range from simple questioning to complex role play for online simulations. There are also grouping strategies, organizing and sequencing strategies, strategies that provide scaffolding for learners, and strategies designed to help learners become more self-directed and autonomous in their learning. Whole books have been written on the subject of *instructional strategies* (e.g., Smith & Ragan, 2005), and therefore we limit our discussion in this chapter to general and specific categories of strategies and how strategies support learning and interaction in instruction. We have provided specific strategy descriptions and a list of resources for further study of instructional strategies on the website for this chapter.

An instructional project may require the use of multiple strategies to support the learning outcomes, convey content, and/or engage the learners. Ultimately, you should select strategies that complement or foster the behavior or learning described in your learning outcomes. Therefore, it is best to begin by determining the assumptions about learning that undergird your outcomes. Once those assumptions are identified, you should be able to group your outcomes under one or more appropriate pedagogical approaches. As with outcomes and assessments, different pedagogical approaches call for the use of different strategies. Consider using this five-step, customizable process for identifying instructional strategies:

1. Revisit and refine the learning context design.
2. Identify assumptions and pedagogical approaches.
3. Identify appropriate interactions and strategies.
4. Select technologies to support the strategies identified (covered in Chapter 9).
5. Seek review and/or approval of the treatment, the aligned outcomes, assessments, strategies, and the technologies (covered in Chapter 9).

Refining the Learning Context Design

Since the learning context provides support for your strategies and activities, its nature will determine what you can do to foster learning. The converse is also true: the way in which you plan to foster learning will influence the nature of the learning context and the delivery technologies you select. Decisions concerning the learning context and strategies are interrelated, underscoring the need to iteratively revisit previous plans and decisions, revising as necessary.

For example, when defining the learning context, you specify the time, place, and dispersion of the instruction, the delivery mode to be used (face to face, online, blended, mobile, etc.), and the type of learner grouping necessary (individual, one-to-one grouping, small group, or large group). To do this, you contemplate questions that suggest the interaction of many factors: Will the learning experience be available on demand or offered during a specific time period? Will it be asynchronous or synchronous? Are learners local or dispersed geographically? Do the identified needs require a face-to-face deployment, or is an online or blended implementation more fitting? Should it be self-paced or foster interaction between the learner and others? Such questions reflect an awareness of how the content, desired learning outcomes, and the learner analysis data can impact design decisions. Table 8.1 provides some examples of how learner analysis data impacts strategy decisions (see the website for this chapter for an expanded version of the table).

In addition to content and needs, there are other project-related factors that impact your design decisions, including:

- *Human and non-human resources and funds* required for both development and implementation, versus the available resources and project budget;
- *Development time* required versus the established project schedule and deadlines;
- *Implementation time* required for a particular strategy, versus the desired length and time allowed for completing instruction;
- *Learner familiarity with and responsiveness to the proposed context and technologies;*

Table 8.1 Examples of How Learner Analysis Data Impacts Design Strategies

Design Factors	Data from Learner Analysis	Possible Design Strategies
Content Treatment	Employees have no experience with equipment they must troubleshoot.	Include hands-on practice troubleshooting with the new equipment or with a simulation of that equipment.
Media Selections	50% of manufacturing line workers did not obtain a high school diploma.	Use multimedia instruction (video or illustrated presentations) to provide highly visual instruction that can be reviewed by learners as needed. Provide illustrated job aids to remind learners of critical procedures.
Structure and Organization	1. Low learner prior knowledge (Instructivist). 2. High learner prior knowledge (Constructivist). 3. Low learner prior knowledge (Connectivist).	1. Use a logical organization reflecting the topic's structure, presenting small units of content from simple to complex. 2. Stimulate recall of relevant prior knowledge and scaffold the learner to explore and build on their prior knowledge. 3. Prompt learners to reflect on what they know, don't know, and need to know. Provide guidance for accessing content.

- *Available infrastructure* to support the use of specific contexts, delivery systems, and technologies;
- *Stakeholder wishes* and other *project constraints*.

Since both instructional *and* practical project factors interact to influence the design, it is a good idea to obtain early approval of your plans for the learning context. Write up a succinct description of the proposed learning context, including your estimate of the human and non-human resources required. Then have your key stakeholders review and approve the plan to ensure that you will have the time, resources, and support necessary to accomplish it. (Refer to the website for this chapter for descriptions of learning contexts and the corresponding required resources and approvals.)

Identifying Assumptions and Pedagogical Approaches

Defining the structural elements of the learning context settles the question of what is *possible* (i.e., in terms of what strategies can be supported by that context). The second question to consider when identifying strategies is: What is appropriate? In an ideal situation (setting aside the practical considerations outlined previously), you select the strategies that are most capable of fostering the type of learning outcomes you and your stakeholders have identified. But we need to take a step back here. What assumptions about learning are reflected by those outcomes? A close study of the outcomes and reflection on your beliefs about learning should reveal your own assumptions; however, you may need to dialogue with key stakeholders to determine their assumptions. Once determined, the assumptions should guide you in choosing one or more appropriate pedagogical approaches (see Figure 8.1). If you have identified more than one type of approach, *regroup* your outcomes under the applicable pedagogical approach, and then begin to select interactions and strategies to address each grouping.

Prior to this point in the process, you probably grouped your outcomes according to a sequence, hierarchy, or content relationship. You may also have used Gagné's and/or Bloom's taxonomies to classify the outcomes by type of learning. Now consider the outcomes from a different perspective and ask yourself: Does each outcome require its own activity or learning experience, or can I optimize the instruction by addressing several outcomes with one activity? Of course, you should also have considered this question when you identified the assessments for the outcomes. Remember, though, we've artificially divided the development of outcomes, assessments, and strategies into separate chapters, when in fact they should all be considered simultaneously. Thinking about this question in connection with the selection of strategies, activities, and learning experiences prompts you to contemplate what you are trying to accomplish

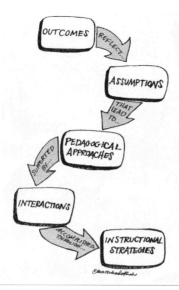

Figure 8.1 From Outcomes to Strategies

General Example

Outcomes: Learners will recall and understand declarative information for future use.

Assumptions: Such outcomes reflect Behaviorist and Cognitivist assumptions concerning the nature of knowledge and the conviction that knowledge should be conveyed to learners in an efficient and effective manner (refer to assumptions in Tables 4.4 and 4.5).

Pedagogical Approach: These assumptions support the practical choice of an Instructivist approach.

Strategies: Learner–content interaction. Present content for learner consumption in an organized and logical fashion to facilitate coding in long-term memory. Provide learners with opportunities to practice recalling the content. Use traditional assessments to test mastery of the outcomes.

Outcomes: Learners will be able to function on teams to use the content to solve problems.

Assumptions: This outcome reflects the Constructivist and Situated assumptions that learning is facilitated when information is directly applied to solving problems in authentic contexts (see Table 4.7).

Pedagogical Approach: Group these outcomes separately under a Constructivist approach.

Strategies: Learner–content and learner-to-learner interaction. Use a strategy like *anchored instruction* to provide learners with a scenario and a related problem to solve. Embed all the information required to solve the problem within the scenario so that higher-order thinking skills are fostered when content is applied to solve the problem. Provide resources on effective problem solving and teamwork, and gradually fade those supports as learners progress.

Outcomes: Learners will keep current on content developments and will connect to share ideas with others who are solving similar problems.

Assumptions: These outcomes reflect Situated and Sociocultural assumptions about learning from models and participation in real-world communities (see Table 4.6). They also reflect a belief that learning, knowing, and cognition are distributed, social, and networked (see Table 4.3).

Pedagogical Approach: Group these outcomes under a Connectivist approach that facilitates legitimate peripheral participation in a community of practice.

Strategies: Set up a social network to foster the development of learner connections/interactions.

at a more basic and practical level. Taking the time to properly reflect on your assumptions, outcomes, and pedagogical approaches is challenging, especially if you are under pressure from a tight schedule, budget, or an anxious client; but the payoffs are big in terms of instructional effectiveness. The general example on p. 154 illustrates the use of all three pedagogical approaches.

Of course, you could use just one of the pedagogical approaches in this example to address all the outcomes, as long as you could identify aligned assumptions, outcomes, and strategies to produce a grounded design. To aid your understanding of this process, here's a more specific example:

Specific Example

A terminal outcome and list of enabling outcomes were identified for an online program to train restaurant employees to store surplus, prepared food. The surplus food was to be donated to community hunger aid agencies, and so it needed to be safely stored until agency representatives could pick it up. The designer identified a terminal outcome and enabling outcomes, and labeled the latter by type of learning. The two main enabling outcomes (1.1 and 1.2) were broken down to show their dependence on several other enabling outcomes (i.e., 1.1.1, 1.1.2, etc.). The outcomes were analyzed to identify the assumptions about learning, and were then regrouped by possible pedagogical approaches (see Table 8.2).

Terminal Outcome 1
Restaurant employees will store surplus prepared food in a safe manner to preserve its wholesomeness up to the time of its donation to an aid agency, displaying knowledge of safe food factors related to temperature control, time to refrigeration, and risks of cross-contamination.

Enabling Outcome 1.1 (Cognitive—Intellectual Skill—Problem Solving)
Recognize a proper and safe food storage environment, distinguishing between safe and unsafe food storage temperatures and time to refrigeration, and identifying cross-contamination risks.

  1.1.1 (Cognitive—Verbal Information)
    List safe temperatures for stored perishable food.
  1.1.2 (Cognitive—Intellectual Skill—Concept)
    Describe time out of refrigeration and temperatures that are acceptable for perishable food.
  1.1.3 (Cognitive—Intellectual Skill—Procedural Rule Application)
    List the procedure for quick-cooling food prior to refrigeration.
  1.1.4 (Cognitive—Intellectual Skill—Concept)
    Describe risks of cross-contamination for food improperly packaged or handled.
    1.1.4.1 (Cognitive—Intellectual Skill—Concept)
      Identify the bacterial risks and consequences of cross-contamination.

Enabling Outcome 1.2 (Psychomotor Skill supported by Cognitive Problem Solving)
Practice safe food storage practices, demonstrating an understanding of the issues of cross-contamination, temperature, time out of refrigeration, and proper quick cooling.

  1.2.1 (Cognitive—Intellectual Skill—Problem Solving)
    Identify proper solutions to scenarios that vary with respect to safe food factors.
    1.2.1.1 (Cognitive—Intellectual Skill—Discrimination)
      Distinguish between safe and unsafe food storage for different perishable foods.

Table 8.2 Grouping Outcomes, Identifying Assumptions, Selecting Pedagogical Approaches

PROJECT DESCRIPTION: Training for restaurant workers who must safely store surplus prepared food prior to donation.

TERMINAL OUTCOME:
Store surplus prepared food in a safe manner to preserve its wholesomeness up to the time of its donation to an aid agency, displaying knowledge of safe food factors related to temperature control, time to refrigeration, and risks of cross-contamination.

Regrouped Learning Outcomes	Related Assumptions	Pedagogical Approaches
1.1.1 (Cognitive—Verbal Information) List safe temperatures for stored perishable food. 1.1.2 (Cognitive—Intellectual Skill—Concept) Describe time out of refrigeration and temperatures that are acceptable for perishable food. 1.1.3 (Cognitive—Intellectual Skill—Procedural Rule Application) List the procedure for quick-cooling food prior to refrigeration. 1.1.4 (Cognitive—Intellectual Skill—Concept) Describe risks of cross-contamination for food improperly packaged or handled. 1.1.4.1 (Cognitive—Intellectual Skill—Concept) Identify the bacterial risks and consequences of cross-contamination. 1.2.1.1 (Cognitive—Intellectual Skill—Discrimination) Distinguish between safe and unsafe food storage for different perishable foods.	Knowledge is objective and absolute, reflecting universal truths about reality, and the goal of instruction is to communicate knowledge and skills and to elicit the desired response or behavior from the learner in the final, real-world performance context. (*Behaviorism*) Learning involves linking new information to prior knowledge, organization, structuring, sequencing and storing that information in memory, and retrieving the information when it is needed. (*Cognitivism*)	*Instructivist* Teach and test learners on this declarative, conceptual, and procedural knowledge. Also provide quick reference aids as an on-the-job reminder.
1.1 (Cognitive—Intellectual Skill—Problem Solving) Recognize a proper and safe food storage environment, distinguishing between safe and unsafe food storage temperatures and time to refrigeration, and identifying cross-contamination risks. 1.2 (Psychomotor Skill supported by Cognitive Intellectual Problem Solving) Practice safe food storage practices, demonstrating an understanding of issues of cross-contamination, temperature, time out of refrigeration, and proper quick cooling. 1.2.1 (Cognitive—Intellectual Skill—Problem Solving) Identify proper solutions to scenarios that vary with respect to safe food factors.	Learners must be actively involved in the learning process to construct meaningful knowledge. Knowledge is embedded in the context in which it is used, and therefore authentic tasks and meaningful, realistic settings best facilitate learning.	*Constructivist* Provide web-based, branching scenarios that simulate real-world situations learners would encounter on the job. Remediate wrong choices.

The process of identifying assumptions and pedagogical approaches and grouping outcomes is involved, but you can use the design guidelines for pedagogical approaches provided in Table 8.3 as you work through the process. Once you've identified the approach or approaches you will take, you are ready to consider how different types of interaction can support those approaches, and the strategies that, in turn, support those interactions (as covered in the next section).

Identifying Appropriate Interactions and Strategies

Basically, all instruction involves one or more types of *interaction* (Thurmond & Wambach, 2004; Yacci, 2000). The interaction may merely be between the learner and the content, or, there may also be design elements that encourage interaction between the learner and:

- An instructor, facilitator, grader or content expert;
- Other learners (through paired, small group, or large group activities);
- The instructional context (through activities designed to prompt exploration or manipulation of elements in a physical project site or a virtual world); or
- His or her own self (through activities designed to prompt reflection on the learner's progress or underlying assumptions).

Interaction can be a goal in itself, or can be used to accomplish other learning outcomes. Instructional interactions are fostered through strategies. These strategies consist of *organizational strategies* that define the structure and flow of learning experiences (Reigeluth & Stein, 1983; Smith & Ragan, 2005), and *engagement strategies* that are designed to involve learners in interactive activities. You should also plan for appropriate *technology delivery* and *instructional management strategies* to deliver and direct learning experiences (covered in Chapters 9 and 11, respectively).

These strategy categories apply to all delivery modes (face to face, online or mobile, blended), although the specific nature of a strategy may differ by time and location of use (synchronous versus asynchronous deliveries, and physical versus virtual locations). For example, the designs for face-to-face and virtual versions of a course would both feature organizational strategies that define the order of topic presentation and the grouping of learners. However, organizational strategies for the online version should also address how the learner will *navigate* through the course, the *functions* that can be completed through the course interface (e.g., printing, submitting feedback and assignments, and finding help), and how the learner can *adapt* the course materials to meet his or her needs (e.g., change font size, use different input devices, or read a transcript of a multimedia presentation that will not play on the learner's system).

As more and more courses are modified for online or blended delivery, the design issue of interaction has taken on more importance. In web courses, designing for interaction is emphasized as one way to deal with the social isolation experienced by some students when instruction moves from a face-to-face environment to a virtual environment (Greenhow, Robelia, & Hughes, 2009; Lee & Paulus, 2001). This isolation is related to a learner's perception of the degree to which others are aware of him or her in the instructional situation (both instructors and peers). This perception is referred to in the literature as *social presence* and has been shown to impact learner motivation and learning (Lowenthal, 2009; Short, Williams & Christie, 1976).

A closer look at current practice reveals *five types of interaction* that are used for face-to-face, blended, and/or fully online environments:

- *Learner-to-Content Interaction*—How do learners interact with content? Learners consume content, manipulate and interpret it to understand it, commit it to memory, recognize

Table 8.3 Design Guidelines and Strategies for Different Pedagogical Approaches

Instructivist Approach	Constructivist Approach	Connectivist Approach
Learning Outcomes—Base on content analysis, applicable state or federal standards, best practices, accreditation requirements, or discipline consensus. Establish and communicate specific outcomes related to knowing and doing that require mastery. **Content**—Tell learners what they will learn (KASIs), teach them, and then test them on the KASIs. Content is usually highly scripted. **Prior Knowledge**—For low levels, design instruction that requires the use of lower-order thinking skills (LOTS). For high levels, require learners to use higher-order thinking skills (HOTS). **Supplantive and Generative Strategies**—For efficiency, use supplantive strategies, especially when time for instruction is limited. Use generative strategies to foster recall of prior knowledge, and the integration, organization, and elaboration of new knowledge. **Structure**—Stimulate learner interest, provide examples and non-examples, and provide opportunities for practice and formative feedback. Instructional models include: mastery learning, programmed instruction, multimedia tutorials, drill and practice, and goal-based scenarios. **Control**—Primarily in the hands of the instructor or the instruction, although learner may be allowed to control pacing and order of content.	**Learning Outcomes**—Establish broad goals based on consensus within a discipline, critical and creative thinking guidelines, process goals, and HOTS, and include interpersonal and affective outcomes. Inform learners of overall goals and have individuals customize personal outcomes to match their interests and goals. Have groups socially negotiate outcomes. **Content**—Prompt learners to build on an established knowledge base, providing access to rich resources or guidance in locating resources. Allow learners choices in content based on their interests. Arrange learning experiences, and guide/scaffold learners during the experience. **Prior Knowledge**—Inform learners if instruction assumes they know and can use LOTS with an established knowledge base. **Supplantive and Generative Strategies**—Use supplantive strategies to prompt recall of relevant prior knowledge, and provide access to remedial materials for those needing a refresher. Use generative strategies to foster deep processing, personal relevance, meaning-making, and knowledge construction. Allow learner control of pacing and scaffold them in the use of metacognitive knowledge and problem solving. **Structure**—Foster transfer of learning by situating learning in real-world contexts, and foster HOTS through interaction with peers, modeling, and imitation and dialogic inquiry. Scaffold learners with multiple sources of information and learner-centered activities that require discussion, creation, and construction. Instructional models include: problem- and project-based learning, scenario- and case-based learning, hypermedia, anchored instruction, cognitive apprenticeships, and the Five Es model.	**Learning Outcomes**—Establish broad goals emphasizing competency in using resources, exploration, self-organizing, choices, and decisions. Encourage learners to define specific outcomes related to the content and their own personal goals, needs, and interests. Foster new forms of social and participatory practices. **Content**—Foster environments where learners are empowered to direct and manage their own learning with respect to both content and process. Provide guidance on navigating, selecting, and connecting to up-to-date content that is relevant to personal preferences and contexts. Encourage sharing of learner-discovered and learner-created content. **Prior Knowledge**—Prior knowledge shapes perceptions and impacts the ability to recognize patterns in information. Prompt learners to contemplate what they know to prepare them for future comparisons between prior and new abilities and connections. Create opportunities for learners to compare their depth of understanding and perspectives on topics and issues with the understanding and perspectives of others. **Supplantive and Generative Strategies**—Use primarily generative strategies to foster learner autonomy and provide learners with practice making connections and reflecting. Supplantive strategies consist of modeling and demonstrating how to make connections, critical contributions, and artifacts, so as to guide processes and facilitate learner growth. Provide scaffolds to help learners: decide which content and individuals are relevant to personal goals; locate, assess, and validate information; make connections between fields, ideas, concepts, and resources (human and technological); and manage an abundance of information through pattern recognition, critical and creative thinking, acceptance of uncertainty and ambiguity, contextualizing, and evaluation to yield trusted sources. **Structure**—Two options: form a group (formal with a membership, governed by rules or guidelines, privacy possible, may be online, blended or F2F instruction); or a network (informal with fluid membership, based on shared interests/practice, norms, MOOCs, rarely F2F). Allow varying levels of participation and contribution. Empower learners to construct personal learning environment, and connections. Network aspects: diversity (different locations, perspectives, cultures, members), autonomy (participants have freedom to set goals, choose tools, make decisions and connections), openness (easy to participate to extent desired, easy access to system and software, open membership, easy to share and interact), and interactivity/connectivity (structure facilitates connections between humans and non-human resources, and the community creates unique connections and knowledge). **Control**—The learner is in control of processes, content and outcomes, but the instructor or the instruction influences and shapes the learning environment. The instructor/ instruction serves as a persistent presence that amplifies, curates, aggregates, filters, models and demonstrates, and facilitates way-finding.

Assessment—Test and reinforce learning primarily with traditional assessments.

Technology—Support strategies with one-to-one and one-to-many technologies (one-way communication technologies, mass media, and two-way web technologies).

Control—Instructor or the instruction provides guidance and scaffolding, with learners controlling the direction of learning processes.

Assessment—Appraise learning through synthesis activities, artifact creation, and other non-traditional assessments.

Technology—Support synchronous and asynchronous opportunities for interaction and dialogue with many-to-many, two-way communication technologies and conferencing tools.

Assessment—If used, base assessment of learning on effectiveness of learner connections, learner contributions to the network, artifact creation, and by appraising the learner's personal learning environment.

Technology—Use many-to-many communication technologies and conferencing tools to support meaning making (bookmarking, tags, RSS, social networking, MOOCs—Massive Open Online Courses, etc.) and to augment, enhance, and extend cognition.

Source: Compiled from: Anderson and Dron (2011); Conole, Galley, and Culver (2011); Deubel (2003); Downes (2012); Drexler (2010); Dron and Anderson (2009); Siemens (2004); Smith and Ragan (2005); Willis (1995).

patterns and trends in it, apply it, analyze and evaluate it, create with it, use it to solve problems, reflect on it, draw conclusions from it and form opinions about it, summarize it, practice its procedures and skills, and apply it to complete assignments or work tasks. *Organizational strategies* for content interaction are used to guide the selection, sequencing, and presentation of the instruction and learning experiences to facilitate learner processing, coding, retrieval, use, and transfer of content. Traditional modes of content presentation used in both physical and virtual environments include lecture and multimedia presentations, *demonstrations,* programmed instruction and tutorials, and readings. This category also includes methods for highlighting information in instructional materials to focus learner attention on key points. *Engagement strategies* provide learners with opportunities to become immersed in the content and to use LOTS and HOTS to interact with it. Traditional means of engaging students with content include discussions, drill-and-practice exercises, games, simulations, experiments, discovery learning activities, problem-solving activities, projects, *synthesis* and application papers, and various assessments. You can provide access to content through a variety of formats, including physical or electronic versions of written materials, live or recorded lectures and presentations, physical or projected images, static or animated electronic images, paper-based or virtual assessments, and web content (e.g., websites, discussion forums, blogs, and wikis).

- *Learner-to-Instructor/Facilitator Interaction*—For most instruction, learners also interact with a course instructor, facilitator, or grader. In face-to-face settings this interaction is direct and immediate, but for virtual environments designers must carefully plan interactions to reduce the amount of isolation and distance that learners may experience. Learners completing self-paced instruction (online or correspondence-based) may also want to contact a grader, a webmaster, or even the designer (to report problems with the instruction). You can support these interactions with regular communication, activities, online discussions, feedback to learners on their performance, and by facilitating feedback from the learners on the course content and organization. Whether designing for physical or virtual environments, or synchronous or asynchronous activities, you must mindfully plan for learner-facilitator interaction, so that learners know how and where to go with their content questions and technical issues. *Organizational strategies* describe how such interactions will occur and include such things as communication plans for feedback and instruction, directions for the mix of online and face-to-face resources in blended courses, policies on late assignments, office hours, and guidelines for grading. *Engagement strategies* provide learners and facilitators with a reason to engage in interactions, and include requirements for the learner to communicate progress to the instructor on independent assignments, and questioning techniques. Both categories of strategies foster social presence and thus lessen the potential for learner isolation and disconnectedness.
- *Learner-to-Context Interaction*—It is important to remember that the learner also interacts with the learning context. Known and potential contextual interactions should be anticipated in the instructional design, whether they involve a face-to-face meeting in a room with terrible lighting, or distractions resulting from a three-year-old demanding the attention of an adult learner during a synchronous online discussion. Contextual design elements can also enhance learning by adding to the realism of the learning experience or by enhancing the development of a community of practice or a community of learning. Regardless, the instructional designer should become familiar with and consider the applicable learning and performance contexts, and consider how factors in those contexts will impact the effectiveness of the learning experience. *Organizational strategies* can help by presenting the instruction and learning experiences in ways that guide the learner and lessen the load on

his or her cognitive processing. *Engagement strategies* can help encourage learners to interact with the learning environment, and include activities that prompt learners to explore a virtual or physical world, guidelines for synchronous interaction, exploratory activities that prompt learners to try out the features of a learning management system.

- *Learner-to-Learner Interaction*—Learners interact with each other in virtual and physical learning environments to discuss content and ideas, seek and respond to others' comments, conduct experiments, collaborate to solve problems, construct meaning, construct projects and other artifacts, share content they've discovered or created, build team and communication skills, and more. Strategies and activities that foster these interactions can be synchronous or asynchronous. They can be designed to refine learners' communication and interpersonal skills, expose them to the prior knowledge and perspectives of others, demonstrate how to participate and contribute to a community of practice and learning, provide opportunities to express and defend their opinions while learning to appreciate the perspectives of others, and provide practice in making connections to knowledge and human and non-human resources. *Organizational strategies* guide the structure, sequencing, and presentation of the learning experiences to facilitate learner cognitive processing, communication, and group processes. *Engagement strategies* encourage learners to interact, requiring them to collaboratively discuss, learn, and process the content, using the content as the hub around which the interaction takes place.
- *Learner-to-Self Interaction*—Reflection on the learning process is important to developing self-directed and lifelong learners. Lee and Paulus (2001) note that when learners interact with themselves, they participate in an internal dialogue about the content, their learning and how the content aligns with their personal goals. This type of metacognitive self-reflection is essential to develop the self-regulatory skills needed for independent learning and instruction. You can use *organizational strategies* to structure the learning experience in a way that encourages spontaneous self-reflection, and add *engagement strategies* to require learner reflection.

Note that when you identify *assessment strategies* to address your learning outcomes, you are defining yet another type of *learner-to-content* interaction. Assessments can also be categorized as *learner-to-instructor* interaction (e.g., an oral exam), *learner-to-learner* interaction (e.g., a peer review or critique), *learner-to-self* interaction (e.g., a self-assessment), and *learner-to-context* interaction (e.g., an assessment to help an individual determine if he has the characteristics to make a good online student). Assessment strategies are addressed in Chapter 7.

Research shows that the way learners perceive the interaction that occurs within a learning environment influences their satisfaction with the experience (Fulford & Zhang, 1993). Table 8.4 lists a variety of strategies that can be used to accomplish multiple types of interaction. The strategies are listed by the applicable *instructional intentions* that a designer or instructor may identify which, in turn, foster certain learning outcomes (as listed in Chapter 6, in Table 6.4). In addition to applying to several types of interaction, most of these strategies can be used in both physical and virtual learning environments, and can be employed in either an asynchronous or synchronous form. For example, discussions foster learner-to-content, learner-to-instructor, and learner-to-learner interactions. You can hold discussions in either face-to-face or virtual environments, and in online environments the discussions can be facilitated synchronously by a live instructor or can be accomplished through an asynchronous discussion board exercise.

Some strategies work better for some applications than others, or they lead to different learning outcomes in different environments. For example, research has shown that asynchronous discussion board activities foster many of the same learning outcomes as face-to-face discussions without the constraints of time and location, and have the added benefit of generating contributions from learners who do not otherwise join in face-to-face class discussions (Chester & Gwynne, 1998). However, remember to consider the learning context and delivery environment, because with more and more learners accessing instruction on mobile phones and tablets, some strategies will not be effective in these more restricted environments (e.g., connectivity and screen size often prove to be limiting factors for mobile deployment). You can search the Internet for details on the individual strategies listed in Table 8.4, or you can consult the descriptions provided on the website for this chapter.

The list of instructional intentions in Table 8.4 overlaps somewhat with Gagné's (1985) types of learning outcomes (verbal information, intellectual skills, cognitive strategies, psychomotor skills, and affective). The website for this chapter features an extensive table that gives examples of strategies to use to foster each of Gagné's types of learning outcomes, as well as strategies to foster interpersonal skills.

Effective Strategies

Many of the strategies addressed in Table 8.4 fall under one or more of *nine categories of effective strategies* that positively impact student achievement (Cawelti, 2004; Marzano et al., 2001). Researcher Robert Marzano and his colleagues conducted a meta-analysis of over 100 research studies to identify strategies that increased student achievement across student populations, content areas, and grade levels. Table 8.5 briefly describes each category of strategies and lists the effect size and percentile rank calculated in the study. Marzano examined experimental research studies that featured a control group of students taught in a traditional manner, and an experimental group of students taught using a new teaching/learning strategy. *Effect size* refers to a statistical means of looking at the significance of differences in student achievement scores between the control and experimental groups. In educational studies, effect sizes of .20 are considered *small but significant*, effect sizes of around .50 have *medium significance*, and effect sizes of .80 or more have *large significance*. In order to understand *percentile gain*, it is first necessary to understand *percentile rank*, which is a measure of where students fall on a continuum from 1 to 99 percent. For example, in a group of 100 students, a student who is at the 85th percentile scores higher than 84 other students. Marzano's study found that students taught with the specified strategy scored a significant number of percentile points higher than students that were not taught with the strategy. A reported percentile gain of 23 means that the student scored 23 percentile points higher than they would have scored without the use of the strategy.

This categorization is very helpful for identifying strategies that are likely to be effective, but remember that your first priority is selecting strategies that support the learning outcomes you've identified. The website for this chapter provides a more complete description and specific strategy examples for each of Marzano's nine categories of effective strategies.

Scaffolding

Strategies can also be categorized by the extent to which they scaffold the learner. Scaffolding is instructional support that facilitates learning, and scaffolding strategies can be categorized as either supplantive or generative. *Supplantive strategies* are those that "supplant" or do more of the mental processing for the learner by explicitly stating instructional goals and providing information on how to think about, structure, and retain the content (Smith & Ragan, 2005). Supplantive strategies are appropriate for novice learners, when information and skills are complicated or are new to learners, when time is limited, or for tasks involving a high degree of physical risk. In contrast, *generative strategies* are those that encourage or allow learners to define their own learning goals, organize the material in whatever manner works best for them, control the sequencing and pace of the instruction, self-monitor their own understanding, and transfer

Table 8.4 Strategy Examples by Instructional Intent and Interaction Type (most strategies have both synchronous and asynchronous formats)

Interaction Type	Motivate learners to engage in learning processes	Present content and communicate expectations	Organize content to aid mental processing	Prompt knowledge/content creation	Scaffold and guide, provide practice and feedback, differentiate and transfer	Promote cooperation and collaboration	Foster Bloom's thinking skills	Build autonomy, metacognitive skills, and personal knowledge management
Learner-to-Content	• Keller's ARCS motivation strategies • Demonstrations and experiments • Multimedia presentations • Generate and test hypotheses • Authentic tasks	• Lecture, presentation, demonstration, experiments • Tutorials and how-tos • Authentic problem scenarios • Simulations • Variety of examples	• Cues, questions, advance organizers • Highlighting text and visuals • Summarizing, taking notes • Similarities and differences • Manage cognitive load • Activate prior knowledge	• Learner-produced content • Concept maps • Minute reflections • Guided discovery • Inquiry • Encourage seeking, making sense of, and sharing	• *K-W-L* (Know—Want to Know—Have Learned) worksheets • Incremental and chunked learning units, formative assessments • Drill and practice, guided and independent practice • Non-linguistic representations • Concept maps • Transfer tasks	• Goal-based learning and anchored instruction • Case-based and scenario-based learning • Problem-based learning • Group projects • Provide primary resources	• Strategies from Churches' (2009) Bloom's Digital Taxonomy • Similarities and differences (compare, contrast, analogies, metaphors) • Use data analytics and data visualization tools	• Provide choices of authentic and relevant experiences with scaffolding • Instruction on cognitive learning strategies • Provide subject-specific strategies • Build self-efficacy • Assign self-reflective tasks
Learner-to-Instructor *and* **Instructor-to-Learner**	• Questioning • Set objectives, expectations • Model desired behavior	• Solicit learner feedback on instruction • Socratic dialogue	• Concept maps • Challenge misconceptions • Reinforce good conceptions	• Make tacit knowledge explicit • *Wait Time I and II* • Coaching	• Prompt feedback on performance • Reinforce effort and provide recognition	• Teamwork skills • Reinforce effort and provide recognition • Guide discussions	• Research guidance and mentoring • Robust feedback	• Reinforce effort and provide recognition • Provide feedback on strategy use
Learner-to-Context	• Video tours of learning environments • Course system scavenger hunt, orientation	• Address issues of access and connectivity • Address technical support needs	• Simulation, role play, games • WebQuests • Guided discovery • Learner pacing	• Data analysis, aggregation, visualization • Instruction on production tools	• Design to accessibility guidelines • Provide accommodations • Technology guides	• Establish group norms • Use online breakout rooms for group work • Critique guides	• Situate problem-solving tasks in authentic settings to promote transfer of thinking skills	• Provide tips on effective study and learning environments • Provide options for accessibility
Learner-to-Learner	• Problem- and project-based learning tasks • Cooperative learning tasks • Discussions	• Peer tutoring • Learner presentations • Peer critiques and editing	• *Anchored instruction* • Team-produced diagrams of processes and concepts	• Tools for team-produced content • Social negotiation	• Cognitive apprenticeship • Reciprocal teaching	• Provide setting for interaction • *Think-Pair-Share, Jigsaw, Fishbowl* • Team building • Debate teams	• Prompt sharing and reflection on multiple perspectives	• Skill inventories and sharing • Share strategies for personal knowledge management
Learner-to-Self	• Personal goals • Self-assessment • Self-monitoring	• Learner reflection on personal goals	• Activate prior knowledge with reviews	• Personal Learning Environments	• Self-checks and opportunities to retake tests	• Self-assessment of group skills • Think-alouds	• Reflection on thinking skills • Learning analytics	• Learner reflection on effectiveness of strategies

Table 8.5 Marzano's Nine Categories of Effective Strategies

Category	Effect Size	Percent Gain
Identify similarities and differences	1.31	45
Summarize and take notes	1.00	34
Reinforce effort and provide recognition	.80	29
Homework and practice	.77	28
Non-linguistic representations	.75	27
Cooperative learning	.73	27
Set objectives and provide feedback	.61	23
Generate and test hypotheses	.61	23
Cues, questions, and advance organizers	.59	22

the knowledge to new contexts. In this way, the learners basically "generate" the majority of the processing (thinking) involved in the learning experience (Smith & Ragan, 2005). One scaffolding strategy that can effectively be used for all pedagogical approaches involves instructor *modeling*. Instructors (or the instruction itself) can model the learning task, and then gradually shift the responsibility for performing the task to the learner. There are many types of scaffolding. For example, the way in which the instruction is organized or presented can also serve as scaffolding, by either mirroring the inherent organization of the content and facilitating learner encoding, or by sequencing the content to reflect a procedure or process to be mastered.

The decision on when to provide more or less scaffolding is a complex one, determined by learner and task characteristics and the instructional context. Table 8.6 illustrates a decision chart that provides guidance on when to use higher and lower levels of scaffolding. In general, you should use more scaffolding when information is complex or when you are instructing novice learners (Kirschner, Sweller, & Clark, 2006), and gradually transition to activities with less scaffolding as learners develop expertise, or when you want to encourage the use of critical thinking skills.

Job aids or *quick reference aids* represent a type of scaffold that focuses on supporting and improving performance. Job aids are generally less costly and time-consuming to develop, implement, and update, and should be used instead of more extensive instruction when:

- Reliance on memory is not essential;
- Its use would enable the task to be performed more efficiently;
- There are a substantial number of steps involved in the job task;
- The activity or task is performed infrequently; and
- The performance involved is complex and there are competing or conflicting activities (unless there is a requirement that the task be performed rapidly) (Lineberry, 1980).

Job aids are often provided without accompanying instruction, but when instruction is provided, it is usually designed to teach individuals how to use the job aids in authentic settings. Job aids can be physical or virtual and may consist of step-by-step instructions illustrated with diagrams or photos, flow charts with decision points, checklists, forms or worksheets, or models that guide through examples of acceptable performance or quality. When designing a job aid, orient the learner to the purpose of the job aid, introduce its format and contents (including the knowledge required for its effective use), and give the learner practice in using the job aid.

We've examined how to foster learning through interaction, looked at a variety of strategies that can be used to foster specific types of *instructional intentions* and *learning outcomes*, and examined strategies categorized by *effectiveness* and by type of *scaffolding*. Next we'll look at some helpful *frameworks* for designing instructional strategies.

Table 8.6 Scaffolding Guidelines

Use Generative Strategies When ...					Use Supplantive Strategies When ...		
Context	**Task**	**Learners**			**Learners**	**Task**	**Context**
Ample time is available for instruction.	Complex task(s)	... have higher prior knowledge.			... have low prior knowledge (novices).	Simple task(s)	Limited time is available for instruction.
Metacognitive goals take priority over subject-specific goals.	Ill-structured task(s)	... have high aptitude.			... have low aptitude.	Well-defined and structured task(s)	Subject-specific goals take priority over the metacognitive.
There are no minimum competency goals for all learners.	Non-hazardous	... have low anxiety.	Lower Levels of Scaffolding ☞	Higher Levels of Scaffolding ☞	... have high anxiety.	Hazardous	Minimum levels of competency are a goal for all learners.
There is low accountability for learner achievement.	Performance level non-critical	... are highly motivated.			... have low motivation.	Performance level critical	There is high accountability for learner achievement.
		... attribute success to internal source.			... attribute success to external source.		
		... possess and use a wide range of cognitive strategies.			... possess few cognitive strategies.		

Source: compiled from information in Smith and Ragan (2005).

Strategy Frameworks

Some claim that the ADDIE model is limited in its application and forever doomed to be a sequential and linear process (Willis, 2009). On the contrary, ADDIE works quite well when implemented as an iterative process, reflecting a policy of continuous improvement. If you are seeking to produce quality instruction, you will naturally revisit and revise your design and employ formative evaluation to test and refine the learning experiences. That said, different pedagogical approaches (reflecting different assumptions about learning) *do* call for different planning processes to select strategies and ways to address content and learning experiences. The key is find and use guidelines (like those in Table 8.3) and a framework that will help you identify strategies to foster the type of learning outcomes you've identified, whether you are using one or several pedagogical approaches. There are several authoritative books and a wealth of web resources on models and frameworks available for use in planning learning strategies (search, for example, "lesson planning frameworks"). A list of resources is provided on the book website for several excellent frameworks and models, including a list of framework resources for problem-based learning, inquiry learning, anchored instruction, cognitive apprenticeship, and more. An effective framework should prompt you to plan for all the major elements of the learning process that a particular pedagogical approach stresses. Five specific frameworks are described in this chapter. They are labeled by pedagogical approach, but with a little reflection you can adjust any of them to use with a different approach or a combination of approaches:

- Gagné's (1965) Nine Events of Instruction (Instructivist approach)
- BSCS Five Es Instructional Model (Constructivist approach)
- Connectivist Learning Environments (Connectivist approach)
- Keller's (1983, 1987) ARCS Motivation Model (use with any approach)
- Scenario Planning Guidelines (use with any approach).

Gagné's (1965) Nine Events of Instruction

For an Instructivist approach to designing a treatment and selecting strategies, one of the most helpful frameworks for planning is Gagné's (1965) Nine Events of Instruction. Robert Gagné (1916–2002) was a seminal thinker in the development of instructional theory and he influenced a generation of educators. His methods are still widely used, having weathered changes in IDT theory and technology for close to fifty years. Gagné identified five types of learning (covered in Chapter 5) and identified a set of internal and external conditions to foster learning that is based on both Behaviorist and Cognitivist assumptions. A close examination of these internal and external conditions (listed in Table 8.7) illustrates why Gagné's work is considered a bridge between Behaviorist and Cognitivist theory. The internal *Conditions for Learning* reflect Cognitive Information Processing (CIP) theory, and the external conditions, or *Nine Events of Instruction*, reflect a Behaviorist emphasis on designing an environment conducive to learning (Gagné, Briggs, & Wager, 1992). As a result, the Nine Events work well as a framework for designing Instructivist learning experiences. Table 8.7 lists generic strategies for use with each of the Nine Events, and the website for this chapter features another version of the chart for use as a planning worksheet. Table 8.8 features an example of a lesson plan that uses Gagné's Nine Events of Instruction as a framework.

Spector (2012) cites Gagné's (1985) Nine Events of Instruction as one of three frameworks he feels have wide applicability for instructional designs, along with Cognitive Apprenticeships (Collins, Brown, & Newman, 1990), and van Merrienboer's (1997) Four-Component Instructional Design Model (4C/ID). You may decide that Gagné's framework works well for you, or you may decide to use a different framework; for example, organizing strategies by the thinking skills you want learners to use (e.g., Bloom's Taxonomy) or by the type of learning they are to pursue (e.g., Gagné's types of learning). You may also choose (or be required) to use a framework common to a specific discipline (e.g., the popular before/during/after reading instruction framework; Vacca, Vacca, & Mraz, 2011) or to a specific career environment (e.g., instructional design handbooks used by various branches of the military), or a template used by your employer. The important thing to remember is that *the way in which an instructor or an instructional design presents and organizes information communicates what is important and can "model" cognitive processes for the learners.* Through this modeling, you can illustrate for the learner how to focus, select, organize, integrate, and apply content as they learn. These practices will eventually foster the development of independent, purposeful, lifelong learners.

BSCS Five Es Instructional Model

The Five Es Instructional model was developed in the late 1980s by Robert Bybee and his colleagues (2006) at the Biological Sciences Curriculum Study (BSCS), a non-profit organization established in 1958 to improve U.S. science education (following the previous year's launch of the Sputnik satellite by the Soviet Union). The Five Es model is "a learning cycle based on a constructivist view of learning" (Morgan & Ansberry, 2007, p. 29), and is designed to facilitate conceptual change by guiding learners as they "redefine, reorganize, elaborate, and change their initial concepts through self-reflection and interaction with their peers and their environment" (Bybee, 1997, p. 176). While it is primarily used to design science-related learning experiences, it has gained acceptance and use in other disciplines, including technology education and mathematics (Bybee et al., 2006, p. 62). Table 8.9 describes the model's five phases, the responsibilities of the instructor during each phase, and the learning strategies to encourage during each phase. While used primarily in face-to-face learning environments, with some adjustments this model could be used for synchronous online learning experiences. The first phase, *Engagement*, is similar to Gagné's first and third learning events, *Gain Attention* and *Stimulate Recall of Prior Knowledge*. What other similarities and differences can you detect between Gagné's Events and the Five Es Model?

Connectivist Learning Environments

According to Siemens and Downes (2008), knowledge and learning are technologically mediated and distributed across networks of connections. To learn, individuals must have (or build) the skills to connect to personally meaningful resources, recognize patterns in the networks, and locate, filter, select from, and manage an overwhelming amount of information. The job of the designer, then, is to build learning environments where learners can practice making those connections and to scaffold learners in developing the skills required to be successful. Table 8.10 provides a framework for planning Connectivist learning environments. The website for this chapter contains a version of this framework with the far right column blank for your use in planning strategies for Connectivist instructional approaches.

Keller's (1983, 1987) ARCS Motivation Model

"Motivation is the process that energizes our knowledge and skills and focuses us on our most important goals … initiating and sustaining the … effort required to achieve a goal … by converting intention into action and … supporting our persistence" (Clark, 2005, p. 14). Motivation is an important factor to consider when determining the type of strategies to use for an instructional design. John Keller's (1987) **ARCS Motivation Model** is a popular tool that will guide you in incorporating motivational strategies into your instruction, and it is also a valuable tool for fostering attitudinal outcomes. ARCS is an acronym that provides a guide for designing instruction:

Table 8.7 Gagné's Nine Events of Instruction

Gagné's Nine Events Events External Conditions	Internal Conditions	Guiding Question for Planning	Strategies to Incorporate the Event
1. Gain Attention	Reception of incoming information	How will you get and keep learner attention?	• Begin with the question "What do you think?" • Use novelty or creativity to present the topic. • Relate the topic to a current event or a subject relevant to the learners.
2. Inform Learners of the Outcomes	Activating expectancy and learner *executive control*	How will you inform learners of the lesson objectives?	• Provide written outcomes or an outline as an advance organizer. • Ask learners what they want to know or think they should know about the topic, then present what you think. (K-W-L charts: Know—Want to Know—Have Learned charts) • Show a video of the desired performance. • Provide a rubric for the activity or task.
3. Stimulate Recall of Prior Knowledge	Retrieval of prior learning to working memory	How will you remind learners of the applicable knowledge that they learned in the past, or their previous related experiences?	• Provide a review or have learners summarize the prerequisite knowledge and/or skills. • Give an ungraded "pretest" on the knowledge or skills learners must recall and use. • Draw, or have learners draw, a concept map of their current perceptions about the topic. • For Intellectual Skills, pose questions to prompt recall of prerequisite rules and concepts. • For Cognitive Strategies, reference related task strategies and relevant intellectual skills. • For Verbal Information, reference familiar, well-organized, and related knowledge. • For Attitudes, reference the situation and actions involved in personal choice, and remind learner of a relevant human role model. • For Motor Skills, remind learners of the executive subroutine and relevant part skills.
4. Present the Stimulus (content or learning activity)	Emphasizing features for the learner's selective perception	How will you teach the information or what type of learning activity or environment will you create to foster learning?	• Give a lecture or multimedia introduction to the new knowledge and/or skills. • Present the content in story form. • Provide a guest speaker. • Present a problem or case and require learners to research the content to determine a solution or analyze the case. • Require learners to take a self-paced tutorial to learn the content. • For Intellectual Skills, display a statement of the rule or concept with an example, emphasizing features of the rule or concept. • For Cognitive Strategies, describe the task, demonstrate the strategy, and describe what the strategy will accomplish for the learner. • For Verbal Information, display visual statements that emphasize distinctive features. • For Attitudes, use a human model to describe the choice and exhibit desired action. • For Motor Skills, display situation existing at the beginning of the skill performance, then demonstrate executive subroutine.

5. Provide Guidance to the Learners	Semantic encoding and cues for retrieval	How will you provide guidance (scaffolding, support) to the learners?	• Demonstrate the skill or apply the knowledge as an example or non-example. • Use questioning to help learners exercise critical thinking skills. • Model the desired behavior or thought processes (cognitive apprenticeship). • Use peer collaboration to conduct an experiment or try out the desired behavior. • Use a physical model or concept maps to portray the relationships. • Intellectual Skills: use examples from many contexts; elaborate to provide retrieval cues. • Cognitive Strategies: describe strategy and give one or more application examples. • Verbal Information: elaborate by relating content to larger bodies of knowledge; use mnemonics and images. • Motor Skills: continue practice with informative feedback.
6. Elicit Performance from the Learners	Responding (also Retrieval)	What type of homework, practice, or learning activities will you provide to help the learners learn?	• Use role plays based on authentic scenarios, and have learners work through case studies or problem scenarios. • Use simulations and games to practice; provide homework. • Have learners provide examples. • Have learners complete projects or construct job aids that display the relevant skills or knowledge they are to have learned.
7. Provide Feedback to the Learners	Establishing reinforcement	How will you inform learners of their progress? How will you encourage, correct, and affirm?	• Correct projects or papers, and indicate whether learner examples are correct/incorrect. • Have peers critique the performance or project. • Suggest alternatives to achieve the same or different results. • Pose "What if?" questions.
8. Assess the Performance of the Learners	Activating retrieval of learning and facilitating reinforcement	How will you know that the learners have learned the material or can do the desired tasks?	• Test the new knowledge or skills, or provide an opportunity to exhibit a new attitude. • Require the development of a project that demonstrates the desired behavior, or provides evidence of application of the learned concepts. • Require learners to suggest alternatives to a procedure, plan, or product presented. • Require the learner to construct a summary of the new information.
9. Enhance the Retention and Transfer of the New Skills, Knowledge, and/or Attitudes	Providing cues and strategies for retrieval and fostering generalization	What will you do to enhance the retention and transfer of the new skills, knowledge, and/or attitudes?	• Remediate if learner exhibits incomplete or unsatisfactory performance. • Provide job aids or memory aids for the future to remind learners of the knowledge or procedures, or to guide them in the desired behavior. • Recommend future knowledge or skills to acquire that build upon the current lesson. • Provide ill-structured authentic problems that will aid future transfer of the learned knowledge or skills.

Source: compiled with information from Gagné (1985); Gagné, Wager, Golas, and Keller (2005); and Gredler (1997).

Table 8.8 Example of a Lesson Plan Using Gagné's Nine Events of Instruction

LESSON TOPIC: Earth Science—Mineral identification by hardness

LEARNING OUTCOMES

- The problem-solving task of identifying minerals by scratch resistance.
- Procedures for checking hardness using a scratch test.
- Concept of hardness.
- Declarative knowledge to include familiarity with the Mohs hardness scale.
- Thinking skills to include remembering the Mohs scale, applying the Mohs scale, and analyzing scratch test results.

GAGNÉ'S 9 EVENTS OF INSTRUCTION

1. **Gaining attention**—Demonstration of scratching a plate of tinted glass with a diamond ring.

2. **Informing the learner of the objective**—"Testing a diamond ring on the showroom display case glass may not be the best way to ensure that you're not getting ripped off when you buy a ring, but there are other reasons why you might want to know how to identify minerals by their hardness. For example, did you know that knowing about mineral hardness can help you select a cleanser that won't scratch your bathroom counter? It can also help you select an eye makeup that won't irritate your eyes. Today you're going to learn a procedure for identifying minerals by using a scratch test to determine hardness according to a scale developed by Friedrich Mohs many years ago."

3. **Stimulating recall of prerequisite learning**—Set out samples of the minerals introduced in previous lessons that will be used in the hardness tests. Use a recall game to review the names of the minerals and their uses with students.

4. **Presenting instruction**—Pass out a copy of the Mohs scale and lecture on the topic of hardness. Demonstrate the scratch test procedure for hardness, using the Mohs scale to identify the hardness of one of the minerals.

5. **Providing learning guidance**—Have two or three students come forward to perform the procedure before the other students using other minerals, offering guidance on proper procedure and results.

6. **Eliciting performance**—Have students work in teams of three to perform the hardness test on a set of five mineral samples. All teams will have the same five minerals.

7. **Providing feedback**—Check one group's results for the class, providing feedback on the results and suggestions for improvement. Have other groups check their results. Solicit questions and clarify any faulty misconceptions.

8. **Assessing performance**—Have students repeat the process individually using a different set of mineral samples. The process should be the same as the final assessment to be administered at the end of the unit.

9. **Enhancing retention and transfer**—provide web-based homework that extends the instruction and provides more examples of mineral identification using the Mohs hardness scale, as well as a mnemonic for remembering the Mohs scale, at http://www.galleries.com/minerals/property/hardness.htm. Provide a "Jeopardy" PowerPoint game to help students review the concepts covered.

- Gain and maintain the learner's *Attention*;
- Provide *Relevance* to make the connection between the instruction and the learner's personal learning goals explicit;
- Encourage the right amount of *Confidence* in the learner so that they make sufficient effort to learn the material; and
- *Satisfy* the learner that their needs will be met by completing the instruction.

You can use ARCS by itself, or in conjunction with any other framework or pedagogical approach. Keller's ARCS model includes both internal and external motivators. Internal or *intrinsic motivators* include things like intriguing or relevant instructional challenges, or instruction that is related to the learner's personal goals or interests. External, or *extrinsic motivators*, include things like praise, money, and grades. The research favors the effectiveness of internal over external motivators; however, there are things you can do in your instruction that will foster both types of motivation. From a review of the research on motivation, Malone and Lepper (1987) identified seven factors that affect a student's intrinsic (internal) motivation:

Table 8.9 BSCS Five Es Instructional Model

Phase	Instructor Responsibilities	Learning Strategies to Foster
ENGAGEMENT—The instructor uses strategies designed to engage learner interest, determine what learners know about the topic, and identify any misconceptions.	• Generate interest and curiosity, raise questions • Assess current learner knowledge and misconceptions **Possible strategies:** Demonstrations and experiments, readings, stories	• Encourage learners to verbalize their questions and reflect on what they know, do not know, and want/need to know • Ask learners to verbalize what interests them **Possible strategies:** K-W-L (Know—Want to Know—Learned), questioning
EXPLORATION—Learners engage in cooperative activities, exploring and creating common experiences to provide a basis for learning concepts and skills.	• Initiate cooperative activities, providing time for learners to explore together • Observe and listen to learner interactions; ask probing questions to guide/redirect, if needed **Possible strategies:** Data collection, model building, experimenting, hypothesis forming and testing, exploring online simulations	• Encourage learners to think creatively about the activity • Provide guidance and scaffold learner hypothesis formation, predictions, and testing • Scaffold learners as they record observations and ideas **Possible strategies:** Procedures or partial procedures for hypothesis formation and testing, forms for recording observations, discussions about what is being observed
EXPLANATION—Learners use their own words to explain their activities, and listen critically to one another, clarifying along with the instructor, clarifying explanations and correcting explanations along with the instructor. Links are made between learner explanations and their previous experiences. Instructor introduces more formal explanations and terminology.	• Have learners explain their experiences using their own words and supportive evidence, then provide formal explanations and vocabulary • Encourage learners to listen critically, clarifying explanations and correcting misconceptions • Explicitly refer to and connect learners' previous experiences to their explanations **Possible strategies:** Questioning, Wait Time I and II, summarizing, graphic organizers, visualizations	• Encourage learners to verbalize explanations to each other and then to the whole group • Model how to listen critically to explanations and respectfully disagree and clarify • Model how to support explanations with evidence **Possible strategies:** Questioning, online discussion forums, critique guidelines, examples and non-examples of supportive evidence
ELABORATION—Learners apply the new concepts and skills in a new situation to build deeper understanding by extending and elaborating on the new knowledge.	• Provide opportunities for learners to apply the new knowledge to new situations • Remind learners of alternative explanations **Possible strategies:** Similar but different activities as those in the Exploration phase	• Encourage learners to apply newly learned explanations, labels, definitions, and skills to new situations, and as a basis for questions, solutions, decisions, and experiments • Remind learners to record observations and explanations **Possible strategies:** Quick reference aids, questioning
EVALUATION—Instructor appraises learner progress toward learning goals by checking understanding through formal and informal assessments and observations. Learners also self-assess.	• Observe and assess learners • Ask open-ended questions to gauge progress toward learning goals • Provide tools to help learners self-assess their learning and group process skills **Possible strategies:** Formal/informal assessments	• Provide opportunities to demonstrate new learning • Encourage learners to use evidence, observations, and explanations to answer open-ended questions • Provide learners with self-assessment instruments and group process assessments to gauge personal progress **Possible strategies:** K-W-L charts, questioning

Source: compiled from Bybee (1997); Bybee et al. (2006); and Morgan and Ansberry (2007).

Table 8.10 Connectivist Learning Environment Planning Framework

Elements	Guiding Questions for Planning	Example Strategies
Goals/Outcomes	Will you establish goals/learning outcomes, or encourage learners to identify their own? What topics, questions, authentic tasks, case studies, examples, or problems will prompt learner exploration of resources?	• Provide broad goals or outcomes, or require the completion of an authentic task or problem. • Provide prompts to enable learners to identify their own learning goals.
Network Structures	What networked environments (social and personal) will you establish, or empower learners to establish, in formal, informal, and non-formal contexts? How will you logistically establish and maintain a vital and engaged community of practice? How will you encourage participation by multiple levels of participants (novices, experts, tutors, apprentices, etc.)?	• Establish a community of practice for in a formal, informal or non-formal context. • Allow learners to select their own networking tools (social bookmarking accounts, blogs, etc.).
Connections/ Interactions	How will you facilitate the learner's ability to create and maintain connections to current, distributed knowledge sources (both human and mediated)? How will you foster interactions between learners, between learners and content, and between learners and the contexts of the network? How will you support learners in building a network of relevant information sources to consult as needed for daily tasks and learning?	• Recommend news feeds, podcasts, blogs, and discussion forums. • Use micro-blogs and social networks to foster social and/or professional networking. Maintain a wiki as a class knowledge repository. • Announce and promote external events to expand the interactions.
Tools	How will you leverage technologies to mediate knowledge and enable learners to extend themselves through tools (language, technology, signals)? What tools are required to enable learners to gather, analyze, and interpret information? What tools are required to enable learners to explain, predict, and communicate results?	• Prompt learners to use network and data visualization tools. • Allow learners to select their own tools or initiate group consensus.
Resources	How will you provide access to expert, relevant, high-quality information resources? How will you guide the learner to authoritative resources? How will you establish the authority of sources? Will you set guidelines or allow the community to critique submitted resources? What, if any, declarative and expert sources of information will you suggest? What generative sources of knowledge will you encourage? How will you encourage and facilitate the sharing of resources? Creation, submission, and exhibition of resources? Rating of resources?	• Provide guidelines on what constitutes authoritative and current sources for your area or topic. • Allow participants to judge the authenticity and value of sources submitted. • Provide access to experts in the field. • Have learners create bookmarking accounts to share useful resources.
Patterns	How will you help the learner to make sense of the complexity and discover meaningful patterns in the mass of information?	• Suggest data analysis and visualization tools. Prompt community discussions concerning trends and patterns.
Personalization	How will you enable the learner to personalize his or her learning space and content?	• Provide models and guidelines.

Scaffold Seeking, Making Sense, and Sharing	How will you support learners in *seeking* information, making *sense* of it, and *sharing* it? How will you model effective connections, appropriate interactions, and effective information management skills? How will you facilitate participant modeling of desired actions, or participant observation of the actions of others? What guidance and support will you provide to learners and how will you "fade" that guidance as learners progress? How will you support learners in self-organizing their own personal learning environment?	• Online tutorials, demonstrations, guidelines, synchronous discussions, and sample networked connections. • Encourage the emergence of participant "tutors" and "senior contributors." • Provide online coaching.
Learner Skills	What skills do learners need to develop? How will you help learners manage an abundance of information and diversity? How will you help learners analyze and extract worthwhile information, make and navigate connections, prune and map connections? How will you prompt learner reflection on skill progress?	• Clarify expectations for learner prior knowledge and skills. • Point learners without prerequisite skills to resources. • Provide incentives for participants to help each other.
Learner Autonomy	How will you foster autonomous, self-directed learners and encourage their efforts to continue learning on their own throughout their lives? In what ways will you allow the learner to govern his or her own learning experience?	• Provide learner choice and options. • Direct learner questions to the group for input. • Promote self-governance.
Diversity	How will you foster a diversity of sources, perspectives, opinions, and inputs? How will you ensure that individual learners are exposed to that diversity and how will you help them make sense of it?	• Recruit a diverse membership, "seed" discussions with diverse/controversial posts, and provide etiquette guidelines.
Openness	How will you establish an open environment that provides ease of access, learner choice for level of participation, ease of interaction, and allows input from external sources?	• Encourage the use of open source tools and provide open membership.
Practice	What opportunities for practice will you provide to learners and how will you do that?	• Prompt tools.
Assessment	If assessment is appropriate, how will you accomplish it? Will you assess learners on their use of content to construct a project or solve a problem? On their ability to find and connect to quality content sources? On the number or quality of contributions to the networked community?	• Provide a few goals or learning areas and have learners develop more specific, personalized objectives. • Provide question "stems" or prompts to help learners develop their own learning outcomes. • Provide a forum for network-based peer assessment.

Adapted from: Anderson and Dron (2011); Conole (2010); Conole and Oliver (2007); Downes (2012); Dron, Anderson, and Siemens (2011); Jarche (2003–2012, 2012); Siemens (2008); Siemens and Conole (2011).

Curiosity—Measures that attract the learners' attention and arouse their curiosity can motivate them to engage in learning activities. You can do this by including unusual or incongruous elements (pictures, examples, or a mystery) in the instruction, by making abrupt changes in the flow or action, or by stimulating the learners' interest by prompting them to wonder about something.

Challenge—Provide learners with an instructional task that is related to their goals and represents an attainable challenge. The task must be difficult enough to maintain the learners' interest but not so difficult that they give up in frustration. Consult your learner analysis data for guidance on the right mix to motivate the learner.

Control/Choice—A sense of control can serve as a powerful motivator. Give learners some control in the learning environment through choices. You can allow the learner to choose the content to access, the order in which to access it, the activities to complete, or the type of assessment to tackle. You should also make the relationship between instructional tasks and learner goals apparent so learners understand the cause and effect relationship between their actions and the results.

Competition—The effects of competition in a learning environment, whether planned or naturally occurring, can motivate learners to engage in the learning tasks, but it can also discourage their participation. There may be some situations where competition is appropriate to produce a desired effect. However, use it with caution and avoid setting up competitive learning situations when your outcomes call for organizational team building.

Cooperation—Cooperation, whether planned or naturally occurring, can motivate learners by promoting satisfaction in helping others achieve personal or group goals. Cooperative strategies are particularly good at fostering team-building and interpersonal skills outcomes.

Recognition—When you acknowledge the accomplishments of learners, the satisfaction they feel at having someone recognize their achievements can motivate them to engage and make the effort to excel at the learning tasks.

Fantasy—Games, visualizing, and using the imagination and mental images can also motivate and engaged learners. The type of fantasy you select should be appropriate for the age level and interests of the learners, but humans never get tired of using their imagination.

Of these seven, *choice* and *challenge* are two of the most effective factors for encouraging and motivating learners.

Table 8.11 provides details on Keller's ARCS model and some examples of strategies that you can use to address each element. The website for this chapter provides other resources related to the ARCS model.

Scenario Planning Guidelines

Authentic experiences provide rich contextual information that facilitates transfer of learning to new situations. When real-world experiences are not logistically possible, are too dangerous, or are financially impractical, they can be simulated with a scenario. You can easily engage a learner's attention with a narrative, maintaining it by providing choices throughout the learning experience. With a scenario, the learner is placed in the middle of a story and becomes invested in working his or her way through it to accomplish the instructional goal. You can use scenarios for individuals or with groups; in face-to-face, blended, or online environments; with synchronous or asynchronous technologies; and for any of the pedagogical approaches. For example, for a more Instructivist approach, you can use Schank's (1996) *Goal-Based Scenario* (GBS) model,

Table 8.11 Keller's ARCS Motivational Strategies

Attention	Relevance	Confidence	Satisfaction
Incongruity and Conflict: Use contradictions, play the "devil's advocate."	*Experience:* Tell learners how new learning will use existing skills. Use analogies to relate current learning to prior experience. Relate content to learner interests.	*Learning Requirements:* Advise learners of requirements (goals and objectives).	*Natural Consequences:* Allow students to use newly acquired skills in realistic, successful settings.
Concreteness: Use visual representations, anecdotes, and biographies.	*Present Worth:* Explicitly state the current value of instruction.	*Difficulty:* Sequence activities in increasing difficulty with continual but reasonable challenge.	*Unexpected Rewards:* Include learner expectation of extrinsic reward (for low interest tasks) or use a surprise reward.
Variability: Change elements including tone of voice, movements, media, instructional formats, layout and design, interaction patterns.	*Future Usefulness:* Relate instruction to future goals (have learners participate in this).	*Expectations:* Use metacognition to forecast outcomes based upon effort; set realistic goals.	*Positive Outcomes:* Provide immediate feedback including praise, personal attention, and knowledge of progress.
Humor: Use puns, humorous analogies and anecdotes, and jokes (in moderation).	*Need Matching:* Give learners the opportunity to achieve, and exercise influence, responsibility, and authority.	*Attributions:* Encourage the learner to internalize **locus of control** by attributing success to himself or herself.	*Avoidance of Negative Influences:* Don't use threats, surveillance practices, or totally external evaluations.
Inquiry Arousal: Use problem-solving activities and constructive practices.	*Modeling:* Use enthusiasm, peer-modeling, etc.	*Self-Confidence:* Foster confidence by providing ungraded pretests and later checks to show progress, and other confidence-building tasks.	*Scheduling:* Repeat reinforcement at fluctuating, non-predictable intervals.
Participation: Use games, simulations, role plays, etc.	*Choice:* Allow learners to have choices in what and how to learn.		

Source: adapted from Keller (1987); Smith and Ragan (2005); Wilson and Linville (1982).

which contains some elements of mastery learning and is based on the Cognitive model of Case-Based Reasoning. You can also use GBS for a Constructivist or Connectivist approach, or you can use the simple guidelines for scenario structure and style illustrated in Table 8.12.

Once you have planned your scenario structure and selected a style, you can select from a wide variety of free web-based tools to create a prototype so you or your reviewers can visualize the scenario. Free online collaboration tools, storyboarding tools, and scenario-building tools will enable you to share your work with others and even simulate the branching progression that would result from learner choices. The website for this chapter provides a list of free and low-cost tools that are currently available, as well as a diagram of the scenario creation process described in Table 8.12.

Selecting Technologies and Seeking Approval of the Plan

Ideally, media and technologies are selected to support the teaching/learning strategies identified for the instruction. Once you've identified a treatment and media and have a plan for the instruction, you should test it, and have it reviewed and approved, as necessary. Chapter 9 provides more detail on the selection of media and the testing and review of your design plan.

Thinking About Evaluation …

Evaluating the success of the instructional strategies you've selected requires you to first look at whether they are aligned to the outcomes and assessments you've identified. If the strategies do not support learners in successfully tackling the assessments, then they will not pass a Level II (Learning) evaluation and the instruction will likely not satisfy them (Level I Reaction evaluation). Failure at these levels almost certainly guarantees that a Level III (Behavior) evaluation and any Level IV (Results) evaluation will also disappoint you and your stakeholders. Consider alignment now to ensure that the evaluation measures you have planned will yield positive results.

Streamlining Outcomes

So in what way can this portion of the design process be streamlined?

- *Sustainable*—As you select strategies, consider the project budget, schedule, and constraints and select those activities that can be implemented and maintained with the resources available for both development and implementation.
- *Optimized*—Using frameworks like those provided in this chapter can speed up the design process and yield a planning form that is easily reviewed by stakeholders. Carefully carrying out the process of identifying approaches and grouping strategies can help you optimize your efforts and provide "chunks" of stand-alone content that can later be reused.
- *Right-Sized*—Be aware that some strategies require more initial effort and outlay of funds than others. Again, seek to not only select strategies to foster your identified learning outcomes, but also select them on the basis of the available resources for development and implementation.
- *Continuous Improvement*—Test your strategies early in the design process with a representative sample of learners to ensure that your approach meets the needs of the learners and will motivate them by providing the right balance of choice and challenge.

Table 8.12 Scenario Development Guidelines

Designing the Scenario Structure
Start by considering the instructional goal and outcomes, and what the learner needs to know, believe, and do to achieve that goal (the KASIs). From that point, the process of designing the scenario structure can be summarized with this diagram (details for each step follow):

Goal, Outcomes, and KASIs → Assessments → Decisions → Challenging Situations → Decision Points and Choices →
→ Consequences → Reference Materials → Feedback/Remediation

1. Goal, Outcomes, and KASIs	What is the ultimate **Goal** of the instruction and the **Outcomes**? What does the Learner need to **Know**, what **Attitudes** should they have, what **Skills** should they be developing, and what **I**nterpersonal interactions and skills should they develop (**KASIs**) to indicate growth or demonstrate mastery of the goal? First think about the *skills* the learner should display (actions) that would lead to accomplishing the goal. Then think about what he or she needs to *know* to carry out those actions/ skills competently (information). Contemplate the type of interpersonal interactions that should occur during the process (communication, cooperation, social negotiation, etc.). Finally, consider the *attitudes* (beliefs, values, etc.) that the learner needs to have about the topic to increase his or her motivation to master the goal.
2. Assessments	Identify the **Assessment** items that will test the learner's grasp of what they should do, know, and believe. Will you assess their mastery based on a traditional test (paper- or web-based questions and answers), through a performance test (using an observation checklist or a self-check), or through the development of a product/ program/process (providing a rubric for guidance)?
3. Decisions	Identify the type of practical and ethical **Decisions** that the learner should make in the course of carrying out those actions/skills, using that knowledge, or displaying those attitudes.
4. Challenging Situations	Identify **Challenging Situations** that would likely prompt those decisions.
5. Decision Points and Choices	Identify the **Decision Points** in those challenging situations and the type of **Choices** that would lead to both good and bad decisions. More specifically, these choices could result in: • The right or wrong use of information, or in failure to locate and access critical information in the first place; • The right or wrong use of skills/actions, or in failure to access available checklists and job aids for appropriate actions; • Actions that reflect appropriate or inappropriate attitudes.
6. Consequences	Identify the **Consequences** of each right or wrong decision (a flow chart can help in visualizing this).
7. Reference Materials	Identify the **Reference Materials** (or job aids) that will be available to help the learner make each decision. What just-in-time materials would inform each decision? This might include documents, memos, checklists, data tables, guidelines, standards and best practices, photos, graphics, case studies, lists of consequences, and more.
8. Feedback and Remediation	Determine the appropriate **Feedback** and **Remediation** necessary to guide the learner in making correct decisions.

(continued on next page)

Table 8.12 Continued

Selecting the Scenario Style
Scenario style consists of the basic storyline and setting, the learner orientation and "hook," and the point of view and voice used.

1. Basic Storyline and Setting	To enhance learner knowledge transfer and use, align the **storyline and setting** to the performance context you've identified for the instruction. Use rich yet concise language to tell the story and use illustrations to visually support the narrative. Language and illustrations should work together to convey the setting and context. The structure and decision points help define the events that should occur and your learner analysis data should inform the definition of any characters used in the story to enable your learners to relate to and engage in the narrative. Consider how you will identify the choices for the learner, how you will relate the consequences of their choices and how you will guide the learner to critical content through the choices and consequences. It's good to identify and build to a climax of some kind so that the learner doesn't just move from one trivial challenge to the next. The climax could be a particularly funny event, an ethical dilemma, a tragic event, or even a change in how choices are presented. Finally, identify a "hook" that will draw the learner into the scenario, and a satisfying ending that will underscore that the scenario was worth his or her time.
2. Learner Orientation	Begin by **orienting the learner** to appropriate goals and outcomes (either explicitly or by having them consider their own goals for learning). You don't want them to get halfway into the instruction and suddenly realize that this isn't the instruction they were seeking. The orientation should not be lengthy (or you'll lose your learner), and should help the learner answer: "How should I use this instruction?" and "How can this instruction help me attain my goals?"
To craft the orientation, go back to your Learner Analysis data and consider what might motivate or interest your learner about the topic. Grab the learner's attention ("hook" them) and engage them in the instruction by stating facts related to a motivation (e.g., "Cervical cancer results in over 250,000 deaths a year …"), by posing a question (e.g., "Did you know that 89% of companies search for candidates online?"), by providing a gripping visual, or by plainly stating the objectives of the instruction (written from the learner's point of view). The style of the orientation should reflect the learner's motivation and the nature of the content (type of learning, seriousness of the topic, and level of attitude change required). For example, a humorous style may work if you're addressing manners; but if you're dealing with life and death issues like mixing chemicals on the job, skip the humor and highlight what can happen if proper procedures are neglected.
3. Point of View and Voice	From whose **point of view** will the scenario unfold? Will you present the choices to the learner to make for himself or herself, or will you ask them to make choices for a character in the scenario? Both of these approaches have challenges and you must decide based on the audience you are trying to engage. If the audience is varied, it may be easier to have the learner make his or her own choices rather than try to come up with a character that will appeal to a wide range of people. After choosing a viewpoint, choose a narrative **voice:**

• First person—The narrative is written from the "I" point of view.
• Second person—The narrative is written using the "you" point of view, with imperative (command) form sentences.
• Third person—The narrative is written from the omniscient point of view, using the pronouns "he," "she," and "it."

Most literary works use either first person or third person voice, but scenarios frequently use either second or first person voice with action verbs. Second person conveys to the learner that they are important because you are looking at things from their point of view. It emphasizes their choices and the benefits and consequences of those choices. |

Writing Tips: Show rather than tell; keep sentences short; write with dialogue; use verbs rather than nouns; cut unnecessary words; avoid jargon and use simpler words; use realistic decisions and describe consequences to convey the bigger picture; use pictures to illustrate choices and probable future actions.

Quality Checks for Continuous Improvement:

- ✓ Are the outcomes, assessments, and strategies all appropriately aligned? Are they written with regard to the prerequisites identified for the instruction?
- ✓ Do the selected strategies reflect the identified pedagogical approach?
- ✓ Are the selected strategies feasible, considering the learning context, learner characteristics, content, and logistical constraints?

Different Career Environments, Different Perspectives

- In some career environments, there are commonly used and accepted strategies that seem to monopolize the instructional design landscape. For example, for many years the majority of corporate environments had large training departments that led face-to-face workshops. More recently, these businesses have cut their training staff and moved to self-paced, online training packages developed for maximum portability using the latest authoring software available. Other businesses have moved to a knowledge management approach, providing point-of-need information and job aids through knowledge management systems and **Electronic Performance Support Systems (EPSS)**.
- In contrast, strategies used in K-12 environments vary widely due to the diversity of ability levels and the accompanying need for differentiation in instructional practices. K-12 teachers use a variety of whole class, small group, and individual activities, and often have to "aim for the middle" in an effort to balance the remediation needs of students who have inadequate prior knowledge and low ability, with the needs of average and gifted students. However, the push for accountability and the mandate to differentiate instruction requires that these teachers plan alternative strategies to meet student needs. As a result, teachers must locate appropriate frameworks that allow for the use of differentiation strategies; see, for example, the Gregory and Kuzmich (2004) Adjustable Learning Grid (p. 58).
- Instruction for health-care environments uses many of the same type of strategies as are used by other sectors for high-stakes training. They make frequent use of simulations, case studies and discussions, clinical experiences, problem-based scenarios, practice exercises, repetition, and immediate feedback (Cook, Levinson, Garside, Dupras, Erwin, & Montori, 2010). Point-of-care quick references, practice guidelines, and patient job aids are also common to provide support for infrequently performed tasks that require high accuracy. Medical and nursing students practice real-world challenges using if-then scenarios and job aid tools. Since medical students are often organized into classes or cohorts to go through their education as a group, designers and instructors use many interactive strategies to promote collaboration and provide opportunities for the students to learn from each other and form an effective team (e.g., the use of electronic and mobile applications).
- You may also be expected to use strategies specific to a particular field or career environment. For example, there are numerous reading strategies used for comprehension as well as for content-area reading requirements in elementary settings. Some business settings use the Six Sigma management strategy, many of the sciences use fieldwork strategies, medical schools use clinical rotations, and military schools use basic training and tactical maneuvers. Finally, some government agencies and high-risk industries put their employees through regulatory and technical training courses and then require that they pass certification tests before advancements.

Test Your Understanding With a Bloom Stretch

Apply	Describe how some or all of the strategies in Table 8.4 could be specifically applied for Instructivist, Constructivist, and Connectivist approaches to address an instructional need.
Analyze	Conduct an Internet search to find examples of motivational strategies that correspond to Keller's ARCS model, including A—Attention, R—Relevance, C—Confidence, and S—Satisfaction. How would your choices differ for Instructivist, Constructivist, and Connectivist approaches?
Evaluate	For a specific learning outcome of your choice, appraise the relative merits of any two frameworks for strategy planning described in this chapter (Gagné's Nine Events, the BSCS Five Es model, the Connectivist tool, Keller's ARCS Motivation Model, and the Scenario Planning Guidelines).
Create	Create sets of matched outcomes, assessments, and strategies for an Instructivist approach, a Constructivist approach, and Connectivist pedagogical approach.

Diving Deeper

Want to know more? When time allows, we encourage you to go deeper using the website resources as a guide for further study:

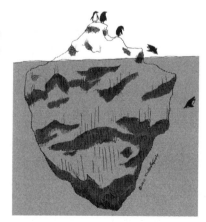

- **Practical Exercises and Examples**—Worked examples and exercises.
- **Job Aids**—Strategy selection worksheets and charts.
- **Resources**—Detailed descriptions of specific strategies and guidelines for using them.

9

Selecting Technologies That Support Instruction

AS USUAL, PEDAGOGY LAGS BEHIND TECHNOLOGY...

Imagine what you could produce if someone gave you a blank, signed check to develop an instructional unit! Unfortunately, it's more likely that you'd be given a budget of $50.00 for media development. Would you know how to produce effective instruction for either scenario, or would you need answers to the following questions?

Inquiring Minds Want to Know …

- What factors determine the type of technology used to deliver instruction?
- How does technology influence learning?
- How do I make the best and most effective use of instructional media?
- What should I remember and understand from this chapter?

    ⇒ The meaning and use of terms like "media," "technology," "media attributes," and "technology affordances";
    ⇒ How technologies foster learning;

⇒   The factors to consider when selecting media; and

⇒   The media-related theories used in the field of IDT.

Jargon Alert!

The terms *media* and *technology* are broad ones that mean different things to different people in different fields. We use these two terms interchangeably. *Media* are used to store and deliver instructional messages. The Latin word for the singular form of *media* (i.e., *medium*) means "middle," and this is a good way to remember that media serve as storage and transmission channels between the sender and receiver in the communication process (refer again to the communications model in Chapter 4). You'll recall that Chapter 1 addressed the dual meanings of the term *technology*, including both a *product* and *process* meaning of the word. When we use *technology* in this chapter, we are referring to its *product* meaning—the hardware and software, or physical *media*, used to convey an instructional message. It is also important to note that there are several terms used to describe the characteristics of different media that foster specific types of learning, including *media attributes, media assets,* and *technology affordances*. Another example of inconsistent terminology exists in the usage of the terms *e-learning, online learning* and *distance education* (Moore, Dickson-Deane, & Galyen, 2011). Not only do the meanings and usage of these terms differ, but the spelling for the term *e-learning* differs, as well. This term, commonly used to describe electronic and Internet-based forms of learning, has *at least* five different spellings: *eLearning, elearning, e-learning, e-Learning,* and *E-Learning*.

Notable Non-Example

So what happens when an instructional designer fails to carefully consider all the factors involved in selecting media and delivery technologies early in the design project?

> *A Mired Media Mindset*—For many years, a seasoned and well-respected professor of Counselor Education—we'll call him Dr. Odom—had taught a Principles of Counseling course that received rave reviews for its applicability and utility for real-life counseling practice. His instructional style and the experiential learning exercises he included in all his courses were credited with building a global reputation for his university's Counselor Education program. Expanding demand for the program prompted the department to offer an online Master's degree. Dr. Odom worked with the university's Distance Learning office to transfer his course to an online format. He was convinced that the course had to be offered using a synchronous conferencing tool so that he could conduct real-time demonstrations and practice sessions for intervention skills and supervision techniques, including active listening, giving feedback, modeling, role-playing and role reversal, and behavior shaping. The Distance Learning representative strongly recommended that he rethink the course and add some asynchronous technologies to avoid dependence on the synchronous system; however, Dr. Odom was adamant. The following fall, the course was implemented in a predominantly synchronous online format on Fridays at 1:00 p.m. in the afternoon. The course enrollment included students from all over the globe, and connectivity issues and time differences (the course occurred at 3:00 a.m. for the Australian students!) were cited as major problems in the end-of-course evaluations. Dr. Odom received the first significantly negative evaluations of his career, and he came to the conclusion that Counselor Education just couldn't be offered as an online course of study. Since Dr. Odom was

a key player in the program, his opposition to the online effort placed his department in a quandary: they could either concede and retreat from the online initiative (missing out on an opportunity to extend their influence in the field of counselor education), or attempt to go around Dr. Odom and risk alienating him. Fortunately for the department, Dr. Odom decided to take early retirement.

Caution!

Neglecting to consider the media and technologies at an early point in the IDT process is a critical mistake that can impact the success of your instruction, especially for distance learning applications where the delivery technology actually is the context. With help from the Distance Learning office, Dr. Odom could have used other media to build a more asynchronous course that better met the needs of global students (e.g., using simulations and video scenarios of the counseling techniques). If you or your stakeholders make critical project decisions prior to contemplating the media mix, your options are likely to be limited and your ability to design cost-effective and successful instruction will be hampered. The selection criteria and recommendations for instructional media and delivery technologies in this chapter can provide a starting point for developing your own guidelines for media selection.

The Challenge

The terms "media" and "technology" refer to a broad spectrum of communication tools used by mankind over the ages. Instructional messages have been shared using available technologies since early times, starting with the ancient cave drawings and extending to the messages conveyed through 21st-century augmented reality and virtual worlds. Today's educators convey instructional messages using a range of both high- and low-tech solutions, in face-to-face and virtual settings, for individuals and for groups. Consider the low- and high-tech groupings below:

- Paper and pencil vs. word-processed files;
- Textbooks vs. eBooks;
- Live lectures vs. audio and video files;
- Face-to-face discussions vs. synchronous and asynchronous online discussions;
- Board games and experiential activities vs. online games and simulations; and
- Real-world projects vs. virtual world experiences.

The list goes on and on. The media you select serves to "deliver" the instructional experience to the learner, much like a straw delivers a milkshake to your mouth.

You may have the luxury of selecting the technology you think best supports the demands of your content, the needs and prior knowledge of the learners, and the requirements of the teaching/learning strategies identified. If that's the case, it probably means that you are acting as the *lone* designer on a project that *you* initiated and that you have *plenty of time and unlimited resources* available to complete the work. If you haven't figured it out by now, that is rarely the case!

In the real world, media decisions are frequently influenced by the desires of clients or employers, budget or schedule limitations, the availability of the media, or by your prior experience with it. There are many factors that influence the selection of media and technologies for instruction, and considering them early in the course of a design project can help you anticipate project challenges and take advantage of the opportunities.

How do Technologies Support and Foster Learning?

Technology can be defined as any tool that helps you take action more efficiently or think better. It includes both *products* and *processes*. Products are both hardware (physical tools such as pencils and paper, white boards, computers, and projectors) and software (digital software programs). Processes cover design procedures and models (including instructional design models). Today, electronic and computer technology allows us to share information and knowledge efficiently and quickly. When such tools enable us to avoid repetitive or time-consuming activities, they free us up to use more complex thinking skills such as analyzing, evaluating, and creating. Jonassen et al. (2002) describe several ways that technology fosters learning, including:

- Serving as tools to support knowledge construction;
- Supporting learning by doing;
- Enabling learners to represent and simulate meaningful real-world problems, situations and contexts, beliefs, perspectives, arguments, and the stories of others;
- Providing a safe, controllable problem space for student thinking;
- Facilitating communication for collaboration, discussion, building consensus, and making meaning; and
- Fostering reflection by enabling learners to articulate and represent their learning in many formats, and mindfully consider where they have come from and where they are headed with respect to their learning goals.

Knowing how technology fosters learning can help you make the best and most effective use of the tools at your disposal. There are other education-related uses for technology, as well. You can use technology to …

- Provide access to content;
- Differentiate instruction to accommodate learners with different needs;
- Gain or maintain attention;
- Establish relevance;
- Instill confidence and ensure satisfaction;
- Remediate or provide access to missing background knowledge;
- Provide for interactivity;
- Help train students' perception; and
- Provide job aids and just-in-time information to support employee productivity.

With all these applications available and new technologies and applications emerging every day, it is important to remember the bottom line: *technology should always be used to meet a specific instructional need!* Learners usually recognize the gratuitous use of technology and may resent it if it does not contribute to their personal learning goals. When a technology is not clearly supporting a learning strategy and there is no solid reason, basis, or justification for its use, it obscures the purpose of the instruction rather than enhancing it. Determine your learners' needs and how technology might support those needs *before* selecting a technology. Doing this enables you to build a justification for the technology you choose, and it helps you to be more accurate in targeting those needs in your design.

It is helpful to think about your plans for using technology as fulfilling one of four educational purposes for both educators and students. Educators frequently use technology as a *productivity tool* to perform administrative tasks related to learning, such as recording grades, administering tests, keeping track of attendance, and developing instruction-related materials. Students learn *from, with,* and *about* technology. They learn *from* it when they complete an online tutorial or listen to a *podcast* lecture on World War II battles. They learn *about* technology when they learn a specific software program or learn how to reformat a computer hard drive. However, the most engaging way to use technology for education is to plan instruction that prompts students to learn *with* technology (Jonassen, 1996b) (see Figure 9.1). In this way, students use technology as a partner, or *mindtool.* The computer is used for tasks it does best (e.g., displaying, storing, and manipulating content), allowing the learner to apply critical thinking skills to analyze, evaluate, and create with the content. According to David Jonassen (1996a), "mindtools represent a constructivist approach for using computers or any other technology, environment, or activity to engage learners in representing, manipulating, and reflecting on what they know, not reproducing what someone tells them. When using a Mindtool, knowledge is built by the learner, not provided by the teacher" (pp. 10–11).

For example, you probably use technology as a *productivity tool* every day for writing emails, grading, keeping track of your finances, communicating with others, and utilizing different software and Internet utilities for pleasure and work. You may learn *about* technology when you learn to use a software program or learn how to use a new digital camera. When you direct your learners to an online tutorial that covers some aspect of instructional content, you are prompting them to learn *from* technology. Finally, if you direct learners to collaborate to develop a comparative government essay using an online wiki, you would be prompting them to learn *with* technology. The wiki is not the focus of their learning task; rather it provides a means for them to collaborate and communicate to facilitate their learning.

Table 9.1 lists ways that technology can serve as mindtools to support some of the categories of effective instructional strategies identified by Marzano and his colleagues (Marzano et al., 2001), as discussed in Chapter 8. The table lists specific examples of how commercial and open source tools—both user- or web-based—can be used to support strategies designed to foster different learning tasks. The website for this chapter provides more examples for supporting Marzano's

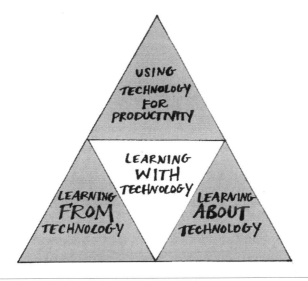

Figure 9.1 Four Educational Purposes of Technology

Table 9.1 How Technologies Can Support Specific Strategies

Marzano's Instructional Strategy Category	Supporting Technologies
Identifying Similarities and Differences	• Use word processing or spreadsheet tables to illustrate similarities and differences; use the "sort" function in Excel to sort by different columns of information, thus enabling learners to see new relationships between compare/contrast items. • Have learners complete a Venn diagram or other graphic organizer (paper-based or online) to illustrate common and unique features between two items (diagram tools are available online or via office software programs for word processing, spreadsheets, and presentations). • Use an online concept map tool to show relationships between concepts.
Summarizing and Note Taking	• Use the notes section of presentation software to share with learners what *you* thought was important from a previous lecture or presentation, and have them compare your notes with the notes they took. • Use online annotation tools to mark up electronic text files, articles, or webpages to focus learner attention on the most important or relevant points. • Have learners use presentation software to provide a summary of their research for a project.
Non-linguistic Representations	• Have learners select a graphic organizer or online diagramming tool to illustrate a concept. • Help learners visualize numeric data by using the charts and graphs in spreadsheet or word processing software. • Study learner concept maps (produced with online mapping tools) to identify their misconceptions.
Cooperative Learning and Feedback	• Have learners review each other's work using the "track changes" or "insert comment" features available in office software, or editing and annotation features available in online collaborative document-sharing programs or wikis. • Teach learners or employees about project scheduling and time management by having them use a spreadsheet program to create a "Gantt" chart for scheduling group work. • Have learners use social bookmarking tools or URLs embedded in spreadsheets to produce a resource on a topic. • Create a "motherblog" to pull the content from individual student blogs into one location. Have students organize their individual blogs as Personal Learning Environments (PLE), using feed readers to "pull" content to their site, and commenting on the best resources to act as curators on a topic. • Use wikis and social networking tools for collaborative work and to provide a vehicle for feedback to and from learners. • Have learners collaboratively create blogs, webpages, or WebQuests using social networking tools such as Squidoo, Weebly, or Zunal. • Require learners to make final research presentations in a webpage format or through virtual pinboard programs, so that peer reviews can be accomplished using the tool's commenting or rating features.

strategy categories with a variety of technologies (e.g., wikis, blogs, social networks, etc.), as well as suggestions and links to specific tools that are currently available online.

So What's Involved? Selecting Technologies to Support Instruction

The process of systematically addressing all the factors and interactions involved in technology selection is a complex challenge, yet it results in a solid justification for your design decisions. Your stakeholders will likely approve a plan for technology selection that you can defend on the basis of valid project factors, but may challenge you on selections or purchases that you make just because the technologies are cheap or are new and impressive. Unfortunately, the ill-defined and changeable nature of design projects can make early or ill-considered decisions seem foolish after just a few days. When possible, strive to make flexible decisions that can be altered to react to project scope changes or new analysis data, and seek early review and approval of your *tentative* plans to ensure that you'll have the required resources to produce effective instruction.

Whether and how well someone learns with a specific technology depends on a complex set of interactions between learner variables, the instruction (Bryant & Hunton, 2000), and the content (see Figure 9.2). For example, the learner must have sufficient prior knowledge about the chosen technology to be able to learn from it, must be motivated by the instruction, and must be capable of mastering the content. The strategies and approach chosen for the instruction should be appropriate for the type and complexity of the content involved. Finally, since the delivery and instructional technologies serve as "channels" through which instructional messages are delivered, they should be chosen to support the instructional strategies you've identified.

Here's a customizable four-step process that you can use as you make technology selections:

1. Consult the project analysis data for information on the learners, the content and the project constraints and resources.
2. Reflect on and identify the support requirements of the strategies and delivery mode you have selected for your design.
3. For each possible technology option, identify its inherent media affordances that could be used to support the learning tasks and strategies.
4. Study media theories and best practices to inform your design (addressed in Chapter 10).

Table 9.2 provides a summary of the details for each step, and more information follows on the factors involved.

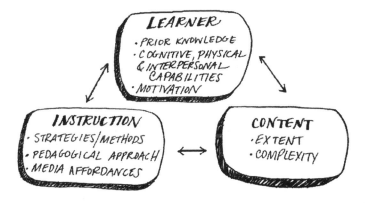

Figure 9.2 Interactions That Impact Media Selections

Table 9.2 Technology Selection Steps and Factors

Selection Steps	Factor Descriptions
1. Consult Project Analysis Data	Consult learner analysis data for information on prior knowledge, motivation (interests and goals), and learner cognitive, physical, and interpersonal capabilities. Consider the challenges involved in aligning the performance and learning contexts, and calculate the complexity and extent of the content. Contemplate how the constraints of the project budget and schedule, and the available resources, will influence your selections. Consider technology affordability, portability, flexibility, reliability, provision for interactivity, ease of use, and appropriateness for the target audience. In judging the appropriateness of a technology, determine whether the target learners and stakeholders will be receptive to it or will resist its adoption.
2. Reflect on the Support Requirements of Strategies and Delivery Modes	The pedagogical approach you take and the strategies you choose to address the desired learning outcomes represent the most important factor to consider when selecting media. Different strategies have different support requirements, and the requirements of a specific strategy often differ based on the delivery mode (e.g., a face-to-face activity versus an online activity, or a synchronous activity versus an asynchronous activity). The delivery mode, in turn, places restrictions on your instructional strategies and content (e.g., for online instruction that will be accessed by both laptop and mobile phone, the size of a mobile screen will restrict the graphics and web layout used).
3. Identify Media Affordances	All media have specific characteristics (affordances or attributes) that make them more or less suitable to support a given instructional strategy in facilitating a learning task or process (including cognitive processes, psychomotor tasks, affective changes or enhancements, and interpersonal skills).
4. Study Media Theories and Best Practices	Media theory and best practice lists have a lot to say about appropriate uses of technology and the design of instructional messages delivered via technology. Studying these theories and best practices will inform your design and empower you to make the best and most efficient use of technology (covered in Chapter 10).

Consulting Project Analysis Data

Your project analysis results provide details on several factors that are related to the learner, the content, the instruction, and the project (constraints and resources). The learner and content analyses should reveal what the learner needs to know about the content, what he or she already knows (prior knowledge and experience), the extent and complexity of the content, and just how motivated the learner is to learn that content. The context analyses and project scope should indicate the infrastructure and support available in both the learning and performance contexts and the resources available to procure and support development and implementation.

All these factors interact to influence your technology choices. For example, if the learner has low motivation, you may want to choose a technology that is new or fun to use to increase motivation. But what if the content is extremely complex and learning it will be a challenge for learners with low levels of prior knowledge or average cognitive abilities? In that case, you should consider the learners' familiarity with the technology to avoid placing additional cognitive load on their mental processing (Paas & van Merrienboer, 1994).

As you consult the data, evaluate your analysis efforts. Are the analysis results adequate or do you need to collect more data? Did your learner analysis ask relevant questions about learner interests, motivations, prior knowledge (of content and media), and attitudes toward different media? Did you determine whether your target learners have the ability to *decipher* information delivered through the media you are considering? The ability to decipher information relates to the learner's developmental literacy and numeracy levels, language literacy level (especially if the learners are non-native speakers of the language used), and physical abilities. For example, exclusively text-based instruction is not the best choice for preschoolers (who couldn't *cognitively* decipher it); audio-based instruction that features technical terms and advanced vocabulary will likely frustrate learners for whom English is a second language; and you definitely wouldn't design small-screen mobile instruction for 80-year-olds or audio instruction for the hearing impaired (who couldn't *physically* decipher the content). This type of information enables you to consider whether there are technology choices that will increase learner accessibility to the instruction.

Your media decisions should also take into account the lifespan of the content and the need and frequency for updating. For example, video instruction is much more difficult to update than written instruction. In addition to the content, consider how different media will support the *learning outcomes* and the *strategies* you've selected. (More specific information on how technologies support learning outcomes and teaching and learning strategies is covered later in this chapter.)

Since your *pedagogical approach* influences the type of strategies you choose, it will naturally also impact your technology decisions. This is another instance where the learning assumptions you espouse may determine pivotal choices in your design. For example, sociocultural and situational theories emphasize that much of our knowledge and experiences are gained through informal learning opportunities in informal settings in the course of everyday life and social interactions, and through social participation in communities of practice (Lave & Wenger, 1991). Therefore, if you are selecting technologies for a Constructivist learning environment, you want the technology to disappear—the more intuitive and transparent the technology, the better the interaction in the learning community. You want the *interaction* to become the focus rather than the technology.

Almost every instructional design project has *constraints* related to context and logistics (where and how the instruction must be delivered), schedule (when it must be completed and when it will be delivered), budget (for development and for delivery), and/or the human and non-human resources available (both for development and for delivery). In addition, you may have to work under the constraints of specific *stakeholder requests* that place limits on what you can do and the technologies you can select. (Previous chapters provided details on how these factors impact projects.)

The nature of the *performance and learning contexts*, and the degree of *alignment* you will be able to accomplish between them, also influences your technology selections. What technologies are being used in the performance context? Whenever possible, select technologies for the learning context that learners will actually be using in the performance context, as well as media that accurately reflect the performance context. The *availability and applicability of existing technologies*, coupled with your project budget and timeline, may also impact your decisions. If the budget and schedule are tight for producing an updated version of an existing training program, you could choose to use the existing technologies to save time and money.

The context also raises issues with respect to the selection of a delivery mode (face to face, online, or blended). The delivery mode is often dictated by your career environment or organization, but once that decision is made there are other related questions to answer, including:

- What factors or conditions should be considered for face-to-face instruction and how could the same strategies be supported in an online environment?
- What mix of activities should I use in a blended environment?
- What should be done face to face and what can be done online?
- How can I make the best use of a limited face-to-face experience?
- Should I use a "flipped classroom" approach? (With a flipped approach, students read or listen to recorded lectures and then class time is used for discussing concepts, clarifying misconceptions, and problem solving.)

Project costs and timelines are often impacted by the amount of *technical expertise and familiarity* possessed by developers with a given technology. Not so long ago, you had to be a programmer and have months of time available to develop e-learning content. That has all changed and you can now find many commercial and e-learning authoring tools that speed up and simplify the development process. Many of these tools fall under the generic label of *rapid authoring tools* and include desktop authoring tools (e.g., Articulate Storyline, Adobe Captivate, and Lectora), server-based tools (e.g., Coursebuilder, Mohive, and Atlantic Link), and PowerPoint plug-ins (e.g., Articulate). The website for this chapter includes links for current rapid authoring tools and reviews.

The familiarity of the target audience with the proposed technology will impact learner ability and willingness to participate in learning experiences delivered via that technology. Logistical factors also apply here, such as the need and ability to transfer and back up instructional material and messages via secure digital means. The amount of influence exerted by these factors is reflected in an often-repeated adage in the field of IDT: "Fast, cheap and good—pick just two!" To summarize, evaluate each media option against what your analysis data and design plan tells you about the following factors:

- Learner needs and characteristics;
- Demands of the content, learning outcomes and the strategies selected to support them;
- Pedagogical approach;
- Project constraints (schedule, budget, and available resources);
- Stakeholder requests;
- Nature of the performance context and design of the learning context;
- Availability and applicability of existing technologies; and
- Technical expertise and familiarity (for development *and* use).

Reflecting on and Identifying Strategy and Delivery Mode Requirements

Chapters 4 and 8 emphasized that strategies are designed to stimulate and foster certain mental processes and actions that are believed to lead to learning, according to a chosen pedagogical approach and theory base. Because of this, different strategies require different kinds of mediated support. For example, feedback strategies require a way to convey messages to the learner; providing cues requires a means of highlighting critical features visually or aurally (Dwyer, 1978); and allowing learners to skip instruction they have already mastered or review information they have forgotten requires a means to "branch" the learner between sections of instruction. Consider both the processing demands of the content and the accompanying strategy requirements to ensure that the delivery and instructional media you select will support the required tasks and mental processes the learner must master or use. Strategy requirements include things like support for demonstrations, motion, drill and practice exercises, multiple examples of skills or concepts, provision for recording learner responses and providing help or cues, and the amount and nature of feedback required to support learner understanding and improvement.

Media choices should also take into account any interactions with the content, strategies, and learner characteristics. These interactions can impact the type and design of a user interface, the duration and pacing of instructional segments, the provision made for accessing instructional materials for review purposes, and the methods used for disseminating and transmitting the instruction.

For example, you may determine that your problem-based learning strategy requires several images to help learners visualize a hypothetical setting and to increase the authenticity of the learning experience. To determine the specific type and format of those images you would consider questions like:

- What is the best graphic representation of the topic and what medium will best illustrate the critical features of the setting?
- What graphics are appropriate for the age level of my learners?

If you are teaching a swimming stroke and decide that a video is appropriate, you would contemplate questions like:

- What video and audio development tools are available that will portray the skill with sufficient fidelity and detail?
- Do I need waterproof equipment to record the elements of the stroke?
- Should I use audio or merely display the required words over the video footage?
- If I do that, what effect will it have on learner mental processing load?
- If audio is required, do I have the expertise and equipment necessary to produce a good script and recording?

For that type of project, you would also need to think about the time available for development and implementation:

- How much time is available to develop the video?
- Are there limits on its length (like ten-minute YouTube videos) that impact its appropriateness for the required content?

Depending on your audience, you may also need to consider whether the materials will have to be translated. For multicultural audiences, you need to consider both the language and any cultural contextual differences that could impact learner receptivity or understanding. It may be easy enough to add subtitles in another language to a video, but if part of your audience would clearly not be able to relate to the visual scenery in the video and it would not be practical to make several versions of the video, you may need to consider a different media choice.

The support requirements of a specific strategy may differ based on the *delivery mode* that you have chosen. For example, suppose you are moving a face-to-face course to an online format, and must figure out how to accomplish the cooperative learning exercises in a virtual environment. In a face-to-face environment, you merely told the students to move their chairs into circles, wrote their task on the board, and then walked from group to group to monitor their progress. For an online version of this strategy, you would have to select a delivery technology such as a synchronous web conferencing tool that provides *breakout* rooms for small group activities, as well as provide a link to a handout or a slide of the task instructions to be displayed in the breakout rooms, and then you would require tool features that allow you to move yourself virtually from room to room to monitor group progress. If you decided to implement that strategy in an asynchronous format, you would need to identify a discussion board tool and provide detailed instructions to guide the students in their asynchronous interactions.

You may find it helpful to begin to categorize technologies in a way that makes sense for the type of instruction that you design. A web search reveals that there are no standard categorizations of instructional technologies, so feel free to invent your own structure (the categorization in Table 9.3 is our own and may help you as you develop a classification of your own). For example, if you design face-to-face instruction, you may want to use a categorization that distinguishes between the technologies used in class and those used for productivity (grading, communicating with students, etc.).

For online instruction, the task of categorizing technologies is a bit more difficult, in part because of the differences in definitions between the terms "distance education," "online learning,"

Table 9.3 A Sample Categorization of Instructional Technologies by Delivery Mode

Face to Face	Online—Web 1.0	Online—Web 2.0	Blended	Mobile
• Paper and writing implements • Manipulatives and real objects • Bulletin boards • White boards • Interactive white boards • Desktop computers, laptops, and mobile devices (phones and tablets) • Projectors and sound systems connected to computer instructional workstations • "Clickers" (student response systems) and cell-phone texting • Software for productivity (grading, administrative purposes) • Software to develop instruction (presentations, spreadsheets, database, illustration, image editing programs, etc.) • Communication technologies (telephone, texting, email, listservs) • Plagiarism detection tools • Collaboration tools	• Tutorials • Drill and practice and assessment programs • Computer-based training and testing • Proprietary and open source Learning Management and Course Management Systems (LMS, CMS) • Hyperlinks • Exploratory simulations and games • Posted recordings and podcasts of lectures and presentations • Desktop instructional production tools and productivity software • Personal webpages • Webpage communities • Forums • Virtual Learning Environments • News groups • Web survey systems • WebQuests • Early search engines • Images, multimedia content, and documents • Form submission • Translation tools • Validators for accessibility	• Software to develop mindtools for learner use • Cloud-based and open source tools and services for creation, mixing/remixing, publishing, sharing, and critiquing, for use by both instructional designers and learners (publishing, video and audio, images and infographics, programs and mobile applications, games, *mashups*, etc.) • Role play and group problem-solving simulations • Blogs, micro-blogs, social networks, multimedia sharing sites, wikis, social bookmarking, review and recommender services, tagging and voting systems • Personal Learning Environments (PLEs) • Real-time voice call systems • Video and audio streaming • Data aggregators, feed readers, learning analytics • Collaboration sites • Proprietary and open source LMSs	• (This category includes many of the technologies listed in other columns) • Proprietary and open source LMS • Communication tools like audiovisual conferencing systems, email, digital drop boxes for assignment submissions, and synchronous and asynchronous discussion and presentation tools. • Group blogs or "motherblogs" • eBooks and eTextbooks • Enterprise learning platforms (institutional administration, tracking, and management for learning, learners, and learning content)	• Personal digital assistants, smartphones, tablets • Mobile phone texting • Augmented reality • Virtual reality • Podcasts, *vodcasts* • Mobile browsers and browser testing systems • e-learning content authoring tools • Authoring tools for mobile applications, for mobile web content, and for cross-platform applications • HTML5 specifications • eBooks, eTextbooks, and audio books • Mobile versions of proprietary and open source LMSs and social media • Learning content delivery solutions for m-learning • Streaming systems • Poll and quiz systems, mobile flash cards, study guides, and learner tracking systems • GPS tours, camera apps, mobile apps and games • Mobile camera applications • Validators for accessibility

"e-learning" (Moore et al., 2011), and, now, m-learning (mobile learning). As the oldest term in this grouping, we define *distance education* as the centuries-old effort to provide access to instruction for geographically distributed learners (Moore et al., 2011), whether that is over the Internet, via cable, or television, or through mailed correspondence course materials. *Online learning* is a form of distance education that is delivered via the Internet (online). Garrison (2011) defines *e-learning* as "electronically mediated asynchronous and synchronous communication for the purpose of constructing and confirming knowledge" (p. 2). Various authors disagree as to whether or not e-learning applies to both instruction delivered over the Internet (or a private Intranet) *and* content delivered via CDs and DVDs, audio and video recordings, and via satellite broadcast and interactive television and cable. We suggest that you use the term that works best for you, but remember: You can cut through the terminology confusion when communicating with stakeholders and others by using a thorough description of the context and structure of your virtual learning environments. Part of the description you use for your context should include whether you are using synchronous and/or asynchronous methods and technologies, and whether you are using Web 1.0 and/or Web 2.0 technologies.

Web 1.0 commonly refers to published, *read-only* content that, once uploaded, is static and does not change unless the owner of the webpage changes it. Web 1.0 content is informational or sales-related. Using Web 1.0 technologies tends to be more Instructivist, since it typically does not include much interaction other than tracking learner progress and providing knowledge of assessment results. However, not all Instructivist web-based instruction can be categorized as Web 1.0, since some Instructivist online learning materials use Web 2.0 technologies to promote interaction.

Web 2.0 is referred to as the *read-write* web (and sometimes the read-write-execute web), and includes technologies that allow everyone to contribute and share content on the web, cloud-based tools to help you create that content, and tools to enable you to categorize the information you find on the web (including social bookmarking tools and tags). Web 2.0 is also social in nature, including technologies like blogs, microblogs, wikis, social networks, feed readers, and media-sharing sites that enable two-way communication and collaboration. Social media and new technology maven Clay Shirky (2009) emphasizes that it is this feature that makes Web 2.0 so powerful because when people change the way they communicate, society itself is changed.

Morris (2011) describes yet another wave of web technologies on the horizon, *Web 3.0—The Semantic Web*. Web 3.0 combines your personal tastes and interests with advances in computer intelligence to enable computers to reason and analyze; to "understand the meaning of information as opposed to simply displaying information" (ibid., p. 43). The Semantic Web is still evolving but promises to improve web searches and functions to provide more relevant information to match your needs, to help you organize and filter the mountain of information you encounter on a daily basis, and to enable you to track your learning progress and customize your learning experiences throughout your lifetime. It is important to realize that Web 2.0 technologies *add to* rather than replace Web 1.0 technologies, and Web 3.0 technologies will likely continue that trend. Therefore, familiarize yourself with the capabilities of all technologies (web-based, mobile-based, blended, and face to face) so you can make choices that foster the learning outcomes and support the teaching/learning strategies you have identified for your instruction. To start that process and get your creative juices flowing, do an image search on the Internet to locate illustrations of Web 1.0 and 2.0 tools used to foster Bloom's thinking skills.

Identifying Media Affordances or Attributes

When we talk about what a technology does best in learning applications, we're basically referring to the unique capabilities that it offers to support specific cognitive processes. All forms of media have characteristics that—to a greater or lesser extent—support the learning processes that your strategies are designed to facilitate. Some strategies and learning tasks can be supported easily by a variety of media, while others may have requirements that can only be supported by the unique characteristics of a specific technology.

Levie and Dickie (1973) first labeled these unique capabilities as *media attributes*. Salomon (1979, 1981) elaborated on their work, emphasizing the importance of alignment between the symbol systems used by the human mind to represent, store, and manipulate information, and those used by media to represent information. You can improve learning by selecting media that facilitate the mental processing the learner must use to master an instructional task. For example, suppose your learners must be able to distinguish between the four chambers of a cow's stomach to remove a foreign object. You could video an operation and zoom in on the chamber to help them focus on the area involved. The ability of a video camera lens to zoom to focus attention is an *attribute* of video technology. Other technologies may also provide the ability to zoom to focus attention, or you may be able to accomplish directing the learner's attention by highlighting the stomach chamber in a static illustration.

The research refers to these unique features of instructional delivery media as both attributes and *affordances of learning environments* (Gaver, 1991; Gibson, 1977; Norman, 1988). Whether you call them media attributes or affordances, a familiarity with how technologies are used to support strategy requirements prepares you to make effective technology choices that will support learner mental processing and instructional purposes.

Figure 9.3 summarizes the iterative process you complete when you select technologies for instruction. Revisiting the goals you've established and the needs those goals are designed to address helps you clarify the main purpose of your instruction. Then, comparing the requirements of the strategies you've selected with the media affordances available enables you to make technology selections that best support the goals. This results in a process of continuous improvement as indicated by the circular nature of the figure.

Table 9.4 provides guidance on how technologies can be used to foster learning at each of the Bloom's levels of thinking skills, and to facilitate collaboration and participation. As you study the chart, consider which applications would be particularly effective for an Instructivist approach, a Constructivist approach, or a Connectivist approach.

According to Spector (2012), "there is no exhaustive taxonomy and account of educational technology affordances, and it is difficult to imagine such an account being made due to the frequent and dramatic changes in technology" (p. 124). However, it is worth contemplating the affordances available to you as you select media. To help you with this task, the website for this

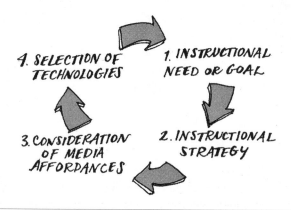

Figure 9.3 Selecting Technologies

chapter provides a multi-page table detailing media attributes from time-honored media forms such as live instructors and print media, to the characteristics of social and emerging technologies including blogs, social networks, and augmented reality.

Studying Best Practices and Media Theories

Once you have selected a specific technology, search out any best practices that exist for developing instruction using that technology. Chapter 11 will address some general production guidelines, but technologies change so frequently that the best source of this type of information is the Internet. (The websites for Chapters 10 and 11 provide links to current sources for production advice and lists of excellent resources on message design principles.)

There are also several theories that address the cognitive demands and challenges of learning with media and technology. Considering how these theories apply to the instruction you are designing can help you make decisions that make the best and most effective use of available technologies. Chapter 10 and the website for that chapter provide information on the following theories related to the design and selection of media for instruction:

- Gestalt Theory;
- Cognitive Load Theory;
- Single and Dual Channel Delivery Theories; and
- Mayer's (2001) Cognitive Theory of Multimedia Learning.

For the sake of your professional credibility alone (and that counts for a lot!), you should really know about two major discussions in our field that relate directly to how you view the role of technology in learning. Both of these issues illustrate the confusion and debate that still rages over the nature of the relationship between instructional messages and the media that convey them. We recommend that you research both issues to determine your viewpoint on them:

1. *Marshall McLuhan's* "the medium is the message"—The 20th-century communications giant Marshall McLuhan is best known for his work on the impact of media on society. McLuhan (1964) distinguishes between the effects of "hot" and "cool" media based on the level of sensory engagement required of an individual. McLuhan and other researchers like Salomon (1983, 1984) maintain that the harder you have to work with a particular medium to understand the message it conveys, the more you will learn. Salomon (ibid.) also found that learners perceive a medium as more difficult if it requires more mental effort to decipher.
2. *Clark vs. Kozma Media Debate*—Chapter 1 provided a brief introduction to the dangers of media comparison studies, which have long been criticized by Richard Clark. His concern over media comparison studies is just one aspect of a larger issue which was the topic of a famous debate between Clark and Robert Kozma over the nature of the effect of media on learning and content (Clark, 1983, 1994; Kozma, 1991, 1994a, 1994b). This classic debate has recently gained renewed strength as Connectivists broach the importance of distributed cognition and the function of technology in facilitating it.

Keeping Up with Emerging Technologies

Every day, new technologies and methods for their educational use are being developed and communicated via the web. As of this writing, a lot of attention is being given to technology strategies to manage the overwhelming amount of information available and strategies for making instruction palatable to learners. For example:

Table 9.4 Fostering Thinking Skills and Collaboration with Technology (website provides current examples of commercial and open source tools)

Thinking Level/ Collaboration	Tools	Example Applications
Remember/ Retrieve	• Bookmark, favorites, and social bookmark tools • Bullet point and highlight tools • Annotation tools • Search engines and alert systems • Video and photo sharing sites • Social and subject matter networks and platforms, blogs, micro-blogs • Aggregators and feed readers • Flashcard and assessment creation tools • Concept or mind mapping tools • Collaborative online spaces • Real objects, visual aids and memory rhymes	• Use browser bookmarks/favorites to mark and organize links to content and resources. • Use social bookmarks to mark content, and share sites and resources with others. • Use bullet points, highlighting, and annotation tools to focus learner attention. • Seek and find content using search engines, and use alert systems to receive notices of new web content on a specific topic. • Use social and subject matter networks, blogs and micro-blogs, and photo and video sharing sites to make connections to human and non-human resources. • "Pull" or gather content from multiple trusted sources, including select bloggers and micro-bloggers, content curators, and experts using feed readers, aggregators, and social media trending programs. • Aid memorization using flashcard and assessment creation tools for drill and practice, concept maps, or mind maps for visual aids and online spaces for collaborative quizzing. • Use memory aids such as manipulatives, visual aids with mnemonics, and rhymes.
Understand	• Search engines and aggregator tools • Word processing software with editing features • Concept or mind mapping tools • Journals and blogs • Wikis and social networking tools • Presentation software • Image and infographic creation tools • Video and audio production tools	• Make sense of topics by using search tools, aggregators, data visualization tools, and trending programs to locate, filter, validate, interpret, and customize information. • Demonstrate understanding by summarizing, elaborating on, and explaining concepts using word processing software, concept mapping tools, physical and virtual reflective journals, and collaborative tools like wikis and the editing capabilities of word processing software. • Present or explain a topic or represent it visually using presentation software or video and audio production tools. • Interpret a topic by using tools to create an image or infographic.
Apply	• Audio/video conferencing tools and Internet-based voice call systems • Geographic mapping programs • Graphics and cartoon creation tools, photo editing tools, 3D imaging tools, multimedia production tools and formats, word processing software, screen capture software, presentation software • Simulations, games, role play, and debates • Checklists, job aids, and reference materials	• Use audio and visual conferencing tools and Internet voice call systems to foster planning and communicating skills and interpersonal interactions. • Use mapping programs to learn navigating, annotating locations with bookmarks and hotspots. • Use image and cartoon creation tools, audiovisual production tools and formats, and screen capture, word processing, or presentation software to demonstrate or record a process or procedure. • Use simulations and games to enable learners to apply learning in authentic contexts. • Use role play and debates to apply knowledge; record, and analyze performances. • Use checklists, job aids, and reference materials to aid in the application of learned material, and to provide point-of-need, on-the-job guidance.
Analyze	• Social bookmarking tools, tags, word clouds, comments, annotation tools • Databases and spreadsheet software • Surveys and web-based survey tools, and survey analysis and data visualization tools	• Categorize and break topics down into parts or group them using social bookmarking tools, tags, word clouds, commenting and annotation tools. • Use databases to explore and represent knowledge categories and relationships. • Use surveys, data visualization tools, and spreadsheet software equipped with a data sort function to and represent information in different ways for analysis.

	Tools	Activities
Evaluate	• Discussions, debates, audiovisual conferencing tools, and collaborative sites • Bulletin boards, white boards, electronic white boards, blogs, wikis, and sharing sites for photos, videos, and documents • Critique sessions, reviews, and rating systems	• Use discussions and debates in face-to-face settings or via audiovisual conferencing tools and collaborative sites to discuss and compare artifacts. • Post artifacts for comparison and post reflections and comments on those artifacts using bulletin boards, white boards and electronic white boards, blogs, wikis, and sharing sites for photos, videos and documents. • Critically comment on the work of others through in-person critiques and reviews, and virtual blog comments, discussion board replies, rating systems, and wiki editing.
Create and Co-Create	• Computer and web-based multimedia production software, and programming tools • Social networks, blogs, wikis, video blogs, social bookmarking tools • Presentation tools • Collaboration and project management tools • Story and simulation creation tools, HTML editors, mobile application creation tools	• Use open source and web-based software to create, mix, and remix videos, audio clips, and songs, and computer programs and scripts. • Use the capabilities of social networks, blogs, wikis, and video blogs to create a personal learning environment where you can curate and share content. • Share resources and learner-created content using bulletin boards, discussion forums, blogs, social networks, Learning Management Systems (LMS), and social bookmarking. • Produce presentations to share in face-to-face and virtual settings. • Use project management tools to collaborate to complete projects of all kinds. • Use tools to create stories, simulations, webpages, and applications for mobile devices.
Participation	• Learning and Course Management Systems (LMS, CMS) • Social networks and network creation platforms, electronic pin boards, social bookmarking, multimedia sharing, wikis, blogs • Audio/video conferencing tools • Email, listservs • Web-based office software tools • Content aggregation technologies (mashups, portals, feed readers, visualization tools)	• Encourage and facilitate participation through Learning or Course Management Systems (LMS, CMS), social networks, electronic bulletin boards, social bookmarking sites, wikis and blogs, and multimedia sharing sites for video, audio, and photos. • Encourage learners to use network creation platforms to start their own networks. • Facilitate participation by using audio/video conferencing tools, email and listservs, and web-based office tools. • Use aggregation technologies to enable learners to collaboratively collect and curate content, share resources, create and socially negotiate meaning.

Source: compiled from Churches (2009); Jarche (2003–2012); and our own brainstorming.

- Thought leaders and designers are developing new technologies and methods for *Personal Knowledge Management* (PKM), *content curation*, and the design of *Personal Learning Environments* (PLEs).
- *Learning analytics* tools, *data visualization* tools, and *infographics* are improving the toolset available for message design, especially when learners must comprehend quantitative data. According to Tufte (2001), "of all methods for analyzing and communicating statistical information, well-designed data graphics are usually the simplest and at the same time the most powerful" (p. 9).
- *Backchannel* interaction at live learning events is also gaining in popularity, providing a record of events that previously were not well documented. Backchannel communication occurs when audience members publish notes and comments to social media (blogs and micro-blogs) during live events such as conference sessions and workshops.
- Learner expectations are being influenced by the prevalence of *Edutainment*—the mixing of instruction with entertaining content (a term which, according to Wikipedia, was first used by Disney in 1948). Fortunately, the increased availability of online production tools enables designers to more easily develop multimedia instruction.
- The learning design rationale for the use of games in instruction, or "*gamification*" (Zichermann & Cunningham, 2011), is becoming more solidly based in theory and research and it is likely that the use of games and simulations will become more mainstream as free development tools become available via the *cloud* (network-based programs and services).
- New standards, best practices and formats for online, face-to-face, blended, and mobile delivery of instruction are being developed, including *HTML5* coding for mobile development and *Tin Can API* (the latest generation of the standards for e-learning development referred to as *SCORM*—Sharable Content Object Reference Model). Tin Can seeks to facilitate the tracking of an individual's formal and informal learning throughout his or her lifetime.
- *Augmented Reality* (AR) layers computer-generated graphics or other sensory information over real-time mobile device displays of the learner's current environment. It often makes use of images, audio, video, geolocation technologies, and data sets to provide information and scaffolding for a variety of educational applications. For example, museums use it to provide additional information on the displays being viewed, national parks use it to supplement self-guided tours with historical or natural images and information, and architects and engineers use it with data sets to help them visualize site information that will impact their designs. AR systems are typically designed for mobile technologies, including smartphones, hand-held tablets and field technologies, and, more recently, head-mounted technologies and contact lenses. Spatial AR systems project images on the surrounding environment and, since they do not generally require the use of personal devices, they hold great promise for collaborative work. However, AR systems require a lot of maintenance and updating because they must align to the learner's environment (you know how annoying it is if your GPS leads you to a street that has been closed for construction!). Due to the fact that the designer has more control over the learning experience, *Virtual Reality* (VR) continues to be used to provide more immersive virtual learning experiences.
- *Telepresence* technologies are becoming more sophisticated, allowing high-quality communication and collaboration between parties separated by a distance. For example, high definition video, full spatial audio technologies and augmented reality systems can be used to project screen-based or hologram-type images of remote experts and colleagues in a very realistic way. These systems are currently used in the commercial world to support high-quality virtual meetings that closely simulate face-to-face meetings. The high definition video can even allow you to see the color change in a person's face when you ask them about that task they were

supposed to have completed. Telepresence systems will soon be used to enhance communication and collaboration in online synchronous courses, enabling course facilitators to do a better job of monitoring engagement and allowing participants to have a learning experience that more closely aligns with that available in face-to-face environments.

Keeping up with recent developments can be a challenge. You should take time to connect to both online and offline sources that can be trusted for worthwhile news on educational technologies and methods. Network with others at work, at conferences, and in professional organizations. Connect with others through online communities of practice, and search out the sites of informative technology bloggers, instructional design mavens, and curators of educational media news. Set up an online Personal Learning Environment (PLE) and subscribe to the blog or micro-blog feeds of experts to pull information about emerging trends into your PLE, where you can organize it for your own use. You can also update the charts in this chapter, create new ones, or locate similar ones online to serve as job aids as you select technologies to address learning outcomes. Customize the worksheets on the website for this book or make them into online job aids.

There are also helpful online tools that can inform your practice and help you make wise technology design choices. For example, Churches' Bloom's Digital Taxonomy (Churches, 2009) and the *Ted Talk* technology videos provide guidance on how to apply technology to address learning needs. You should also regularly search for technology applications in journal articles, books, and on technology blogs; check out "best website" and "best e-learning" awards for inspiration; and review the New Media Consortium's (NMC) annual *Horizon Report* on new and emerging technologies being used for instruction. The professional community for IT leaders and practitioners, EDUCAUSE, regularly publishes the *7 Things You Should Know About* series that provides details and design factors to consider when exploring new learning technologies and instructional practices. These concise briefs provide a description of what the technology or practice is and how it works, and how it is being used to promote learning. The bad news is that there is an overwhelming amount of information on the web concerning educational technology use; but the good news is that an increasing number of technology tools and methods are being developed to help you manage the information overload.

Thinking About Evaluation …

- *Level I Reaction*—When technologies are used in instruction, every learner reaction survey should include questions about how the technology worked, whether it was easy to use or learn, and whether technology issues interrupted the flow of learning. When making technology selections, be sure to consider the receptivity of the learners and facilitators to the technologies under consideration, and ponder the type of questions that you can ask in a Level I evaluation to determine how the technology impacted the learning experience.
- *Level II Learning*—When you select delivery and instructional technologies, consider how you will assess learning. How will the selection of media impact the assessments for the instruction? Are there options that will make assessment or collection and reporting of assessment data easier or more comprehensive? What learning analytics tools, assessment development, and reporting tools are available? Will the planned assessments be easy to access by learners and will they find them easy to use? Will the planned assessments satisfy learners that they have learned what was needed to fulfill their personal goals (a combination of a Level I and II consideration)?
- *Level III Behavior*—Measuring a change in behavior and the transfer of learning (its actual implementation in the performance setting) can often be facilitated by technology. What

technologies are available that can help you measure the use of learned skills and knowledge in the performance context? Can you use technologies to collect learner-report data on transfer? Are there technologies available that will enable you to observe the transfer of learning?

· *Level IV Results*—Because the delivery technologies and development costs for instructional media are often the most expensive line items on the budgets of instructional design projects, evaluating the effective use of technology is an important part of calculating results and the return on investment (ROI). Be sure to keep accurate records of the different technology options you considered and the pros and cons you weighed when making your decisions. Record benchmark and learning analytics data on technology use in your organization before and after the instructional project, as well as information on learner familiarity with the technologies selected, to provide data for later Level IV comparisons.

Streamlining Technology Selection

So in what way can the process of selecting delivery and instructional technologies be streamlined? Here are a few measures you can take during the selection process, and Chapter 11 provides more that are related to the actual development of delivery and instructional media.

· *Sustainable*—When possible, select technologies and media that can be used by other efforts in your organization, and factor in the expected lifespan of the instruction when considering costly technology choices.

· *Optimized*—When selecting media and technologies, consider whether the revision of existing materials is an option. Also, identify technologies already in use in your organization and evaluate whether their use for the instruction would help optimize your project design. Use rapid authoring tools to automate much of the multimedia production process and save on development costs. Tom Kuhlmann, the Rapid E-Learning Blogger, reports in his book on rapid e-learning (2007) that outside vendors charge companies anywhere from $25,000 to $45,000 for the development of an hour's worth of instruction (p. 9). When budgets are tight, technology decisions count!

· *Redundant*—Be sure to select technologies that will provide learners with alternatives to meet their differing physical and cognitive access requirements. Whenever possible, identify low- *and* high-tech solutions for your instruction, and consider producing a version of the main content via a low-tech medium, both to provide a backup in case of technology failure and to accommodate learners with special needs. What backup plan can you enact to ensure that learners can access the main content if technical issues arise? Can you produce a backup version that will also accommodate special needs? (For example, providing written transcripts of multimedia presentations that can be read by a screen reader, and considering how to continue a synchronous discussion if the video and audio go out on your conferencing system.) Low-tech versions of instruction are also often in a format that learners can easily refer back to for review purposes and remediation, when necessary.

· *Right-Sized*—Guard against media selections that are made on the basis of someone's favorite technology (your favorites or a stakeholder's). Right-size your instruction by enacting this personal rule: *use the lowest-tech solution that sufficiently supports the strategies and learning experiences you've identified.*

· *Continuously Improving*—Keep a record of your successes with particular technologies, as well as the challenges or negative technology experiences. Consult your "lessons learned" or pass them along to others to improve future technology selections.

Different Career Environments, Different Perspectives

Most technologies applied to learning efforts are eventually used across all career environments, although the purposes for which they are used may differ. Social networks provide an excellent illustration of this fact. For example, to see how social media are used in government settings, visit http://www.howto.gov/social-media). The rate of adoption of new technologies can also vary by career environment. For example, the widespread adoption and use of search engines in K-12 education has taken longer than in some other environments due to the logistical difficulties involved in filtering out unacceptable content. Logistical considerations may also factor into your decisions on delivery technologies and hardware platforms for specific geographic locations, where either the availability of connectivity or prevalence of certain preferred hardware platforms—such as the mobile phone in South Africa (Hutton, 2011)—necessitate different technology choices.

Technology decisions are also impacted by the popularity of certain tools in various career environments. With respect to social networks, LinkedIn® is bylined as the "world's largest professional network" and is more popular for networking in business environments than is the otherwise highly popular Facebook®. Often, popularity varies geographically. Facebook® is clearly the most popular general-purpose social networking site in the United States and in many other countries (Stevens, 2008), but it is banned in China, where QZone® is the leading social network (Cosenza, 2012). Depending on your instructional goals, you might also decide to create or use an existing special use social network. Either way, technology selections should always include consideration of the lifespan of the instruction and whether a particular technology is likely to be around or be supported for that long.

While medical education continues to emphasize clinical, face-to-face training (e.g., the first two years of medical school are typically face to face), they also make use of a wide variety of technologies to deliver content and promote interaction between students. Medical school textbooks are often web-based and allow students to search, pull out, and annotate information for both present and future use, and they use some of the most sophisticated simulation systems and mannequins available. These schools typically use learning management and tracking and assessment systems designed specifically for the health-care field (e.g., Ilios®, KnowledgeMap®, One45®, TUSK®, LCMS+®, OASIS® On-line Applicant Status and Information System, and OpalQM® quality management system, and E*Value® residency management system).

Do your research and determine what technologies are commonly used in your career environment and locality. Remember that the choices of other organizations in your field, preferences typical of your locality, and kinds of instructional applications may reflect logistical or practical factors that should be considered in your decisions.

In the business world, technology tools often serve an educational purpose (delivering training, tracking employee professional development, providing productivity information), as well as a marketing function. New uses for existing and emerging technologies are constantly being developed. According to Haig (2011) private sector organizational use of technology is continuing to evolve most noticeably in these areas:

- *E-learning*—Technologies are providing a variety of delivery options for online training and learning.
- *Social Collaboration*—Internet, intranet, and mobile technologies provide a forum for interaction, allowing people to access information, communicate across distances and time zones, take university courses, access executive coaching, collaborate on joint work projects, and manage and supervise remotely.
- *User-Created Content*—Learners are no longer just consumers of information and instruction, now they can create it, and organizations benefit by capturing the wisdom of their

members and employees who publish, edit, review and share podcasts, videos, hyperlinked documents, websites, and more.

- *Just-in-time Training and Electronic Performance Support Systems (EPSS)*—Often referred to as *point-of-need support,* companies are developing and integrating knowledge management (KM) systems, personal knowledge management (PKM) systems, and electronically based performance support systems (EPSS) to scaffold employees with easy access to information, training, reference files, and social networking and collaboration applications. These systems provide just-in-time information and self-paced training units and tutorials. They also capture and store the knowledge, expertise, and interaction of employees for future use and to guard against valuable information loss when employees leave the organization.

Test Your Understanding With a Bloom Stretch

Apply	Apply the information from this chapter to identify both good and bad examples of technology selections on the Internet.
Analyze	Analyze a unit of instruction of your choice to identify the technologies selected and the strategies they were chosen to support. Do the technologies used adequately support the learning outcomes and strategies?
Evaluate	For a specific learning outcome of your choice, identify the pros and cons of two technology alternatives. Which alternative would you choose for that learning application and why?
Create	Create a technology plan for a unit of instruction of your choice. Include a description of all media elements, how those selections support the desired learning outcomes and identified strategies, and the factors you considered in your selections. Use all this information to justify your media selections.

Diving Deeper

Want to know more? When time allows, we encourage you to go deeper using the website resources as a guide for further study:

- **Practical Exercises and Examples**—Worked examples and exercises.
- **Job Aids**—Technology analysis and selection job aids.
- **Resources**—Links to resources and researchers and practitioners responsible for advancing knowledge about topics like reusable learning objects and SCORM, and media theory.

10
Designing and Delivering an Effective Message

ERNEST BRACES FOR "INSTRUCTIONAL IMPACT" BETWEEN MEDIA & MESSAGE.

Which is more important, the medium or the message? As you design the instructional message, you'll realize the importance of having the medium and message working together to support a productive learning event. Understanding the basics of *message design* will help you avoid the potential clash (or "crash," as in the image above) between your selected delivery approach and the content you wish to convey. This chapter will help you focus on maximizing "instructional impact" by appropriately organizing the learning environment to create an effective instructional message.

Message design and delivery is not an afterthought. It's something you think about from the very moment you begin an instructional project. Information design guru Edward Tufte says that "Good design is clear thinking made visible" (as cited in Bisbort, 1999, para. 35). For the instructional designer, good *message design* is clear thinking effectively communicated, whether through the written word, through visual and/or aural media, or by designing a message that appeals to any or all of the human senses. Instructional message design is defined as the "specification and manipulation of media for the purpose of producing learning" (Bishop, in press). So much research and development has been done in the realm of instructional message design that it has seemingly become its own discipline. As with learning theories, there are entire books written on the subject by researchers and practitioners from a variety of disciplines who regularly present new developments that impact practice. By streamlining the topic of message design to fit in one chapter, we are likely omitting important work that you might want to use in your IDT practice, so be sure to refer to our companion website for additional resources and references to continue to build your knowledge base. Also, a caveat—many efforts in the realm of message design focus primarily on the visual design aspects. We interpret the term more broadly to include all forms of information presentation, from the spoken word to virtual worlds—all possible types of educational communication.

Inquiring Minds Want to Know ...

- What are the characteristics of an effective instructional message?
- What factors should I consider when designing the presentation and flow of an instructional message?
- What theories inform the design of instructional messages?
- What should I remember and understand from this chapter?

  ⇒ The guidelines for designing effective instructional messages;
  ⇒ The factors to consider when designing the flow of instruction and how to design delivery media that will support that flow; and
  ⇒ The process for evaluating the effectiveness of message design decisions.

Jargon Alert!

Guidelines for message design have evolved from a wide range of fields, including instructional technology, graphic arts, educational psychology, human-computer interaction, and visual literacy. As a result, there are a variety of terms that refer to planning and developing effective instructional messages, including *information design*, *visual design*, and *graphic design*, just to name a few. Realize, too, that many terms used in message design originated in the publishing and photographic industries. Fortunately, many of these terms have been standardized by the proprietary and open source software programs that are now available.

Notable Non-Examples

So what happens when an instructional designer fails to carefully design the message presentation and does not give sufficient consideration to the selection of delivery technologies? Take a look at these non-examples to see what *not* to do when designing instruction:

An Aborted Early Adoption—About a year after the 2003 introduction of the popular 3D virtual world Second Life (SL), the educational technology coordinator of Logan City School District became excited about using SL to support collaboration in K-12 classrooms. He was eager to help the system's teachers adopt the use of SL in their classrooms, given its great instructional potential. In order to introduce the teachers to this virtual reality-based forum, he planned an online training session to give the educators the chance to engage in a real-time SL conference so they could learn about the features and educational possibilities. Excited teachers from all over the district signed up to participate in the virtual workshop, but shortly after logging in they became frustrated and disengaged. They had no prior knowledge of how to manipulate their avatar to maneuver through the school's "SL island," and there was no clear indication of how to get to the designated virtual classroom space within SL for the training event. There were no visual cues to guide their navigation and the complexity of the environment made it nearly impossible to figure out how to get assistance. The teachers were expecting to converse and ask questions using the audio communication channel, but were dismayed to learn that, due to system constraints, they would have to communicate solely through the text chat feature. After thirty minutes of attempting to assist teachers individually using only the virtual chat tool, the coordinator decided to cancel the remainder of the session. He announced that he would rethink the workshop design and the design of the SL learning space to guide teachers in their early learning about the virtual world system.

Conflicting Design Priorities—A veterinary professor worked collaboratively with an instructional development team to create case-based software to help students learn to diagnose diseases. The program presented a case with a description of a sick animal and a set of correlating laboratory results. After students studied the lab results related to the case, they were to identify the animal's symptoms using specific clinical terms. The team's interface designer drafted a prototype of the program with a drop-down menu that students could use to select appropriate symptoms. As the professor reviewed this portion of the prototype, she became agitated and complained that the design did not align with the requirement that students be able to recall the symptoms from memory and accurately spell them. The interface designer expressed his concern that students would not be able to progress to the diagnosis stage if they correctly identified the symptom, but misspelled it. Clearly, the professor's instructional design and the team member's interface design were at odds. In the end, priority was given to a "fill in the blank" interface design that would support the professor's targeted learning outcome of accurately identifying and spelling the symptoms.

Caution!

A critical mistake in the IDT process is to neglect the mindful design of the message presentation until very late in the process. Waiting on these tasks until after other critical project decisions have been made can limit your options and hamper your ability to design an effective instructional message. Another common mistake is to think that a presentation and flow that makes sense to you will automatically also be intuitive for the learner. As you can see from these real-life examples, a well-planned learning event can inadvertently be compromised by the organization or presentation of the instructional information. Take note of the media selection criteria and recommendations for message design and flow presented in this chapter, and you can avoid having your instructional designs labeled as notable non-examples.

Characteristics of an Effective Instructional Message

In planning and organizing your learning experience, it's helpful to know that there are two primary characteristics of an effective instructional message: *accessibility* and *support of your overall design plan*. Both of these aspects are, in turn, supported by your knowledge of learning theories that relate specifically to the effective design of instructional messages. We address how to make learning accessible and how to support your design plan later in the chapter, but here's a brief overview of four theories that can enhance your ability to design effective messages.

Gestalt

Gestalt is the German word for "form," "essence," or "shape" (Betteridge, 1965). Gestalt psychology had its genesis in the early 1900s, through publications and experiments conducted by Max Wertheimer (1923), Kurt Koffka (1935), and Wolfgang Köhler (1929). Their writings and research form the foundation for the modern study of perception. The basic idea behind this branch of psychology is that the brain is holistic, and has self-organizing tendencies that enable it to understand external stimuli as a whole form rather than as parts. You can apply this theory to your practice of IDT by using Gestalt grouping laws in the design of your instructional messages. These grouping laws address visual stimuli, but there are also similar laws that have been proposed for other stimuli, including aural, tactile, gustatory, and olfactory stimuli (Bregman, 1990; Kubovy & van Valkenburg, 2001). Wertheimer (1923) was the first to introduce these visual Gestalt principles or laws of grouping, and he and others continued to study visual perception and refine the laws (Köhler, 1929; Koffka, 1935; Metzger, 1936/2006).

A related concept is that of *figure/ground perception*, which refers to the ability of the viewer to distinguish an object from its surrounding background (Rubin, 1915/1921). Color combinations, shading, placement, and other design decisions can affect how easy it is to perceive an object or figure from the background (the artistic work of M.C. Escher illustrates how the distinction between figure and ground can sometimes be quite ambiguous). Since some learners have difficulty with figure/ground associations, you can use the grouping laws to organize and display information in a way that helps them distinguish between objects. The grouping laws most often discussed and applied by instructional designers include:

- *Proximity*—You can help learners see many elements as being part of a whole if you group them in close proximity to each other.
- *Closure*—You can help learners perceive items as being part of a whole by visually grouping or coloring them as parts of a closed figure.
- *Continuity*—You can help learners see individual items as part of a whole by aligning them visually with each other.
- *Similarity*—You can help learners perceive things as a group by displaying them using similar visual attributes including color, size, orientation, shape, or degree of lightness/darkness.
- *Simplicity*—You can use symmetry, regularity, and smoothness to organize elements and help learners perceive them as simple, coherent figures.

Refer to the website for this chapter for examples of these grouping laws and ideas for using them to design effective messages. The website also provides resources that will allow you to further investigate the use of Gestalt principles in your message design.

Cognitive Load Theory

John Sweller's (1988) *Cognitive Load Theory* builds on the work of G.A. Miller (1956), who was the first to suggest that our working memory is limited in how much information it can process. Cognitive load theory defines three types of load on working memory: intrinsic load, germane load, and extraneous load. *Intrinsic load* refers to the type and amount of mental processing required by a learning task, based on its inherent complexity. For example, for a vast portion of the population, the inherent load for processing information about rocket science is greater than that involved in reading a comic book. *Extraneous load* refers to the unnecessary, increased demand on mental processing (i.e., "noise") that results from the way in which the content is presented. For example, extraneous load can result if content is organized in an illogical manner, if nice-to-know information is mixed in with essential information, and if the designer uses colors that cannot be distinguished by a color-blind learner. Finally, *germane load* is processing that relates directly to the content and helps the learner to perceive and process the information more easily. For example, you can incorporate germane load by chunking content, organizing it logically, identifying similarities and differences, and providing visual or auditory cues to guide learners. In your message design efforts, you should seek to:

- Decrease *extraneous* cognitive load by eliminating confusing or competing instructional formats, and irrelevant or non-essential activities and information;
- Increase *germane* load by making content relevant and meaningful to the learner, by using logical organization and by following grouping (Gestalt) and visual design principles to make content easier to process; and
- Manage *intrinsic* load (which is generally thought to be unchangeable) by using methods to increase germane load through organizing, segmenting, and sequencing complex material to help the learner in their mental processing efforts.

Dual-Coding Theory

Allan Paivio (1969, 1971, 1986, 1991) was the first to introduce the theory of cognition referred to as *Dual-Coding Theory*. He postulated that the brain processes visual and verbal information separately using two distinct mental channels, producing separate mental representations for the two types of information. This theory is controversial due to some of its limitations; nevertheless, it has been used by many as a basis for research studies and it is a key component in Mayer's Cognitive Theory of Multimedia Learning.

Cognitive Theory of Multimedia Learning

Richard E. Mayer's (2001) *Cognitive Theory of Multimedia Learning* (CTML) uses cognitive theory to support ten design principles that facilitate learning processing of content conveyed through multimedia. In addition to Paivio's Dual-Coding Theory (1969), Mayer's CTML draws support from cognitive science on the limited capacity of working memory (Miller, 1956) and cognitive load limits (Sweller, 1988), the importance of active mental processing (accomplished by making connections between word-based and image-based representations of knowledge), and the methods used to facilitate effective information transfer (such as worked examples). Mayer's principles can be divided by the type of load involved:

Principles to Reduce Extraneous Load

1. *Coherence Principle*—Facilitate learning by reducing nice-to-know information and concentrating on essential information.
2. *Signaling Principle*—Facilitate learning by highlighting essential information.
3. *Redundancy Principle*—Facilitate learning by using appropriate redundancy to support one mediated form of content with another form, being careful not to use multiple forms that cause a conflict between the learner's processing channels (e.g., support animation with related aural narration but do not add on-screen text, because the learner can process the narration aurally and the animation visually, but the addition of on-screen text introduces an additional visual processing task that conflicts with the processing of the animation).

4. *Spatial Contiguity Principle*—Place the descriptive text for a visual close to the visual element it describes rather than far away, to facilitate learning.
5. *Temporal Contiguity Principle*—Facilitate learning from video and animation by ensuring that the descriptive audio narration corresponds to what is displayed on the screen.

Principles to Manage Intrinsic Load

6. *Segmenting Principle*—Chunk instruction and present it in segments that are paced to match the learner's mental processing capabilities.
7. *Pre-Training Principle*—Present foundational terms and essential characteristics prior to presenting a narrated multimedia presentation that features those terms and characteristics to facilitate learning.
8. *Modality Principle*—To avoid conflicts in mental processing, present graphics with aural narration rather than graphics with printed text.

Principles to Foster Germane Load

9. *Multimedia Principle*—facilitate learner connections between their verbal and pictorial models of content by using both words and pictures.
10. *Personalization Principle*—facilitate learning by using a more informal, conversational style of communication.

Throughout this chapter we will provide examples of how you can apply these theories in your message designs. You can also refer to the website for this chapter for more examples and for suggested resources that will guide you in investigating these theories further (see, for example, Clark & Mayer, 2008).

Making Learning Accessible

The first stage in effective message design is ensuring that the content and activities are *accessible* to the learner. When instruction is accessible, the learner can access it technically, physically, and cognitively. From a technical perspective, you must design the instruction so that learners can easily retrieve it and utilize it. In the first Notable Non-Example, the failure of the technology coordinator's SL workshop was due, in part, to the fact that participants didn't have access to the audio channel for real-time, synchronous communication. Without that feature, the teachers had to rely on conveying their technical problems via the text chat. The technology coordinator was also limited to using the chat tool as he attempted to help the participants resolve their technical issues. While text chats are effective in some situations, in this learning context the participants needed the ability to engage in real-time, detailed conversation to support their troubleshooting efforts. The technology coordinator might have had more success if he had planned a face-to-face workshop where participants explored the virtual world using their own workstations or laptops, and could receive one-on-one help from several knowledgeable assistants.

To access instruction physically and cognitively (mentally), the learner must be able to perceive the instructional message so that it can be processed. Much has been written about the phenomenon of perception and its role in creating educational products (Alessi & Trollip, 2001; Barry, 1994; Fleming & Levie, 1993; Lohr, 2003; Rieber, 1994; Winn, 1993). Winn states that "perception can be thought of as a set of physiological and psychological processes by means of which we make sense of our environment" (p. 57). As he goes on to indicate, perception is the earliest stage of cognition and, as such, it predetermines what happens later in the processing of information. Often, we think of perception as primarily visual, but our perceptions are influenced by inputs from all our senses. Perception can vary by individual, so it is important to consider how to help learners with differing physical and mental abilities access the intended communication and effectively process it. Thankfully, experts in the area of message design have devised strategies to address perceptual needs to enhance access for learners (Clark & Lyons, 2004; Lohr, 2003).

Another aspect of cognitive access relates to the learner's ability to encode, understand, and retrieve the instructional communication once it is incorporated into memory (Alessi & Trollip, 2001). In this area, principles of organization and repetition provide guidance in terms of strategies that you can use to enhance the recall and application of new knowledge, skills, and attitudes. For example, you can use organizational charts or concept maps as visual techniques to delineate relationships. You can also use multiple representations of information to enhance learning and provide access to a broader range of learners. This practice is supported by Mayer's principles of "multimedia learning" (2001, 2009) described earlier. Message design that incorporates these principles will utilize multiple forms of media to represent concepts through words (printed or spoken), as well as images (diagrams, illustrations, photographs, animations, or video) (Mayer, 2001, 2009, in press; Mayer & Sims, 1994). For example, if you use an animation to demonstrate the process of drug absorption into the body, you can also use narration to describe the process being illustrated by the animation. In that way, you would provide reinforcement of the intended instructional message. However, you should be aware that such use of multiple media is not always productive. For example, in an online course, you might have the option to play a narration of text that is present on the screen. Because we process written and spoken words at different rates, this use of narration could cause interference in learning. Also, since the audible narration and on-screen text are processed by different channels (as described by Paivio's (1986) Dual-Coding Theory), and if the narration and visual text are not well-aligned, the learner could become confused and the increased extraneous cognitive load could hamper the learning process.

Supporting the Overall Learning Design Plan

The second important characteristic of an effective message design is its *ability to support existing instructional design decisions*. By now you have determined who the learners are, as well as the targeted learning outcomes, the desired assessment strategies, and the instructional method by which the learners will engage with the content. Additionally, you may have already chosen the delivery medium, which becomes the development framework for the learning environment. Your message design determines how information and activities are presented to learners, as well as whether and how they are able to interact with the learning environment. For example, in the computer-based veterinary diagnostic tool described in the second Notable Non-Example, the instructional strategy included the use of case-based scenarios of sick animals. The instruction was designed to include everything the learners needed to diagnose the case by providing textual descriptions of each animal's symptoms, an image of the animal, and the correlating lab report data. The instructional method chosen (case studies) influenced the message design decisions, such as how the relevant information was presented and what the learners were able to do with it.

As Richard Clark pointed out many years ago (1994), the good news is that, while teaching methods are usually constrained to one delivery mode, they can typically be supported by various forms of media. So, if factors such as logistics or cost are an issue, it's good to know that a little creativity in the message design process can provide different avenues to reach the same instructional goal. To illustrate, our previous example of using an animation to demonstrate drug absorption in the body could also be effectively conveyed by using a series of still images with a text explanation. Given the power of today's computing technologies and the creative energy of the instructional designer, it has become much easier to design instructional messages that support a wide array of teaching approaches.

At this point in the ADDIE process, you have a great deal of information—details about the target audience and their relevant characteristics, the instructional and performance context, and the instructional goal and intended learning outcomes. You have also selected the assessment method(s), the interactions and supporting strategies, and the delivery media. The message design process requires you to consider all of this information as you plan how to convey the learning experience. This may seem somewhat overwhelming, but we hope you will benefit from a "streamlined" approach to developing your own effective educational communications. Read on!

So What's Involved? Elements of Effective Message Presentation and Flow

We've listed a three-step process below for designing an effective message presentation and flow. A brief description of the steps is provided here, and in the remainder of the chapter we'll discuss more about the "why" and "how" of designing your message.

1. *Design the presentation of the message,* based on best practices, principles of good message design, and learner needs and characteristics. For messages with a visual element, the presentation is often referred to as the "look" of the message, but you must consider message presentation for aural, tactile, and olfactory messages, as well, so we will frequently refer to presentation as the "form" of instruction in this chapter.
2. *Design the flow and "feel" of the instructional message,* based on best practices for the use of technology to support the strategies chosen, usability and universal design principles, and learner needs and characteristics.
3. *Test your design formatively* with stakeholders and representatives of the target population.

Figure 10.1 Select Technologies to Support the Nature of the Targeted Learner Outcome

The process of organizing and laying out the content of an instructional message requires you to design both a presentation and a flow for the learning event. *Message presentation* involves determining the form of instructional information and the manner in which it is organized and presented to the learner. *Message flow* refers to how the learner will access and progress through the instruction. Message flow involves navigation, usability, accessibility, scalability, and considering what would be logical or intuitive for your target audience. Together, all these aspects of message presentation and flow are commonly referred to as the "look and feel" of the instructional product, particularly when designing software or e-learning. Designers in other fields (such as architectural design) use the broader term "form and function." This phrase is more accurate for our use, because not all instruction has a visual element (e.g., educational podcasts), and the principles we'll discuss in this chapter apply to all forms of instruction.

Message Design: Presentation

The presentation, or form, of an instructional product is not just decorative in nature. When you design the message presentation (and the flow), you are designing the specifics of the conditions, events, and strategies you identified as most likely to lead to the learning outcomes desired. (Remember our previous discussions of Gagné's events of instruction, Keller's ARCS model of motivation, and Bloom's taxonomy of learning outcomes?) You may have a dynamite plan to provide engaging, online scenario-based instruction that allows the learner to choose their path through the content, but if you use a confusing screen design or one that simply contains too much information, your learner may become frustrated and never complete the instruction. Ultimately, the way the instructional information is physically presented can impact your success in communicating the message, so it's clear that this part of the process is vastly important!

There are several elements that you should consider when designing your instructional message. Note, however, that the specifics of how you address each element depend on the medium selected as the means of instructional delivery. Effective design of the message presentation and flow requires a grasp of the capabilities of the media chosen to deliver the message. In many cases, the delivery media has already been determined, such as an organization-wide learning management system, and so the message design will be constrained to the features of that system. The good news is that many such systems are becoming more flexible in their content presentation options so that designers and instructors are not limited to a narrow choice of message design features. Each design situation varies—in some cases the media selection has been done prior to the message design phase, but in other cases, designers may have the opportunity to select delivery media based on the message design needs of the instructional event. For guidance on the affordances provided by various delivery media, you can refer to the website resources for Chapter 9.

As mentioned earlier, your message design decisions are also impacted by logistics and available resources. An organization may rely heavily on a classroom-based training approach, given heavy investments in regional training facilities. If this describes your situation, you should focus on how to help instructors select and organize appropriate content and how to use message design principles to develop supporting materials that learners may use on the job. Logistics and resources drive a lot of decision making in all aspects of ID, but especially so in message design, given the specialized skills and knowledge required to create an effective instructional message.

Given all of the factors related to the presentation aspect of message design described thus far, the possibilities and limitations may seem overwhelming. However, there are just three questions you need to answer to make these decisions:

- What kind of information should I use in the presentation of the instructional message?
- How should I organize and deliver the instructional message?
- What will the learner do with the instructional information?

What Kind of Information Should I Use?

To begin the message design process, you must first determine the kind of information needed to convey your instructional message. Consider your analysis data and the targeted learning outcomes, instructional strategies, the delivery media, and the associated resources and constraints, and it often becomes clear how content would best be presented. For example, if your instructional strategy requires the learner to label the chambers of a virtual heart using a computer-based tutorial, then the information types are largely predetermined (an image of the heart with the chambers clearly delineated) and your next step is to decide how to organize the message and activities on the screen.

Some of the early work done in the area of message design (Levie & Dickie, 1973) analyzed a series of physical media attributes, many of which were described in Chapter 9 as considerations for media selection. One category of attributes emphasized in this research was *sign types*—in other words, how ideas or concepts are presented, and Levie and Dickie (1973) proposed that information is either iconic or digital. Iconic representations concretely present an actual depiction of an object (like drawings, photographs, video, etc.). Digital representations are abstract, such as the use of text or spoken words (since words or sounds only reflect the object or concept through the verbal associations we have learned for them). In the previous example, a line drawing or a photograph of the chambers of the heart would be iconic, since each of those images resembles the actual composition of the heart. The word "ventricle" would be digital, since it is an abstract representation of this portion of the heart. In this scenario, combination of images and text is a necessary physical element of the design in order to support your instructional strategy of labeling the chambers of the heart.

Levie and Dickie (1973) identified other physical characteristics that you may need to consider in the message design process. The *sensory modality* (i.e., auditory, visual, tactile, etc.) may be an important factor, given the characteristics of your learners. While learners with the ability to perceive and process images can easily rely on photographs or animations to perceive the instructional message, those with visual challenges will need a different modality to acquire the information. The *level of realism* relates to how closely the instructional message parallels reality. Is a lecture presentation an effective way to convey the process of glacier meltdown, or would a video depicting this phenomenon more effectively communicate the idea? Closely related to this feature is the *amount of detail* that you need to convey through the message. Determining the right amount of realism and related details to include in the learning environment are important considerations in the physical design of your program.

A Word of Caution

Innovations in computing technologies provide an amazing array of message design possibilities, including flashy features that contribute to the "wow" factor of your instruction. You may think that a trendy approach will appeal to, and perhaps motivate, your learners (for now, think "gamification" or anything related to social media), but experts encourage us to avoid what Rieber (1994) calls "pyrotechnics" and what Clark and Lyons (2004) call "eye candy." These terms refer to the use of extraneous and perhaps distracting design features just because it's possible. However, this type of approach can just as easily contribute to extraneous cognitive load. When considering using the newest, latest trends to influence how your instructional message is portrayed, think about the good advice in Chapter 9 related to low-tech solutions versus high-tech solutions. If the feature is necessary for learning, then by all means use it. If another lower-tech approach can be used to convey the message, you may be increasing learner access (both technically and cognitively) in using the lower-tech solution.

How Should the Instructional Information Be Organized and Delivered?

Once you've decided on the type of information to include, then you are ready to consider how to organize and present your message. Related to our previous discussion, one aspect of organization is deciding how much information to include. When considering the amount of instructional content to include and how to arrange it, use findings from relevant cognitive load research to inform your decisions. For over fifty years, scientists have investigated the demands on human cognitive processing. Miller (1956) determined that our short-term memory can store 7+/–2 items, and anything beyond that cannot be effectively processed. Since then, cognitive load researchers have emphasized the need for "a universal set of learning principles that are proven to result in efficient instructional environments as a consequence of leveraging human cognitive learning processes" (Clark et al., 2006, p. 7). Research in the area of cognitive load has investigated different strategies to minimize extraneous load, such as avoiding too much information on the screen. Some cognitive load is positive, supporting learner engagement with the planned instructional event. However, we can try to eliminate the unnecessary or excessive information that the learner is exposed to at one time, and one way to do that is by thoughtfully planning the learner's visual field. There are some learners whose cognitive style limits their ability to discern the salient cues within print- or computer-based programs, and those learners are said to be "field dependent" (Witkin, 1977). To address the needs of these learners, the visual field must contain only pertinent information arranged in a way that makes the communication meaningful. In the first Notable Non-Example, teachers were placed in a virtual environment which was filled with excessive information that made the navigation of that program difficult, especially without the provision of visual cues to help learners focus on the pertinent details, such as navigation mechanisms to move avatars through the virtual world. You can help all learners, both field-dependent and field-independent, by including only relevant visual features and essential content.

Once you have determined what information to include in the instructional program, the next step is to plan how the information should be organized and presented. Much of your message design efforts will focus on aspects of visual design, particularly for computer-based or print-based programs. Table 10.1 features the principles of visual message design suggested by Thompson (1994). These factors should serve as considerations as you plan the aesthetics of your learning event.

Design principles are implemented through the use of the features of the delivery medium, such as light, color, texture, motion, sound, and (more recently) touch and smell (in high-end simulation environments, for example). The use of these elements to convey information requires a skillful blend of art and science, as almost every element has correlating design guidance from experts in related disciplines. For instance, Williams (2008) and Rieber (1994) provide suggestions related to the use of color to convey meaning. And, each of these design elements requires some artistic sense and awareness of the technical capacity of the delivery mode to support the planned design. Therefore, while some knowledge of graphic arts or digital art production is helpful, you may have to rely on some outside assistance in the production aspect of message design. Whether you create the educational program or you call in external expertise, it's good to be aware of the elements of visual design, as well as strategies for how to implement them in the message design process. Table 10.2 summarizes excellent guidance from Clark and Lyons (2004), advice that is based on the integration of theory presented

Table 10.1 Visual Message Design Principles

Design Principle	Description
Simplicity	• The inclusion of only essential information in order for the viewer to understand the targeted concept. For example, the use of one illustration per step in a procedure will help learners focus on only the relevant information for that step.
Clarity	• The ability of the visual to clearly communicate intended meaning to the viewer. Interpretation will depend on designer's awareness of audience characteristics and prior knowledge.
Balance	• Placement of visual components to distribute the "weight" of elements equally through the frame. Formally balanced visuals share equal weight on both sides of the frame and can be perceived as less interesting. Informally balanced images use asymmetrical placement of objects, with "lighter" objects at the top of the frame and "heavier" objects at the bottom. Informal balance maintains viewer attention better, as patterns are less predictable.
Harmony	• Defining how well all components of the visual field relate and complement each other. Harmony can be achieved through the use of drawing style, color, texture, size, and text style.
Organization	• The arrangement or placement of the visual elements. Optimal organization will create a clear path for the eye to follow, which can be achieved through proximity and/or the use of visual cues such as numbers, arrows, lines, or circles.
Emphasis	• Establishing the area of intended focus, or focal point, of the image. This principle may be seen in conflict with the principle of harmony, but selection between these principles will depend on instructional design priorities.
Legibility	• The degree to which the viewer can "read" the design, a principle that refers to both text and images.
Unity	• The placement of components of a visual field so that they are viewed as a cohesive whole or unit.
Perspective	• The representation of the spatial relationship of objects to approximate how they actually appear to the human eye. Converging lines appear to recede in the distance, for example.
Point of view (POV)	• Apparent location of the viewer in relation to the visual field. An objective POV puts the learner as external to the field, while a subjective POV places the learner within the field, engaged in the activity or event.
Framing	• Depicts the boundaries of the visual field, determining what is included and excluded. Inner frames can be used within a larger field to isolate certain components of the visual.

Source: adapted from Thompson (1994).

earlier in this chapter with design principles. These strategies are centered on the type of intended learning outcome for your program, broken into five potential content types: procedures, concepts, facts, processes, and principles.

By letting the learning outcomes drive the design choices, you can then consider the principles of message design supported by the attributes or features of the learning environment to create a productive and successful instructional event!

Before You Begin

Whether you are creating an instructor-led presentation or developing a virtual world educational event, it helps to put your ideas on paper. Yes—paper! Duarte (2008) suggests that storyboarding is an essential element of planning effective communication and she contends that using paper to do so allows for greater freedom for brainstorming and enhanced creativity. Figure 5.2 in Chapter 5 provided an example of a paper prototype that can be used early in the testing process to obtain stakeholder and target learner feedback. In addition to storyboards, you can use flow charts, diagrams, concept maps, infographics, and other graphic organizers to help you and your stakeholders visualize the design.

Table 10.2 Visual Message Design Strategies

Type of Learning Outcome	Message Design Strategies
Procedures	• Use diagrams to illustrate procedures that are complex. • Use full screen captures with numbered action steps. • Use narration with animations for memory support. • Keep numbered steps within short-term memory limitations (7 +/− 2).
Concepts	• To teach concrete concepts, place two or more visual examples in close proximity to each other, as well as near a definition in text. • Use cuing features such as arrows, circles, and callouts to call attention to discriminating features. • Use visual analogies to convey abstract concepts. • Make computer-based visuals interactive in order to engage learners (i.e., drag and drop, selections, etc.). • Use organizational visuals to demonstrate hierarchical relationships.
Facts	• Use visual information that will be accessible when needed in the instruction and the performance context. • Group related facts in proximity to aid learning. • Engage learners with factual visuals by asking them to answer related questions or apply the information in an authentic situation. • Avoid extraneous detail to reduce unnecessary cognitive load.
Processes	• Organize illustrations of individual process steps. • Place graphics in their authentic spatial arrangements. • Convey abstract processes using visual analogies. • Reduce cognitive load by providing narration with animations, as well as ability to pause, replay, and magnify key aspects of animation.
Principles	• Develop checklists, forms, or worksheets to guide the application of principles. • Design an interface that replicates the performance context. • Use models that simulate the application of principles. • Combine static visuals with questions to engage learner. • Avoid extraneous detail or excessive complexity so as to obscure the targeted principles in action (as in the first Notable Non-Example).

Source: adapted from Clark and Lyons (2004).

Message Design: Flow

The final question that should guide your message design planning is: What will the learner do with the instructional information? This question addresses the *flow* of the instructional event or program. In message design, flow is the "feel" of the instructional experience and its exact nature depends on the technology you've chosen to convey your instructional message. For computer- and web-based instruction, flow refers to the ease of navigation, the usability of the interface design, and the learner's awareness of how to work through the instructional program or activities. Head, Lockee, and Oliver (2002) describe the abilities of delivery media to support learner engagement with the instruction as the medium's "functional attributes" (p. 263). The American Society for Training and Development (Sanders, 2003) devised an evaluation system that identifies some of these factors in considering the effectiveness of e-learning programs. Their interface design standards center on the following questions:

- *Orientation*—Does the design indicate to learners where they are in the program?
- *Tracking*—Does the design indicate to learners what instruction they have begun and what units they have completed?
- *Navigation*—Does the design allow the learner to easily start, exit, move forward, move backward, save, and return to top level of the course as they wish?

- *Optional navigation devices*—Does the design permit learners to access additional information or to mark their location within a program?
- *Operational support*—Does the design provide easy access to technical assistance?

These guiding questions can serve your message design efforts as you consider the flow of the activities within the instructional event and design how learners will engage with the activities and content.

Flow should also be planned from the "macro" perspective. In other words, it's important to consider how the program or learning event will be accessed and delivered in a general sense and how its message design features may impact learner participation and program scalability. For example, if computer-based training is developed to include audio narration and to be delivered asynchronously, will all learners have access to equipment to control the audio output, such as speakers or headphones? If learners will engage in the program at their desks, headphones may be essential so as to not impact their surrounding colleagues. For programs that require heavy bandwidth because of a high level of realism incorporated into the design, will learners have access to that necessary bandwidth on the receiving end, particularly in remote locations? These kinds of technical and logistical aspects of message design should be determined as soon as possible in the planning process so that the final instructional product or event won't be limited in its use due to these kinds of factors.

You can use the following chart as a job aid to help you address the applicable principles of effective message design. As you have read in this chapter, the presentation and flow of your instruction can be guided by the three questions in the left column, questions related to access and instructional design support. Use Table 10.3 to specify ID considerations that should have priority in your planning, and then jot down some message design strategies related to how you will convey the content and activities based on those considerations.

Table 10.3 Message Design Planning Aid

Guiding Questions	ID Considerations	Message Design Strategies
• **Type of information**: What kind of information should be used in the presentation of the instructional message?		
• **Organization and Delivery**: How should the instructional message be organized and delivered?		
• **Use of the Content**: What will the learner do with the instructional information?		

Thinking About Evaluation ...

A bad message design can often ruin or obscure an instructional message. If you fail to consider and formatively test the message design elements of your instruction prior to implementation, you can jeopardize your attempts to measure learner reaction to your instruction (Level I), learning (Level II), a change in behavior or transfer of learning (Level III), and the ultimate results or impact of the instruction on your organization (Level IV). For example, your instruction may be topnotch, fun, and engaging, but if your color scheme is distracting, learner reactions will probably be negative (Level I). If a course is poorly organized or contains too much extraneous information, the results of learner assessments will likely not reflect adequate learning (Level II). If you use a virtual world to train employees but do not pay adequate attention to mirroring the performance context, learner transfer will suffer (Level III). Finally, if the message design approach is not scalable because of high-end visualization techniques, it will be difficult to realize results that impact the entire organization without reaching a critical mass of learners (Level IV).

To ensure that your message design is accessible and supportive of your instructional design, consider these formative evaluation criteria offered by Lohr (2003). While her criteria were initially designed for visual evaluation, they work well for general message design principles as well. When you pilot test your plans with representative learners, ask them the following questions:

1. Effectiveness

    a. Does the design address the content accurately?
    b. Does the design portray an appropriate amount of information?
    c. Does the design convey the intended learning outcome?

2. Efficiency

    a. Does the design make key information accessible to the learner?
    b. Does the design help the learner connect the information to learning or performance context?
    c. Does the organization of the design convey the necessary sequence or hierarchy of information?

3. Appeal

    a. Is all information important and relevant to the learner?
    b. Is the information aesthetically appealing? If not, what should be modified, added, or eliminated?
    c. Does the design attract and maintain the learner's attention?

Asking these questions of a few learners from your target audience can provide valuable information in terms of necessary revisions to make the instructional message design more effective. While formative evaluation is important throughout the ID process, its use is critical during message design to ensure that the "look and feel" of the final product supports learning instead of obscuring the instructional message.

Streamlining Message Design

So in what way can the process of designing the message and delivery be streamlined? Here's a list of things you can do to make this process more …

- *Sustainable*—When designing the learning context and the instructional message, think about the longevity of the instructional content, as well as the delivery mode and the need to maintain the instruction. Select a design that will be sustainable in the future.
- *Optimized*—Message design is all about optimizing the effectiveness of the instructional message. By using principles featured in this chapter, you can select the optimal arrangement of the content and activities to ensure the accessibility and effectiveness of the learning event.
- *Redundant*—As Mayer (2001) points out, redundancy can help reinforce the instructional content. Use his evidence-based multimedia learning principles to design programs that incorporate redundant information in a supportive and effective way.
- *Right-Sized*—The "size" of the instructional event can refer to different aspects of the message design. In terms of the amount of content, you must be careful to present information

in a manner that aligns with the learner's capacity to process information, avoiding cognitive overload. From a technological perspective, message design decisions can also impose processing demands on the instructional delivery system, causing a literal system overload. Be sure that your delivery mode will support the kinds of message design approaches and features that you have planned before launching into full-scale development. You should also consider the systems that the learner will be using. For example, if the target learner is likely to have limited bandwidth, you should avoid large-sized images that will increase the time required to download and display those images.

• *Continuously Improving*—Utilizing formative evaluation will help ensure that your message design plans meet learner needs and adequately facilitate the learning experience. Don't forgo this stage—it's essential for success!

Different Career Environments, Different Perspectives

Perhaps more so than any other phase of the design process, message design can require a diverse set of skills. As Morrison, Ross, and Kemp (2007) point out, in larger corporate settings, message design may be a team effort, with personnel specializing in graphic arts, print production, videography, etc. In smaller organizations, which typically have fewer resources, the instructional designer may also serve as the message design specialist. This is also often the case in educational institutions, both K-12 and higher education. Either way, it's important to have a handle on message design principles and strategies, whether you are responsible for directing a team that carries out your ultimate message design plan or you are the sole designer extraordinaire.

Test Your Understanding With a Bloom Stretch

Apply	Apply one of the message design theories described earlier in the chapter to create one "frame" of instruction (print-based or computer-based). Describe how your product demonstrates the principles inherent in that particular theory.
Analyze	Use Table 10.1 to analyze an online unit of instruction. You may also want to use one of the free annotation and markup tools to comment on the presentation and flow of the instruction (see the website for a list of current, recommended tools).
Evaluate	Find websites that offer examples of good message design and poor message design. (http://www.websitesthatsuck.com is a great place to start!)
Create	Create your own message design for one specific learning outcome. To really put your creative juices to the test—create several different designs using different media for instruction. You will be able to test the idea that different forms of media can be used to convey the same instructional event. Give it a shot!

Diving Deeper

Want to know more? When time allows, we encourage you to research more about message design and flow for instruction. The website resources for this chapter can get you started:

- **Practical Exercises and Examples**—Worked examples and exercises for message design.
- **Job Aids**—Examples of message design tools and job aids.
- **Resources**—Links to resources on message design and theories related to the topic.

11
Producing and Implementing Instruction

For several decades guides were produced that claimed to supply everything you needed to know about producing instructional materials (Lockwood, 1998; Minor & Frye, 1977). The ever-broadening range of possibilities for self-production and publication has changed that, though, along with the range of competencies you might expect to see in an IDT job advertisement. For example, imagine the variation in tasks for the following scenarios:

- You are a secondary teacher producing a lesson plan and print handouts for three sections of a biology lab that you will personally facilitate;
- You manage a corporate team of instructional and graphic designers, programmers, and subject matter experts producing an online, multimedia self-paced *module* on cost estimating for a multicultural audience of petrochemical construction engineers;
- You are designing and coordinating a day-long train-the-trainer workshop on conflict resolution for human resource department managers, to be delivered face to face at three different data centers;

- You have a contract to produce a multi-purpose hands-free job aid for a client's employees that must be delivered both online and in a physical format.

You can easily imagine the differences in the required production tasks, schedules, budgets, coordination and communication, and implementation procedures involved, and that is why there are no all-inclusive production and implementation guides currently available in our field. However, there are some general steps that apply to almost every instructional project, as well as some project management activities and implementation recommendations that can help you organize and effectively monitor your projects, whether you are working alone or as part of a team. Armed with this information, you can easily locate production and implementation recommendations and best practices for the specific media and delivery mode you've identified for an instructional design project.

Inquiring Minds Want to Know …

- What planning and project management tasks are critical to the success of any design/development effort?
- What personal organizational and record-keeping tasks should I use, regardless of whether I am working alone or on a team?
- What specialized activities are required to produce different types of mediated instruction?
- What communication and tracking practices can lead to a successful team production effort?
- What formative and summative evaluation measures contribute to the quality of instructional products?
- What copyright laws and universal design guidelines should inform my instructional design?
- What should I remember and understand from this chapter?

    ⇒ The basic functions involved in all instructional production efforts;
    ⇒ How to incorporate evaluation efforts into every phase of the ADDIE process;
    ⇒ The meaning and implications of terms like accessibility, universal design, differentiation, accommodation, copyright, fair use, return on investment (ROI).

Jargon Alert!

Most IDT process models (including ADDIE) use the term *development* to refer to the actual building of instructional materials. However, taking a cue from David Merrill (2002, p. 41), we use the term *production*. We do this to avoid the confusion caused by the fact that much of the literature uses both *instructional design* and *instructional development* to describe the *overall* design/development process. Just do an Internet search on "steps in instructional design" and then on "steps in instructional development," and you'll see that the results for each search yield basically the same process steps. On the other hand, when you "produce" instruction, it's clear that you are actually constructing the physical materials that will be used to facilitate learning. Note, too, that many discussions of *evaluation* use that word and *assessment* interchangeably, so determine whether the author/speaker is referring to the evaluation of an instructional product/program or the assessment of an individual's learning. Finally, your stakeholders may not be familiar with Kirkpatrick's (Kirkpatrick & Kirkpatrick, 2006) evaluation levels, so use language they can understand to determine how they will judge the success of your efforts. As emphasized throughout this book, you should decide on your formative and summative evaluation plans and procure the applicable benchmark measurements at the *beginning* of your project to enable you to make valid comparisons and gauge your success at the *end* of the project.

Notable Non-Example

So what happens when an instructional designer goes about the development process in a haphazard and unorganized manner? Take a look at this non-example to see what *not* to do when developing instruction:

Management Mishaps—With several years' experience developing training simulations, Barker Thornton easily landed a job with a government contractor to manage the design and development of a simulation-based training program on critical disaster reaction procedures for the U.S. Department of State Bureau of International Narcotics and Law Enforcement Affairs (INL). As project manager of the non-personal services contract, Barker did a great job of identifying the key milestones and work-flow for the project, but his lack of experience managing other people and working on a government contract proved to cause problems later in the project. His supervisor at the contracting company assured Barker that any issues with the INL would be handled at a higher level. He also emphasized that the project would use INL SMEs who had proven to be helpful on previous contracts, and that the project team members were all very experienced and should have no problems working together to complete the deliverables on time and within budget. Barker wondered if he should complete the training programs offered by the Small Business Administration on government contracting and working with government agencies, but his supervisor wanted to avoid any delays on the project and assured him that he could handle any issues. All went well until the fifth week of the two-month contract. The graphic designer on the project team had to go on leave to recover from injuries sustained in a car accident, and she had just gotten started on the final animations and visuals. Barker drew on his network of contacts to find a subcontractor to handle the graphics work, but the schedule began to slip and they missed several important milestones. With one week left before the original deadline, Barker scheduled a meeting with his supervisor to discuss some concerns and ask for an extension to the schedule. Barker was concerned that his programmer had insisted on taking the following Monday off, even though he had not informed Barker in advance so it could be included on the schedule, and the programming was to be completed that Wednesday. He also explained that he couldn't get enough clients to commit to testing the product prototype, and asked whether two team members who were former government employees could test the product instead. Finally, the outside graphic designer had approached him about intellectual property rights and for permission to use his work for another client. His supervisor frowned and said, "First off, our contract with the INL includes hefty monetary penalties for variances and project schedule extensions that are our fault, and if we have to delay the deadline the penalties will come out of your pay. You were hired to handle things like this. Secondly, Bob and Anne may be too familiar with the prototype to adequately test it, and besides, if there are major issues with the product and we don't catch them, using former government employees to approve the prototype could be considered a conflict of interest. We *don't* want that! Finally, you tell that subcontractor that he should have brought up the issue of intellectual property before he signed the contract with us. We're already stretching the goodwill of the INL and I don't want to risk future contracts just because some graphic designer needs something for his portfolio!" Barker left the office with a sick feeling in his stomach, convinced that he wouldn't be doing any more projects for this government contractor.

Caution!

Both novice and experienced designers can easily neglect important communication and project tracking practices that are pivotal to the success of a project. In addition, working on government contracts requires familiarity with the regulations and issues characteristic of government agencies and work. Attention to the details of project management, people management, and project-specific regulations and considerations can help you carry out a successful instructional design project, whether you are working alone or on a team.

So What's Involved? Production and Implementation

Successful instructional design projects are both planned *and* managed effectively. Due to the ill-structured nature of design, every project will have unique production and implementation elements that you must identify and carefully plan and execute. You can add those unique elements to the following, customizable list of essential tasks common to almost all IDT projects:

1. Examine existing materials for possible use in the current project.
2. Identify the project management requirements.
3. Identify production tasks (general and project-specific).
4. Establish standards for accessibility, safety and privacy, and quality.
5. Manage the production and formative testing of the instruction.
6. Guide implementation and promote adoption.
7. Evaluate and revise for continuous improvement.

Examining Existing Materials

Critically examine any related existing instruction, information, and/or images to determine whether and how they might be used for the current instructional design project. This includes materials and previous versions of the instruction available from the sponsoring organization, products available on the commercial market, and materials that are in the public domain. You may be able to appropriate or adapt these materials to reduce the production time and costs necessary for your project. With that in mind, evaluate the existing materials against project content and quality specifications, and conduct an Internet search to find guidelines for the appraisal of specific materials such as textbooks, presentations, and online courseware. It is also wise to use any available criteria and best practices for applicable subject- or media-specific instruction (e.g., quality standards for emergency response operations, best practices for the use of asynchronous discussion boards, etc.).

One of the major issues to consider when using existing materials is *copyright*. Copyright laws were enacted in the United States as early as 1790, and the current law (1976) has been updated (1998) with provisions to protect the intellectual property rights of individuals as soon as a creative work is fixed in a tangible medium of expression (written form, electronic form, etc.). The law protects the individual's rights concerning their creations, including the right to copy, make derivative works, distribute, publicly perform, publicly display, and the right to "prevent any intentional distortion, mutilation, or other modification" to the work if that modification would damage the author's honor or reputation (U.S. Copyright Law, Section 106A). The law applies to all kinds of creative works, including books, articles, music, choreography, plays, photographs, drawings and other illustrations, programming code, and more. Thoroughly research the nature and origin of the existing materials that you are considering for inclusion in your instruction—when in doubt, check it out!

When you reuse or update existing materials that were developed by or for your organization, copyright is usually not an issue, but it is still wise to obtain the appropriate permissions to use, alter, or remix it. If you are producing instruction for a non-profit educational endeavor (e.g., K-12 or college instruction), you may be able to use *a portion* of an existing work under the fair use exception provision of the U.S. Copyright Law. Consider this description of *fair use* from Chapter 2, Section 107, of the Copyright Law of the United States:

> The fair use of a copyrighted work, including such use by reproduction in copies or phonorecords or by any other means specified by that section, for purposes such as criticism, comment, news reporting, teaching (including multiple copies for classroom use), scholarship, or research, is not an infringement of copyright. In determining whether the use made of a work in any particular case is a fair use the factors to be considered shall include (1) the purpose and character of the use, including whether such use is of a commercial nature or is for nonprofit educational purposes; (2) the nature of the copyrighted work; (3) the amount and substantiality of the portion used in relation to the copyrighted work as a whole; and (4) the effect of the use upon the potential market for or value of the copyrighted work.

The fair use provision does not give specific guidance on the amount of a work that you can use, but educational institutions generally provide guidelines or even specific restrictions for the amounts allowed for each type of media. For example, universities often recommend that both face-to-face and online instructors restrict their use of copyrighted materials to a single chapter from a book, three minutes of a film or video, thirty seconds of a song or music video, and up to five illustrations or photographs by the same artist (Butler, 2004). In addition, you must *always* provide attribution, properly citing the source. Of course, if you are producing instruction for a commercial enterprise, you must obtain written permission to use copyrighted materials and must provide proper attribution, even when using materials in the public domain. If you work in the public domain, you should also check to find out if your company or organization has an established policy concerning the use of copyrighted works, including software and company documents.

The duration of the copyright for a work, if not renewed, can be as much as the life of the author plus seventy years. If the copyright on a creative work expires, it is considered to be in the *public domain,* the term used to refer to the status of works for which the copyright has expired, been forfeited, or for which copyright is not applicable. Such works can generally be used without concern as to copyright restrictions, although you should always provide proper attribution. In general, copyrightable works published in the United States prior to 1923 are now in the public domain, and works produced by or for the U.S. government are usually also in the public domain, although there are some exceptions. You should therefore always verify the status of any work you use. For example, you might think you could make an animated film from one of the fairy tales produced by the Brothers Grimm, since those tales were published in the early 1800s and should therefore be in the public domain. However, you would have to choose a tale carefully, because many of them were made into animated movies by the Disney company and are now protected by a Disney-held copyright (for more on this topic, search the Internet for C.G.P. Grey's video on copyright).

In particular, copyright issues are particularly complicated with respect to the use of web-based materials in instruction. What web-based materials are okay to use? Ask yourself the following questions when considering material that you locate online:

- Is it fair to use this, or am I infringing on someone's ability to make a living?
- If I determine that it is OK to use this information, how should I credit the source?
- Is this information accurate, or did the source publish lies or half-truths?
- Will participating in this online social network endanger the learners, their families, or damage their current or future reputations?
- What cautions should be communicated to learners to aid them in protecting their privacy and the privacy of others when they publish information on the web?

The answers to these questions are critical and, if not considered carefully, the issues involved can lead to lawsuits. Therefore, it is appropriate and essential that you conduct a thorough examination of the issues and ethical use policies involved, prior to launching instruction.

If you are not sure of the copyrighted status of an existing resource, you should seek to find a comparable version in the public domain or produce the resource yourself. The term *copyleft* refers to special licenses that you can apply to make the use of your creative work free, and to require that all future modified versions of that work be free of copyright restrictions, as well. More and more authors are distributing their work under a Creative Commons license (see http://creativecommons.org) or other similar licenses (e.g., the GNU General Public License). An Internet search and sites like http://www.copyright.gov/, http://www.thecopyrightsite.org/ and http://www.spa.org can provide you with more specific guidelines on copyright. Individuals and companies should protect themselves and their employees by developing and publicizing policies concerning copyright and software piracy.

A thorough evaluation of existing materials also requires that you accurately judge the authority, credibility, and value of web resources. Web-based resources are convenient, but part of your job as a designer is to emphasize to learners that not everything found on the Internet is authoritative and accurate (or freely available to copy and use). Some sites can appear quite authoritative but, in reality, represent sources of misinformation. To illustrate the challenges involved in judging credibility, see if you can identify specific features that provide clues to the nature of this spoof site: http://www.dhmo.org. The website for this chapter provides links to guidelines on evaluating web resources, and on the type of information and literacy skills essential for instructional designers.

You can also use web-based activities to guide learners to use existing materials without fear of copyright infringement. One such activity is a *WebQuest*. First suggested by Bernie Dodge and Tom March in 1995, the WebQuest is an inquiry-oriented activity that guides learner exploration of web resources, optimizes learner search time, and prevents learner access and use of questionable content. The literature supports the use of WebQuests as an instructional approach that integrates structured inquiry and the use of technology (Gohagan, 1999; Kachina, 2012; March, 2000; Milson, 2002; Milson & Downey, 2001; Molebash & Dodge, 2003). According to Dodge (1997), well-designed WebQuests should provide:

- An introduction or advance organizer that provides background information;
- A search task that is interesting and achievable;
- A set of weblinks to guide completion of the search task (serving to focus the learner on the *use* of information rather than the search itself, foster the use of higher-order thinking skills, and prevent unproductive web searches);
- A description of the step-by-step process learners should use to accomplish the task;
- Some form of guidance for organizing the information located (e.g., questions, outlines, concept maps, diagrams, or other graphic organizers); and
- A conclusion that reiterates the purpose of the assignment, what the students have learned, and a summary of the activity.

An Internet search on WebQuests will provide a variety of examples. Similar learning outcomes can also be accomplished with virtual field trips and through the use of social bookmarking and curation sites.

Identifying Project Management Requirements

Whether you are working alone or on a team, effective planning and project management techniques are essential to the success of your effort. Adequate planning of the design and production process requires that you work with your stakeholders and collaborators. Together you will establish project tasks, deliverable specifications, and schedule milestones, as well as communication procedures and teamwork roles and responsibilities. You must also address review and testing requirements, quality standards, guidelines for resource use, and a project budget. Finally, urge your stakeholders to commit to a set of priorities for the project in anticipation of inevitable future tradeoffs between time, budget, and quality. Once these elements are established, you will integrate the project tasks and identify critical task dependencies to develop an overall schedule. As the project gets underway, you must monitor the progress of the design/development effort so you can effectively manage the project schedule, costs, risks, and quality. Effective management strategies allow you to schedule activities and allocate resources to implement and deliver the instruction as originally planned (Smith & Ragan, 2005, p. 128).

Develop a project scope document to provide a blueprint for tracking and monitoring the many tasks involved. Your scope document should include a project budget, schedule, and a description of the deliverables. If approved by all parties, the scope document serves as a common reference point for the project and a source of accountability. The website for this chapter provides an example of a project scope document and guidelines for its development.

Project Tasks, Deliverables, and Milestones

The nature of the instruction that you are developing determines the specific production tasks. For example, an instructional video requires the development of a script and storyboard, and an instructional website or online courseware requires programming. Some project tasks, such as reviews and testing, are common to all projects. Identify the specific deliverables that you will produce, and then determine what production tasks are required to produce those deliverables. Almost all projects include a planning phase and require time to review literature, gather data, and determine the content to be included. Other tasks are specific to the media or type of instruction (see "Identifying Production Tasks").

Here are several general management tasks that are typical for instructional design projects:

- Develop a sequence of the tasks and identify task dependencies, overlaps, and tasks that can be carried out concurrently.
- Produce a work-flow diagram or *work breakdown structure* that provides a graphic representation of all the project activities and end products in a hierarchy that illustrates everything that must be completed to finish the project. The work breakdown structure "is the basis for time estimating, resource allocation, and cost estimating and collection" (Richman, 2002, p. 75), and it should include all analysis, design, and production activities. This includes tasks related to project management, project documentation, implementation, evaluation, and handling the final project paperwork.
- For each task, estimate the time required and identify a start and end date.
- From this information, generate a schedule that illustrates the critical path of the project, so that all parties know how their contributions impact the final product, the work of others on the team, and the final schedule.

A Gantt chart is a specific type of project schedule that does a good job of illustrating the dependencies between tasks and functions. Schedules that illustrate project dependencies can help team members, client reviewers, and subcontractors visualize how their own progress (or lack of progress) impacts the project schedule and costs. There are other process and project management tools that can improve the creative productivity of a team, including brainstorming tools, interactive visualization tools for illustrating shared data, electronic management and editing systems for working collaboratively on documents and projects, calendar and scheduling support tools, audit trail managers, work-flow management tools, and tools to facilitate review, feedback, and revision processes. The website for this chapter includes examples of Gantt charts, work-flow diagrams, and links to productivity tools.

You should also develop a budget that includes the human and non-human resources required for the project, and that reflects the anticipated costs of delays. What if your estimate of the time or resources required to complete the project or its major project phases does not match the stakeholder's deadlines and cost expectations? Address this issue as soon as you determine a problem so that you can renegotiate the deadlines (delaying the project), employ additional resources to complete within the original deadline (increasing the costs), or reduce the scope or quality of the project (delivering less). In other words, you are giving the stakeholders a choice: *fast, cheap, good: pick two.*

Communication, Project Responsibilities, and Teamwork

Early in the project, establish when and how you will communicate with the applicable key stakeholders, team members and subcontractors. According to Spector (2012), "the International Board of Standards for Training, Performance and Instruction (ibstpi; see www.ibstpi.org) found that professional practitioners in the fields of instructional design and training management ranked communication skills as the most critical skills required in performance of their jobs and everyday tasks" (p. 83). How are your interpersonal and communication skills? Seek to determine your own communication strengths and weaknesses, as well as those of any team members, early in the project. There are many commercially available personality and skills inventories that can help improve self-awareness, interpersonal skills, and group processes (e.g., the DiSC® Personality Profile rating individual Dominance, Influence, Steadiness and Compliance; the Johari Window technique for self-reflection on working relationships; and the Myers-Briggs® Personality test).

A regular schedule of communication between stakeholders and project team members helps you identify and resolve issues before they become problems that impact the project schedule and costs. With your stakeholders and collaborators, agree upon the frequency and type of communications and the communication tools to be used for the project. Figure 11.1 provides an example of a chart that can be used to communicate with stakeholders concerning the flow of a project, project responsibilities, deliverables, and key milestones and dependencies.

You should also include a communication plan in your project scope document that features:

- The mode, frequency, location (physical or virtual), and nature of planned communications such as team meetings, SME meetings, reviews, and evaluative tests;
- The individuals who will be present and contribute at each meeting;
- How the agenda for meetings will be communicated and when;
- The type of topics to be discussed and decisions to be made at meetings, vs. through email or in one-to-one phone conversations or meetings;
- The reviewers and review responsibilities and hierarchy;
- How variances and reviews are to be addressed; and
- The tools to be used for different communications.

	ANALYSIS	DESIGN	DEVELOPMENT	IMPLEMENTATION	EVALUATION
Instructional designer/ developer responsibilities	• Analyze needs and desired performance • Analyze target learner • Identify constraints and resources • Analyze content/ jobs/tasks • Identify instructional goal(s) • Develop terminal outcomes • Address plans for formative and summative evaluation	• Identify desired knowledge, skills and attitudes (KSAs) • Identify and classify enabling outcomes • Prioritize outcomes • Determine relationships between outcomes • Sequence outcomes • Detail content • Develop assessments • Identify teaching/ learning strategies • Select delivery systems and media/ technologies • Revisit analyses	• Establish formats, templates, color schemes, etc. • Develop prototype of instructional materials • Edit content and apply quality control • Identify data collection tools and develop testing plan • Conduct prototype testing • Revise instruction based on testing results • Revisit analyses and design parameters	• Produce Management and/or Implementation Plan/Guidelines • Outline recommended quality control measures • Implement, or facilitate implementation of the instruction • Formatively evaluate instruction during implementation • Revisit analyses, design parameters and development specifications	• Conduct summative evaluation • Revisit analyses, design parameters, and development specifications in light of evaluation data • Produce Evaluation and Future Revision Recommendations Report
Deliverable	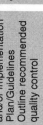 *Proposal, Contract, Initial Design Document*	 *Revised Design Document*	 *Prototype Materials, Testing Plan, Final Instructional Products*	 *Management/ Implementation Plan/ Guidelines*	*Evaluation Report and Future Recommendations*
Stakeholder responsibilities	• Meet with designer(s) to discuss project scope and contract • Review, and verify or comment on Initial Design Document	• Meet with designer(s) • Identify outcome priorities and content • Review, and verify or comment on Revised Design Document	• Meet with designer(s) • Recommend testing participants • Review and test prototype materials	• Meet with designer(s) to discuss implementation logistics • Meet to discuss implications of evaluation results	• Finalize contractual agreement with designer/developer

Figure 11.1 Instructional Design/Development Process Chart

Source: Adapted from and inspired by K. Indermill, By Design.

The tools you use will depend on access issues for all parties involved, including availability of the necessary equipment and connections. Possibilities include email, conferencing systems, shared databases, electronic bulletin boards, news groups, chatrooms, and more. There are many virtual workspace tools available that facilitate the type of collaboration essential to instructional design/development team projects. These tools enable teams to share and work cooperatively on documents and prototypes, comment on the work of other team members, and solicit feedback from SMEs and reviewers. When identifying tools for prototype testing, be sure to identify the specific equipment and systems to be used and the measures that will be taken to protect participant privacy. (See more on testing later in this chapter.)

If you have ever tackled a project as the coordinator or member of a team, you know that the quality of the coordination and teamwork can make or break the project. Every project needs some structure and a coordination process to provide the control necessary to produce a quality product. However, do not jeopardize the project by creating a complex project management system that creates inefficiencies or frustrates your colleagues or stakeholders. Teamwork skills are important for all project parties, both during the instructional design/development process and during implementation of the instruction. There are thousands of books, websites, and tips available on the subject of effective teamwork, and the website for this chapter features some suggestions of excellent resources on the topic.

The plan for communication described previously is just one aspect of project management that you must attend to if you are managing a team effort. Clark (2005) emphasizes that, ideally, the members of a team "collectively possess all of the skills required to achieve team goals" (p. 13). He goes on to state that, while each member may have played all the available team roles at one time, for the effectiveness of the team each member should be assigned to a position in which he or she excels. This promotes interdependence in pursuit of a goal. Clark also stresses that a key role of a team manager or leader (or of all members in a leaderless team) is to achieve five motivational goals (pp. 14–15):

1. Foster mutual respect for the expertise of all team members;
2. Help weaker team members believe that their effort is vital to team success;
3. Support a shared belief in the cooperative capabilities of the team;
4. Hold individual team members accountable for their contributions to the team effort (to prevent "social loafing"); and
5. Direct the team's competitive spirit outside the team and the organization, rather than internally.

As a project team manager, you must also gather regular detailed status updates from team members, monitor team member progress on tasks against the schedule estimates, and provide follow-up notes and action items for meetings to keep all parties on task. Work with your team members to identify potential issues, risks, and variances in the project scope or schedule, as well as external changes from clients, which may impact both the project progress and costs and then take the necessary actions to resolve these project challenges. Monitor the feedback received from SMEs and reviewers to ensure that it is addressed in project revisions or to help team members determine how to respond.

Part of your job, whether you work alone or on a team, is to secure your position and promote the work that you do. Instructional designers frequently bemoan the fact that few in the profession know how to effectively market themselves and their skills to convince others of the value-added that their work contributes to organizational effectiveness (Larson, 2004). Since the role of the instructional designer is not well understood outside the profession, you must communicate your value to the organizations you serve and share your success stories. It is an unfortunate fact that when times get hard, the first to get cut from the job rolls are often those in the training department, so don't be shy about reporting what you've accomplished and the impact your work is having on your organization's bottom line.

Identifying Production Tasks

Production consists of the processes used to physically complete the development of the instruction as outlined in your design/development plan or project scope document. Production is usually the longest activity in the ADDIE process and it consumes the most energy and resources. It involves both general and specific production tasks and the management of those daily activities, as well as prototype testing at critical points to ensure that the project design is on the right track, quality monitoring, and the incorporation of feedback and review comments to improve the final product.

Project production almost always includes writing tasks, whether for print materials, multimedia presentations, website or online course content, or audio and video scripts. The style of writing usually varies slightly for different media, applications, and audiences. For example, the style of writing may include more detail for print-based materials or it may need to be clear and abbreviated if used to support visuals in a multimedia presentation. For audiovisual scripts, you may need to use an informal, conversational style for certain audiences or a more professional, research-based style for others. In general, a brief, concise style is appreciated by learners for all instructional applications. You can find helpful tips for writing for specific media through an Internet search and on the website for this chapter. Writing-related production tasks to include in the project schedule include content outlines, rough draft preparations, SME and team member reviews, proofing and editing, and completion and review of final drafts. The identification and acquisition/production of visuals are also common production tasks to add to the schedule, although the detailed sub-tasks involved will vary by the type of visual media being developed.

Multimedia instruction typically includes tasks related to scripting and storyboarding, development and approval of a camera shot list or a sound effects list, the recording and editing of audio and visual content, programming code, preparation of support materials, and testing and revisions. In their book *Multimedia for Learning: Methods and Development*, Alessi and Trollip (2001) list the production elements that should be included in the schedule for specific multimedia formats that are developed for either web delivery or stand-alone delivery (delivered via a computer, a DVD player, etc.). These multimedia formats include tutorials, hypermedia, practice drills, simulations, educational games, tools (e.g., construction sets, electronic performance support systems, *microworlds*, modeling and simulation tools, and multimedia construction tools), open-ended learning environments (such as problem-based or scenario-based authentic environments), and assessments. They recommend that if one of these formats is used to deliver a complete learning experience (as opposed to being just one element of the learning environment), it should be designed to accomplish these four phases of instruction: presentation of information, learner guidance, provision for learner practice, and assessment of learning (p. 7). Most multimedia projects also require planning and production of introductory material, learner controls, information presentation, help functions, procedures for temporarily and permanently exiting the instruction, media credits, accessibility formats, and promotion and marketing efforts.

All instructional projects should include the testing of prototypes, whether they are paper-based or mediated versions or portions of the final product (Nistor, Dehne, & Drews, 2010). If you are developing instruction for international audiences, you may need to include tasks related to language translation or multiple tasks dedicated to developing versions of the instruction for different localities. You will likely also need to include tasks related to the development of facilitator and implementation aids such as test banks, classroom exercises, grader guidelines, and implementation guides.

Web-based and software-based instructional products should include tasks related to software programming and testing, and for any type of instruction you should factor in the time and expertise required to develop alternate forms of the instruction to ensure that it is accessible to physically and mentally challenged learners. Finally, be sure to include tasks related to duplication and dissemination of any physical materials produced for multiple locations. Here are just two examples of the type of production tasks you might identify for specific instructional products:

- For the development of a blended learning course:
  - Identification and procurement of supplemental reading materials (articles, book chapters, etc.);
  - Development of multimedia presentations;
  - Preparation of asynchronous discussion board prompts and guidelines;
  - Setup of the assignments, tests, and the grading center for the learning management system used to house the materials; and
  - Arrangement for the use of a synchronous discussion tool and development of materials to be used with it (if synchronous sessions are used).
- For the development of an electronic performance support system (EPSS) for a company:
  - Programming of the software and user interface providing access to the system;
  - Development of a social networking tool to foster employee interaction;
  - Development of a profile management system to individualize the software for users;
  - Instructions and tools to enable employees to make and upload digital video and audio content;
  - Job aid production;
  - Digital images and graphics to model and prompt skill usage;
  - Attractive graphics and interface design to enhance usability of site;
  - The production of content in alternate formats to enhance accessibility;
  - Accessibility testing and programming;
  - Utilities for running employee tools with media on a hand-held device;
  - Record-keeping capabilities and storage in company databases;
  - Creation of hard-copy, CD, and download versions of the software and documentation,
  - Creation of company reference documentation and strategy information; and
  - Design and creation of examples, testimonials, and tips.

When you identify the specific production tasks, you should also attempt to estimate the time required to complete those tasks. Development time estimates for instructor-led training (face-to-face or synchronous virtual instruction) are frequently cited in terms of the number of hours required to develop a half-day, day, or several days of instruction. Estimates of the time required to develop asynchronous e-learning are frequently cited as a ratio of development hours to hours of instruction. The amount of development time required depends on the expertise and work habits of your development team members, as well as the complexity of the content and media being developed (Clark, 1995–2012).

Some organizations have made estimates that you can use to develop your schedule if your team members are not able to estimate their own time requirements. Even if your team members provide estimates, Defelice and Kapp (2010) warn that these self-reported hours can be flawed due to accidental misreporting of hours or the tendency to forget to report work hours, discrepancies in how different people categorize work tasks, discrepancies between individual productivity due to learning curve, overly confident team members who underestimate the time required, and hours spent thinking about or working on the project at home that employees may not include in previous task hour reports. You should also keep in mind that estimates based on the number of hours required to complete certain tasks must be adjusted for worker efficiency before calculating the days required for activities on your project schedule. It is not unreasonable to figure an individual's efficiency at 60%, meaning that for an eight-hour day that individual would likely contribute only about four hours and forty-five minutes towards progress on their project responsibilities.

Many estimates provided by organizations use a measure of complexity based on the level of interactivity involved in the instructional materials, and they are reported as a ratio of development time hours to hours of learning or *seat time* (hours of time spent by the learner in a learning environment). These estimates tend to change rapidly as pedagogical approaches to instruction evolve. For example, a 2000 report by Brandon Hall, editor and publisher of the *Multimedia & Internet Training Newsletter,* estimates a 50% reduction in seat time when converting classroom instruction to e-learning (Rosen, 2000). However, according to Schlenker (2008), "learning design is becoming less about presentation, and more about conversation" (para. 1), and therefore these seat time estimates may change as more social media and networked activities are included in instruction.

You should be aware that organizations use different definitions for the levels of interactivity, and these levels and the associated development time estimates tend to become outdated quickly as development tools become more sophisticated (decreasing development time estimates) and expectations rise (increasing development time estimates). For example, Langevin Learning Services (2011) estimated that instructor-led training requires 25 to 60 development hours per hour of instruction, and 75 to 500 hours per hour of web- or computer-based training (depending on the complexity of the content and the instructional approach). The E-Learning Practitioner blog by Prakash Bebington (2008–2011) provides a measure of web-based training complexity that states that simple, on-screen text training with linear navigation requires 120–240 soft skills design/development person-hours and 60–120 hard skills design/development person-hours per learning hour. In contrast, Bebington (2008–2011) estimates that complex web-based training with simulations, audio, full interactivity, and decision-based branched navigation requires 1,920–3,840 soft skills design/development person-hours and 960–1,920 hard skills design/development person-hours per learning hour.

In 2002, the E-Learning Guild surveyed its membership and published the following categories and development times per hour of e-learning:

Simple Asynchronous (static HTML pages with text and graphics)—117 hours
Simple Synchronous (static HTML pages with text and graphics)—86 hours
Average Asynchronous (all the above plus Flash, JavaScript, animated GIFs)—191 hours
Average Synchronous (all the above plus Flash, JavaScript, animated GIFs)—147 hours
Complex Asynchronous (all the above, plus audio, video, interactive simulations)—276 hours
Complex Synchronous (all the above, plus audio, video, interactive simulations)—222 hours

In 2010, Brandon Hall and Chapman Alliance surveyed nearly 4,000 learning professionals at 249 companies to determine the average time to develop various types of instruction. They reported a ratio of development hours to hours of instruction in the range of:

Instructor-led training	43:1
Level 1 e-learning (Basic)	79:1
Level 2 e-learning (Interactive)	184:1
Level 3 e-learning (Advanced)	490:1

However, according to Jon Matejcek (2010), these figures do not take into account several things. He emphasizes that economies of scale reduce the amount of development time required as the developer becomes familiar with both the content and the development tool. He also states that subject matter complexity can impact these estimates.

Finally, Kapp and Defelice (2009) surveyed industry peers in both 2003 and 2009 to compare estimates of the time required to design and develop one hour of training. Note the variability of the numbers, which is influenced by the sophistication of the software used to incorporate interactivity into the instruction. The factors Kapp and Defelice cited as influencing the estimates included: the complexity of the content; the treatment of the content with respect to the expertise level of the learners; the design experience of the designers, developers, and subject matter experts; the availability and completeness of documentation; and the specificity provided by survey respondents concerning the level of interaction (e.g., electronic page turners versus more sophisticated simulations, discussion boards, games, virtual coaches, streaming multimedia content, etc.).

	2003 Estimates	2009 Estimates
Stand-up classroom training	20–70 hours	43–185 hours
Self-instructional print	80–125 hours	40–93 hours
No template e-learning, limited interactivity	100–150 hours	93–152 hours
No template e-learning, moderate interactivity	250–400 hours	122–186 hours
No template e-learning, high interactivity	400–600 hours	154–243 hours
Template e-learning, limited interactivity	40–100 hours	73–365 hours
Template e-learning, moderate interactivity	150–200 hours	90–240 hours
Template e-learning, high interactivity	60–300 hours	132–324 hours

When estimating the amount of time devoted to different aspects of the schedule, Bebington (2008–2011) suggests that you budget about 40–60% of the total available development time to analysis, design, and production tasks. Another 10–15% should be allocated for project management tasks, and another 10–15% for testing and quality assurance efforts. The remainder of the time should be reserved for any unforeseen contingencies.

In some cases (particularly with Connectivist applications), you can leverage learner-created content and thus lower your production time and costs. Having learners produce mediated content to demonstrate their learning serves to both engage learners and foster their learning. You can even include learner updating as a maintenance plan for your instruction, designing individual or collaborative learner activities that involve testing URLs in the instruction to locate dead links, and exploration activities to find more current web-based content. Leveraging learner contributions in this way can be used in any career environment, although you should consider learner familiarity with the technologies involved prior to implementing the strategy. Many companies use powerful knowledge management systems to capture employee knowledge and rapidly evolving content so that it can be shared across distances and time. This type of system is particularly valuable in organizations subject to frequently changing regulations or standards that require employees to have current content knowledge for successful and effective operations.

So what competencies are required to produce instruction? Ritzhaupt, Martin, and Daniels (2010) conducted a job announcement analysis and a survey of practicing IDT professionals to identify the multimedia competencies required to produce instruction. They compared their results from both investigations to come up with knowledge, skill, and ability competencies that were most frequently cited. Keep in mind that you may not need all these competencies, depending on your role on a project and your ability to outsource portions of the design/development effort. For the knowledge, skills, and abilities domains, Table 11.1 lists the collection of competencies from the job announcements and survey of professionals (in order of importance):

Table 11.1 Multimedia Knowledge, Skills, and Abilities Cited by Professionals and Job Ads

Knowledge	Skills	Abilities
• Knowledge of instructional design models and principles. • Knowledge of presentation software, word processing and desktop publishing software, web authoring tools, and screen recording software. • Knowledge of software for creation and editing of bitmap images, vector images, and audio and video content. • Knowledge of assessment methods. • Knowledge of Web 2.0 technologies, learning management systems, copyright laws, and cognitive theories of learning.	• Oral and written communication skills. • Interpersonal communication skills. • Computer programming and scripting skills. • Project management skills. • Organizational skills. • Troubleshooting, customer service, editing and proofing, and time management skills. • Web design, print design, and graphics design skills. • Video production skills.	• Ability to create effective instructional products. • Ability to work well with others in teams. • Ability to work with diverse constituencies (e.g., SMEs, clients). • Ability to work under deadlines, independently, and to manage teams. • Ability to apply sound ID principles, conduct a needs assessment, and formative and summative evaluations. • Ability to teach face to face. • Ability to apply multimedia principles to design and development, to operate computer hardware, to adapt and learn new technology and processes, and to work with synchronous technology.

You can compare the results from Ritzhaupt et al.'s (2010) study with your own competencies and those of your design/development team to identify gaps and areas for professional development.

Establishing Standards for Accessibility, Safety, Privacy, and Quality

What if you have a variety of learners for whom your instruction must provide a range of options for access or understanding?

Accessibility

One of the most valuable features of technology is its use to reach learners with a variety of cognitive learning abilities and/or physical disabilities. *Accessibility* is the term used to describe the degree to which instruction is available to all learners, even those with special needs or disabilities. When applied to web-based instruction, it also addresses issues of access related to connectivity and availability of instructional and communications equipment.

Traditionally, the majority of instruction in Western schools and universities has been presented in linguistic form, either as a lecture or written materials. However, many learn more readily from non-linguistic (usually visual) representations. Technology provides options for providing students with these non-linguistic representations and with tools that enable learners to create their own representations. This is one way that technology is used for *differentiation*—to provide learners with different ways to access, process and learn content. Carol Tomlinson (2001) explains that an instructor who practices differentiation "proactively plans and carries out varied approaches to content, process, and product in anticipation of and in response to student differences in readiness, interest, and learning needs" (p. 7). The term is typically used in K-12 settings but it is a concept that applies to all career environments.

Providing access to content in a variety of representations and formats is also helpful for learners whose native language is something other than English, and it can provide options for reaching a broader learning audience. For example, what if you had to provide quality control training for employees who must be certified in quality assessment, for managers and supervisors who have to oversee process quality, and for front-line personnel who must identify and flag low-quality products on the production line? Learners across these three groups would probably have a wide range of educational backgrounds (from vocational-technical school degrees to graduate degrees) and prior knowledge and experience, and technology could be used within a single quality control program to differentiate and ensure that each group has access to the information required to help them meet their learning goals.

A related term—*accommodation*—refers to a form of scaffolding that supports students through a change in the delivery of instruction or the method of student performance *without* changing the content or conceptual difficulty of the curriculum. It often features the use of assistive technologies, but it can also consist merely of a low-tech strategy. For example, providing students with cues to important passages in a reading selection can be accomplished with a low-tech solution like sticky notes or through a more high-tech solution involving the highlighting of text in an electronic pdf document. An *adaptation* is a change in the delivery of instruction *and/or* the conceptual difficulty and content to assist an individual to learn in the least restrictive environment. Ebeling (1998) cites nine ways to adapt instruction to facilitate learning. With some reflection, you can use these methods for both challenged and gifted learners:

1. *Size*—Adjust the size or length of an assignment.
2. *Time*—Adapt the amount of time allowed to complete a task or a test.
3. *Complexity*—Adjust the type of test problem or the level of skill required to complete a learning task to better match the learner's readiness and abilities.
4. *Participation*—Adjust the type of participation required of a learner (e.g., allow them to listen to a text selection instead of having to read it).
5. *Environment*—Make physical adjustments to the learning environment to meet the learner's needs or enhance their ability to learn.
6. *Input*—Adapt the way in which instruction is delivered to aid learner comprehension.
7. *Output*—Allow learners to use different ways of demonstrating their learning.
8. *Support*—Provide a variety of human and mechanical scaffolds to help with learning tasks.
9. *Goals*—Adjust expectations for learners.

Universal design is related to the concepts of differentiation and accommodation, but is used to refer to "least restrictive" design elements and plans for buildings, environments, products, and instruction. Universal design elements and strategies are built into and integrated with the design from the very beginning of the process, rather than added later as a special adjustment that might draw unnecessary attention to a learner or make him or her feel different. Examples include the use of ramps in place of stairs rather than in addition to stairs, or the use of a color-blind friendly color scheme for a webpage rather than providing an alternate view of the webpage. The three primary principles of Universal Design for Learning (UDL) emphasize flexible approaches that can be customized and adjusted for individual needs, including CAST (2011):

1. Multiple means of representation

   • Providing options for perceiving information through different senses;
   • Providing information in linguistic and non-linguistic forms, multiple languages, and multiple media; and

- Providing options for comprehension through the presentation or activation of background knowledge; highlighting of patterns, critical features, big ideas, and relationships; guiding information processing, visualization, and manipulation; and maximizing transfer and generalization of knowledge.

2. Multiple means of action and expression

- Provide options for physical actions including alternatives for navigating and selecting (e.g., using a mouse, the keyboard, or voice activation to navigate through a webpage), responding and composing (e.g., allowing hand-written, typed, or voice recordings of an assigned essay), and interaction (e.g., providing alternative requirements for rate, timing, speed, and range of motor action required to interact); and access to assistive technologies like joysticks and webpage magnifiers.
- Provide options for expression and communication, including multiple media for communication, multiple tools for construction and composition; and use incremental scaffolding, plenty of opportunities for practice, and differentiated models, feedback, and examples to build learner fluencies.
- Provide options for executive functions through scaffolds that support and guide goal-setting, planning, and strategy development, the management of information and resources, and the learner's capacity for monitoring progress.

3. Multiple means of cognitive engagement

- Provide options for recruiting interest by optimizing individual choice and autonomy, optimizing relevance, value, and authenticity, and by minimizing threats and distractions.
- Provide options for sustaining effort and persistence by heightening the salience of goals and objectives, varying demands and resources to optimize challenge, fostering collaboration and communication, and increasing mastery-oriented feedback.
- Provide options for *self-regulation* by promoting expectations and beliefs that optimize motivation, facilitating personal coping skills and strategies, and developing self-assessment and reflection.

(Refer to http://www.udlcenter.org for examples of all the UDL principles.)

In addition to these general UDL principles, you can obtain specific accessibility guidelines for web-based instruction from portions of the 1998 Section 508 Amendment to the U.S. Rehabilitation Act. The applicable portions are listed below, and you can find links to additional resources on Section 508 compliance on the website for this chapter.

- 1194.21 Software Applications & Operating Systems
- 1194.22 Web-based Intranet & Internet Information & Applications
- 1194.24 Video and Multimedia Products
- 1194.31 Functional Performance Criteria
- 1194.41 Information, Documentation & Support

Technology improves instruction for *all* learners, but is particularly helpful for those with cognitive and physical disabilities. *Assistive technology* can be defined as "any item, piece of equipment or product system, whether acquired commercially off the shelf, modified or customized, that is used to increase, maintain, or improve the functional capabilities of children with disabilities" (Public Law 101–476, Individuals with Disabilities Education Act, IDEA; http://idea.ed.gov/). The required modifications to instruction that make it accessible to all learners can often be accomplished through technology, and often those changes make the instruction more interesting and engaging for *all* learners. Of course, wheelchairs, Braille, and hearing aids are often some

Figure 11.2 Accessibility Applies to All Aspects of Education

of the first examples that come to mind when considering assistive technologies, but there are many other examples of technologies that can help challenged learners:

- Braille readers, text-to-speech, screen readers and screen magnifiers, video for viewing sign language, hearing aids and audio books for the visually impaired and hearing impaired;
- Augmented and alternative communication (AAC) devices, including low- to high-tech solutions such as gestures, speech generating devices, photographs and pictures, adapted mice and joysticks, eye tracking, and switch access scanning.
- Assistive technologies for cognition (ATC), e.g., reminder systems and planning systems that help learners with cognitive processes such as attention, memory, self-regulation, and planning.
- Prosthetics (artificial eyes, hearing aids, replacement limbs, etc.), technologies to assist those with mobility impairments, and sports-related assistive technologies.

Safety and Privacy

Along with accessibility, you should consider the issues of learner safety and privacy when designing web-based instruction. Ask yourself questions like:

- Will participating in this online social network endanger the learners, their families, or damage their current or future reputations?
- What cautions should be communicated to learners to aid them in protecting their privacy and the privacy of others when they publish information on the web?

The answers to such questions are critical and, if not considered carefully, the issues involved could lead to lawsuits or, in extreme cases, bodily injury or death. Therefore, it is appropriate and essential that you conduct a thorough examination of the safety and privacy issues involved, prior to launching instruction. You can use resources on the web to familiarize yourself with these other important terms related to accessibility, learner safety, and privacy: Acceptable Use Policy (AUP), the Children's Internet Protection Act (CIPA), the Children's Online Privacy Protection Act (COPPA), the Family Educational Rights and Privacy Act (FERPA), Netiquette, cyberbullying, phishing, spyware and malware, adware and spam, and virus protection.

Quality

Every design project should be built on standards that will yield a quality instructional product that is accessible and effective. Design/development teams need established quality standards, guidelines, and policies that provide working parameters and define responsibilities and the interrelationships between job functions. In addition to standards for accessibility and universal design, you should define both general and specific quality standards for the content you are covering, the teaching and learning strategies used, and the delivery and instructional technologies that support those strategies. Examples of such standards include:

- Performance and mastery standards for learners;
- The international World Wide Web Consortium's (W3C) development standards for the web;
- Interoperability and SCORM compliance ("SCORM" stands for "Sharable Content Object Reference Model," and is a set of technical standards for e-learning software products, the current version of which is referred to as Tin Can API), including content packaging, run-time environment, and metadata;
- Overall seat time maximum and minimum hours, optimal class size and limits, and response times for providing feedback to learners;
- The maximum number of clicks required to access information;
- Course flow and design standards, including established templates, style guides, and production guidelines for instruction;
- Grammar, punctuation, and readability/reading level standards;
- Course content structure and course site maps;
- Essential deliverables for each type of instruction (face to face, online, blended, and mobile); and
- Best practices and guidelines for specific media, such as the international Aviation Industry Computer-Based Training Committee's (AICC) specifications for web-based training (at http://www.aicc.org).

As just one example, the definition and use of design templates and style guidelines can contribute to product quality, save project time and money by standardizing the development process, and can provide a consistent look and feel. Some criticize the use of templates, claiming that they inhibit creative and novel approaches to instruction. However, the format and size limits that characterize templates can also benefit a design effort by forcing writers to chunk information, guiding graphic designers in producing appropriately sized illustrations and multimedia elements, reminding programmers of the need to integrate accessibility features, and by simplifying and standardizing navigation controls. Design templates can be developed for storyboards and audio scripts, page and screen layouts, and help files. Style guidelines often establish standards for headings and titling, font sizes and styles, color schemes (to promote both consistency and visibility), the behavior of pop-up windows and hyperlinks, the use of breadcrumb trails, and graphic user interface features.

Your organization or institution may have established metrics for judging the quality of instruction, or you can locate quality rubrics for judging the effectiveness of different delivery modes through an Internet search. For example, one of the more popular systems for evaluating online instruction is the Quality Matters™ (QM) Program (http://www.qmprogram.org/). QM is a faculty-centered process for assessing the quality of online and blended instruction, and it is used in both higher education and K-12 career environments. The program uses a rubric with eight general and forty specific quality standards to assess instruction and assure quality and continuous improvement (http://www.qmprogram.org/rubric). QM also incorporates a peer review process and professional development initiatives. Whether you use an established program like QM or define your own quality criteria, seek to establish those standards early in the design process so that you can measure quality as an aspect of your project evaluation.

Managing the Production and Formative Testing of the Instruction

The success of an instructional design and development project is often judged by how well it stays within the original schedule and budget limits. Since schedule and budget overruns frequently occur during production, you must closely monitor and manage this stage of the process. This basically requires effective time and cost management, and involves the collection of status data from all parties involved in the production effort, tracking of progress, and mitigation of project risks and schedule and budget overruns.

In addition to managing the production schedule and costs, you must also take steps to control quality. During production, the instructional materials should be checked by an editor and proofreader, and reviewed by SMEs and stakeholders for content accuracy. Reviews and approvals by SMEs and key stakeholders should occur at several points in the process (see the example of a review and approval log in Table 11.2).

Table 11.2 Example Review and Approval Log

Description	Submit Date	Reviewers	Requested Approval Date	Approve/Deny/ Modify	Initials/ Date	Reviewer Comments
Initial project scope	9/25	Jim Tarkee, Amanda Greig	10/3	□ Approve As Is □ Modify Content □ Deny		
Design plan and content detail	10/15	Jim Tarkee, Amanda Greig, and assigned SMEs	10/23	□ Approve As Is □ Modify Content □ Deny		
Aligned outcomes, assessments, and strategies	10/30	Jim Tarkee, Amanda Greig, and assigned SMEs	11/7	□ Approve As Is □ Modify Content □ Deny		
Paper prototype review	11/14	Jim Tarkee, Amanda Greig, & assigned SMEs	11/22	□ Approve As Is □ Modify Content □ Deny		
Usability test revisions	11/30	Jim Tarkee, Amanda Greig	12/15	□ Approve As Is □ Modify Content □ Deny		
Final instruction	12/29	Jim Tarkee, Amanda Greig, and assigned SMEs	1/15	□ Approve As Is □ Modify Content □ Deny		

Prototypes should be produced early in the process and formatively tested to ensure quality and improve the effectiveness of the instruction. In Chapter 5 you considered how to develop interim paper prototypes for review of content. Both paper prototypes and more sophisticated software-based prototypes can be tested for usability, feasibility, and effectiveness. An iterative cycle of prototype production, testing, and revision based on feedback and test results—sometimes referred to as *rapid prototyping* or *agile development*—fosters a policy of continuous improvement that ultimately improves the quality and effectiveness of the final instruction.

Usability testing is carried out to determine if the instruction operates correctly, if it meets the content and functionality specifications, if it operates on different equipment, platforms, and browsers, and if learners can operate it and perceive its usefulness and purpose. Hix and Hartson (1993) stress that usability is concerned with effectiveness, efficiency, and ease of use. Testing usability generally involves a monitored and recorded observation of the use and functional testing of the prototype by participants who are representative of the target learner group. Participants are asked to use a think-aloud procedure as they explore the instruction, verbalizing their thoughts, questions, and issues with the instruction. Often, the participant also completes a satisfaction survey or is interviewed following the test to identify their concerns and clarify their comments. There is no substitute for the feedback you obtain when actual members of the target learner group usability-test your instruction; however, you may also wish to have stakeholders, reviewers, or SMEs participate in a usability test for the purpose of evaluating the quality and completeness of the instruction. Carrying out several cycles of usability testing during the course of your design/development project enables you to make iterative modifications that produce more effective instruction.

All instructional materials should be tested formatively, but you should increase the scheduled design and testing time for materials that are asynchronous and self-paced. This is because a live, experienced instructor can address missing or erroneous content or misconceptions in a face-to-face class or synchronous online session, but asynchronous and self-paced materials must be able to stand on their own. Additional testing should also be scheduled for materials that would be costly to update or correct (either monetarily or in terms of human risk). The website for this chapter provides a usability testing example and guidelines, examples of test participant profiles, and a participant task handout and reaction survey.

Some project managers also carry out a *feasibility test* to identify whether the supports are in place in the learner's environment to encourage the implementation and use of the instruction. This type of test usually identifies any supports or barriers that should be addressed when the instruction is disseminated. To determine feasibility, you must allow learners in the target environment to use a fairly robust prototype of the instruction. Feasibility can often be assessed in conjunction with a *pilot test* of the instruction. A pilot test also involves the participation of members of the target learner group who test a rough draft of the complete instruction. Pilot testing serves to identify the effects produced by the instruction in the learning environment and any related environments such as school or home. Helpful tools for both pilot and feasibility testing include observation checklists, targeted behavior data, goal attainment scales, social responsiveness scales, interviews, progress reports, rubric-based reviews, satisfaction surveys and interviews, and usage records (either in-person observations or electronic usage logs).

Guiding Implementation and Promoting Adoption

So, you've monitored and guided the instructional project through an iterative process of analysis, design/development, and production, testing and modifying it along the way to ensure certain levels of quality and effectiveness. Now you're ready to implement it. Sounds like you're done, doesn't it? But no—implementation typically consists of a lot more than merely placing instruction online or stepping into a classroom to facilitate training. Implementation involves both preparing for and actually delivering the instruction, and the extent of the preparation required varies with the type of delivery mode, the scope and geographical distribution of the instruction, and the receptivity of those for whom it is intended. Table 11.3 provides a few examples of how the preparation for implementation can vary based on delivery mode and factors related to distribution. The website for this chapter provides an example of an implementation guide for a face-to-face technical unit.

Prior to implementation you must schedule the logistics of the instruction so that its functional aspects remain transparent and learning processes are not hampered. You also continue to carry out formative evaluation measures (similar to those described for the production effort), taking notes on what works and does not work so that you can make the appropriate revisions.

Implementation preparations frequently include a plan for communication with learners, scheduling the logistical aspects of training, providing technical and content support for learners, training facilitators and support staff, and providing technical support for instructors and others involved in the effort. The type of delivery mode and media you use for the instruction may also require coordination or logistical planning, especially if you will be offering a global, synchronous online program across time zones.

Depending on your role and the type of organization sponsoring the instruction, you may also be required to provide marketing support for the instruction. This could involve front-end market research to establish customer or learner need for the instruction, as well as a market need. It might also include advertising and learner recruitment. Front-end market research activities may include:

- Situation analysis to identify basic underlying characteristics of the industry, and the economic, technical, and social environments;
- Definition of the target market, learning product concept brainstorming and support plans;
- Competition analysis to identify actual and potential competitors for each market opportunity; and
- Development of marketing tactics.

Advertising and learner recruitment may be handled through another entity in your organization, or you may need to utilize traditional advertising methods and social media to inform and recruit learners. Often, you may also have to consider and plan to address issues of *adoption*. Learning experiences typically involve change and can therefore be considered innovations. Rogers' (2003) Diffusion of Innovation Model attempts to describe how an innovation is introduced and the many variables that determine its rate of adoption. As Rogers explains it, "diffusion is the process by which an innovation is communicated through certain channels over time among the members of a social system" (p. 11). Instructional designers must often take on the role of change agent to convince learners or organizations to adopt a new or innovative learning product, program, or system. The adoption process typically involves the following stages:

1. *Knowledge*—the learner or organization is introduced to the learning innovation but lacks information about it;
2. *Persuasion*—the learner or organization becomes interested in the innovation, seeks to learn more about it, and forms either a favorable or unfavorable impression of it;

Table 11.3 Examples of Preparation for Implementation by Type of Instruction

Delivery Mode and Time/Location	Implementation Preparations
Face to face, delivered by designer/developer	• Lesson plans, syllabus, and implementation notes. • List of, and procurement of, equipment and supplies for course/workshop. • Schedule for instruction, and arrangement for physical training facility. • Reproduction of learner materials (handouts, etc.). • Arrangements for learner technical support. • Marketing and advertisement (depending on the sponsoring organization).
Face to face, delivered by someone other than the designer/developer	All the above, plus: • An implementation guide that includes required equipment and supplies, grading guidelines and/or assignment rubrics or checklists (see implementation guide example in the website resources for this chapter). • Arrangements for facilitator technical support. • Arrangements for learner instructional support.
Stand-alone unit of **online asynchronous** instruction	• List of all software and plug-ins used in development and required for implementation, with version dates and URLs and/or phone numbers to use for potential maintenance issues, updates, and/or troubleshooting. • List of media credits for any images or videos used, with full citations for attribution and URLs. • A file of original documents and images with versions clearly indicated. • If learner performance on assessments will be recorded, and if feedback will be exchanged between a facilitator and the learner, a database must be set up to record and track learner input, and a plan must be established for communication between the facilitator and learner (via the instructional system itself, email, or other means). • Guidelines for asynchronous interactions and discussions, and peer critiques. • A list of resources and supplemental materials for students, and a central location for those materials with clear instructions on how to access them. • If using a learning management system (LMS), organize the user interface to provide buttons or links that clearly guide the learner to the content presentations, learning activities and resources, instructional schedule, assessments, assignment submissions, and grades. • Arrangements for learner instructional and technical support.
Online synchronous instruction facilitated by someone other than the designer/developer	Similar requirements as for asynchronous instruction, plus: • Scheduling of synchronous tools use, and publication and communication of the synchronous instruction schedule with learners and other stakeholders (technical staff, guest speakers, assistants, site coordinators, etc.). If instruction will be delivered across multiple time zones, this schedule should include the start and end times of each synchronous schedule for each time zone. • Instructions for learners on what to do and how to obtain help if they experience connectivity issues during the synchronous sessions. • Instructions for learners and training for facilitators on how the synchronous tools work for the systems being used. • Backup recordings and hard copies of presentations for learners to review if they miss the session or wish to revisit the session content. • An implementation guide that includes a schedule for the instruction with topics and time estimates, the required systems with contact numbers and email addresses for help with those systems, grading guidelines and/or assignment rubrics or checklists (see implementation guide example in the website resources for this chapter). • Arrangements for facilitator training and technical support. • Arrangements for learner instructional and technical support.

Blended instruction	Similar implementation requirements as for the above face-to-face and online implementations, varying based on the mix of asynchronous and synchronous instruction and the familiarity of the instructional facilitator with the content and course materials. Also requires:
	• A plan for the coordination between face-to-face activities and online activities, with guidance for learners concerning where to find resources and tools for the assigned activities, where to submit assignments, and a communication plan that is clear and considerate of the learners' time.
	• Established policies on: how online classes factor into faculty teaching loads, compensation structures, how incompletes will be handled, how final assessment for the instruction is integrated with final assessment for the program.
	• Established policies on: grading, late work, academic honesty, learner interactions, and potential facilitator-student conflicts.

3. *Decision*—the learner or organization weighs the pros and cons of using the innovation and decides whether to adopt or reject it;
4. *Implementation*—the learner or organization uses the innovation and makes a judgment concerning its usefulness; and
5. *Confirmation*—the learner or organization evaluates the results of implementing the innovation and integrates it into his or her life or organization.

Within any organization there are several types of adopters, including *innovators* (those who are the first to adopt an innovation, typically about 2.5% of the organization), *early adopters* (those who are opinion leaders, typically up to 13.5% of the organization), *early majority* (a large portion of the organization at 34% who adopt later in the process), *late majority* (34% of the organization who are skeptics and adopt later), and *laggards* (at 16%, the last in an organization to adopt due to an aversion to change and change agents) (Rogers, 2003, p. 282). As a change agent, you must seek to encourage adoption by convincing opinion leaders and gatekeepers in your organization of the value of the instructional innovation. You must also build buy-in for the learning experience, seek to integrate the learning experience into the larger organizational framework and mission to build its sustainability, and convince others of its ease of use and cost-effectiveness. Finally, if you are delivering a learning product to a client, be sure to provide an orientation to the instruction when you hand it over, highlighting its value to the client's mission or organizational goals.

Evaluating and Revising for Continuous Improvement

SOMETIMES YOU NEED MORE THAN JUST A LEVEL I EVALUATION.

Figure 11.3 Failing to Plan for Evaluation is Planning to Fail

Planning for a successful instructional design means beginning with the end in mind. It is at this point in the project that the importance of your evaluation plan and the quality of your initial benchmark measurements (addressed in Chapter 1) become evident. After implementation you must carry out the *summative evaluations* that you planned early in the life of your project. As noted in earlier chapters, successful summative evaluation depends on how well you consider and embed evaluation measures in every activity of the design/development process. This practice promotes the "continuous improvement" and excellence of your instructional products and your process. At the beginning of a project you focus your evaluation and outline a plan that identifies the key questions your evaluation effort will answer and the stakeholders who will be involved in the evaluation measurements. Summative evaluation consists of putting that plan into action using debriefing sessions, final product reviews, and evaluation measurements for Kirkpatrick's four levels (discussed in more detail later in this chapter).

Following implementation of the instruction, conduct a *debriefing session* with your team and/ or stakeholders to: (a) identify project successes and areas for improvement, (b) highlight and document key lessons learned for the future, (c) analyze whether the product was delivered on time, within budget, and to the scope and quality standards originally established, and (d) compare the project outcomes and stakeholder satisfaction to the original project goals and specifications. Ask questions of yourself and of your team, such as: Were the clients or project stakeholders satisfied with the instruction delivered? Was the design/development team satisfied with the quality of the instruction delivered? Encourage team members to identify key lessons learned and ways to improve future team design/development efforts. Make sure that all final tasks have been completed and all promised deliverables have been turned over to the client or key stakeholder and that all required project records and evaluations have been completed and reported.

You should also address the results of SME and stakeholder final *reviews and feedback*. More and more, instructional design is a process that involves close collaboration with others, whether subject matter experts, colleagues, clients, learners, or product end users. Therefore, the instruction you produce will likely be subject to review and revision (or at least feedback) from others. If you are both the designer and instructor, you may never design instructional content that requires review by others, but you may wish to obtain feedback from others to improve your design, and you will doubtless submit other things that require review (e.g., final papers, proposals, product descriptions, journal articles, or book chapters).

Due to variations in the quality and applicability of the feedback you receive, you may not always choose to use it, or you may decide to make changes that are slightly different from what the reviewer intended. Therefore, it is important to have a systematic process for responding to the feedback from others who review your work. This is especially important when a client or SME will be involved in the development and/or delivery of the proposed instruction, and will be aware of whether or not you have addressed their previous concerns (Morrison, 1985). It is important to document your design decisions in response to the reviews so that you can both remember and justify any design elements or decisions that may be challenged later in the process. A handy way to accomplish this is to compile a summary table of the issues raised by a reviewer and notes on how you addressed those issues. A one- or two-paragraph summary of what you gleaned from the review and how it improved the design (or was not applicable to the design) should accompany the table.

If you decide to ignore a reviewer's comments, you must justify why you have decided to do so. Be sure to acknowledge their concerns and clarify their main points. Verifying this information will lead you to an appropriate solution in a more efficient manner. Present a resolution, stating or outlining in writing the specifics of what you will do and will not do, presenting any applicable alternatives. Check back to verify your understanding and to gain approval. Table 11.4 provides

Table 11.4 Review Response Example

Content/Design Element Addressed (Include Location)	Comment, Recommendation, or Issue Raised by Reviewer	Whether and How Comment Was Addressed
Banana box photo on page 3 of the assessment	Client was concerned about using a banana box photo. Banana boxes are commonly used to transport non-perishable food donations, but if used for perishable food, it might fall through the hole in the box bottom.	Photographed a different type of box to use in the assessment and will emphasize in the scenario feedback that any box used for food donation transport should have a full lid and bottom.
Photo descriptions on the job aids	Client requested that the descriptive text on the job aids be placed as close as possible to the photo being described.	Replaced photos with line drawings that had the relevant items labeled.
Job aids	Client suggested using the term "quick reference aid" instead of "job aid." Also recommended deleting the job aid for how to lift heavy objects to avoid the impression that it gives that it is OK for volunteers to lift heavy objects. Volunteers should not lift heavy objects.	Agree to change "job aid" to "quick reference aid" throughout the instructional materials. Will also delete the job aid on lifting.

a chart format that works well for documenting how you have decided to respond to a reviewer's comments.

You will recall that we introduced Kirkpatrick's *four-level evaluation* model in Chapter 1. Kirkpatrick recommends that you start at the beginning of your project by defining your expectations for the results you want to see in your summative evaluation after implementation, and then work backwards to build a chain of evidence by collecting benchmark data for all four levels, and defining the measurements you will take during and after the implementation. Ask yourself: What will success look like and what are the key factors that will contribute to that success (Level IV Results)? What critical behaviors and organizational drivers would be required to achieve success (Level III Behavior or Transfer)? What knowledge, skills, and abilities should the learner perform on the job (Level II Learning)? What type of learning environment and conditions will support the learner's efforts and enjoyment (Level I Reaction)? In this way, the model serves as both a planning and an evaluation tool.

Once the instruction has been implemented, begin the summative evaluation with the Level I learner reaction surveys and the assessments of learning (Level II). You may need to present your results for Levels I and II now, and possibly for Level IV (Impact/Results) if you have access to all the data, and then add the behavior change data for Level III when it is available. After a period of time, you can measure Level III (Behavior change/Transfer) by observing whether the learners are using the new critical behaviors on the job.

You may be able to use learning analytics as a basis for some of your Level II Learning evaluation. Learning analytics involves collecting, interpreting, and reporting data about how and where learning occurs for a learner to determine academic progress, predict future performance, and identify potential learning issues. Large amounts of learner data, profile information, and curricular information can be gathered from learning management systems, social networking tools, and other online learning experiences. Learning analytics programs then evaluate and report this information to the learner or instructor so that measures can be taken to improve learning outcomes, personalize learning spaces, and recommend instructional interventions and adaptations.

IDT job advertisements increasingly indicate that candidates should be able to calculate the return on investment (ROI) for instructional and training expenditures. Kirkpatrick's fourth level (Impact/Results) addresses ROI (Kirkpatrick & Kirkpatrick, 2006); however, Dr. Jack J. Phillips, a recognized authority on accountability, measurement, and evaluation, has suggested that a fifth level devoted to ROI should be added to Kirkpatrick's model (Brewer, 2007; Phillips, 2005). The website for this chapter provides information and resources on calculating ROI as part of your Level IV evaluation.

Kirkpatrick and Kirkpatrick (2006) devote an entire chapter of their book *Evaluating Training Programs* to the topic of evaluating e-learning. They stress that a Level I evaluation can serve to monitor the emotional acceptance of e-learning which, to some learners, is a new experience. To gauge learner reaction to e-learning (Level II), they suggest asking learners to vote on the e-learning design, arranging for them to comment on their e-learning experiences on a discussion forum or blog, gathering their feedback in a chat-based focus group, automatically recording access and participation statistics through the system, and embedding several short (one or two question) evaluations periodically throughout the e-learning instruction. An evaluation of learning (Level II) for an online course should address the quality, quantity, and thoroughness of the assessment involved (Garrison, 2011). Kirkpatrick and Kirkpatrick (2006) stress that Level II evaluations are much easier for e-learning since you can automate assessment administration, scoring, recording, and reporting. Some systems also allow you to immediately compare assessment results to required standards and competencies, and to use the results of those comparisons as the basis for suggested remediation and enrichment.

For Level III evaluations of e-learning (Behavior change/Transfer), Kirkpatrick and Kirkpatrick (2006) suggest sending electronic questionnaires to the supervisors of those who have been trained. If considered early in the process, you can have the supervisors compare trained and untrained employees before and after training to document any improvements and more directly link those improvements to the training. The same systems and questionnaires you use to evaluate the success of the training can also be used to evaluate an individual's job performance (thus optimizing your efforts and associating the costs of the Level III evaluation to a function that is necessary for, and may then be paid for by, the operations department). You can also utilize the systems that employees work with to measure whether they are applying the information and skills they learned in the instruction. For example, if you taught them how to use certain reference materials or job aids that are available online, you can determine whether and how often they access those aids.

Such practices can also contribute to a Level IV (Results/Impact) evaluation by enabling you to quantify things like productivity before and after instruction. In general, an effective Level IV evaluation requires a clear picture of the strategic intent of the e-learning program (Garrison, 2011) so that you have a goal for your evaluation and comparisons. Metrics for evaluating impact for e-learning are much the same as those used for other types of instruction, with the exception of the use of social media and networks. For example, how would you determine the impact or ROI for a community of practice (CoP)? Etienne Wenger (the father of CoP) and his colleagues Beverly Trayner and Maartin de Laat (2011) have come up with a means to address this challenge, and you may want to refer to their work as a model for Level IV evaluations of the social media strategies you use in your instructional designs (see Wenger, Trayner, & de Laat, 2011).

While Kirkpatrick's (1998) model is the best known, there are other models and approaches that you can use to evaluate your instruction. In addition to Kirkpatrick's systems, Preskill and Russ-Eft (2005) describe numerous other models, including: a behavioral objectives approach, responsive evaluation, goal-free evaluation, adversary/judicial approaches, consumer-oriented approaches, expertise/accreditation approaches, utilization-focused evaluation, participatory/collaborative evaluation, empowerment evaluation, organizational learning, theory-driven evaluation, and the success case method (pp. 101–103). Roger Kaufman, Guerra-Lopez, and Platt

(2005) offered a five-level evaluation model as an alternative to Kirkpatrick's model. Kaufman's levels include:

> *Level 1*—Resources and Processes, which focuses on how organizational factors such as available resources and processes impact learner satisfaction;
>
> *Level 2*—Acquisition, which focuses on the micro-benefits to individuals and groups and achievement of targeted outcomes (for both instructional and non-instructional solutions);
>
> *Level 3*—Application, which focuses on micro-benefits resulting when individuals apply the newly acquired knowledge and skills on the job;
>
> *Level 4*—Organizational payoffs, which focus on the macro-benefits impacting the organization;
>
> *Level 5*—Societal contributions, which focus on the mega-level contributions made by the organization to its community or to society as a whole.

Select an approach that aligns with the purpose of your evaluation and what you need to be able to do with the results. Using an approach familiar to your stakeholders is also a good idea, since by doing so you are more likely to meet their expectations.

Streamlining Production and Implementation

Successful production and implementation efforts are those that are aligned to organizational goals, and streamlined to be effective, efficient, and sustainable.

- *Sustainable*—Examine your design/development process and identify those activities that do not add significant value and that your client or employer would likely refuse to fund if consulted. Eliminate those activities or, if you still feel the activity is essential, investigate whether it can cost-effectively be outsourced or in some way simplified so that it takes less time. Limit the number of SMEs consulted and allowed to review the materials, since disagreements between several SMEs on content can extend the schedule for development. Build sustainability into your design/development process by using best practices and planning for unanticipated absences by cross-training team members and thus reducing reliance on just a few key team members.

- *Optimized*—Identify learning elements or units that can be optimized by serving multiple purposes in your instructional program, and generic materials that can be leveraged by other instructional projects and entities in your organization. Use templates to standardize the design and optimize the development process. Settle on an agreed-upon number of unique layouts and designs and discourage adding new ones. If there is more of a need to share information with the learner than to actually instruct them on a complex skill, consider designing the instruction around job aids to optimize it. Embed informal learning opportunities in your organization's work-flow to provide just-in-time resources and training, and use incentives to encourage individuals to access and share ideas in communities of practice. Establish formal processes, templates, and guidelines that can help streamline the production process.

- *Sustainable and Optimized*—It is a fact that as you move from traditional face-to-face instructional formats to more high-tech formats the amount of required development time and effort increases. Therefore, you should seek to use less costly formats and production processes when: you expect the content to change rapidly or need frequent updating, the instruction will have a short shelf life, you have a limited budget, the instruction must be produced and implemented in a short time period, you are repurposing existing content, and/or the topic can be easily explained with words and does not require visuals or animation (Rosen, 2009).

- *Appropriately Redundant*—Keep a careful record and track all draft versions of the instructional elements and review comments, including written drafts, images, audio and video recordings, instructor guidelines, help files and FAQs, interface designs, etc. Failure to do so may result in undesirable redundancy that compromises the quality of your final materials.
- *Right-Sized*—Be very clear with SMEs concerning deadlines for adding new content, because if you allow them to continue to add items throughout the design/development process, your project will likely fall behind schedule due to project creep.
- *Continuously Improving*—Whenever possible, tie your evaluation measurements to client-recorded benchmarks that illustrate the need for training. Build support for your initiatives by aligning them with your organization's mission and goals, emphasizing that the success of your projects are dependent on the contributions of everyone in the organization. Emphasize that formal and informal learning opportunities are the key to responding to and managing change.

Different Career Environments, Different Perspectives

- Some government agencies use the PADDIE model, which consists of the ADDIE stages plus a Project Management stage. In addition, some government agencies require the preparation of a Training Implementation Matrix (TIM) that defines the organization, planning, and administration of qualification and certification training programs for employees and the responsibility, authority, and methods for conducting training. This type of document also describes the education and experience requirements necessary for trainers in the organization to ensure that they are qualified to carry out their assigned duties.
- Process improvement programs in corporate environments stress the development of a culture that encourages the constant evaluation of tasks to eliminate those that do not add value. Training programs to foster this type of culture and the supporting attitudes are evaluated both formatively and summatively.
- In higher education, production work is either done by faculty members or is completed by departments devoted to helping faculty produce instructional materials or move face-to-face courses to an online format. Colleges and universities typically make use of course or learning management systems (LMS) to deliver both blended and online courses. Most use proprietary LMSs, but some institutions have devoted resources towards open source LMSs. In both situations technical support for faculty and students is an issue, since proprietary systems are not always immediately responsive to faculty and student needs, and open source systems require that the institution dedicate both human and non-human resources to provide the necessary support.
- Additional concerns in K-12 environments include accomplishing production with limited resources and dealing with the challenges of unpredictable Internet filtering systems.
- Instructional designers working in the health-care environment are frequently in charge of their own projects and must work with development teams or outside vendors to effectively manage the schedule, budget, and quality of the final product. Evaluations are prioritized and are generally carried out on a regular basis to satisfy accrediting agencies and/or funding sources and to improve the quality of care through quality instruction.

Diving Deeper

Want to know more? Check out these website resources:

- **Practical Exercises and Examples**—Worked examples and exercises for project management and evaluation, and Bloom Stretch exercises.
- **Job Aids**—Samples of design documents, usability test task lists and reaction survey, and other relevant job aids.
- **Resources**—Links to resources on learning analytics, ROI, Section 508 compliance, copyright, and more.

Wrapping It Up: Pursuing Continuous Improvement in Your Professional Practice

Test Your Understanding With a Bloom Stretch

Remember and Understand	Reproduce the ADDIE model from this book (or your own, elaborated version of it), and concisely articulate the activities and iterative process involved to a client, friend, or relative. Ideally, your audiences will be able to understand your description and dialogue with you about the implications of the process for a potential project (client), for your reputation and ability to keep a conversation going (friend), or for the demands that the process might place on your time and availability (spouse or relative).
Apply	Apply the streamlined ADDIE activities to successfully design and develop effective instruction and learning experiences.
Analyze	Analyze the scope of an instructional design project to determine how best to address project needs, streamlining the process to use only those activities that are necessary for the given content, context, learners, and project goals.
Evaluate	Compare the process described in this book to other design/development models and processes, ascertain the strengths and weaknesses of the activities involved, and identify the activities and processes that work best for you.
Create	Revise and/or elaborate the process described in this book to create your own, streamlining to produce a process that is sustainable, optimized, appropriately redundant, right-sized, and continuously improving! (And please feel free to engage in our learning process by sending us your suggestions for improving this book!)

Glossary

Accommodation	Changing existing knowledge (schema and scripts) to incorporate new information. Any modification of an assimilatory scheme or structure by the elements it assimilates (Piaget, 1970). This term also refers to a form of scaffolding that supports students through a change in the delivery of instruction or the method of student performance without changing the content or conceptual difficulty of the curriculum. It often features the use of assistive technologies, but it can also consist merely of a low-tech strategy.
Adaptation	A change in the delivery of instruction, and/or the conceptual difficulty and content to assist an individual to learn in the least restrictive environment.
Alternative assessment	Evaluation instruments and procedures other than objective-style tests. Includes the evaluation of live performances, products, and attitudes. Format includes directions for the learner and a scoring rubric (Dick, Carey, & Carey, 2008).
Analyzing skills	A core thinking skill that involves clarifying information by examining the parts and relationships between the parts and the whole.
Anchored instruction	A problem-based approach that provides all the information within a scenario that a learner needs to solve the problem. Used frequently in K-12 environments, this strategy is based on situated cognition and is designed to provide a meaningful context and realistic, interesting problems for learners (Smith & Ragan, 2005).
Andragogy	The learning strategies, instructional frameworks, and theory related to teaching the adult learner (as opposed to "pedagogy," the teaching of children), which was developed and popularized by Malcolm Knowles (Simonson, Smaldino, Albright, & Zvacek, 2009).
Applying skills	A core thinking skill that uses learned concepts to solve a new problem in appropriate ways.
Aptitude-treatment interaction (ATI) research	A field of research that studies the interaction between learner aptitudes and instructional treatments (or strategies that are used during instruction). The goal of this type of research is to create instruction that best matches an individual learner's aptitude.

Aptitudes and instructional treatments interact in complex ways and are influenced by task and situation variables (Seels & Richey, 1994).

ARCS
The acronym for Keller's model of motivation theory, which stands for "Attention, Relevance, Confidence, and Satisfaction" (Keller, 1983).

Assimilation
A cognitive process to integrate external elements into evolving or completed structures (Piaget, 1970). It occurs when a learner perceives new objects or events in terms of existing schemes or operations (Driscoll, 1994).

Asynchronous learning
Learning experiences for which there is a delay between the sending and receiving of instructional messages, communications, and feedback. Asynchronous learning is typically electronically mediated (Lewis & Whitlock, 2003).

Attention
Conscious control of mental focus on particular information.

Attitudes
Personal principles, beliefs, and values that influence an individual's behavior.

Authentic assessment
Assessment in meaningful real-life contexts in which newly acquired skills will ultimately be applied (Dick, Carey, & Carey, 2008).

Blended learning
A mix of learning experiences that includes learning in a supervised physical location away from home, and through online delivery where the student has control over the time, place, path, and/or the pace of the learning experiences (Staker & Horn, 2012). Also known as *hybrid learning*.

Bloom's taxonomy
Bloom's Taxonomy of Educational Objectives (Bloom, Engelhart, Furst, Hill, & Krathwohl, 1956) is a classification of cognitive, psychomotor, and affective learning outcomes. The most popular of the classifications is the handbook for cognitive objectives (thinking skills), and the most commonly used version of that taxonomy today is the revision completed in 2001 (Anderson & Krathwohl, 2001). Churches (2009) applied Bloom's Revised Taxonomy to digital media.

Chunking
An instructional strategy that divides information into manageable "chunks," or units, which are ultimately combined to construct a more complex lesson (Dabbagh & Bannan-Ritland, 2005). A related concept is George Miller's (1956) "magical number 7, plus or minus 2," which refers to the average number of objects a learner can hold in working memory.

Classifying
Grouping entities on the basis of their common attributes.

Cognitive apprenticeship
An instructional strategy that pairs a less experienced learner with an expert to learn a skill along with implicit and tacit knowledge, and to receive coaching and mentoring (Brown, Collins, & Duguid, 1989).

Cognitive Flexibility Theory
A constructivist theory that focuses on the nature of learning in complex, ill-structured domains, and concerns the ability to adapt and change one's mental organization of knowledge and mental management of solution strategies to solve new, unexpected problems (Spiro, Coulson, Feltovich, & Anderson, 1988).

Cognitivism
A learning theory in which learning is viewed as active mental processing to store new knowledge in memory and retrieve knowledge from memory. Cognitivism emphasizes the structure of knowledge and

	external conditions that support internal mental processes known as schema (Woolfolk, 2005).
Cognitive Load Theory	Cognitive Load Theory defines three types of load on working memory: intrinsic load, germane load, and extraneous load. *Intrinsic load* refers to the type and amount of mental processing required by a learning task, based on its inherent complexity. *Extraneous load* refers to the unnecessary, increased demand on mental processing (i.e., "noise") that results from the way in which the content is presented. *Germane load* is processing that relates directly to the content and helps the learner to perceive and process the information more easily (Sweller, 1988).
Cognitive Theory of Multimedia Learning	The use of cognitive theory to support ten design principles that facilitate the learning of content conveyed through multimedia (Mayer, 2001, 2009, in press).
Component Display Theory	An instructional theory consisting of component displays of instruction (descriptive theory) and the prescriptive relationships between these component displays and different kinds of instruction (prescriptive theory); this theory is based on the premise that there are different relationships between content ideas and that selecting an appropriate content structure and its instantiation provides the basis for more appropriately selecting instructional modules and their organization (Merrill, 1994).
Concept	A set of objects, events, symbols, situations, and so on, that can be grouped together on the basis of one or more shared characteristics and given a common identifying label or symbol. Concept learning refers to the capacity to identify members of the concepts category (Dick, Carey, & Carey, 2008).
Concept formation	Organizing information about an entity and associating the information with a label or word.
Connectivism	A philosophy that maintains that knowledge exists in the world rather than merely in the head of an individual, and learning consists of connections made by the learner to build a network of information sources to consult as needed when completing a related task. Some claim that Connectivism is a theory of learning (Downes, 2012; Siemens, 2004).
Constraints	Every instructional design project is subject to constraints, or limits, on the parameters of the project. Constraints may include non-negotiable design specifications that have been dictated by key stakeholders, as well as limits on the amount of time and/or human and non-human resources available to complete the project.
Constructivism	A learning theory in which learning is viewed as an internal process of constructing meaning by combining existing knowledge with new knowledge gained through experiences in the social, cultural, and physical world. Constructivism emphasizes the processes and social interactions in which a student engages for learning (Woolfolk, 2005). A school of psychology which holds that learning occurs because personal knowledge is constructed by an active and self-regulated learner who solves problems by deriving meaning from

experience and the context in which that experience takes place (Seels & Richey, 1994).

Content curation   The act of organizing, maintaining, and commenting on a collection of information artifacts on a topic of interest.

Creative thinking   The ability to think fluently, flexibly, and originally about a topic. To form new combinations of ideas to fulfill a need, to produce an original or appropriate solution to a problem or challenge for the domain in question.

Critical thinking   Reasonable, objective, and logical reflective thinking that is focused on deciding what to believe or do, while being aware of one's own biases. The ability to analyze arguments, see other points of view, and reach sound conclusions.

Curriculum   A structured series of instructional topics and materials intended to address specific learning goals and outcomes.

Declarative information   Factual information.

Delivery system   Term used to describe the means by which instruction will be provided to learners. Includes instructor-led instruction, distance education, computer-based instruction, and self-instructional materials (Dick, Carey, & Carey, 2008).

Demonstration   A dynamic presentation where specific parts or processes are identified and the function or activities performed by each component is explained (Merrill, 1994).

Differentiation   A term used primarily in K-12 environments that refers to efforts to provide learners with different ways to access, process, and learn content in consideration of learner differences in readiness, interest, and learning needs (Tomlinson, 2001).

Discrimination   Distinguishing one stimulus from another and responding differently to the various stimuli (Dick, Carey, & Carey, 2008).

Disequilibrium   Opposite status of *equilibrium*. It occurs when new stimuli do not fit existing schema.

Divergent   An interdisplay relationship in which the critical attributes of two examples are as different as possible while sharing the same critical attributes (Merrill, 1994).

Dual-Coding Theory   Theory that suggests that the brain processes visual and verbal information separately using two distinct mental channels, producing separate mental representations for the two types of information (Paivio, 1969, 1971, 1986, 1991).

Effect size   Refers to a statistical means of looking at the significance of differences in student achievement scores between a control and an experimental group.

Elaborate   To encode information and connect it to prior knowledge and experiences by adding details, explanations, examples, or other relevant information from prior knowledge.

e-learning   Also *eLearning*, *e-Learning*, and *E-Learning*. This term refers to "instruction delivered on a computer by way of CD-ROM, Internet, or intranet" (Clark & Mayer, 2003, p. 13), or to "the use of Internet technologies to deliver a broad array of solutions that enhance knowledge and performance" (Rosenberg, 2000, p. 28).

Electronic Performance Support System (EPSS)	A computer software program or a component of a larger system that supports users and helps improve their performance by providing point-of-need information, tutorials, guidance, and job aids (Lewis & Whitlock, 2003). Also, a combination of hardware and software components which provides an "infobase," expert system, job aids, and tools and other elements, to support performance of tasks (Seels & Richey, 1994).
Encode	To store information in long-term memory.
Entry skills	Specific competencies or skills a learner must have mastered before entering a given instructional activity (Dick, Carey, & Carey, 2008). See also *Prerequisites*.
EPSS	See *Electronic Performance Support System.*
Equilibrium	The mental state of balance indicating that new knowledge aligns well with previous knowledge. When new information does not align with the learner's existing schema, the learner must use *assimilation* or *accommodation* to regain equilibrium (Driscoll, 1994).
Evaluating skills	Core thinking skills that involve assessing the worth, value, and/or reasonableness and quality of ideas or objects.
Evaluation	A systematic, planned, and purposeful activity of judging the merit, worth, value, or effectiveness of an instructional program or product, for the purpose of enhancing knowledge and decision making (Lewis & Whitlock, 2003; Russ-Eft & Preskill, 2001).
Executive control	Evaluating, planning, and regulating the declarative, procedural, and conditional information involved in a task.
Exemplifying	A situation in which the student tries to find in memory a previously learned instance of the information (Merrill, 1994).
Feedback	Information provided to learners about the correctness of their responses to practice questions in the instruction (Dick, Carey, & Carey, 2008). A secondary presentation consisting of information about the nature of the student's response; the response may include the correct answer to the question (Merrill, 1994).
Figure/ground perception	The ability of the viewer to distinguish an object from its surrounding background (Rubin, 1915/1921).
Fishbowl strategy	A teaching strategy that helps learners practice contributing and listening in a discussion. Learners sit in two concentric circles—those in the inner circle carry on a discussion, and those in the outer circle observe the process. After a while, those in the outer circle move to the inner circle and vice versa, or the facilitator can call upon inner-circle participants who have made substantive contributions to the discussion and allow them to select their replacement from the outer circle. When used to discuss an assigned reading selection, this strategy also encourages learners to complete those readings. Questions can be supplied with the readings, learners can be asked to bring questions to ask others in the fishbowl, or the facilitator can broach questions at the beginning of the discussion.
Front-end analysis	A process used for evaluating instructional needs and identifying alternative approaches to meeting those needs. It includes a variety of activities, including (but not limited to) performance analysis, needs

	assessment, job analysis, training delivery options, and feasibility analysis (Dick, Carey, & Carey, 2008).
Generative strategies	Strategies designed to encourage or allow learners to define their own learning goals, organize the material in whatever manner works best for them, control the sequencing and pace of the instruction, self-monitor their own understanding, and transfer the knowledge to new contexts. In this way, the learners basically "generate" the majority of the processing (thinking) involved in the learning experience (Smith & Ragan, 2005).
Gestalt	A branch of psychology that proposes that the brain is holistic, and has self-organizing tendencies that enable it to understand external stimuli as a whole form rather than as parts (Wertheimer, 1923).
Goal	A broad, general statement of an instructional intent, expressed in terms of what learners will be able to do (Dick, Carey, & Carey, 2008).
Goal analysis	The technique used to analyze a goal to identify the sequence of operations and decisions required to achieve it (Dick, Carey, & Carey, 2008).
Goal-Based Scenarios	A structured learning program used in physical and virtual environments that provides a simulation or scenario to motivate learners to engage and develop skills rather than memorize facts (Schank, 1996).
Granularity	The extent to which an instructional system is broken down, divided, or organized into small units to enable flexible sequencing, branching, and shorter "chunks" for study and learning. Many instructional programs are divided into modules, units, lessons, etc. (Lewis & Whitlock, 2003).
Hybrid learning	See *Blended learning.*
Ill-structured	Situation in which neither the exact rules to be applied nor the exact nature of the solution is identified in the problem statement. Multiple solutions may be acceptable (Dick, Carey, & Carey, 2008).
Inferring	Identifying what may be reasonably true by building on and going beyond the available information.
Instructional strategy	An overall plan of activities to achieve an instructional goal. The strategy includes the sequence of intermediate objectives and the learning activities leading to the instructional goal as well as specification of student groupings, media, and the delivery system. The instructional activities typically include pre-instructional activities, content presentation, learner participation, assessment, and follow-through activities (Dick, Carey, & Carey, 2008). Specifications for selecting and sequencing events and activities within a lesson (Seels & Richey, 1994).
Instructivism	An approach to instruction for which the instruction or an instructor presents content, monitors, and guides learner performance in a practice environment and provides feedback, the learner performs the goal task, and their performance is assessed. Also described as a "directed" learning environment (Sharma, Oliver, & Hannafin, 2007).
Jigsaw	A cooperative learning strategy used with small groups of learners that requires each member of the group to specialize in one area of content and then teach the rest of the group that content.

Job aid	A support for performing a job that is in either paper or electronic form and serves to relieve the learner's reliance on memory during the performance of a complex task. Also referred to as a *quick reference aid*.
Job analysis	The process of gathering, analyzing, and synthesizing descriptions of what people do, or should do, in their jobs (Dick, Carey, & Carey, 2008).
KASI	An acronym that stands for "Knowledge, Attitudes, Skills and Inter-personal" abilities. During content analysis the designer determines which KASIs are desirable and should be included in the instruction being developed. See also *KSA*.
Kirkpatrick's Model	Donald Kirkpatrick developed a four-level model that recommends evaluating instruction with respect to: Level I Learner Reaction, Level II Learning, Level III Behavior (change in behavior or transfer of new knowledge and skills), and Level IV Results (also known as Impact). (Kirkpatrick & Kirkpatrick, 2006).
Knowledge domain	A body of information commonly associated with a particular content area or field of study.
Knowledge management	Also referred to as *point-of-need* and *just-in-time* support, this term refers to management of information and performance support materials that scaffold workers and learners with easy access to information, training, reference files, and social networking and collaboration applications. These systems provide just-in-time information and self-paced training units and tutorials. They also capture and store the knowledge, expertise, and interaction of employees for future use and to guard against valuable information loss when employees leave the organization.
KSA	A common acronym in the field of instructional design and training development that stands for Knowledge, Skills and Attitudes. During content analysis, instructional designers determine which KSAs are desirable and should be included in the instruction being developed.
K-W-L strategy	Know—Want to Know—Learned is a reading strategy that guides reading and inquiry using a frame or worksheet that requires learners identify what they already Know about a topic, what they Want to know, and (following the reading or inquiry) what they have Learned about the topic.
Learner analysis	The determination of pertinent characteristics of members of the target population. Often includes prior knowledge and attitudes toward the content to be taught, as well as attitudes toward the organization and work environment (Dick, Carey, & Carey, 2008).
Learning analytics	Learning analytics involves collecting, interpreting, and reporting data about how and where learning occurs for a learner to determine academic progress, predict future performance, and identify potential learning issues.
Learning context	The actual physical location (or locations) in which the instruction that is under development will be used (Dick, Carey, & Carey, 2008).
Learning hierarchy analysis	A method of content analysis that involves the analysis of how learners mentally process information while performing tasks. A learning

hierarchy is a structure which describes what the learner must be able to do before something else can be learned and which illustrates the dependencies and relationships between the elements to be learned (Merrill, 1994).

Learning object "A learning object is any entity, digital or non-digital, which can be used, re-used and referenced during technology-supported teaching" (from the IEEE 1484.12.1-2002 Learning Object Metadata standard, IEEE, 2002). Learning object repositories are online, searchable collections of digital educational resources.

Locus of control Also referred to as *locus of causality*, this term refers to the extent to which a learner believes that he or she controls the events that affect their learning (Rotter, 1954).

Mashup A combination of existing works, data, presentations, or functionality to create a new entity.

Message design The specification and manipulation of media for the purpose of producing learning (Bishop, in press).

Metacognition Awareness and control of one's thinking, including commitment, attitudes, and attention. Often defined as "thinking about thinking."

Microworlds A term coined by Seymore Papert to describe exploratory learning environments that Jonassen (2000) says are basically discovery spaces and simulations of "real-world phenomena in which learners can navigate, manipulate or create objects, and test their effects on one another" (p. 157), and they can assume many forms in different learning domains.

Mindtools "[C]omputer applications that require students to think in meaningful ways in order to use the application to represent what they know" (Jonassen, 2000, p. 4), and they serve as tools that learners use as intellectual partners to build knowledge.

Misconception A situation in which the student focuses on some irrelevant attribute as a critical attribute and thereby excludes examples which do not have this attribute and includes non-examples which do have this attribute (Merrill, 1994).

Mnemonics A set of encoding strategies that involve linking bits of information together through visual or semantic connections.

Module An instructional package with a single integrated theme that provides the information needed to develop mastery of specified knowledge and skills and serves as one component of a total course or curriculum (Dick, Carey, & Carey, 2008).

MOOC A Massive Open Online Course provides open access to an unlimited number of interested individuals wishing to learn online. MOOCs are frequently offered by established universities who allow open participation without credit. Sometimes they will establish additional requirements for participants desiring credit.

Needs analysis The formal process of identifying discrepancies between current outcomes or conditions and desired outcomes or conditions for an organization or individual (Dick, Carey, & Carey, 2008). Also known as *needs assessment*.

Objective A statement of what the learners will be expected to do when they have completed a specified course of instruction, stated in terms of observable performances. Also known as *performance objective, behavioral objective,* and *instructional objective* (Dick, Carey, & Carey, 2008).

Paraphrasing A situation in which the student reformulates the information in his or her own words (Merrill, 1994).

Pedagogy The methods, strategies, and practices of teaching, specifically teaching children and young adults.

Performance analysis An analytical process used to locate, analyze, and correct job or product performance problems (Dick, Carey, & Carey, 2008).

Performance context The setting in which it is hoped that learners will successfully use the skills they are learning; includes both the physical and social aspects of the setting (Dick, Carey, & Carey, 2008).

Performance support system Scaffolds or supports to improve the performance of an employee or learner. See also *Electronic Performance Support System.*

Personal Learning Environment (PLE) Systems that empower learners to take control of and manage their own learning. These systems can be physical or virtual and the term has been used more recently in conjunction with an emphasis on lifelong learning.

Pilot test Trying out instruction or a portion of the instruction with learners representative of the target audience for the purpose of revising and improving the instruction prior to implementation (Lewis & Whitlock, 2003).

Podcast An electronic digital file of a multimedia presentation available for subscription, downloading, or streaming via the Internet. It may consist of audio, video, portable document format (pdf) documents, and/or ePub files.

Posttests See *Pretests.*

Prerequisites A term used to describe entry skills and/or knowledge necessary for taking the instruction (Dick, Carey, & Carey, 2008). See also *Entry skills.*

Pretests A method of measuring learning by using a written, oral, knowledge- or skill-based test before and after instruction. The difference between the learner's performance on the pretest and the *posttest* is taken as a measure of what was learned. Such tests, however, are subject to other influences and may not reflect actual learning (e.g., if the learner is not feeling well when the test is taken, misunderstands the instructions given for taking the tests, etc.) (Davies, 1981).

Prior knowledge A universally acknowledged prerequisite for learning, prior knowledge refers to content or experiences previously learned that relates to the new topic or task to be learned. A learner's prior knowledge interacts with new information and instruction, and can be sufficient for assimilating the new knowledge, or it may be incomplete, lacking, or incompatible with the knowledge to be learned.

Problem solving Analyzing a perplexing or difficult situation for the purpose of generating a solution.

Procedural knowledge Knowledge about the various actions or processes important to a task.

Prototype A preliminary model of instruction used for review and testing purposes.

Psychomotor skill	Execution of a sequence of major or subtle physical actions to achieve a specified result. All skills employ some type of physical action; the physical action in a psychomotor skill is the focus of the new learning and is not merely the vehicle for expressing an intellectual skill (Dick, Carey, & Carey, 2008).
Reciprocal teaching	A strategy for increasing reading comprehension developed by Palincsar and Brown (1984), that has been proven effective through extensive research. The strategy emphasizes the skills of generating questions, clarifying, summarizing, and predicting. It requires students to summarize what they have read and generate questions about the reading. One learner role-plays as the teacher and questions the other learners; the teacher functions as a model and coach to assist learners and learners ask questions for clarification.
Rehearsal	An encoding strategy that involves repeated processing of information.
Remembering skills	A core thinking skill that involves proper encoding and conscious effort to store knowledge in long-term memory so that it can be recalled or recognized when necessary for future use (Sprenger, 2005).
Retrieval	Accessing or remembering previously encoded information.
ROI	Acronym for "return on investment." In training and development it is a comparison between the costs incurred for training and the benefits realized from training (Phillips, 2005).
Rubric	A document that lays out the expectations for an assignment by listing criteria that serve as guidelines for learners and as scoring points for grading. Some rubrics describe different levels of quality and provide point values to be scored for each level.
Scaffolds	Scaffolds are different types of support (e.g., hints, examples, worksheets, question prompts, etc.) that assist learners when they are not able to complete a learning task on their own (Wood, Bruner, & Ross, 1976).
Schema	Mental knowledge structures associated with a specific state, event, or concept.
SCORM	Acronym for "Sharable Content Object Reference Model"—a set of standards and specifications that defines communication between the content of web-based instruction and a Learning Management System (LMS). It also defines how to package the content into a ZIP file so that it is easily transferred. The current version of SCORM (2004) provides for adaptive sequencing so that rules can be defined to control a learner's access to areas of the content.
Scripts	Mental scripts are schema that describe events. They are temporally organized representations of a common sequence of events, or schema about procedural knowledge that include everyday events (Schank & Abelson, 1977).
Self-regulation	Controlling one's learning by checking or monitoring one's progress toward a goal. Self-generated thoughts, feelings, and actions that are planned and cyclically adapted for the attainment of personal goals (Boekaerts, Pintrich, & Zeidner, 2005).
Situated learning	The concept that learning occurs best through engagement in a

process or activity that should be placed in (situated in) a context that is relevant to the learner and the knowledge to be gained (Lave & Wenger, 1991).

SMART objectives "Specific, Measurable, Action-oriented, Realistic, and Timely" objectives (Smith, 1994).

Sociological shift A paradigm shift that involves how an individual looks at society and elements within a society. In the field of instructional design, this term refers to a designer's ability to view the design challenge or topic from the viewpoint of the target culture, especially if that culture is different from the designer's culture.

Stakeholder Any individual or group with a "stake" or interest in the instruction being designed and developed. Stakeholders vary by career environment and can include the designer, learners, employees, users, facilitators or instructors, managers, company owners, community residents, patients, etc.

Subject matter expert A person knowledgeable about a particular content area (Dick, Carey, & Carey, 2008); often given the acronym "SME."

Supplantive strategies Strategies designed to "supplant" or do more of the mental processing for the learner by explicitly stating instructional goals and providing information on how to think about, structure, and retain the content.

Synchronous learning Learning experiences carried out in real time, featuring immediate sending and receipt of messages and information amongst participants. This term is typically applied to electronically mediated learning environments but can also be used to refer to face-to-face instructional environments (Lewis & Whitlock, 2003).

Synthesis Core thinking skills that involve connecting or combining information.

Think-aloud strategy A strategy that requires that learners verbalize their thoughts when reading, solving math problems, or responding to questions posed by others. Instructors should model thinking aloud to demonstrate practical and effective ways of approaching problems and other cognitively demanding tasks.

Think-Pair-Share strategy A strategy for engaging learners in a lesson by posing a question, allowing quiet time for learners to reflect and write their individual responses, then pairing students to discuss their answers, and asking each pair to share their conclusions, observations, or viewpoints to the whole group (Walsh & Sattes, 2005).

Transfer Transfer is "the ability to use and apply knowledge and skills learned in one situation or environment to another situation or environment" (Mariano, 2009). There are several different types of transfer mentioned in the instructional design literature: *positive transfer, negative transfer, vertical transfer, lateral transfer, near transfer* and *far transfer* (Haskell, 2000). Methods for fostering transfer of learning include deep learning, awareness and control of cognition (metacognition), learning discrete facts *and* the principles that undergird that knowledge, and instruction that includes multiple and varied examples and contexts (Mariano, 2009).

Understanding skills   A lower-order thinking skill that involves interpreting, exemplifying, classifying, summarizing, inferring, comparing, and explaining.

Vodcast   "Video-on-demand"-casts, or online delivery of video content that is one form of a podcast. See also *Podcast*.

Wait Time I and II   Also recorded as *Wait Time 1 and 2*. Instructional strategies used when questioning learners. Wait Time I refers to the amount of time that elapses after a question is asked, and Wait Time II is the amount of time elapsing between a learner's response to a question and the questioner's reaction or comment to that question. Both strategies are intended to encourage learner reflection and elaboration (Walsh & Sattes, 2005).

Well-structured   Situation in which the nature of the solution is well understood and there is a generally preferred set of rules to follow to determine the solution to a problem (Jonassen, 1997).

References

Ainsworth, L. (2003). *Power standards: Identifying the standards that matter the most.* Englewood, CO: Advanced Learning Press.

Alessi, S.M., & Trollip, S.R. (2001). *Multimedia for learning: Methods and development* (3rd ed.). Boston: Allyn & Bacon.

Allen, C.M., Pike, W.Y., Lacy, L.W., Jung, L., & Wiederhold, M. (2010). *Using biological and environmental malodors to enhance medical simulation training.* Presented at the Interservice/Industry Training, Simulation & Education Conference (I/ITSEC), December 3–6, 2012, Orlando, FL.

Allen, I., & Seaman, J. (2007). *Making the grade: Online education in the United States, 2006: Midwestern edition.* Wellesley, MA: Sloan Consortium.

Allen, M.W. (2003). *Michael Allen's guide to e-learning.* San Francisco: Wiley.

Allen, W.C. (2006). Overview and evolution of the ADDIE training system. *Advances in Developing Human Resources, 8,* 430–441.

American Association of School Administrators (AASA) (2002). Using data to improve schools: What's working. Retrieved November 8, 2007 from: http://aasa.files.cms-plus.com/PDFs/Publications/UsingDataToImproveSchools.pdf

Anastasi, A. (1958). *Differential psychology: Individual and group difference in behaviour* (3rd ed.). New York: Macmillan.

Anderson, L., & Krathwohl, D.A. (2001). *Taxonomy for learning, teaching and assessing: A revision of Bloom's taxonomy of educational objectives.* New York: Longman.

Anderson, T., & Dron, J. (2011). Three generations of distance education pedagogy. *International Review of Research in Open & Distance Learning, 12*(3), 80–97.

Ausubel, D. (1960). The use of advance organizers in the learning and retention of meaningful verbal material. *Journal of Educational Psychology, 51,* 267–272.

Ausubel, D. (1968). *Educational psychology: A cognitive view.* New York: Holt, Rinehart & Winston.

Ausubel, D. (1980). Schemata, cognitive structure, and advance organizers: A reply to Anderson, Spiro, and Anderson. *American Educational Research Journal, 17*(3), 211–218.

Baddeley, A. (2003). Working memory: Looking back and looking forward. *Nature Reviews Neuroscience, 4*(10), 829–839.

Bandura, A. (1977). *Social learning theory.* Englewood Cliffs, NJ: Prentice Hall.

Bandura, A. (1986). *Social foundations of thought and action: A social cognitive theory.* Englewood Cliffs, NJ: Prentice-Hall.

Bandura, A. (1991). *Psychological modeling: Conflicting theories.* Chicago: Aldine-Atherton.

Bandura, A. (1997). *Self-efficacy: The exercise of control.* New York: W.H. Freeman.

Bandura, A., & Schunk, D.H. (1981). Cultivating competence, self-efficacy, and intrinsic interest through proximal self-motivation. *Journal of Personality and Social Psychology, 41,* 568–578.

Barry, A.M.S. (1994). Perceptual aesthetics and visual language. In D.M. Moore & F.M. Dwyer (Eds.), *Visual literacy: A spectrum of visual learning* (pp. 113–132). Englewood Cliffs, NJ: Educational Technology Publications.

Bartell, S.M. (2001). Training's new role in learning organizations. *Innovations in Education and Teaching International, 38*(4), 354–363.

Basdogan, C., & Loftin, R.B. (2008). Multimodal display systems: Haptic, olfactory, gustatory, and vestibular. In D. Schmorrow, J. Cohn, & D. Nicholson, (Eds.), *The PSI Handbook of virtual environments for training and education: Developments for the military and beyond* (pp. 116–135). Westport, CN: Praeger Security International.

Bebington, P. (2008–2011). WBT course complexity. Blog: *The E-Learning Practitioner.* https://sites.google.com/site/prakashbebington/project-management-resources/wbt-course-complexity-levels

Benjamin, S. (1989). A closer look at needs analysis and needs assessment: Whatever happened to the systems approach? *Performance & Instruction, 28*(9), 12–16.

Benson, R., & Samarawickrema, G. (2009). Addressing the context of e-learning: Using transactional distance theory to inform design. *Distance Education, 30*(1), 5–21.

Berlo, D.K. (1960). *The process of communication.* New York: Holt, Rinehart & Winston.

Berrett, D. (2012). How "flipping" the classroom can improve the traditional lecture. *Chronicle of Higher Education, 58*(25), A16–A18.

Betteridge, H.T. (Ed.) (1965). *The new Cassell's German dictionary: German–English, English–German.* New York: Funk & Wagnalls.

Biehler, R., & Snowman, J. (1993). *Psychology applied to teaching* (7th ed.). Boston: Houghton Mifflin Co.

Biggs, J.B. (1999). *Teaching for quality learning at university: What the student does.* Buckingham: Society for Research into Higher Education/Open University Press.

Bisbort, A. (1999). *Escaping flatworld.* Retrieved October 1, 2012 from: http://www.edwardtufte.com/tufte/advocate_1099

Bishop, M.J. (in press). Instructional message design: Past, present, and future relevance. In J.M. Spector, M.D. Merrill, J. Elen, & M.J. Bishop (Eds.), *Handbook of research on educational communications and technology* (4th ed.). New York: Springer.

Blondy, L.C. (2007). Evaluation and application of andragogical assumptions to the adult online learning environment. *Journal of Interactive Online Learning, 6*(2), 116–130.

Bloom, B.S., Engelhart, M.D., Furst, E.J., Hill, W.H., & Krathwohl, D.R. (1956). *Taxonomy of educational objectives: The classification of educational goals; Handbook I: Cognitive domain.* New York: Longmans, Green.

Boekaerts, M., Pintrich, P.R., & Zeidner, M. (2005). *Handbook of self-regulation.* Burlington, MA: Elsevier Academic Press.

Bonk, C.J., & Cunningham, D.J. (1998). Searching for learner-centered, constructivist, and sociocultural components of collaborative educational learning tools. In C.J. Bonk & K.S. King, (Eds.), *Electronic collaborators: Learner-centered technologies for literacy, apprenticeship, and discourse* (pp. 25–50). New York: Routledge.

Bransford, J.D., Brown, A.L., & Cocking, R.R. (2000). *How people learn: Brain, mind, experience, and school.* Washington, DC: National Academy Press. Available online at: http://newton.nap.edu/html/howpeople1/

Branson, R.K., & Reiser, R.A. (2009). In memoriam: Robert M. Morgan: A key figure in the history of educational technology. *Educational Technology, 49*(6), 62–63.

Bregman, A. (1990). *Auditory scene analysis: The perceptual organization of sound.* Boston: MIT Press.

Brewer, T.K. (2007). User of Phillips' five level training evaluation and return on investment framework in the U.S. non-profit sector. Unpublished dissertation. University of North Texas.

Brey, K.H. (1971). The missing midwife: Why a training program failed. *South Asian Review, 5*(1), 41–52.

Briggs, L.J., Gustafson, K.L., & Tillman, M.H. (Eds.) (1991). *Instructional design: Principles and applications* (2nd ed.). Englewood Cliffs, NJ: Educational Technology Publications.

Brown, A.L. (1987). Metacognition, executive control, self-regulation, and other more mysterious mechanisms. In F.E. Weinert & R.H. Kluwe (Eds.), *Metacognition, motivation, and understanding* (pp. 65–116). Hillsdale, NJ: Lawrence Erlbaum Associates.

Brown, J.S., Collins, A., & Duguid, S. (1989). Situated cognition and the culture of learning. *Educational Researcher, 18*(1), 32–42.

Bruner, J. (1962). Act of discovery. *Harvard Educational Review, 31*(1), 21–32.

Bruner, J. (1966). *Toward a theory of instruction.* Cambridge, MA: Belknap Press.

Bruner, J. (1978). The role of dialogue in language acquisition. In A. Sinclair, R.J. Jarvella, & W. Levelt (Eds.), *The child's concept of language* (pp. 241–255). New York: Springer-Verlag.

Bruner, J.R., Goodnow, J.J., & Austin, G.A. (1956). *A study of thinking.* New York: Wiley.

Bryant, S.M., & Hunton, J.E. (2000). The use of technology in the delivery of instruction: Implications for accounting education and education researchers. *Issues in Accounting Education, 15*(1), 129–162.

Burton, J.K., Moore, D.M., & Magliaro, S.G. (1996). Behaviorism and instructional technology. In D.H. Jonassen (Ed.), *Handbook of Research for Educational Communications and Technology* (pp. 46–73). New York: Macmillan.

Buss, A., & Poley, W. (1979). *Individual differences: Traits and factors.* New York: Gardner Press.

Butler, R. (2004). *Copyright for teachers and librarians.* New York: Neal-Schuman.

Bybee, R.W. (1997). *Achieving scientific literacy: From purposes to practices.* Portsmouth, NH: Heinemann.

Bybee, R., Taylor, J.A., Gardner, A., Van Scotter, P., Carlson, J., Westbrook, A., & Landes, N. (2006). *The BSCS 5E instructional model: Origins and effectiveness.* Colorado Springs, CO: BSCS.

Cabral-Cardoso, C.J. (2001). Too academic to get a proper job? The difficult transition of Ph.D.s to the "real world" of industry. *Career Development International, 6*(4), 212–217.

Carroll, J.B. (1993). *Human cognitive abilities: A survey of factor-analytic studies.* Cambridge, UK: Cambridge University Press.

Carroll, L. (1871). *Through the looking glass and what Alice found there.* London: Macmillan.

Cassidy, V.M. (1950). *The effectiveness of self-teaching devices in facilitating learning.* Unpublished dissertation. Columbus: Ohio State University.

CAST (2011). *Universal design for learning guidelines version 2.0.* Wakefield, MA: Author. Available at: http://www.udlcenter.org/aboutudl/udlguidelines

Castejon, J.L., Perez, A.M., & Gilar, R. (2010). Confirmatory factor analysis of project spectrum activities: A second g factor or multiple intelligences? *Intelligence, 38,* 481–496.

Cawelti, G. (Ed.) (2004). *Handbook of research on improving student achievement.* Arlington, VA: Educational Research Service.

Cennamo, K., & Kalk, D. (2005). *Real world instructional design.* Independence, KY: Wadsworth.

Chase, C.I. (1999). *Contemporary assessment for educators.* New York: Longman.

Chastain, K. (1975). An examination of the basic assumptions of "individualized" instruction. *Modern Language Journal, 59*(7), 334–344.

Chester, A., & Gwynne, G. (1998). Online teaching: Encouraging collaboration through anonymity. *Journal of Computer-Mediated Communication, 4*(2). Retrieved June 13, 1012 from: http://jcmc.indiana.edu/vol4/issue2/chester.html

Chickering, A.W., & Gamson, Z.F. (1987). Seven principles for good practice in undergraduate education. *American Association of Higher Education Bulletin, 39*(7), 3–7.

Chickering, A.W., & Gamson, Z.F. (1999). Development and adaptations of the Seven Principles for good practice in undergraduate education. *New Directions for Teaching and Learning, 80,* 75–81.

Churches, A. (2009). Bloom's digital taxonomy. *Educational Origami.* Retrieved June 13, 2012 from: http://edorigami.wikispaces.com/Bloom's+Digital+Taxonomy

Clark, D. (1995–2012). Estimating costs and time in instructional design. Website: *Big Dog & Little Dog's Performance Juxtaposition.* Available at: http://www.nwlink.com/~donclark/hrd/costs.html

Clark, R.C., & Lyons, C. (2004). *Graphics for learning: Proven guidelines for planning, design, and evaluating visuals in training materials.* San Francisco: Pfeiffer.

Clark, R.C., & Mayer, R.E. (2003). *E-Learning and the science of instruction.* San Francisco: Pfeiffer.

Clark, R.C., & Mayer, R.E. (2008). *E-Learning and the science of instruction: Proven guidelines for consumers and designers of multimedia learning* (2nd ed.). San Francisco: Pfeiffer.

Clark, R.C., Nguyen, F., & Sweller, J. (2006). *Efficiency in learning: Evidence-based guidelines to manage cognitive load.* San Francisco: Pfeiffer.

Clark, R.E. (1983). Reconsidering research on learning from media. *Review of Educational Research, 53*(4), 445–459.

Clark, R.E. (1994). Media will never influence learning. *Educational Technology Research & Development, 42*(2), 21–29.

Clark, R.E. (2005). Research-tested team motivation strategies. *Performance Improvement, 44*(1), 13–16.

Clark, R.E., & Feldon, D.F. (2005). Five common but questionable principles of multimedia learning. In R.E. Mayer (Ed.), *The Cambridge Handbook of Multimedia Learning* (pp. 97–115). New York: Cambridge University Press.

Coffield, F., Moseley, D., Hall, E., & Ecclestone, K. (2004a). *Learning styles and pedagogy in post-16 learning: A systematic and critical review.* London: Learning Skills Network.

Coffield, F., Moseley, D., Hall, E., & Ecclestone, K. (2004b). *Should we be using learning styles? What research has to say to practice.* London: Learning and Skills Research Centre.

Collins, A., Brown, A.S., & Newman, S.E. (1990). Cognitive apprenticeship: Teaching the crafts of reading, writing, and mathematics. In L.B. Resnick (Ed.), *Knowing, learning, and instruction: Essays in honor of Robert Glaser* (pp. 453–494). Hillsdale, NJ: Lawrence Erlbaum.

Colliver, J.A. (2002). Constructivism: The view of knowledge that ended philosophy or a theory of learning and instruction? *Teaching and Learning in Medicine, 14*(1), 49–51.

Conole, G. (2010). Theory and methodology in networked learning. Website: *Cloudworks.* Available at: http://www.slideshare.net/grainne/theory-and-methodology-in-networked-learning

Conole, G., Galley, R., & Culver, J. (2011). Frameworks for understanding the nature of interactions, networking, and community in a social networking site for academic practice. *International Review of Research in Open & Distance Learning, 12*(3), 119–138.

Conole, G., & Oliver, M. (2007). *Contemporary perspective in e-learning research: Themes, methods and impact on practice.* London: RoutledgeFalmer.

Cook, D.A., Levinson, A.J., Garside, S., Dupras, D.M., Erwin, P.J., & Montori, V.M. (2010). Instructional design variations in internet-based learning for health professions education: A systematic review and meta-analysis. *Academic Medicine, 85*(5), 909–922.

Cook, G.A. (1993). *George Herbert Mead: The making of a social pragmatist.* Chicago: University of Illinois Press.

Cook, V. (2012). Learning everywhere, all the time. *Delta Kappa Gamma Bulletin,* 48–51.

Copeland, L., & Griggs, L. (1985). *Going international: How to make friends and deal effectively in the global marketplace.* New York: Random House.

Cormier, D. (2008). Rhizomatic education: Community as curriculum. *Innovate, 4*(5). Available at: http://innovateonline.info/?view=article&id=550

Cosenza, V. (2012). World map of social networks. Blog: *VincosBlog.* Available at: http://vincos.it/world-map-of-social-networks/

Covey, S.R. (1989). *The seven habits of highly effective people: Powerful lessons in personal change.* New York: Simon & Schuster.

Cronbach, L., & Snow, R. (1981). *Aptitudes and instructional methods: A handbook for research on interactions* (2nd ed.). New York: Irvington.

Dabbagh, N., & Bannan-Ritland, B. (2005). *Online learning: Concepts, strategies, and application.* Upper Saddle River, NJ: Pearson.

Dave, R.H. (1970). Psychomotor levels. In R.J. Armstrong (Ed.), *Developing and writing behavioral objectives* (pp. 33–34). Tucson, AZ: Educational Innovators Press.

Davies, I. (1981). *Instructional technique.* New York: McGraw-Hill.

Deal, T.E., & Kennedy, A.A. (1982). *Corporate cultures: The rites and rituals of corporate life.* Reading, MA: Addison-Wesley.

Defelice, R.A. & Kapp, K.M. (2010). Reducing the time to develop one hour of training. Learning circuits: ASTD's source for e-learning. Retrieved from http://www.astd.org/Publications/Newsletters/ASTD-Links/ASTD-Links-Articles/2010/03/Reducing-the-Time-to-Develop-One-Hour-of-Instruction

Delors, J., et al. (1996). Learning: The treasure within. *Report to UNESCO of the International Commission on Education for the Twenty-first Century.* Paris: UNESCO.

Deubel, P. (2003). An investigation of Behaviorist and Cognitive approaches to instructional multimedia design. *Journal of Educational Multimedia and Hypermedia, 12*(1), 63–90.

Dewey, J. (1896). The reflex arc concept in psychology. *Psychological Review, 3,* 357–370.

Dewey, J. (1929). *The sources of a science of education.* New York: Horace Liveright.

Dewey, J. (1933). *How we think* (rev ed.). Boston: D.C. Heath.

Dewey, J. (1938). *Experience and education.* New York: Collier Books.

Dick, W., Carey, L., & Carey, J.O. (2005). *The systematic design of instruction* (6th ed.). Boston: Allyn & Bacon.

Dick, W., Carey, L., & Carey, J.O. (2008). *The systematic design of instruction* (7th ed.). Upper Saddle River, NJ: Pearson.

Dodge, B. (1997, May 5). *Some thoughts about WebQuests.* Available at: http://webquest.sdsu.edu/about_webquests.html

Dooley, K.E., Lindner, J.R., & Dooley, L.M. (2005). *Advanced methods in distance education: Applications and practices for educators, administrators, and learners.* Hershey, PA: Information Science Publishing.

Downes, S. (2006, October 16). Learning networks and connective knowledge. *Instructional Technology Forum: Paper 92.* http://it.coe.uga.edu/itforum/paper92/paper92.html

Downes, S. (2007, February 3). What connectivism is. Blog: *Half an Hour.* Available at: http://halfanhour.blogspot.com/2007/02/what-connectivism-is.html

Downes, S. (2012). *Connectivism and connective knowledge: Essays on meaning and learning networks.* Canada: Author. Available at: http://www.downes.ca/files/Connective_Knowledge-19May2012.pdf

Draxler, A., & Carneiro, R. (2008). Editorial. *European Journal of Education, 43,* 145–148.

Drexler, W. (2010). The networked student model for construction of personal learning environments: Balancing teacher control and student autonomy. *Australasian Journal of Educational Technology, 26*(3), 369–385.

Driscoll, M.P. (1994). *Psychology of learning for instruction.* Needham Heights, MA: Allyn & Bacon.

Driscoll, M.P. (2004). *Psychology of learning for instruction* (3rd ed.). Boston: Allyn & Bacon.

Dron, J., & Anderson, T. (2009). How the crowd can teach. In S. Hatzipanagos & S. Warburton (Eds.), *Handbook of research on social software and developing community ontologies* (pp. 1–17). Hershey, PA: Information Science Reference/IGI Global Publishing.

Dron, J., Anderson, T., & Siemens, G. (2011). Putting things in context: Designing social media for education. *Proceedings of the European Conference on e-learning* (pp. 178–186).

Duarte, N. (2008). *Slide:ology: The art and science of creating great presentations.* Sebastopol, CA: O'Reilly.

Dwyer, F. (1978). *Strategies for improving visual learning.* University Park, PA: Learning Services.

Earl, L., & Katz, S. (2006). *Rethinking classroom assessment with purpose in mind. Assessment for learning, assessment as learning, assessment of learning.* Western and Northern Canadian Protocol for Collaboration in Education (WNCP). Available at: http://www.wncp.ca/media/40539/rethink.pdf

Ebeling, D. (1998). Adapting your teaching for any learning style. *Lutheran Education, 133*(4), 219–224.

Edmundson, A. (2007). The cultural adaptation process (CAP) model: Designing e-learning for another culture. In A. Edmundson (Ed.), *Globalized e-learning cultural challenges* (pp. 267–290). Hershey, PA: Idea Group, Inc.

Educause. (2009). *7 things you should know about personal learning environments.* Available at: http://www.educause.edu/ir/library/pdf/ELI7049.pdf

Ertmer, P.A., & Newby, T.J. (1993). Behaviorism, cognitivism, constructivism: Comparing critical features from an instructional design perspective. *Performance Improvement Quarterly, 6*(4), 50–72.

Ferreira, F. (2011). What cultural lenses do you wear? How to see the cultural perspective behind someone's actions. *Toastmaster, 77*(2), 8–11.

Fink, L.D. (2003). *Creating significant learning experiences: An integrated approach to designing college courses.* San Francisco: Jossey-Bass.

Fleming, M., & Levie, W.H. (Eds.) (1993). *Instructional message design: Principles from the behavioral and cognitive sciences* (2nd ed.). Englewood Cliffs, NJ: Educational Technology Publications.

Fulford, C.P., & Zhang, S. (1993). Perceptions of interaction: The critical predictor in distance education. *American Journal of Distance Education, 7*(3), 8–21.

Gagné, R.M. (1965). *The conditions of learning and theory of instruction* (1st ed.). New York: Holt, Rinehart & Winston.

Gagné, R.M. (1985). *The conditions of learning and theory of instruction* (4th ed.). New York: Holt, Rinehart & Winston.

Gagné, R.M., & Briggs, L.J. (1974). *Principles of instructional design* (2nd ed.). New York: Holt, Rinehart & Winston.

Gagné, R.M., & Medsker, K.L. (1996). *The conditions of learning: Training applications.* Fort Worth, TX: Harcourt Brace College Publishers.

Gagné, R.M., Briggs, L.J., & Wager, W.W. (1992). *Principles of instructional design* (4th ed.). Fort Worth, TX: Harcourt Brace Jovanovich.

Gagné, R.M., Wager, W.W., Golas, K.C., & Keller, J.M. (2005). Principles of instructional design (5th ed.). Belmont, CA: Wadsworth.

Gardner, H. (1983). *Frames of mind: The theory of multiple intelligences.* New York: Basic Books.

Gardner, H. (2006). On failing to grasp the core of MI theory: A response to Visser et al. *Intelligence, 34,* 503–505.

Gardner, H., & Moran, S. (2006). The science of multiple intelligences theory: A response to Lynn Waterhouse. *Educational Psychologist, 41*(4), 227–232.

Garrison, D.R. (2011). *E-Learning in the 21st century* (2nd ed.). New York: Routledge.

Garrison, D.R., & Anderson, T. (2003). *E-learning in the 21st century: A framework for research and practice.* New York: Routledge.

Garrison, D.R., Anderson, T., & Archer, W. (2000). Critical inquiry in a text-based environment: Computer conferencing in higher education. *Internet and Higher Education 2*(2–3), 87–105.

Gaver, W.W. (1991). Technology affordances. In S.P. Robertson, G.M. Olson, and J.S. Olson (Eds.), *Proceedings of the ACM CHI 91 Human Factors in Computing Systems Conference, April 28–June 5, 1991* (pp. 79–84). New Orleans, LA.

Gibson, J.J. (1977). The theory of affordances. In R. Shaw & J. Bransford (Eds.), *Perceiving, acting and knowing* (pp. 67–82). Hillsdale, NJ: Erlbaum.

Gibson, A.M., & Slate, J.R. (2010). Student engagement at two-year institutions: Age and generational status differences. *Community College Journal of Research and Practice, 34*(5), 371–385.

Glaser, R. (1976). Components of a psychology of instruction: Towards a science of design. *Review of Educational Research, 46*(1), 1–24.

Gohagan, D. (1999). Computer-facilitated instructional strategies for education: Designing WebQuests. *Journal of Technology and Human Services, 16*, 145–159.

Gottlieb, M. (2003). *Large scale assessment of English language learners: Addressing educational accountability in K-12 settings.* TESOL Professional Papers #6. TESOL.

Gredler, M.E. (1997). *Learning and instruction: Theory into practice.* Upper Saddle River, NJ: Prentice-Hall, Inc.

Greenhow, C., Robelia, B., & Hughes, J. (2009). Learning, teaching, and scholarship in a digital age: Web 2.0 and classroom research: What path should we take now? *Educational Researcher, 38*, 246–259.

Gregory, G.H., & Kuzmich, L. (2004). *Data driven differentiation in the standards-based classroom.* Thousand Oaks, CA: Corwin Press.

Grimwald, A. (2001). Industry vs. academia: Survey results, March 2001. *Scientist, 15*(8), 28. Available at: http://www.the-scientist.com

Guthrie, E.R. (1930). Conditioning as a principle of learning. *Psychological Review, 37*, 412–428.

Haig, C. (2011). TrendSpotters: Tech and design. Column: *Performance Xpress TrendSpotters.* Available at: http://www.performancexpress.org/2011/02/trendspotterstech-and-design/

Hall, E.T. (1976). *Beyond culture.* New York: Anchor Books.

Hannafin, M.J., & Hill, J.R. (2002). Epistemology and the design of learning environments. In R.A. Reiser & J.V. Dempsey (Eds.), *Trends and Issues in Instructional Design and Technology.* New Jersey: Merrill Prentice Hall.

Hannafin, M.J., West, R.E., & Shepherd, C.E. (2009). The cognitive demands of student-centered, web-based multimedia: Current and emerging perspectives. In R. Zheng (Ed.), *Cognitive effects of multimedia learning* (pp. 194–216). Hershey, PA: Information Science Reference/IGI Global Publishing.

Harrow, A.J. (1972). *A taxonomy of the psychomotor domain: A guide for developing behavioral objectives.* New York: David McKay.

Haskell, R.E. (2000). *Transfer of learning: Cognition and instruction.* Waltham, MA: Academic Press.

Hattie, J.A. (1992). Towards a model of schooling: A synthesis of meta-analyses. *Australian Journal of Education, 36*, 5–13.

Hattie, J.A. (1999). Influences on students' learning. Inaugural lecture, University of Auckland, New Zealand.

Head, J.T., Lockee, B.B., & Oliver, K.M. (2002). Method, media, mode: Clarifying the discussion of distance education effectiveness. *Quarterly Review of Distance Education, 3*(3), 261–268.

Heinich, R. (1968). The teacher in an instructional system. In F.G. Knirk & J.W. Childs (Eds.), *Instructional Technology: A Book of Readings.* New York: Holt, Rinehart & Winston.

Henderson, L. (1996). Instructional design of interactive multimedia: A cultural critique. *Education Technology Research & Development, 44*(4), 85–104.

Heylighen, F. (1993). *Epistemology, introduction. Principia Cybernetica.* Available at: http://pespmc1.vub.ac.be/EPISTEMI.html

Hill, J.R., Song, L., & West, R.E. (2009). Social learning theory and web-based learning environments: A review of research and discussion of implications. *American Journal of Distance Education, 23*, 88–103.

Hix, D., & Hartson, H.R. (1993). *Developing user interfaces: Ensuring usability through product and process.* New York: John Wiley & Sons.

Hofstede, G. (1986). Cultural differences in teaching and learning. *International Journal of Intercultural Relations, 10*, 301–320.

Holton, E.F., Wilson, L.S., & Bates, R.A. (2009). Toward development of a generalized instrument to measure andragogy. *Human Resource Development Quarterly, 20*(2), 169–193.

Hutton, J. (2011, September 30). Mobile phones dominate in South Africa. Blog: *nielsenwire.* Available at http://blog.nielsen.com/nielsenwire/global/mobile-phones-dominate-in-south-africa/

IEEE (2002). IEEE Standard for Learning Object Metadata, 1484.12.1-2002. http://ltsc.ieee.org/wg12/index.html

James, W. (1904). Does consciousness exist? *Journal of Philosophy, Psychology, and Scientific Methods, 1*(18), 477–491.

Janzen, K.J., Perry, B., & Edwards, M. (2011). Aligning the quantum perspective of learning to instructional design: Exploring the seven definitive questions. *International Review of Research in Open and Distance Learning, 12*(7), 56–73.

Jarche, H. (2003–2012). *Work is learning and learning is the work.* Web log. Available at: http://www.jarche.com

Jarche, H. (2012). *Seek, sense, share: Personal knowledge management (PKM) guide.* Available at: http://www.jarche.com/2012/09/pkm-book-alpha-version/

Jonassen, D.H. (1996a). *Computers as mindtools for schools: Engaging critical thinking.* Upper Saddle River, NJ: Merrill.

Jonassen, D.H. (1996b). Learning from, learning about, and learning with computing: A rationale for mindtools. In D.H. Jonassen, *Computers in the classroom: Mindtools for critical thinking* (pp. 3–22). Columbus, OH: Merrill/Prentice-Hall.

Jonassen, D.H. (1997). Instructional design model for well-structured and ill-structured problem-solving learning outcomes. *Educational Technology: Research and Development, 45*(1), 65–95.

Jonassen, D.H. (2000). *Computers as mindtools for schools: Engaging critical thinking* (2nd ed.). Upper Saddle River, NJ: Merrill.

Jonassen, D.H. (2006). *Modeling with technology: Mindtools for conceptual change* (3rd ed.). Boston: Allyn & Bacon.

Jonassen, D.H. (2011). Supporting problem solving in PBL. *Interdisciplinary Journal of Problem-Based Learning, 5*(2), Article 8. Available at: http://dx.doi.org/10.7771/1541-5015.1256

Jonassen, D.H., & Grabowski, B.L. (1993). *Handbook of individual differences, learning, and instruction.* Hillsdale, NJ: Lawrence Erlbaum.

Jonassen, D.H., & Land, S.M. (Eds.) (2012). *Theoretical foundations of learning environments* (2nd ed.). New York: Routledge.

Jonassen, D.H., & Tessmer, M. (1996/7). An outcomes-based taxonomy for the design, evaluation, and research of instructional systems. *Training Research Journal, 2.* Available at: http://tecfa.unige.ch/

Jonassen, D.H., Tessmer, M., & Hannum, W.H. (1999). *Task analysis methods for instructional design.* Mahwah, NJ: Lawrence Erlbaum Associates.

Jonassen, D.H., Howland, J., Moore, J., & Marra, R.M. (2002). *Learning to solve problems with technology: A constructivist perspective* (2nd ed.) Upper Saddle River, NJ: Prentice Hall.

Jones, B.F., Palincsar, A.S., Ogle, D.S., & Carr, E.G. (1987). *Strategic teaching and learning: Cognitive instruction in the content areas.* Alexandria, VA: Association for Supervision and Curriculum Development.

Kachina, O.A. (2012). Using WebQuests in the social sciences classroom. *Contemporary Issues in Education Research, 5*(3), 185–200.

Kanuka, H., & Anderson, T. (1999). Using Constructivism in technology-mediated learning: Constructing order out of chaos in the literature. *Radical Pedagogy, 2*(1). Available at: http://radicalpedagogy.icaap.org/content/issue1_2/02kanuka1_2.html

Kapp, K.M., & Defelice, R.A. (2009). Time to develop one hour of training. Learning Circuits: ASTD's Source for E-Learning. Retrieved from http://www.astd.org/Publications/Newsletters/Learning-Circuits/Learning-Circuits-Archives/2009/08/Time-to-Develop-One-Hour-of-Training

Kaufman, R., Guerra-Lopez, I.J., & Platt, W.A. (Eds.) (2005). *Practical evaluation for educators: Finding what works and what doesn't.* Thousand Oaks, CA: Corwin Press.

Keen, A. (2007). *The cult of the amateur: How today's internet is killing our culture.* New York: Doubleday/Currency.

Keller, J.M. (1983). Motivational design of instruction. In C.M. Reigeluth (Ed.), *Instructional-design theories and models: An overview of their current status,* (pp. 383–433). Hillsdale, NJ: Lawrence Erlbaum Associates.

Keller, J.M. (1987). Strategies for stimulating the motivation to learn. *Performance & Instruction, 26*(8), 1–7.

King, J. (1998). Practitioner perceptions of critical data for analysis of three types of training. Unpublished doctoral dissertation, University of Northern Colorado, Greeley. Program in Educational Technology.

Kinzie, M.B., Cohn, W.F., Julian, M.F., & Knaus, W.A. (2002). A user-centered model for web site design: Needs assessment, user interface design, and rapid prototyping. *Journal of the American Medical Informatics Association, 9*(4), 320–330.

Kirkpatrick, D.L. (1998). The four levels: An overview. In D.L. Kirkpatrick, *Evaluating training programs: The four levels* (2nd ed.). San Francisco: Berrett-Koehler.

Kirkpatrick, D.L., & Kirkpatrick, J.D. (2006). *Evaluating training programs: The four levels* (3rd ed.). Berrett-Koehler Publishers.

Kirschner, P.A., Sweller, J., & Clark, R.E. (2006). Why minimal guidance during instruction does not work: An analysis of the failure of constructivist, discovery, problem-based, experiential, and inquiry-based teaching. *Educational Psychologist, 41*(2), 75–86.

Knowles, M.S. (1970). *Modern practice of adult education: Andragogy versus pedagogy.* New York: Association Press.

Koffka, K. (1935). *Principles of Gestalt psychology.* New York: Harcourt, Brace.

Köhler, W. (1929). *Gestalt psychology.* New York: Liveright.

Kolb, D.A. (1984). *Experiential learning: Experience as the source of learning and development.* Englewood Cliffs, NJ: Prentice-Hall.

Kop, R., & Hill, A. (2008). Connectivism: Learning theory of the future or vestige of the past? *International Review of Research in Open and Distance Learning, 9*(3), 1–13. http://www.irrodl.org/index.php/irrodl/article/view/523/1103

Kozma, R.B. (1991). Learning with media. *Review of Educational Research, 61* (Summer 1991), 179–211.

Kozma, R.B. (1994a). Will media influence learning? Reframing the debate. *Educational Technology Research & Development, 42*(2), 7–19.

Kozma, R.B. (1994b). A reply: Media and methods. *Educational Technology Research & Development, 42*(3), 11–14.

Krathwohl, D.R. (2002). A revision of bloom's taxonomy: An overview. *Theory into Practice, 41*(4), 212–218.

Krathwohl, D.R., Bloom, B.S., & Masia, B.B. (1973). *Taxonomy of educational objectives, the classification of educational goals. Handbook II: Affective domain.* New York: David McKay.

Kubovy, M., & van Valkenburg, D. (2001). Auditory and visual objects. *Cognition, 80,* 97–126.

Kuhlmann, T. (2007). *Insider's guide to becoming a rapid e-learning pro.* Available at: http://www.articulate.com/rapid-elearning

Lamancusa, J.S., & Pauley, L.L. (2011). Development and implementation of an intermediate design course using active learning. *118th ASEE Annual Conference & Exposition, Conference Proceedings.*

Langevin Learning Services (2011, November 17). The mystery of determining instructional design time. Blog: *Langevin Blog.* Available at: http://www.langevin.com/blog/2011/11/17/the-mystery-of-determining-instructional-design-time/

Larson, M.B. (2004). Survey and case study analyses of the professional preparation of instructional design and technology (IDT) graduates for different career environments. Unpublished doctoral dissertation, Virginia Polytechnic Institute and State University, Blacksburg.

Lave, J. (1988). *Cognition in practice: Mind, mathematics, and culture in everyday life.* Cambridge: Cambridge University Press.

Lave, J. & Wenger, E. (1991). *Situated learning: Legitimate peripheral participation.* Cambridge: Cambridge University Press.

Lee, M.M., & Paulus, T. (2001). An instructional design theory for interactions in Web-based learning environments. In *Leadership and Technology: Keys to Transforming Education, Annual Proceedings of the Association for Educational Communication and Technology, 1* (pp. 245–250).

Lengel, R.H., & Daft, R.L. (1988). The selection of communication media as an executive skill. *Academy of Management Executive, 2*(3), 225–232.

Levie, W.H., & Dickie, K.E. (1973). The analysis and application of media. In R.M.W. Travers (Ed.), *The second handbook of research on teaching* (pp. 858–882). Chicago: Rand-McNally.

Lewis, R., & Whitlock, Q. (2003). *How to plan and manage an e-learning programme.* Farnham, UK: Gower Publishing Co.

Lineberry, C.S. (1980). *The instructional design library: Job aids.* Englewood Cliffs, NJ: Educational Technology Publications.

Lockee, B.B. (1996). Development of a hypermedia template using whole language instructional methods for the preservation of native American languages. Unpublished doctoral dissertation, Virginia Polytechnic Institute and State University, Blacksburg.

Lockwood, F. (1998). *The design and production of self-instructional materials.* New York: Routledge.

Lohr, L.L. (2003). *Creating graphics for learning and performance: Lessons in visual literacy.* Upper Saddle River, NJ: Merrill Prentice Hall.

Lowenthal, P.R. (2009). The evolution and influence of social presence theory on online learning. In T.T. Kidd (Ed.), *Online education and adult learning: New frontiers for teaching practices* (pp. 124–139). Hershey, PA: IGI Global.

Mager, R.F. (1975). *Preparing instructional objectives* (2nd ed.). Belmont, California: Pitman Learning.

Makin, L., White, M., & Owen, M. (1996). Creation or constraint: Teacher response to children's artmaking in Anglo-Australian and Asian-Australian child care centres. *Studies in Art Education, 37*(4), 226–244.

Malone, T.W., & Lepper, M.R. (1987). Making learning fun: A taxonomy of intrinsic motivations for learning. In R.E. Snow & M.J. Farr (Eds.), *Aptitude, learning and instruction: III. Conative and affective process analyses* (pp. 223–253). Hilsdale, NJ: Erlbaum.

Manfra, L. (2005). School survey 2005: Research—Its role in North American design education. *Metropolis, 25*(1), 132–134. Research summary at: http://www.metropolismag.com/PDF_files/SchoolSurvey2005.pdf

March, T. (2000). WebQuests 101. *Multimedia Schools, 7*(5), 55–58.

Mariano, G. (2009). Fostering transfer in multimedia instructional environments. In R. Zheng, (Ed.), *Cognitive effects of multimedia learning* (pp. 237–259). Hershey, PA: Information Science Reference/IGI Global Publishing.

Marzano, R.J. (1998). *A theory-based meta-analysis of research on instruction.* Aurora, CO: Mid-Continent Research for Education and Learning.

Marzano, R.J. (2006). *Classroom assessment and grading that work.* Alexandria, VA: ASCD.

Marzano, R.J., & Kendall, J.S. (Eds.) (2007). *The new taxonomy of educational objectives* (2nd ed.) Thousand Oaks, CA: Corwin Press.

Marzano, R.J., & Kendall, J.S. (2008) *Designing and assessing educational objectives: Applying the new taxonomy.* Thousand Oaks, CA: Corwin Press.

Marzano, R.J., Pickering, D.J., & Pollock, J.E. (2001). *Classroom instruction that works: Research-based strategies for increasing student achievement.* Alexandria, VA: ASCD.

Maslow, A. (1954). *Motivation and personality.* New York: Harper.

Matejcek, J. (2010, November 15). Why eLearning development ratios can be hazardous to your career. Blog: *Dasche & Thomson's Social Learning Blog.* Available at: http://www.dashe.com/blog/elearning/why-elearning-development-ratios-can-be-hazardous-to-your-career

Mayer, R.E. (2001). *Multimedia learning.* New York: Cambridge University Press.

Mayer, R.E. (2009). *Multimedia learning* (2nd ed.). Cambridge, MA: Cambridge University Press.

Mayer, R. (in press). Multimedia instruction. In J.M. Spector, M.D. Merrill, J. Elen, & M.J. Bishop (Eds.), *Handbook of research on educational communications and technology* (4th ed.). New York: Springer.

Mayer, R.E., & Sims, V.K. (1994). For whom is a picture worth a thousand words? Extensions of a dual-coding theory of multimedia learning. *Journal of Educational Psychology, 86*(3), 389–401.

McCune, V., & Entwistle, N. (2000). The deep approach to learning: analytic abstraction and idiosyncratic development. Paper presented at the Innovations in Higher Education conference, August 30–September 2, 2000. Helsinki, Finland.

McLoughlin, C. (1999). Culturally responsive technology use: Developing an online community of learners. *British Journal of Educational Technology, 30*(3), 231–243.

McLuhan, M. (1964). *Understanding media: The extensions of man.* New York: McGraw-Hill.

Merrill, M.D. (1983). Component display theory. In C.M. Reigeluth (Ed.), *Instructional design theories and models: An overview of their current states* (pp. 279–333). Hillsdale, NJ: Lawrence Erlbaum Associates.

Merrill, M.D. (1994). *Instructional design theory.* Englewood Cliffs, NJ: Educational Technology Publications, Inc.

Merrill, M.D. (2000). Instructional strategies and learning styles: Which takes precedence? In R.A. Reiser & J.V. Dempsey (Eds.), *Trends and issues in instructional technology.* Upper Saddle River, NJ: Prentice Hall.

Merrill, M.D. (2002). A pebble-in-the-pond model for instructional design. *Performance Improvement, 41*(7), 39–44.

Merrill, M.D., Li, Z., & Jones, M.K. (1991). Second generation instructional design (ID2). *Educational Technology, 30*(1), 7–11 and *30*(2), 7–14.

Metzger, W. (2006). *Laws of seeing*. Cambridge, MA: MIT Press. (Original work published in German in 1936).

Miller, G.A. (1956). The magical number seven, plus or minus two: Some limits on our capacity for processing information. *Psychological Review, 63*(2), 81–97.

Milson, A.J. (2002). The Internet and inquiry learning: Integrating medium and method in a sixth grade social studies classroom. *Theory and Research in Social Education, 30*(3), 330–353.

Milson, A.J., & Downey, P. (2001). WebQuest: Using Internet resources for cooperative inquiry. *Social Education, 65*, 144–146.

Minor, E.O., & Frye, H.R. (1977). *Techniques for producing visual instructional media* (2nd ed.). New York: McGraw-Hill.

Molebash, P., & Dodge, B. (2003). Kick starting inquiry with WebQuests and web inquiry projects. *Social Education 67*(7), 158–163.

Moore, C. (2008). Be an elearning action hero. Website: *Cathy Moore: Let's save the world from boring elearning!* Available at: http://blog.cathy-moore.com/2008/05/be-an-elearning-action-hero/

Moore, D., Bates, A., & Grundling, J. (2002). Instructional design. In A.K. Mishra & J. Bartrram (Eds.), *Skills development through distance education*. Vancouver: The Commonwealth of Learning. Available at: http://www.col.org/SiteCollectionDocuments/Skills_Development.pdf

Moore, J.L., Dickson-Deane, C., & Galyen, K. (2011). e-Learning, online learning, and distance learning environments: Are they the same? *Internet and Higher Education, 14*, 129–135.

Moore, M.G. (1993). Theory of transactional distance. In D. Keegan (Ed.) *Theoretical principles of distance education* (pp. 22–38). New York: Routledge.

Morgan, E., & Ansberry, K. (2007). BSCS 5e instructional model. In K. Ansberry & E. Morgan, *More picture-perfect science lessons: Using children's books to guide inquiry, K-4*. Arlington, VA: NSTA Press.

Morgan, M. (1985). Reward-induced decrements and increments in intrinsic motivation. *Review of Educational Research, 54*(1), 5–30.

Morris, R.D. (2011). Web 3.0: Implications for online learning. *TechTrends, 55*(1), 42–46.

Morrison, G.R. (1985). Nonviolent instructional development: Working with the subject matter expert. *Performance & Instruction Journal* (June), 25–27.

Morrison, G.R., Ross, S.M., & Kemp, J.E. (2007). *Designing effective instruction: Applications of instructional design* (5th ed.). New York: Wiley.

National Education Association (NEA). (2011). *Teacher leader model standards*. A report by the Teacher Leadership Exploratory Consortium. Available at: https://www.nea.org/.../TeacherLeaderModelStandards2011.pdf

NCREL (2004). *Alternative assessments*. Retrieved March 8, 2007 from: http://www.ncrel.org/sdrs/areas/issues/methods/assment/as8lk30.htm

Neidorf, R. (2006). *Teach beyond your reach: An instructor's guide to developing and running successful distance learning classes, workshops, training sessions and more*. Medford, NJ: Information Today, Inc.

Nielsen, L. (2012). Nine ways to assess without standardized tests. *Technology & Learning, 32*(11), 30.

Nistor, N., Dehne, A., & Drews, F.T. (2010). Mass customization of teaching and training in organizations: Design principles and prototype evaluation. *Studies in Continuing Education, 32*(3), 251–267.

Norman, D.A. (1988). *The psychology of everyday things*. New York: Basic Books.

Norman, D.A. (2002). *The design of everyday things*. New York: Basic Books.

Oblinger, D.G. (Ed.) (2006). Learning spaces. Website: *Educause*. http://www.educause.edu

Oblinger, D.G., & Oblinger, J.L. (Eds.) (2005). Educating the net generation. Website: *Educause*. http://www.educause.edu/educatingthenetgen/

Paas, F.G.W.C., & van Merrienboer, J.J.G. (1994). Instructional control of cognitive load in the training of complex cognitive tasks. *Educational Psychology Review, 6*, 351–371.

Paivio, A (1969). Mental imagery in associative learning and memory. *Psychological Review, 76*(3), 241–263.

Paivio, A (1971). *Imagery and verbal processes*. New York: Holt, Rinehart and Winston.

Paivio, A (1986). *Mental representations: A dual coding approach*. Oxford, UK: Oxford University Press.

Paivio, A. (1991). Dual coding theory: Retrospect and current status. *Canadian Journal of Psychology, 45*(3), 255–287.

Palincsar, A.S., & Brown, A.L. (1984). Reciprocal teaching of comprehension-fostering and monitoring activities. *Cognition and Instruction, 1*, 117–175.

Papert, S., & Harel, I. (1991). *Constructionism*. Norwood, NJ: Ablex Publishing.

Pavlov, I.P. (1927). *Conditioned reflexes*. London: Oxford University Press.

Peterson, J.C. (1931). The value of guidance in reading for information. *Transactions of the Kansas Academy of Science, 33*, 41–47.

Phillips, J.J. (2005). *ROI at work*. Alexandria, VA: ASTD.

Piaget, J. (1969). *Science of education and the psychology of the child*. New York: Viking Press.

Piaget, J. (1970). Piaget's theory. In P.H. Mussen (Ed.), *Carmichael's manual of child psychology*, Vol. 1 (3rd ed.). New York: Wiley.

Piaget, J. (1977). *The development of thought: Equilibration of cognitive structures*. New York: Viking Press. (Original: *L'Equilibration des structures cognitives* (1975).)

Piaget, J. (1985). *Equilibration of cognitive structures*. Chicago: University of Chicago Press.

Picciano, A., & Seaman, J. (2007). *K-12 online learning: A survey of U.S. school district administrators*. Needham, MA: Sloan Consortium.

Piskurich, G.M., (2000). *Rapid instructional design: Learning ID fast and right*. San Francisco: Jossey-Bass Pfeiffer.

Prensky, M. (2001a). Digital natives, digital immigrants. *On the Horizon, 9*(5).

Prensky, M. (2001b). Digital natives, digital immigrants, Part II: Do they really think differently? *On the Horizon, 9*(6).

Prensky, M. (2005). Listen to the natives. *Educational Leadership, 63*(4), 8–13.

Preskill, H., & Russ-Eft, D. (2005). *Building evaluation capacity: 72 activities for teaching and training.* Thousand Oaks, CA: Sage.

Reeves, T.C. (1994). Evaluating what really matters in computer-based education. In M. Wild & D. Kirkpatrick (Eds.), *Computer education: New perspectives* (pp. 219–246). Perth, Australia: MASTEC.

Reigeluth, C.M., & Carr-Chellman, A. (2006). A common language and knowledge base for ID? Available at: http://it.coe. uga.edu/itforum/paper91/Paper91.html

Reigeluth, C.M., & Stein, F.S. (1983). The elaboration theory of instruction. In C.M. Reigeluth (Ed.), *Instructional design theories and models: An overview of their current states.* Hillsdale, NJ: Lawrence Erlbaum.

Reiser, R.A. (2001a). A history of instructional design and technology: Part I: A history of instructional media. *Educational Technology Research and Development, 49*(1), 53–64.

Reiser, R.A. (2001b). A history of instructional design and technology: Part II: A history of instructional design. *Educational Technology Research and Development, 49*(2), 57–67.

Reiser, R.A. (2002). A history of instructional design and technology. In R.A. Reiser & J.V. Dempsey (Eds.), *Trends and issues in instructional design and technology.* Upper Saddle River, NJ: Merrill Prentice Hall.

Reiser, R.A., & Dempsey, J.V. (2007). *Trends and issues in instructional design and technology* (2nd ed.). Upper Saddle River, NJ: Pearson.

Reiser, R.A., & Dick, W. (1996). *Instructional planning: A guide for teachers* (2nd ed.). Boston: Allyn & Bacon.

Revelle, W. (2008). The contribution of reinforcement sensitivity theory to personality theory. In P.J. Corr (Ed.), *The reinforcement sensitivity theory of personality* (pp. 508–527). Cambridge: Cambridge University Press.

Revelle, W., Wilt, J., & Condon, D.M. (2011). Individual differences and differential psychology: A brief history and prospect. In T. Chamorro-Premuzic, A. Furnham, & S. von Stumm (Eds.), *The Wiley-Blackwell handbook of individual differences.* Hoboken, NJ: Wiley-Blackwell.

Richards, J. (2005). A review of the research literature on effective instructional strategies. Unpublished literature review for Edvantia, Inc. Charleston, WV: Edvantia.

Richey, R.C., Klein, J.D., & Tracey, M.W. (2011). *The instructional design knowledge base: Theory, research, and practice.* New York: Routledge.

Richman, L. (2002). *Project management step-by-step.* New York: Amacom.

Rieber, L.P. (1994). *Computers, graphics, and learning.* Madison, WI: WCB Brown & Benchmark.

Rieber, L.P. (2009). Supporting discovery-based learning within simulations. In R. Zheng (Ed.), *Cognitive effects of multimedia learning* (pp. 217–236). Hershey, PA: Information Science Reference/IGI Global Publishing.

Ritzhaupt, A., Martin, F., & Daniels, K. (2010). Multimedia competencies for an educational technologist: A survey of professionals and job announcement analysis. *Journal of Educational Multimedia and Hypermedia, 19*(4), 421–449.

Rogers, E.M. (2003). *Diffusion of innovations* (5th ed.). New York: The Free Press.

Rosen, A. (2009). *E-Learning 2.0: Proven practices and emerging technologies to achieve results.* New York: American Management Association.

Rosen, M. (July 30, 2000). Specific needs influence type of web-based training. *Puget Sound Business Journal.* Available at: http://www.bizjournals.com/seattle/stories/2000/07/31/focus20.html

Rosenberg, M. (2000). *E-Learning: Strategies for delivering knowledge in the digital age.* New York: McGraw Hill.

Rotter, J.B. (1954). *Social learning and clinical psychology.* New York: Prentice-Hall.

Rovai, A.P., Ponton, M.K., & Baker, J.D. (2008). *Distance learning in higher education: A programmatic approach to planning, design, instruction, evaluation, and accreditation.* New York: Teachers College Press.

Rowland, G. (1993). Designing and instructional design. *Educational Technology Research & Design, 41*(1), 79–91.

Rubin, E. (1921). *Visuell wahrgenommene Figuren.* Copenhagen, Denmark: Glydenalske Boghandel. (Original work published in Danish in 1915.)

Ruff, H.A., & Lawson, K.R. (1990). Development of sustained, focused attention in young children during free play. *Developmental Psychology, 26,* 85–93.

Russ-Eft, D., & Preskill, H. (2001). *Evaluation in organizations: A systematic approach to enhancing learning, performance and change.* New York: Basic Books.

Saettler, L.P. (2004). *The evolution of American educational technology.* Charlotte, NC: Information Age Publishing.

Saklofske, D.H., & Zeidner, M. (1995). *International handbook of personality and intelligence.* Springer.

Salomon, G. (1979). *Interaction of media, cognition, and learning.* San Francisco: Jossey-Bass.

Salomon, G. (1981). *Communication and education.* Beverly Hills, CA: Sage.

Salomon, G. (1983). Television watching and mental effort: A social psychological view. In J. Bryant & D.R. Anderson (Eds.), *Children's understanding of television* (pp. 181–198). New York: Academic.

Salomon, G. (1984). Television is "easy" and print is "tough": The differential investment of mental effort in learning as a function of perceptions and attributions. *Journal of Educational Psychology, 76,* 647–658.

Salomon, G., Perkins, D., & Globerson, T. (1991). Partners in cognition: Extending intelligence with intelligent technologies. *Educational Researcher, 20*(4), 2–9.

Sanders, E.S. (2003). *E-learning courseware certification (ECC) standards (1.5).* Alexandria, VA: ASTD.

Scandura, J.M. (2001). Structural learning theory: Current status and recent developments. *Instructional Science, 29*(4), 311–336. Available at http://www.scandura.com/publications.htm

Schank, R.C. (1996). Goal-based scenarios: Case-based reasoning meets learning by doing. In D. Leake (Ed.), *Case-based reasoning: Experiences, lessons & future directions* (pp. 295–347). Palo Alto, CA: AAAI Press/MIT Press. Available at: http://cogprints.org/635/1/CBRMeetsLBD_for_Leake.html

Schank, R., & Abelson, R. (1977). *Scripts, plans, goals and understanding: An inquiry into human knowledge structure.* Hillsdale, NJ: Lawrence Erlbaum.

Schlenker, B. (2008). Conversation 2.0. *Training, 32.*

Schön, D.A. (1987). *Educating the Reflective Practitioner.* San Francisco: Jossey-Bass.

Schunk, D.H. (1983). Reward contingencies and the development of children's skills and self efficacy. *Journal of Educational Psychology, 75,* 511–518.

Schwartz, D.L., Lindgren, R., & Lewis, S. (2009). Constructivism in an age of non-constructivist assessments. In S. Tobias & T.M. Duffy (Eds.), *Constructivist theory applied to instruction: Success or failure* (pp. 34–61). New York: Taylor & Francis.

Seels, B.B., & Richey, R.C. (1994). *Instructional technology: The definition and domains of the field.* Washington, DC: Association for Educational Communications and Technology.

Sharma, P., Oliver, K.M., & Hannafin, M.J. (2007). Teaching and learning in directed environments. In M. Moore (Ed.), *Handbook of distance education* (2nd ed.) (pp. 259–270). Mahwah, NJ: Lawrence Erlbaum.

Shirky, C. (2009). *Here comes everybody: The power of organizing without organizations.* New York: Penguin Books.

Short, J., Williams, E., & Christie, B. (1976). *The social psychology of telecommunications.* London: John Wiley.

Siemens, G. (2004). Connectivism: A learning theory for the digital age. *elearnspace everything elearning.* Available at: http://www.elearnspace.org/Articles/connectivism.htm

Siemens, G. (2005–2012). Connectivism: A learning theory for today's learner. Website: *Connectivism.* Available at: http://www.connectivism.ca/

Siemens, G. (2008). About: Description of connectivism. Website: *Connectivism.* Available at: http://www.connectivism.ca/about.html

Siemens, G. (2010, March 6). *TEDxNYED—George Siemens—03/06/10.* Video file. Retrieved from: http://www.youtube.com/watch?v=4BH-uLO6ovI

Siemens, G., & Conole, G. (2011). Editorial. Special issue—Connectivism: Design and delivery of social networked learning. *International Review of Research in Open and Distance Learning, 12*(3).

Siemens, G., & Downes, S. (2008, November 24). Connectivism and connective knowledge online course support wiki. Available at: http://ltc.umanitoba.ca/wiki/Connectivism

Simao, A.B. (2008). *USDA APHIS leadership program evaluation report.* Frederick, MD: Professional Development Center.

Simonson, M. (2003). Dan Coldeway, 1949–2003: Professor and distance educator. *Quarterly Review of Distance Education, 4*(2), vii–viii.

Simonson, M., Smaldino, S., Albright, M., & Zvacek, S. (2009). *Teaching and learning at a distance: Foundations of distance education* (4th ed.). Boston: Allyn & Bacon.

Simpson, E.J. (1972). *The classification of educational objectives in the psychomotor domain.* Washington, DC: Gryphon House.

Skinner, B.F. (1953). *Science and human behavior.* New York: Macmillan.

Skinner, B.F. (1954). The science of learning and the art of teaching. *Harvard Educational Review, 24,* 86–97.

Skinner, B.F. (1968). *The technology of teaching.* New York: Appleton-Century-Crofts.

Skinner, B.F. (1969). *Contingencies of reinforcement: A theoretical analysis.* New York: Appleton-Century-Crofts.

Slaughter, S., & Leslie, L. (1997). *Academic capitalism: Politics, policies and the entrepreneurial university.* Baltimore: Johns Hopkins University Press.

Sleezer, C.M. (1993). Training needs assessment at work: A dynamic process. *Human Resource Development Quarterly, 4*(3), 247–264.

Smith, H. (1994). *The 10 natural laws of successful time and life management.* New York: Warner Books.

Smith, M.K. (2002) Malcolm Knowles, informal adult education, self-direction and andragogy. Website: *The encyclopedia of informal education.* Available at: http://www.infed.org/thinkers/et-knowl.htm. Last updated October 20, 2005.

Smith, P.L., & Ragan, T.J. (2005). *Instructional design* (3rd ed.). Hoboken, NJ: John Wiley & Sons.

Spearman, C. (1904). "General intelligence," objectively determined and measured. *American Journal of Psychology, 15,* 201–293.

Spector, J.M. (2001). A philosophy of instructional design for the 21st century? *Journal of Structural Learning & Intelligent Systems, 14*(4), 307–318.

Spector, J.M. (2012). *Foundations of educational technology: Integrative approaches and interdisciplinary perspectives.* New York: Routledge.

Spiro, R.J., Coulson, R.L, Feltovich, P.J., & Anderson, D. (1988). Cognitive flexibility theory: Advanced knowledge acquisition in ill-structured domains. In V. Patel (Ed.), *Proceedings of the 10th Annual Conference of the Cognitive Science Society.* Hillsdale, NJ: Erlbaum.

Sprenger, M. (2005). *How to teach so students remember.* Alexandria, VA: ASCD.

Staker, H.C., & Horn, M.B. (2012). *Classifying K-12 blended learning.* Mountain View, CA: Innosight Institute.

Stepich, D.A., & Ertmer, P.A. (2010). "Teaching" instructional design expertise: Strategies to support students' problem-finding skills. *Technology, Instruction, Cognition and Learning, 7,* 147–170.

Stevens, T. (June 14, 2008). Facebook surpasses MySpace as world's most popular social network. Website: *Switched.* Available at: http://www.switched.com/2008/06/14/

Stokes-Hendriks, T.L. (2002). *Individual differences: A review.* Downsview, Ontario: A report sponsored by the Defence and Civil Institute of Environmental Medicine.

Sullivan, H., & Higgins, N. (1983). *Teaching for competence.* New York: Teachers College.

Sweller, J. (1988). Cognitive load during problem solving: Effects on learning. *Cognitive Science 12*(2), 257–285.

Tasker, M., & Packham, D. (1993). Industry and higher education: A question of values. *Studies in Higher Education, 18*(2), 127–136.

Taylor, B., & Kroth, M. (2009). A single conversation with a wise man is better than ten years of study: A model for testing methodologies for pedagogy or andragogy. *Journal of the Scholarship of Teaching and Learning, 9*(2), 42–56.

Terry, M. (2001). Translating learning style theory into university teaching practices: An article based on Kolb's experiential learning model. *Journal of College Reading and Learning, 32*(1), 68–85.

Thompson, M.E. (1994). Design considerations of visuals. In D.M. Moore and F.M. Dwyer (Eds.), *Visual literacy: A spectrum of visual learning* (pp. 165–182). Englewood Cliffs, NJ: Educational Technology Publications.

Thorndike, E.L. (1911). *Animal intelligence.* New York: Macmillan.

Thurmond, V., & Wambach, K. (2004). Understanding interactions in distance education: A review of the literature. *International Journal of Instructional Technology and Distance Learning, 1*(1), 9–26. Available at: http://www.itdl.org/journal/jan_04/article02.htm

Tolman, E.C. (1932). *Purposive behavior in animals and men.* New York: Century.

Tolman, E.C. (1948). Cognitive maps in rats and men. *Psychological Review, 55*, 189–208.

Tomei, L., & Balmert, M. (2001). The virtual tour: A web-based teaching strategy. *Learning & Leading with Technology, 28*(6), 6–13.

Tomlinson, C.A. (2001). *How to differentiate instruction in mixed-ability classrooms* (2nd ed.) Alexandria, VA: Association for Supervision and Curriculum Development.

Trimby, M.J. (1982). Entry level competencies for team members and supervisors/managers on instructional development teams in business and industry. Doctoral dissertation, Michigan State University. *Dissertation Abstracts International, 43*, 0346.

Tschofen, C., & Mackness, J. (2012). Connectivism and dimensions of individual experience. *International Review of Research in Open & Distance Learning, 13*(1), 124–143.

Tufte, E.R. (2001). *The visual display of quantitative information* (2nd ed.). Cheshire, CT: Graphics Press.

Underbakke, M., Borg, J.M., & Peterson, D. (1993). Researching and developing the knowledge base for teaching higher order thinking. *Theory into Practice, 32*(3), 138–146.

Useem, J., Useem, R., & Donoghue, J. (1963). Men in the middle of the third culture: The roles of American and non-western people in cross-cultural administration. *Human Organization, 22*(3), 169–179.

Vacca, R.T., Vacca, J.L., & Mraz, M. (2011). *Content area reading: Literacy and learning across the curriculum* (10th ed.). Boston: Pearson.

van Merrienboer, J.J.G. (1997). *Training complex cognitive skills: A four-component instructional design model for technical training.* Englewood Cliffs, NJ: Educational Technology Publications.

van Tiem, D.M. (2004). *Fundamentals of human performance technology* (2nd ed.). Silver Springs, MD: International Society for Performance Improvement.

Visser, B.A., Ashton, M.C., & Vernon, P.A. (2006a). Beyond g: putting multiple intelligences theory to the test. *Intelligence, 34*, 487–502.

Visser, B.A., Ashton, M.C., & Vernon, P.A. (2006b). G and the measurement of multiple intelligences: A response to Gardner. *Intelligence, 34*, 507–510.

von Glasersfeld, E. (1995). A constructivist approach to teaching. In L. Steffe & J. Gale (Eds.), *Constructivism in education.* Mahwah, NJ: Lawrence Erlbaum Associates.

Vygotsky, L.S. (1978). *Mind and society: The development of higher psychological processes.* Cambridge, MA: Harvard University Press.

Walsh, J.A., & Sattes, B.D. (2005). *Quality questioning: Research-based practice to engage every learner.* Thousand Oaks, CA: Corwin Press.

Watson, J.B. (1913). Psychology as the Behaviorist views it. *Psychological Review, 20*, 158–177.

Watson, J.B. (1925). *Behaviorism.* New York: W.W. Norton.

Wenger, E. (1999). *Communities of practice: Learning, meaning, and identity.* Cambridge: Cambridge University Press.

Wenger, E., McDermott, R., & Snyder, W.M. (2002). *Cultivating communities of practice.* Boston: Harvard Business Press.

Wenger, E., Trayner, B., & de Laat, M. (2011). *Promoting and assessing value creation in networks: A conceptual framework.* The Netherlands: Ruud de Moor Centrum. Available at: http://wenger-trayner.com/documents/Wenger_Trayner_DeLaat_Value_creation.pdf

Wenglinsky, H. (2002, February 13). How schools matter: The link between teacher classroom practices and student academic performance. *Education Policy Analysis Archives, 10*(12). Available: http://epaa.asu.edu/epaa/v10n12/

Wertheimer, M. (1923). Laws of organization in perceptual forms. First published as Untersuchungen zur Lehre von der Gestalt II, in *Psychologische Forschung, 4*, 301–350. Translation published in W. Ellis (1938), *A source book of Gestalt psychology* (pp. 71–88). London: Routledge & Kegan Paul. Available at: http://psy.ed.asu.edu/~classics/Wertheimer/Forms/forms.htm

Weston, C., & Cranton, P. (1986). Selecting instructional strategies. *Journal of Higher Education, 57*(3), 259–288.

Wiggins, G.P., & McTighe, J. (2005). *Understanding by design* (2nd ed.). Upper Saddle River, NJ: Merrill/Prentice Hall.

Wiley, D.A., & Edwards, E.K. (2002). *Online self-organizing social systems: The decentralized future of online learning.* Available at: http://opencontent.org/docs/ososs.pdf

Williams, R. (2008). *The non-designer's design book: Design and typographic principles for the visual novice* (3rd ed.). Berkeley, CA: PeachPit Press.

Willis, B.D. (1993). *Distance education: A practical guide.* Englewood Cliffs, NJ: Educational Technology Publications.

Willis, J. (1995). Recursive, reflective instructional design model based on constructivist-interpretivist theory. *Educational Technology, 35*(6), 5–23.

Willis, J. (2006). *Research-based strategies to ignite student learning: Insights from a neurologist and classroom teacher.* Alexandria, VA: Association for Supervision and Curriculum Development.

Willis, J. (2009). Pedagogical ID versus process ID: Two perspectives in contemporary instructional design theory. *International Journal of Technology in Teaching and Learning, 5*(2), 93–105.

Wilson, T.D., & Linville, P.W. (1982). Improving the academic performance of college freshmen: Attribution theory revisited. *Journal of Personal and Social Psychology, 42*, 367–376.

Winn, W. (1993). Perception principles. In M. Fleming & H. Levie (Eds.), *Instructional message design: Principles from the behavioral and cognitive sciences.* (2nd ed.) (pp. 55–126). Englewood Cliffs, NJ: Educational Technology Publications.

Witkin, H.A. (1977). Field-dependent and field-independent cognitive styles and their educational implications. *Review of Educational Research, 47*(4), 1–64.

Wood, P., Bruner, J., & Ross, G. (1976). The role of tutoring in problem-solving. *Journal of Child Psychology and Psychiatry and Allied Disciplines, 17*, 89–100.

Woolfolk, A. (2005). *Educational psychology* (9th ed.). Boston: Allyn & Bacon.

Yacci, M. (2000) Interactivity demystified: A structural definition for distance education and instructional CBT. *Educational Technology, 40*(4), 5–16.

Zichermann, G., & Cunningham, C. (2011). *Gamification by design: Implementing game mechanics in web and mobile apps.* Sebastopol: O'Reilly Media.

Index

Page numbers in bold refer to figures and tables

accessibility 234–237
accommodation *see* accessibility
ADDIE viii, 8–11
affective domain **104**
alternative assessments 135, 136
ARCS Theory of Motivation 81
assessments 132; *academic prompts* 138; aligning
   with learning outcomes 133, 138, 140–141, **142**;
   alternative 135, 136; *authentic* 136; *Connectivist*
   141, **142**, 143; *Constructivist* 141, **142**; *criterion-
   referenced* 135; *curricular alignment* 139; *data-driven
   decision making* 144–145; defining for instruction 134,
   160; designing 134–135; *feedback* on 142–144;
   informal 135; *instructional alignment* 140;
   Instructivist 141, **142**; *norm-referenced* 135;
   peer assessments 138; *performance tasks* 138;
   plagiarism on 144; as *practice* 143; *projects* 138;
   self-assessments 137, **138**; *strategic alignment* 139;
   traditional 136
Association for Educational Communications and
   Technology 4
assumptions, learning 153–157
asynchronous learning 13, 14
attitudes **104**, **127**
authentic assessments 136

BSCS 5 Es Instructional Model 167, **171**
behavioral objectives 117
Behavioral Theory **82**
Behaviorists 77; *see also* Behavioral Theory
best practices 35
blended learning 14; *see also hybrid* learning
Bloom's Revised Taxonomy of Cognitive Outcomes
   101–102, **142**
Bloom's Revised Taxonomy of Educational
   Objectives viii
Bloom's Thinking Skills **124**, 125, **126, 127, 142**
Branson, R. 4
Briggs, L. 3, 4
Bruner, J. 3

career environments 16, 39–40, 58–59, 88–89, 113,
   129–130, 147–148, 179, 201, 249
Clark, R. E. 15, 55, 195, 209

Clark vs. Kozma media debate 195
cognitive apprenticeship 78
Cognitive Constructivism 77
cognitive domain **104**
Cognitive Load Theory 81
cognitive strategies **106, 127**
Cognitive Theory **83**
Cognitive Theory of Multimedia Learning 81
cognitivist objectives 117
Cognitivists 77; *see also* Cognitive Theory
collaboration 14
communication 70–72
competency 16, **17**
Connectivist approach 79, **80, 158**
Connectivist assessment 141, **142**, 143
Connectivist learning 3
Connectivist learning environments 167, **172–173**
constraints 32–33
Constructivist approach 78, 79, **80, 158**
Constructivist assessment 141, **142**
Constructivists 77
content analysis 91–93; methods **98–99**; process
   of 94–96
content classification 101
content mapping 108–111
content scope 92, 111
context: alignment between learning and
   performance 63; analyzing 63–64, 152–153;
   communication in the learning 70–72; cultural 60,
   72–75; of instruction 60; learning 60, **64**, 66–69;
   performance 60, 61, 64–65; theoretical 60, 75–85
continuous evaluation 10
continuous improvement 10, 12, 39, 58
continuously improving viii, 10, 88
curriculum alignment 36

data-driven decision making 144–145
declarative knowledge 102
delivery mode 187
design 5–6
Design of Everyday Things, The 4
Dewey, J. 3
distributed cognition 78
domains of learning 101, 102, **104–105**

electronic performance support systems 15
emerging technologies 195, 198–199
engagement strategies 157, 160, 161
epistemology 76, **80**
equilibrium 77
evaluation 10–11, 38, 56–57, 86–87, 112, 129, 133, 144–146, 176, 244–248; of message design 216–217; selection 199–200
extrinsic motivators 170

feedback 143–144
formative evaluation 10

Gagné, R. 3, 4, 102
Gagné's five types of learning outcomes 102, **104–105, 106, 127**
Gagné's Nine Events of Instruction 166–170
generative strategies 164, **165**
geographic location 13
goal analysis 92
Goal-Based Scenario 174, 176

higher-order thinking skills (HOTS) 101, 124
human performance technology 4
hybrid learning 14

implementation 240–244
individual differences 50; age and generational differences 54; cognitive styles, learning styles, and learning preferences 55–56; gender, ethnicity, race, and cultural background 54; intelligence and mental capabilities 52; motivation 53; physical capabilities 52; prior knowledge and experiences 53
individualized instruction 51
instruction, definition of 3
instructional alignment 36
instructional design: definition of 2, 4, 5; history of 4
instructional design and technology viii
instructional design process 8–9
instructional goals 34; definition of 34; factors that shape 34; specifying 36
instructional intentions 157, **163**
instructional strategies 149, 150, 151–152, 162, 164
instructional systems design 4
instructional technologist 4
instructional technology 4
Instructivist approach 78, **80, 158**
Instructivist assessment 141, **142**
intellectual skills **106, 127**
interaction 157; types of 157–161, **163**
interpersonal skills domain **105**
Intrinsic motivators 170
iterative instructional design 8–9

KASI 97–100, 103, **107**, 108, 109
Keller's ARCS Motivational Model 170–174, **175**
key questions 10
Kirkpatrick, D. 10
Kirkpatrick's Four Level Evaluation Model 10–11, 38, 56–57, 86–87, 112, 129, 133, 144–146, 199–200
knowledge, skills, attitude, interpersonal skills *see* KASI

learner analysis 42; data sources for **48**; gathering data for 45; process of 43–44; scope of 45–49
learner characteristics 44–45, **46–47**

learning, nature of 3
learning outcomes 115, 116; ABCDs of **119**; aligning with assessments and strategies 128, 133, 140–141, **142**, 151, 153–157; communicating 128; confusion with learning activities 122; *Connectivist* 121, **158**; *Constructivist* 121, **158**; defining 117–118; *Instructivist* 121, **158**; *learning strategies* 149, 150, 153–157
learning theories, importance of 15
lower-order thinking skills (LOTS) 124

Marzano's Nine Categories of Effective Strategies 162, **164**
McLuhan, M. 195
media 182
media affordances 182, 187, **188**, 193–195
media assets *see* media affordances
media attributes *see* media affordances
media comparison studies 15, 195
media selection *see* technology selection
media theories 195
message design 203, 204; characteristics of effective 205–210; elements of 210–216
metacognition 125
mindtool 185
Morgan, R. 4

needs 21, 28, 33
needs analysis 21–23, 26–27, 29–31
needs assessment 21, 22; *see also* needs analysis
non-instructional solutions 28, 34
Norman, D. 4, 6

objectives 117
online learning 14
optimized instruction viii
optimized instructional design 12, 38–39, 57, 113, 129, 146, 176, 217, 248; redundant instructional design 12, 87, 146, 200, 217, 248, 249
organizational climate 75
organizational strategies 157, 159, 161

pedagogical approaches 78, **80**, 153–157, 166–176
peer assessments 138
Performance Support Systems 15
Personal Learning Environments 14
plagiarism 144
practice 143
pretests 135
prior knowledge 125
problems 6, 21; ill-structured 6–7; nature of design 6; well-structured 6
production 223–226; managing 239–240; tasks 230–234
productivity tool 185
project creep viii
project management 226–230
psychomotor domain **105**
psychomotor skills **105, 127**

quality 238–239

redundancy, appropriate viii
resources 32–33
return on investment 15
right-sized instruction viii

right-sized instructional design 12, 88, 113, 129, 146, 176, 200, 217–218, 249; continuous improvement 12, 88, 113, 129, 146–147, 176–177, 200, 218, 249; instructional design competencies 16
rubric 137

scaffolding 77, 162–164, **165**
scenario planning guidelines 174, **177–178**
schema 77; *see also* continuous evaluation
self-assessments 137, **138**
self-direction 14
situated learning theory 64
Situated theorists 77
Social Constructivism 77
social presence 157
Sociocultural theorists 77; *see also* Sociocultural, Social, and Situated Theory
Sociocultural, Social, and Situated Theory **84**
Spector, M. 3
stakeholder 24–25
subject matter expert 25
summative evaluation 10
supplantive strategies 162, **165**

sustainable instruction viii
sustainable instructional design 12, 39, 57, 87, 113, 129, 146, 176, 200, 217, 248
synchronous learning 13
systematic design 8
systemic design 8

taxonomies of learning 101, 102, **104–105, 106**
teaching strategies 149, 150
technology 182, 184, 195, 198–199; definition of 6
technology delivery strategies 157
technology selection 182, 183, 211; process 187–193
technology-supported learning 184–187
thinking skills 124
time and place 13
traditional face-to-face instruction 14
Transactional Distance, theory of 81

universal design 235–237

verbal information **106, 127**

Zone of Proximal Development 77

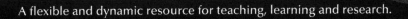